Critical Ac[illegible]
for *Traveler*[illegible]

"The *Travelers' Tales* series is altogether remarkable."
—Jan Morris, author of *Journeys*, *Locations*, and *Hong Kong*

"For the thoughtful traveler, these books are an invaluable resource. There's nothing like them on the market."
—Pico Iyer, author of *Video Night in Kathmandu*

"This is the stuff memories can be duplicated from."
—Karen Krebsbach, *Foreign Service Journal*

"I can't think of a better way to get comfortable with a destination than by delving into *Travelers' Tales*...before reading a guidebook, before seeing a travel agent. The series helps visitors refine their interests and readies them to communicate with the peoples they come in contact with...."
—Paul Glassman, Society of American Travel Writers

"...*Travelers' Tales* is a valuable addition to any predeparture reading list."
—Tony Wheeler, publisher, Lonely Planet Publications

"*Travelers' Tales* delivers something most guidebooks only promise: a real sense of what a country is all about...."
—Steve Silk, *Hartford Courant*

"...*Travelers' Tales* is a useful and enlightening addition to the travel bookshelves...providing a real service for those who enjoy reading first-person accounts of a destination before seeing it for themselves."
—Bill Newlin, publisher, Moon Publications

"The *Travelers' Tales* series should become required reading for anyone visiting a foreign country who wants to truly step off the tourist track and experience another culture, another place, firsthand."
—Nancy Paradis, *St. Petersburg Times*

"Like having been there, done it, seen it. If there's one thing traditional guidebooks lack, it's the really juicy travel information, the personal stories about back alleys and brief encounters. The *Travelers' Tales* series fills this gap with an approach that's all anecdotes, no directions."
—Jim Gullo, *Diversion*

Other Travelers' Tales Books

Country and Regional Guides

America, Brazil, France, India, Italy, Japan, Mexico, Nepal, Spain, Thailand; Grand Canyon, Hong Kong, Paris, and San Francisco

Women's Travel

A Woman's World, Women in the Wild, A Mother's World, Safety and Security for Women Who Travel, Gutsy Women, Gutsy Mamas

Body & Soul

The Road Within, Love & Romance, Food, The Fearless Diner, The Gift of Travel

Special Interest

Danger!, There's No Toilet Paper on the Road Less Traveled, The Penny Pincher's Passport to Luxury Travel, A Dog's World, Family Travel

Footsteps

Kite Strings of the Southern Cross, The Sword of Heaven

TRAVELERS' TALES GUIDES

HAWAI'I

TRUE STORIES OF THE ISLAND SPIRIT

Collected and Edited by

RICK AND MARCIE CARROLL

Series Editors

JAMES O'REILLY AND LARRY HABEGGER

TRAVELERS' TALES
SAN FRANCISCO

Travelers' Tales Hawai'i: True Stories of the Island Spirit
Collected and Edited by Rick and Marcie Carroll

Cover and interior design by Judy Anderson, Susan Bailey, and Kathryn Heflin
Cover photograph: Copyright © Rita Ariyoshi/Ariyoshi Ink. Photographed at Hui Noeau; Hawaiian girl draped in ferns dancing the hula.
Map by Keith Granger
Page Layout by Cynthia Lamb, using the fonts BemboCI and Boulevard

Library of Congress Cataloging-in-Publication Data

Hawai'i: true stories of the island spirit / collected and edited by Rick and Marcie Carroll.
p. cm. — (Travelers' Tales guides)
Includes indexes.
ISBN 1-885211-35-X
1. Hawaii—Description and travel. I. Carroll, Rick, 1943– II. Carroll, Marcie. III. Series.
DU623.Z5H36 1999
996.9—dc21 99-26910
CIP

First Edition
Printed in the United States of America
10 9 8 7 6 5 4 3 2 1

In what other land save this one is the commonest form of greeting not "Good day," nor "How d'ye do," but "Love"? That greeting is Aloha—*love, I love you, my love to you...*

—Jack London

Table of Contents

Part Two
Some Things to Do

Part Three
Going Your Own Way

Part Four
In the Shadows

Part Five
The Last Word

⋆ ⋆ ⋆

The Next Step

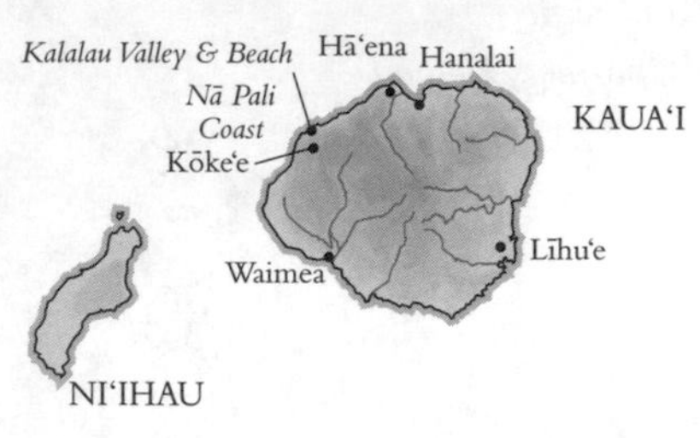

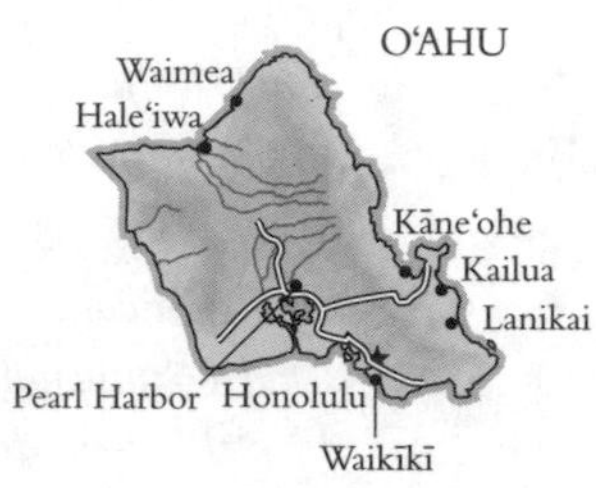

Pacific Ocean

Hawaiian Islands

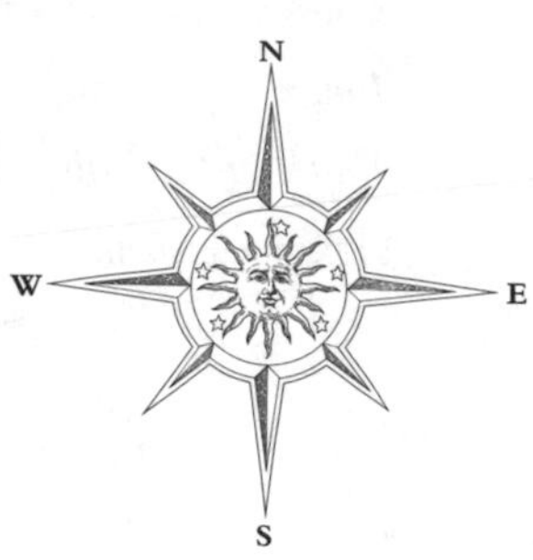

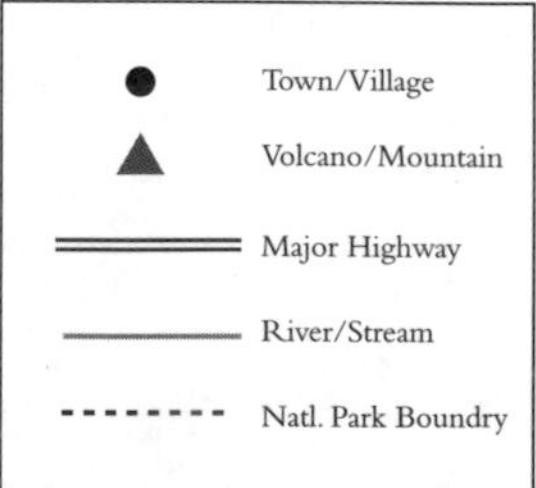

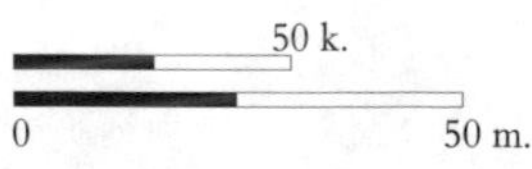

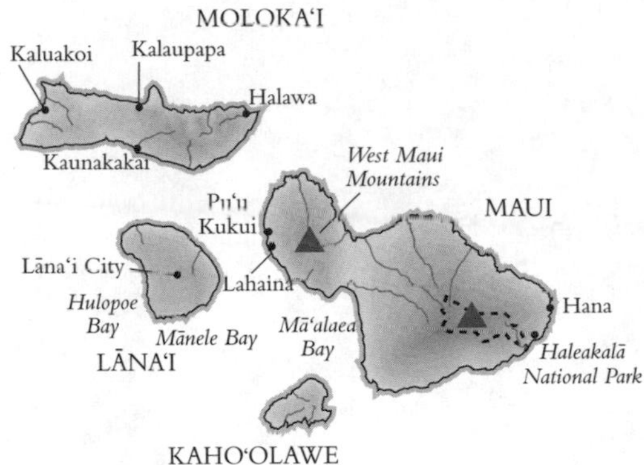
MOLOKA'I
Kaluakoi
Kalaupapa
Halawa
Kaunakakai
West Maui
Mountains
MAUI
Pu'u
Kukui
Lāna'i City
Lahaina
Hulopoe
Bay
Mānele Bay
Mā'alaea
Bay
LĀNA'I
Hana
Haleakalā
National Park
KAHO'OLAWE

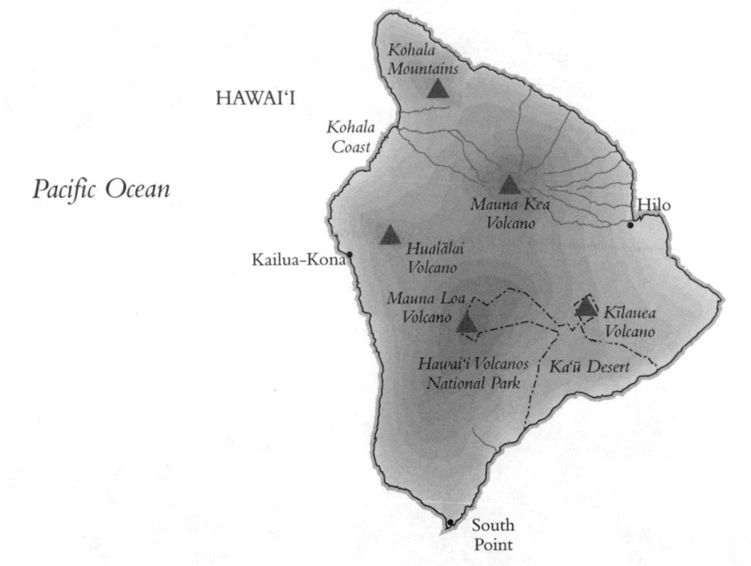
Kohala
Mountains
HAWAI'I
Kohala
Coast
Pacific Ocean
Mauna Kea
Volcano
Hilo
Hualālai
Volcano
Kailua-Kona
Mauna Loa
Volcano
Kīlauea
Volcano
Hawai'i Volcanos
National Park
Ka'ū Desert
South
Point

Hawai'i: An Introduction

This New Year's morning we celebrated Hawai'i on a dark, cool North Shore beach watching 20- to 25-foot waves roll in from across the sea, molten mercury and platinum in the moonlight. Dawn broke, and a reverential crowd assembled on the beach. Mesmerized by the heaving, foaming, roaring might of the sea, we all stood quiet, except for a collective gasp that escaped when a lone surfer grabbed one of those spumy summits and rode it, twisting and turning, then spilled, surfaced in the wash, shook himself and rode out for more. It was one of the rare times in fifteen years in Hawai'i that we saw the fabled waves, biggest in the world, at Waimea Bay. We wish we could have shared the morning with you, who care enough about these Islands to read on and seek more. But that's how it is with Hawai'i. To enjoy its special moments, spiritual, physical, or personal, you have to be at the right place in the right frame of mind, open and ready to receive.

Hawai'i is more about reception than transmission. That makes it hard to capture in writing. It's always been so—the ancients left their legacy in chants and dances, stories passed down by spoken word and illustrated by petroglyph or by hula, another passed-down tradition that defies writing. We feel our modern authors have crossed that difficult barrier and written meaningfully about Hawai'i, that their collective experiences take the reader a step beyond the usual interpretation to capture something of the essence of this magical mystery place and how to experience it and grow from the experience. A contemporary vision of Hawai'i, if you will.

Some of the writers are well-known; some are never before published. They range from native Hawaiians to first-time visitors and include poets and professors, surfers and drifters, a shaman, a Pulitzer Prize–winning biographer. They hail from several countries, ages, and states of mind. They share not only the good fortune to discover the special reality of Hawai'i but also the talent to write about it in a way that helps explain why the most remote island chain on the planet is one of the best known and most yearned-for destinations under the sun.

Together they represent a very readable collection, not one that exhausts every important topic or point of view, not one that defines the heart of the Pacific at the new millennium, but hopefully one that exposes new possibilities and deepens understanding. One that points out experiences you may want to pursue. *Travelers' Tales Hawai'i* is a unique collection of stories about the true spirit of the Islands.

Let us hasten to add that there is another Hawai'i, entertaining and fulfilling enough to sustain a four-day package tour if the flight's not too long. It's the version experienced by most of the seven million people who come to the Islands each year, many who search not just for warmth and beauty but for a fictionalized destination of photo ops and must-dos and then move on to some other theme park next year. Maybe it's just as well. Not everyone can stay. Not everyone "gets" Hawai'i. Not everyone wants to. But if you do, if you can step out of your world and connect with a moonlit monster wave or a seductive hula hand or a Pacific kiss or a steamy piece of newborn lava, it could change your life. It did ours.

When we left San Francisco for the Islands in the early '80s, a colleague asked, "What will you do after you get a tan?"

What we did was listen and learn about Hawai'i and ourselves, and now, we and our authors present our discoveries to you.

Aloha.

—Rick and Marcie Carroll
Ka'a'awa, Hawai'i

A Note on Spelling and Meaning

The Hawaiian language, which sounds like a waterfall set to speech, was suppressed and nearly lost for much of the twentieth century. Recently widespread efforts to recapture and preserve the culture have led to language immersion schools for children and night school language classes for devoted adults. Right now, both official languages of Hawai'i—English and Hawaiian—are thriving, along with the unofficial language, pidgin.

So just how do you pronounce *humuhumunukunukuāpua'a* anyway? Break it into couplets—*humu-humu, nuku-nuku, a-pu, a-a* and remember the song ("Little Grass Shack." It gets you ahead on Ke-ala-ke-kua too). Hawaiian was not born written. It was verbal, rich, and musical, spoken with enough drama to carry the entire history down among families and hula schools and warrior chants. Missionaries dressed it in writing, as surely as they dressed the naked. They wrote what they heard, not necessarily correctly. With only seven consonants, speakers eked maximum duty from vowels (sometimes four in a row, as in the Honolulu neighborhood Aiea—Aye-eh-ya), often using the trusty 'okina (glottal stop), and kahakō to separate and alter sound and meaning. *A'a* means a small root or artery. *'A'a* means to dare. *'A'ā* is the clinker lava. And *'ā'ā* means speechlessness. Nonetheless, the vowels are always pronounced the same—a close-mouthed uh for "a," eh for "e," ee for "i," oh for "o," and oo for "u."

Hawaiians don't always agree on English spellings of their words; Mary Kawena Pukui's *Hawaiian Dictionary* is the most respected resource.

—RC & MC

PART ONE

Essence of Hawai‘i

RICK BASS

Paradise Rising

Discovering Hawai'i, where there's no place to go but up.

I WAS AFRAID I WOULDN'T LIKE HAWAI'I. I HAD EXPECTED TO BE homesick for the good, crisp weather of Montana the whole time I was there. I imagined it seething with traffic, sun and glimmer. I imagined that the Islands would be overrun with game-show winners and lit up with the terrible smiles of newlyweds.

If I head into Hawai'i's high mountains, I thought, into its upland rainforests, into its tortured, barren, exquisitely beautiful lava fields, I could stay clear of the crowded beaches. I was determined not to view Hawai'i as "paradise," not to even use that word, that cliché. For a while, at first, I saw the Islands as beautiful floating prisons—each Island destined to an extremely short life, drifting to oblivion. And while that's true, I soon found that there was also no other word—it was a paradise. A short one, like the one day of life given to a mayfly in the spring, but paradise nonetheless.

We went to the Big Island first—the youngest one, the only one where lava still flows—and headed straight for the mountain village of Volcano, just outside Hawai'i Volcanoes National Park. I don't know if I can describe how glorious, how serene it felt to stand in the high rainforest on that incredibly young, incredibly healthy mountain. The village is green, with every leaf shape, every assemblage of plants new and different to me, so that the effect is like going back in time to childhood, when the woods were so new and untamed.

The first evening, I went alone up into Hawai'i Volcanoes National Park after closing and walked around in the dusk, gawking at the alien place I'd been dropped into. Steam rose from the trees—little rifts in the hot earth had worked up to the surface—and it was windy and cold. Water dripped from the green bushes along the hiking trails. It's all or nothing at Volcanoes—beautiful, twisted, folded sheets of hardened lava spread for great distances, as if on the moon, or, in places spared by the lava, birdsong and lush greenery. Such jungle islands, around which the lava flowed and then hardened, are called *kīpuka*, and they are of tremendous ecological significance.

Life—and the rapid evolution characteristic of Hawai'i, or any new landform—proceeds at a startlingly brisk pace. The last thing a visitor should do in Hawai'i, however, is hurry up. You just rest, and watch. You look. More than 90 percent of the species in the Hawaiian Islands are found nowhere else. This is their sacred home. Every time I blink, 90 percent of what comes into my field of vision is new.

I head up toward the great Southwest Rift, a beautiful prairie of twisted rough *'a'ā* (pronounced ah-ah) lava. All through Hawai'i there are gorgeous stone walls built from lava rock, iridescent black and iron bloodred, rock fences being swarmed under with greenery, and I'm jealous. I want to have such rocks for my stone wall in Montana, which suddenly seems as ponderous and sledge-footed—as freighted—as a dinosaur. Everywhere I look I see the lightness of things, the youth of the planet. It is like looking at a scrapbook of one's parents when they were children: You think, so this is what it was like....

The lava fields are treacherous, but the park has a wonderful system of hiking trails. Normally I abhor trails; they lead to violent erosion. But in this unfamiliar place they're welcome. Up here, I have them to myself. The crunch of the crushed volcano rock underfoot reminds me of the cinder running tracks in high school, and I realize that's exactly what it is: ground cinders. There's no soil for me to disturb or erode on these trails; it hasn't even formed yet.

You don't think of molten rock—magma, lava—as being the source of life. But each volcano rises from the sea to become an Island, and each Island blocks the trade winds that blow from northeast to southwest. This creates rain showers on the windward mountain slopes, which create life—lush rainforests.

I walk out across the Southwest Rift, into an astonishing copper sky of sunset, and then I head back to the park entrance, to the bar at the Volcano House hotel, to watch a bit of tape-delayed *Monday Night Football.* I'm the only customer in the place. A few tourists in shorts walk around in the parking lot, hunched against the chill, high-elevation winds.

A full moon casts a silver-blue glow on the guts of Kīlauea—the Halema'uma'u crater that only ten years ago was a pool of roiling lava. It could happen again at any time—is due, in fact, at any time. The magma is only two miles below me; it is boiling, searching for a rift or fissure, straining to make one, to launch still more lava into the air. Two miles down is not very far for such a force. Any day now.

That night, lying in bed a short distance from the park, I remember reading how the last eruption of the crater gave hikers out on the trails only about a three-hour warning. It could go off while I sleep! It could explode (I'm a heavy sleeper), flow down the road, make a left at the Kīlauea Lodge, and turn cottage number six into a *kīpuka*. Or worse!

Volcanoes and molten lava—it's delicious, in this age of arrogance, to rediscover humility.

The next day we walk, my wife Elizabeth and I and our nine-month-old daughter, Mary Katherine. We take the Kīpuka Puaulu Trail into a beautiful dense *kīpuka* forest. Later, we walk across the floor of Kīlauea's crater—all lava wasteland, all glorious, both for what it is (three square miles of cooled lava) and for what it will soon become (a seedbed for Hawai'i's diversity, Hawai'i's writhing, lovely forests).

Say the words out loud—*pāhoehoe* (puh-ho-eh-ho-eh) lava, the smooth, ropy, almost intestinal kind, and *'a'ā,* the chunky, savage, bombed-looking pieces. Most dramatic to me are the incredible, ghostly lava trees, where the lava crept up on a standing tree and covered it but then drained away—joining back up with the rest of the lava flow, leaving a hardened crust around the now-dead tree, branches still intact (but cloaked in lava), still lifted to the sky.

What happens when the lava flows up and over a tree but does *not* recede is just as startling. The lava engulfs a tree, but the tree's sap and moisture keep it from burning up completely. When the lava eventually hardens, the fried tree trunk inside that lava smolders, dries, rots and disappears, leaving a perfect hole, or "tree mold," looking for all the world as if someone has drilled a well out in the lava field. Big holes, little holes, all perfectly round, the only clue that once there was a green forest.

The smooth *pāhoehoe* lava is hotter than the rough *'a'ā*—and as long as the *pāhoehoe* retains its gas, the lava remains hotter, which produces the smoother, more liquid flow. As the gas escapes and the lava cools, the flow of lava slows and turns into the rougher *'a'ā.*

I tell you, I love this stuff. I promise not to do too much sciencespeak, but I'm a modern man, European stock, and I can't resist it. To look at the lava we're walking across and to try to *understand,* to look back into the mysterious, recent past, to see the clues, the story—it's not unlike following the tracks of animals in the snow, back in Montana.

Walking across the crunchy, twisted lava, around the edge of the napping Kīlauea, I'm refreshed, and humbled. Looking out at a new world of nothing but rock, with nothing but sunlight above and empty sky (though lichens are beginning to form on some of the lava)—looking out at the rubble of lava, is like gazing at the pattern, the blueprint, for the possibility of life. It's a lovely, spiritual, sobering moment—or at least it is until a helicopter comes bopping up over the rim of the crater, defiling the sound of the wind. The helicopter hovers, banks, casts a commercial eye down into the crater, then whirls away, departs like a motorized pterodactyl; and somehow, where before I felt awe, I now feel slightly foolish. And it is not a good trade, awe for foolishness.

Not knowing the sacred dos and don'ts of these Islands, I pick up a fist-sized piece of *'a'ā* to take home to a friend's son, noting that the rock is the same age as the boy. It is only by chance, later in the day, that I hear one of the park rangers telling a visitor about the drawerful of letters that the Park Service gets from people who have taken lava back to the Mainland only to have bad luck suddenly descend upon them. Broken legs, back injuries, financial catastrophes, car wrecks—nothing subtle, says the ranger. Serious, heavy-handed stuff from Madame Pele, the fire goddess, the power and meaning beneath the Pacific Plate. And accidents befall the rock snatchers whether they're aware of the "curse" or not.

I'm just overhearing this conversation, mind you. No one's got me made. The rock's *still in the back of the car,* just riding around with me. I haven't tried to take it away from its home—yet. I'll just think on it a bit, and try to rationalize. But Madame Pele, it's for a *little boy....*

The thought stays in my mind, however, and puts its roots into my brain and slowly strengthens its hold there, expanding ever so slightly all the while, like water freezing in a wedge between two rocks. And it acts like a filter, changing still further the way I look at the Island, so that finally, the morning we leave the Big Island, I drive the tiny, winding road up to the 6,600-foot trailhead that leads to the summit of Mauna Loa. I return the lava rock I've got stashed in the car to the base of Mauna Loa—back to its source—and know, in that way we rarely feel anymore, that I have done something right.

Rick Bass is the author of a dozen books, including The Sky, The Stars, The Wilderness. *He lives on a remote Montana ranch.*

*

Hawaiians created chants as trail guides, according to Hawaiian historian John Pa II. Everyone memorized them so they would know the physical characteristics of the Islands and could find their way.

The sun sends a streak of light on Mauna Loa.
The clouds go scurrying by
There is a rumble on the mountaintop

That echoes from the mountain of Kona, the calm,
Hilo stands directly in the rain.
Hamākua's cliffs are tall,
Kohala is buffeted by the wind,
Kauiki reaches and touches the sky....

—RC & MC

SUE HALPERN

Hawai'i on the Wild Side

Adventurer, beware: the beauty of Kaua'i's North Shore masks elemental dangers.

NOTHING—NOTHING—PREPARES ME FOR THE WAVES. NOT THE matter-of-fact announcements every half hour the night before on the hotel TV station to "never turn your back to the sea," as if the sea were a pickpocket, or a man with a gun. Not the genial injunction in the book I pick up on the plane from Honolulu to Princeville, at the northern end of the island, where the next day I will be setting out on a five-day kayak trip along Nā Pali Coast. "Don't be seduced into a false sense of safety by the friendly blue sky and the lovely turquoise water," it says of this particular place. And not even this, from *Gilman's Journal of a Canoe Voyage Along the Kaua'i Pali, Made in 1845:*

> "The sun was just rising when we reached the point where the great *pali*, or precipices, begin. These precipices are one of the grandest wonders of the Islands, but the danger of examining them on the passage deters many persons from visiting them. There are those who will travel by land 60 miles around rather than sail these 15 by canoe, and I was warned not to try. But with me, curiosity was stronger than caution."

With me too, though standing on the beach at Hāʻena that first morning, my curiosity was of a more mundane sort: how to use the double-bladed paddle. Earlier, when I had called from the Mainland, Micco Godinez, the outfitter, had assured me that this five-day gambol down Nā Pali was suitable for people whose primary aquatic experience was in a canoe, on a lake. There are other ways, of course, to see what is considered to be Hawai'i's most magnificent, least-developed coast.

There are helicopter rides, tour boats, and motorized life rafts, but only in a kayak would I have no choice but to scroll through the landscape. In a kayak, the landscape wouldn't go by so much as it would be revealed, stroke by stroke, like a painting.

If you are going to paddle, you have to launch your boat through the surf. This morning, we are told, it's not too bad, maybe four feet, tops, though tops is the operative word when you are sitting in a molded plastic boat six inches above sea level. Get under a four-foot wave as it starts to spill, and you will probably lose your boat, or worse. Just paddle hard, someone said, and keep the boat straight. But how? Micco picks up a paddle, holds it out in front of him, and cranks it through the air like a pair of bicycle pedals. "Push, don't pull," he says. End of lesson.

Jack, a middle-aged insurance agent from Los Angeles who is making his second trip down Nā Pali, launches first, then Sandy, a competitive paddler and nurse who will be our cook for the next few days, then Rob and Leah, who are celebrating their second anniversary, then me. Micco gives my kayak a push and suddenly I am on my own, digging at the water with my paddle, and pulling, not pushing, as a sheer *pali* of water moves faster toward me than I toward it, and Micco is yelling something, and so are Jack and Sandy and Rob and Leah, and I find I have almost no choice but to turn my back to the sea because that seems to be where my boat wants to go until I will it to go straight, and the boat and I ski over the first wave just as it is starting to snarl, and on to the second, and then to the third, which is less a mountain than a mogul. Afterward, the water flattens out, and it's as if I've gone through a door, and the sound in the room is what you hear when you put your ear to a seashell, and then I realize it is me, breathing.

The sky, by the way, is neither friendly nor blue. It is mottled gray and dripping. Sandy pulls up behind me and says the natives call rain "liquid sunshine." This suggests a kind of denial, I think, until a swell turns my boat northward, and I see the Makana Cliffs 1,500 feet above me, and they are covered with a luminous green fur.

Our flotilla glides along the cliffs, about a quarter mile out. Even at a distance, the coastal rock is massive, daunting. Thousands of years of erosion have serrated its ridges, which are as sharp as knives. My mind tries out an assortment of metaphors to get at what it looks like—a giant green relief map, a stand of enormous conifers—but none of them will do. We have entered the realm of the ineffable. It is 10:35 in the morning. We have been in the water an hour. My arms say it's been a long time, but the ancient headlands say otherwise.

According to Micco, the trade winds are supposed to push us down the coast, but today they're not cooperating. There is wind from the south and wind from the west, and the effect is to churn the ocean like butter. On top of this wash, my boat feels like a bathtub toy. Later, in Joseph Conrad's *The Mirror of the Sea,* I find a passage that in its physical description bears almost no resemblance to this day; as to how the day feels, though, it is remarkably precise:

> "The grayness of the whole immense surface, the wind furrows upon the faces of the waves, the great masses of foam, tossed about and waving, like matted, white locks, give to the sea in a gale an appearance of hoary age, lusterless, dull, without gleams...."

We pass a cave whose entrance is draped with a waterfall, and another, shaped like a horseshoe, with openings at either end, but the surf is too high to get at them. No one seems to care. By midday we are a much less enthusiastic navy than we were at daybreak. All our concerns now are elemental, having to do with the sun, the wind, the water. Most of us are seasick and losing fluid faster than it can be replaced. The nice, gentle float along Nā Pali that I had envisioned is beginning to seem quixotic. Although I knew we would be paddling in open water, it had never occurred to me to take account of the sea. It would just be there for me in my boat, the way the highway is there for me in my car. I am relieved when Micco says that once we round the next point, about a mile away, there will be a beach called Kalalau where we can go ashore and camp.

What I see from my tent at Kalalau is this: a narrow strip of sand, a pond of stale seawater, a wide strip of sand, the Pacific. The pond collected in winter, when the tide was up, and it now has no place to drain. Beyond it, the beach slopes downward, and the effect, when looking out to the horizon, is to obscure the shore break. From my tent, the sand appears to meet the ocean with an affable handshake. In fact, the waves are about a story high and collapse like walls, one upon the next. Coming into shore, an experienced paddler might be able to charge through the debris and avoid getting pelted. Anyone else—those like me, for instance—will find themselves boatless in the drink, being pounded and tugged at, swimming to no avail, suddenly aware that drowning is a possibility, and knowing for an instant, maybe longer, what drowning would be.

Over dinner—tuna steak grilled on a Coleman stove, chilled wine, tossed salad—we recall the day's events as if giving a toast at a bachelor party. "How many different ways are there to say 'throw up'?" someone asks, and everyone laughs just a little too hard. It is not lost on us that coming through today's gauntlet means only that we will have to go through tomorrow's and the next day's and the days' after that. No one says anything about it.

Our party is up at dawn, looking expectantly out to sea. We are scheduled to take off this morning if the surf is down, but it's not down, and we are waiting, waiting, and eating nervously. Sandy has fixed eggs and pancakes and muffins and sausage while Micco, an old surfer, paces the beach, reading the waves. Twice he comes back with the news that it's hopeless, a judgment that is later confirmed when a Zodiac raft is unable to find a channel to land and bypasses Kalalau, stranding the twelve people scheduled to ride it back to civilization. But both times Micco resumes his watch, and when he returns around 11 a.m., he tells us we're going out. The waves are now eight feet high, but he thinks we can make it. And somehow, somehow we do.

I once stood transfixed on Kaua'i's fabled Lumaha'i Beach as a new husband posed his young bride with her back to the Pacific just as a rogue wave broke over her head. She disappeared under water, tugged out to sea. Only her shoes remained in the golden sand. Then, the next wave spat her back on shore.

Locals have another name for Lumaha'i, the picturesque beach where Mitzi Gaynor washed "that man right outta my hair" in the Hollywood classic *South Pacific.* They call it "Tourist Beach," because young honeymooners and others pose at the surf line, backs to the ocean, and more than a few are drowned each year by the furious waves that hurl onshore and suck away whatever was there.

—RC & MC

It is three miles to the beach at Miloli'i. The sea is still sloppy. Strung out over a quarter mile, we sing rounds to ward off sickness. Behind us the jagged coast, wrapped in fog, stands in silhouette. We pass Honopū, where twin beaches precede a broad, contoured valley, measuring our slow passage against spectral black cliffs. A tour boat that's just come from Miloli'i stops to visit. The captain cannot believe we made it through the waves at Kalalau. Miloli'i is even worse, he says, throwing down cold cans of soda into our kayaks as his passengers take our pictures. We resume singing.

Miloli'i is not worse. It is not better. It is best—a crescent beach below a balcony of land. The balcony is grassy and flat and sheltered by a towering rampart. There is an open-air pavilion, where Sandy sets up our kitchen, and an outdoor sink, shower, and toilet.

Somehow we've been upgraded to first class. Micco has arranged for a motorboat to arrive later, stocked with wine and chocolate, fresh guava juice, vegetables, cold beer, and other essentials. Our group is giddy, about to get giddier. We are nine miles down the Nā Pali Coast, and none of us doubts any longer that we'll make it all the way. The question now is whether any of us will want to.

At dusk, Micco leads an expedition to Nu'alolo Kai, a beach between where we are and where we have been. For once the water is polished. We skate along. Sluggish green sea turtles acknowledge our presence, craning their necks to get a look, sinking away. Brown boobies fly overhead, and tropic birds. The red sky is liquid. We ride the shoulder of the western arm of rock that holds Nu'alolo Kai in its embrace. The rock is the color of milk chocolate and full of holes. We are so small here, and so alone, we could be survivors of a shipwreck. But our kayaks are under us, even as their shadows disappear. In Gilman I read:

> "When we had passed about two thirds of the Pali we came to a little bay making in between two arms or points of land, on the shore of which we noticed several canoes, and a few miserable huts.... A few rods back from the beach rise the cliffs, in some places perpendicular for 500 feet.... Along the base of one side are ranged the houses, which form a striking contrast with the black mass of rock rising behind them."

This is the place, the miserable huts are gone, the people having gone first. Micco takes us to a stone well, filled with hoary water, and to the remains of a temple. There are chickens, gangs of them, on the ground and in the trees, flapping their wings, flying. There are burial caves along the eastern cliff wall, but their occupants are all gone. There are shrouds in some and guano everywhere and a feeling not of being in the presence of the sacred but of the deified.

Back at Miloli'i our little group sits around a campfire making S'mores and drinking whisky. We are subdued, talking quietly, if at all. It is clear that having reached Canaan, having reached it by holding our arms out in front of us and pushing, not pulling, we will soon have to give it up. Jack's voice breaks the logjam of silence. "What *is* the meaning of life?" he asks plaintively. "Is there a meaning? What do I work for? It's all I know how to do." His voice drifts off to sea, punctuated by the tide. No one attempts an answer. Down on the beach, we have seen a humpback whale breaching, turning cartwheels like an 85-pound gymnast.

I wake with my hands crabbed and a satisfying ache in my shoulders, covered with a filament of sand from a night outside sleeping on the dunes. The rainwater that flows from the shower is colder than the ocean. I stand under it, exposed to the mountain wall, letting my body chill. My senses are in full possession of me. A draft of honeysuckle blows by. The curling ocean is a voluptuary. It is easy to think this from such a height. At breakfast, Micco says we'll be going higher. There's a waterfall he wants us to see, a short climb into the landscape. I put on hiking boots and a bathing suit, and we set out in search of the trail.

It's not hard to find. It seems that every helicopter turning inland to view the falls follows it. The helicopters are like cicadas, invisible through the dense thatch of trees, but chattering louder even than the rush of water over rocks. We cross those rocks every few minutes, jumping from one to the other as the stream breaks around them. Of course I fall in. My boots fill with water and mud. I fall in again. I can't recover my balance. I slip on dry ground.

We pick our way into a keyhole gorge with walls that rise a few hundred vertical feet and water that falls from the top. The main chamber is one flight up, but there are no stairs. Micco starts climbing the porous rock as if it were a ladder, hand over hand at first, then sideways, across it and around a bend, where he drops down. When it is my turn, I run my hand over the pocked stone like a blind person trying to understand the particular arrangement of a new face. And though I don't understand it, I find myself climbing up anyway, hugging the wall as if it were a friend that had come to stop me from suicide. Which is maybe what it is to be spread-eagled above a sluice of boulders and a rushing stream, attached to the earth by an inch or two at best. It occurs to me that if I think I'm going to fall, I will fall. It is not an encouraging thought. Micco, seeing my fear and fearing it, calls out precise instructions, telling me where to put my left foot, then my right, my left hand, then my right. When I finally drop down into the canyon I am bloody and bruised, and all too conscious, as I have been before on this trip, that there is no way out but the way I came in.

Early the next morning, when the sun is just scaling the backside of the *pali*, with the moon still aloft, a few of us slip into the water to paddle back to Nu'alolo Kai. We give up miles generously, happy to be going in the wrong direction. At Nu'alolo Kai, we put on mask and flippers and snorkel through the coral. The water is alive with wildly colored fish that change hues as the sun ascends. The fish are not shy. They crowd me, trying to get at the bag of fish food I am carrying. They peck at my fingers and bang into my mask. They let me swim among them. Just before nine o'clock a fleet of tour boats arrives, and within minutes the water is filled with a school of jabbering people who drive us away.

Back at Miloli'i, our camp is breaking up. The kitchen is gone, the tents are folded. It's just a matter of loading the boats and taking off. By noon, when we finish, the sun is keen. There is no wind. Micco says that no wind is almost as bad as too much wind, since we will have to work harder, with little relief. On his advice we each stand under the shower and saturate our clothes with the last freshwater we will know for miles.

But a wind comes up, a very gentle one, and it puts a guiding hand on the back of my kayak. I am coasting, barely using my paddle, covering miles in minutes. There is no need to rush today, and I let the boat drift for a while, stalling for time. The sky is a glorious, oceanic blue, and the ocean its glorious double. Onshore, the Nā Pali cliffs stand unflinching, even where rainwater spouts over them and runs hundreds of feet down their face. Polihale State Park, where the trip ends, is in sight nearly the whole way. It is a signature Hawaiian beach, a fifteen-mile cradle of hot white sand.

What cannot be seen is the shore break, and the waves. Micco says they are there, but we have been seduced by the friendly blue sky and the lovely turquoise water, and we are dumb to any dangers. It's as if we have learned nothing on this trip.

Having gotten there first, Rob and Leah go first toward land, and are the first to be swept overboard by a wave that whacks them from behind. I can see them bobbing in the water, far from their kayak. Meanwhile, Jack closes in on the beach, oblivious to the fugitive boat and its absent pilots. Then suddenly, he too, is separated from his kayak, which gets away on the backwash and is carried out to sea.

Sandy disappears. I can't see her or her boat, and won't for minutes. I am out in the open water alone, and my kayak is rocking stern to bow as the waves pass under it, and I am doing everything in my power to keep it perpendicular to the rollers behind me, which I cannot see. Micco, who has already landed, swims out to guide me in. It takes him a while, diving through the waves, pushing against the current, and when he gets to me he grabs the front of the kayak and hangs his body like an anchor. He wants me to slide out of the boat and swim to safety; he'll paddle in. "Micco," I say before he has a chance to tell me this. "I'm not too scared right now." I am not sure what I mean by this, but to him apparently, it suggests that I don't need his help. He lets go and swims away, and I am on my own, fully on my own, whether I want to be or not. A surge comes along and picks up my kayak and me and carries us close to shore, and another comes and another, and the boat rides up the beach, and I step out, not a little triumphantly. A large hairy man I have never seen before rushes over and throws his arms around me. I think that this is some Hawaiian custom I don't know about, having never successfully landed a kayak in big surf before, so I lean into his flesh and let him drag me up the beach a few feet.

"Never turn your back to the sea," he says, galloping away as a swell of water plows into the kayak which would have plowed into me had I still been standing there, marveling at my mastery of wind and water.

Sue Halpern lives in the Adirondack Mountains of New York, which explains in part, she says, "why, I've been to Hawai'i five times in the past ten years." Now writing Two Wings and a Prayer, *a book about monarch butterflies as the ultimate adventurers, she is the author of* Migrations to Solitude *and the editor-at-large of* DoubleTake Magazine. *Her Nā Pali adventure story won a Hawai'i Convention and Visitors Bureau travel writing award. "The prize was an all-expenses-paid trip to Honolulu, which I was completely eager to accept but was otherwise engaged (in the birthing room) at the time." Married to writer Bill McKibben, she is the mother of a daughter.*

⋆

"Water is a kind of Destiny," Gaston Bachelard wrote. "A being dedicated to water is a being in flux...water always flows, always falls, always ends in horizontal death...death associated with water is more dreamlike than death associated with earth: the pain of water is infinite."

The raging main. The fear not injury but death by drowning.

"Those are pearls that were his eyes." Immersions/baptisms/transformations/cleansings/dissolutions. A "sea change into something rich and strange."

Notable local drownings: Hawaiian activists George Helm and Kimo Mitchell (their surfboard found thirteen miles off the island of Lāna'i); waterman Eddie Aikau; waterman José Angel. All lost at sea. Lost at sea.

("I go down with the guys who are out," says surfer Charlie Walker in Bruce Jenkins' *North Shore Chronicles*. "I go down with Eddie (Aikau)—every time I go out. I see him. I see life, I see death. I see every mistake I've made.")

Poet Steve Smith: "I was not waving but drowning."

Surfer Fred Van Dyke: "I was held down.... I'd swim frantically up ten feet, see light, but then get sucked back down again."

But also, being in the water as counterphobic. Buzzy Trent: "Waves are not measured in feet or inches, they are measured in increments of fear."

Of Greg Noll—"Da Bull'—at Mākaha in 1969, Fred Hemmings testified, in Noll's memoir: "All of us were onshore as he finally stroked into a wave that filled the whole horizon...it was a death-wish wave. He elevator-dropped to the bottom. The wave broke over him.... I think he was glad to be alive. I *know* he was lucky to be alive." On the beach, Noll's friend, Buffalo Keaulana, greeted him with a beer. "'Good ting you men make 'em, Brudda,'" Keaulana said. "'Cause no way I was comin' in afta you. I was jus' goin' wave good-by and say 'Aloo-ha.'"

Though this day has become story—the biggest wave ever attempted? —Noll's wife writes that it was quite a while before her husband—who seemed always to enjoy the wipeouts as much as the rides, who would laugh underwater, pinned down at the bottom, waiting for the wave to release him—would speak of that day at all. (It is perhaps not surprising that having tested this limit—and survived—Noll subsequently made a decision to give up surfing altogether.)

—Thomas Farber, *On Water*

LEON EDEL

My Cool, Green Place

A former New Yorker confesses his long love affair with Hawai'i.

WHEN I FIRST CAME TO THE ISLANDS, I DISCOVERED THAT MY EYES were starved for greenness. Even today, after my long feast, I find no satiety in lushness of leaf and shrub, spread of ferns—so many varieties—a universal rustle. The trees grow with determination. No cutting back lasts very long. As I look around me and feel the stirring of rooted things, I think of Yeats's "Byzantium." "The young in one another's arms, birds in the trees...sensual music." The young are very often not in one another's arms but in the arms of the ocean—they surf compulsively—they are hypnotized by great waves and the sea's treacherous and ceaseless seduction. When they are not on surfboards, they tinker with motors. I suppose some few are also linked to their computers.

As for Yeats's, "sensual music," I wonder sometimes what I, now a bookish old man (with mildew, bookworms, silverfish feeding on my books), did before I yielded to so much solicitation of the senses. In the big cities, I used to close my eyes to the monotonous street landscape, and my ears became inattentive while screening out city noise. Nature is full of agreeable sounds here, and we live in a kind of sybaritic awareness of exotic tastes and smells. I find myself accepting the periodic visit of the night-flying termites, who in amorous delight shed their wings during the love-flights; and there are also the armored skittering roaches with space-age antennae who take general possession of tropical climates. One learns to live with them as a form of life.

Everything proliferates, even germs, although Hawai'i seems to have more problems with chemical poisons than bacteria. The local health record is excellent; longevity is distinctly in fashion. There was a time when senescent gentlemen and ladies, down by the seawall, used to walk their dogs at the cocktail hour with leash in one hand and a martini in the other. Congeries of insects, and every now and then a gecko, hum amid the multitudes of plants. Some plants (the experts tell me) have unique mutations and are particular to these Islands. We live in continuing and exhilarating proof of Darwin.

Rice birds swoop in the cassias, cardinals and bulbuls serenade us regularly, and the chattering mynahs are everywhere. Gray days are rare. This gives grayness a particular value.

Up on this cool hilltop, I wonder that I have come to cherish gray as much as the dazzling light of the equatorial sun. It heightens the colors; it makes for contrasts. The greens are deeper; the yellows and reds shine and flame. With so many bright days, I am regularly reminded that I live in a land with a monotony of good weather (with occasional welcome variations and unwelcome hurricanes at long intervals). The ever-refreshing trade winds are the Islands' air conditioning (I wonder how much longer they will be able to keep us cool; they were intended to air-condition thatched huts, not skyscrapers.)

The uninitiated complain that there are no seasons in Hawai'i. But after a while one becomes aware of subtle signals. Certain flowers bloom only in the summer—the ginger spreading its sweetness in gardens and in the mountains, for example—others in the winter, and yet others—the shower trees, the gardenias—in the spring. The golden plover returns from the north in September. There are many secret whispers. One loses all sense of time—but not season—in this bewitchment.

On our front lawn, there stands a short, stocky, determined-looking tree with thick, shining, intensely green leaves. Each leaf looks like an oversized hand stretched toward the coarse, green-brown, melon-sized fruit that weigh down the branches. That tree delights me every time I look at it. It reminds me of my childhood readings of Robert Louis Stevenson, Jack London, Herman Melville and of tales of piracy on the high seas I used to read in the *Boy's Own Annual.* In those stories, sailing ships lowered anchor in tropical coves, rugged Western seamen bargained with natives for breadfruit and papaya. I had always wondered about the fruity bread, and now I have it on my doorstep. It takes a good deal of preparation, much scraping and pounding, to get it cooked properly into succulent softness. Today, the modern equivalent of these Western sailors knock at our door—mainly Tongans and Samoans who have migrated here—and ask whether we plan to eat our breadfruit or whether they may pick it. We consent, on condition that they don't break the branches. With mangoes we are less fussy: they take less preparation. They too signal the season, for there are summer and winter mangoes.

Do I make Hawai'i sound like a twentieth-century Eden—a safe refuge from the space age? If I yield completely to the beauty and seduction of these Islands—those mysterious smoky mountains and haunted and impenetrable valleys and rugged, seamed cliffs—it would be very easy to "go native." But I get a sufficiently paradisiacal sense by my aloofness from the shop-filled tourist centers and the hotel strips.

One can still discover what Hawai'i must have felt like in the time of Melville, before "progress" hit the Islands. Much wealth has poured in since statehood. This has been the fate of Hawai'i from the time that Captain Cook tied up his ships at the Island of Hawai'i, the Big Island. Suddenly, the eighteenth century burst upon a very subtle and organized Stone Age culture. The Hawaiians were asked to take a great—an impossible—leap across the centuries, the kind of leap we invite Third World countries to take today in order to be like us.

Such historical athleticism never comes naturally. It certainly is not as easy as the Western world believes. The consequences of

Cook's eruption into the Hawaiian Islands can be seen even now as alien centuries penetrate somnolent valleys. The number of pure Hawaiians has dwindled. There has been constant dilution, particularly since the Hawaiians were a friendly and welcoming people. Hawaiian types can be singled out within the admixtures—straight black hair, well-defined sensuous lips, dark soulful eyes, high cheekbones. They were always large and unusually tall. There is no person more graceful than a big Hawaiian woman carrying her floating obesity with ineffable grace. She is as light on her feet as a young girl in performing a hula. Her caloric unconcern is welcome in a diet-conscious age. The Hawaiians in their racial mix with Chinese, Japanese, Portuguese, Irish, English, Filipino showed a true cosmopolitanism of their own. The climate ministered to their relaxed good nature and their confidence in a providing world.

The original friendliness and acceptance have been translated commercially into something called the "aloha spirit"—"aloha" meaning all the kinds of affection of which humans are capable.

> More often than not, going back to a place where you've had a special experience is disappointing. With that in mind, I returned with my family to Kona Village Resort on the Big Island…and yet, despite my wariness, the rapture began again. Was it the octopus we saw while snorkeling, the grass skirt one of my daughters wove under the tutelage of a sweet crafts director, the dinner we ate after waiting for the local manta ray to show up by the dining hall, the lack of telephones and television, the stroll under the stars to our grass-thatched *hale,* the wind blowing over our bed, the sincere kindness of the staff? No, I am convinced there is a dimensional portal here, that when you are in Kona Village, you are not on earth at all. How else can I explain that four days lasted three months?
>
> —James O'Reilly, "Kona Dreamtime"

But after living here awhile, one sees some shadows within the aloha spirit. The rapid growth of the population has frayed tempers—just as the pouring of cement increases the Islands' heat.

People ask me what my life in Honolulu is like. It is pretty much what it would be almost anywhere—without the hassle, and with local adaptation. In New York, I used to move within a 75-block area—East Side and West Side and down to Washington Square where I worked. In Honolulu, a city of less than a million, I move in a three- to five-mile radius. This is very comfortable. I drive myself to the beach in twelve minutes. If I am too lazy to swim or find the glare too uncomfortable, I wait for the late afternoon coolness and take a leisurely walk. Living on a hill, I must first do some climbing. At the top I feel myself the king of all I survey.

In Hawai'i everyone is so intermingled with everyone that nobody can sit up until 2 a.m. discussing burning social issues. For one thing, there aren't any. Take race, which is so divisive in California. The governor of Hawai'i is a Filipino-American who beat out an Italian-American and a Japanese-American for the right to succeed a Hawaiian-American and work with the state's two senators, a Japanese-American and a Hawaiian-American who were preceded by a Chinese-American.

—Art Hoppe, "The Mindless Vacation," *San Francisco Chronicle*

The Pacific Ocean near the shores of O'ahu defies description—one has to comb among the jewel colors to get the different shades, the variety of jade greens and blues ranging from dark blue to turquoise; and the coast itself, with the spread of coral reef, adds luminescence I never knew in Atlantic waters.

Having walked around the top of my hill, I descend through unpolluted air past guardian dogs that bark their vigilance at me. I pass houses ranging from solid elegance to bourgeois shabbiness; but none is downright shanty town. Ferns and tī leaves and Italianate cypresses turn even the most humble into graceful abodes.

The Hawaiian environment suits me. I am—especially in my old age—no longer wedded to the ephemera of existence. In this community I find it distinctly agreeable to be reminded (even more than in the East) of faraway places, other ways of life, other peoples, other kinds of speech. We are more polyglot than Manhattan can be. The difference resides in the fact that we look toward Asia rather than Europe. The presence of open space not yet overrun by the private sector, the immensity of sea and sky and the absence of industrialization make Hawai'i a kind of old-fashioned frontier state in the very midst of her modernity. Tourism is a kind of industry, but it involves subtle pollutions. It is easy to count one's blessings.

Honolulu has its music, its restaurants, its museums and a fine Academy of Art. It has had to create its own culture. Like "Old New York" of defunct aristocracy, it has a certain kind of "society" here—a mixture of descendants of the American missionaries and descendants of the old Hawaiian *ali'i* (nobility), plus the transient military elite. It has shaped newer immigrants—the Japanese and Chinese having long found a prosperity comparable to that of the Americans. The Tongans and the Samoans and Filipinos are also here. They have taken over from the earlier upwardly mobile workers.

It is not difficult to discover Hawai'i's natural past—the same valleys, volcanoes, mountains, cliffs, and waterfalls exist as they did when Herman Melville came to Hawai'i in the 1840s or Robert Louis Stevenson in the 1890s. But in these Islands, where so much perishes only to be renewed, there are also a few human abodes and fragile monuments extant, some of them hidden away.

I have always found it moving to stand on the site where Captain Cook died in his fateful encounter with Hawaiians two centuries ago. Or to visit the impressive restoration of the Place of Refuge National Historical Park at Hōnaunau in Kona, which goes back to early times. Drawings of this ancient temple, terraced with rocks, were made by voyagers in the eighteenth century. In

Kailua-Kona, there still stands the house known as Hulihe'e, built in 1837 by the High Chief Kuakini, who became governor first of the Island of Hawai'i and later of O'ahu.

On Moloka'i, one can visit Father Damien's former leper settlement at Kalaupapa, and it is remembered that Stevenson came there shortly after Damien's death and watched a group of young leper girls playing croquet. Later, he sent them a new croquet set and the gift of a piano. On Maui, at Lahaina, where Hawaiian royalty held its court at certain periods, there are some royal tombs and relics of the whaling days. A grand sight on O'ahu is the restored palace of King Kalākaua, completed in 1882, which television viewers often see in *Hawai'i Five-O* reruns: It is the only royal palace in the United States. Queen Emma's mid-nineteenth-century summer villa is still visitable in the Nu'uanu Valley near the Pali on O'ahu. Emma was Kamehameha IV's queen, and her villa bears the splendid name of Hānaiakamalama—a beautiful building in a splendid setting. The Pali, itself, in the wilder part

> Years ago, when I was first traveling in the Pacific, Hawai'i seemed to me to be the westernmost point of the United States. A colony, yes, but American. Avis, McDonald's, Hertz, Hilton. A farther California. But then one day, jogging in Kapi'olani Park in Honolulu, in the shadow of Diamond Head, I stopped to watch an incredibly violent rugby game, one team Samoans, the other Tongans. And suddenly, it came clear: Hawai'i was the northeastern corner of Polynesia; Easter Island, the southeastern corner; the Marquesas, Tahiti, Tonga, Samoa, and New Zealand thus Polynesian points west and south. Honolulu, in this view, is a kind of Rome of the Pacific, various islanders making their way north and east to the imperial city.
>
> —Thomas Farber, *On Water*

of Honolulu, is spectacular—a row of steep, serried cliffs over which Kamehameha I drove armies he defeated in the eighteenth century, when he made himself master of the Island.

On occasion, it occurs to me that I am an escapist. But "escape" from what? Thoreau found it difficult enough in his time. I can't escape my phone, which rings at 4 a.m. and gets me out of deep sleep when some New Yorker forgets we are six hours behind the Eastern Seaboard. On such occasion it is I who explain to the parochial callers that the comfortable midmorning telephone hour happens to be the middle of the night. With telephone, express deliveries, fast-flying jets, one does not "escape" anything, and one can readily flee Island claustrophobia. One is in touch, in, I think, a hundred agreeable ways.

My feeling essentially is not that of being an escapee, but rather having found within our American civilization a rare place where I've been able—without overindulgence—to have my cake and to eat as much of it as my caloric intake allows. "Lucky you live Hawai'i" is a pidgin remark one hears often in the Islands. Different people will measure their luck in different ways. I measure mine as enabling me to have the best of my two worlds. To be sure, I am an ocean and a continent removed from my old stamping grounds—but they are in reality only ten hours away. And when I visit them, I think of my cool, green place that awaits my return. I think then of the hibiscus and the plumeria blossoms blown over my lawn and the sound of the ocean breaking with a regular beat and feel a great contentment—that sense of indolence which Pliny the Younger felt to be a beatitude of the leisure life.

Leon Edel, Pulitzer Prize–winning biographer of Henry James, died September 5, 1997, in Honolulu, where he had lived since 1972. He was 89. A former professor of English and American Letters at New York University, Edel received both the Pulitzer and the National Book Award in 1963 for the second and third volumes of his five-volume biography of James, the American novelist and critic.

⋆

I recall being advised when I first visited Honolulu that if I left the keys in a car in Waikīkī, I could look for it stripped down in 'Ewa Beach. There is no particular reason to go to 'Ewa, no shops, no businesses, no famous views, no place to eat or even walk far; there is only the fact that the place is there, intact, a plantation town from another period. There is a school, a post office, a grocery. There is the Immaculate Conception Roman Catholic Church, there is the 'Ewa Hongwanji Mission.

'Ewa was a company town, and its identical houses are arranged down a single street, the street that leads to the sugar mill. Just one house on this street stands out: a house built of the same frame as the other but not exactly a bungalow, a house transliterated from the New England style, a *haole* house, a manager's house larger than any other house for miles around. A Honolulu psychiatrist once told me, when I asked if he saw any characteristic Island syndrome, that, yes, among the children of the planter families, children raised among the memories of the place's colonial past, he did. It was the conviction that they were being watched, being observed, and not living up to what was expected of them. In 'Ewa one understands how that conviction might take hold. In 'Ewa one watches the larger house.

On my desk in Los Angeles, I keep a clock on Honolulu time, and around five o 'clock by that clock I imagine driving through 'Ewa at that time of day, when the mill and the frame bungalows swim in the softened light like amber, and I imagine driving on down through 'Ewa Beach and onto that tract of military housing at Iroquois Point, a place as rigidly structured and culturally isolated in one way as 'Ewa is another. From the shoreline at Iroquois Point, one looks across the curve of the coast at Waikīkī, a circumstance so poignant that it stops discussion, a view in which there is written each of the tensions of Honolulu life. Quite often people tell me that Honolulu is a place of no interest. I can only think that they have not yet noticed.

—Joan Didion, "Going 'Ewa," *New West*

JAMES D. HOUSTON

* * *

Fire in the Night

A hands-on encounter with the work of the fire goddess Pele.

AMONG VOLCANO BUFFS, THERE IS A LITTLE RITE OF PASSAGE, whereby you stick your hand-ax into moving lava and bring away a gob of the molten stuff. In order to do this, you have to be where the lava is flowing and hot, then you have to get your body in close enough to reach down toward the edge of the flow, and it usually means you have to walk or stand at least a few seconds on some pretty thin crust.

My chance came one night when I was traveling in the company of Jack Lockwood, a specialist in Volcanic Hazards with the U.S. Geological Survey. He is a trim and wiry fellow, with wild hair and a devilish grin, a man from New England who has found this Island, its craters and flows, to be his natural habitat. He loves it here, he loves the look of the ropey *pāhoehoe*, the many shapes it takes. He will stop the car to study the way today's flow has poured over yesterday's, making a drapery of knobs and drips. He will remark upon the metallic sheen in the late sun and then point out that newer lava can be crumbled with your shoe, while the stuff that came through yesterday has already hardened under a rainfall and thus is firmer.

We park where the yellow line of the coast road disappears

under a ten-foot wall of new rock. We get out the packs, the gloves, the canteens, the flashlights, the hardhats. Jack's hat is custom-made, with his name in raised letters on the metal. His hard-toe boots are scuffed ragged with threads of rock-torn leather. I was going to wear running shoes for this expedition, until he told me no. "Where we're going," he said while we were packing, "the soles could peel right off."

Hunkered on the asphalt, lacing up the high-top boots I've borrowed, I can already feel it shimmering toward us. Minutes later we are hiking through furnace heat, over lava that has rolled across here just a few hours ago. Through cracks and fissures, you can see the molten underlayer showing, three or four inches below the dark surface.

"You can actually walk on it fifteen or twenty minutes after it starts to harden," Jack says, "as long as you have an inch of surface underfoot."

Soon the red slits are everywhere, and we're crossing what appears to be several acres of recent flow. Jack plunges ahead with great purpose, with long firm strides, planting each foot and leaning forward as he walks, as if there is a path to be followed and we are on it—though of course there is no path, no prior footprints, no markers of any kind to guide us across terrain that wasn't here this morning.

"Jack," I say, "have you ever stepped into a soft spot? I mean, got burned, fallen through?"

He shakes his head vigorously. "Nope."

"How do you know where to step?"

He stops and looks at me with his mischievous eyes, his beard and squint reminding me of a young John Huston. "You just pick your way and pay attention as you go. It's partly experience and partly faith."

"Faith?"

"You have to put your trust in Pele. Tell her you come out here with respect, and she'll take care of you."

As he plunges on, I want to trust in Pele, whose crater/home is about fifteen miles upslope from where we're walking. We have already talked about her, while driving down Chain of Craters Road, and I know he means what he just said. But I have to confess that at the moment I am putting my full trust in Lockwood, placing my feet where he places his, stepping in his steps as we stride and leap from rock to rock.

Eventually the heat subsides, and we're hiking over cooler stuff, though none of it is very old.

"Everything you see has flowed through in the last six months," he says.

Two and a half miles of the coast road have recently been covered, as well as the old settlement of Kamoamoa, near where we parked. Inland we can see some of what remains of Royal Gardens, a subdivision laid out in the early 1970s, laid right across a slope of the East Rift Zone. In the Royal Gardens grid, cross streets were named for tropical flowers—Gardenia, *Pīkake*—while the broader main streets sound noble—Kamehameha, Prince. I have been up there. You have to be careful when you turn a corner. Take a left, and you are liable to come upon a charcoal heap the size of a football field, with a fallen street sign poking through to remind you that this had been the intersection where Ali'i Drive met Plumeria Boulevard, where home-bound motorists once slowed down to look both ways before crossing.

From the shoreline now, it looks as if great vats of black paint have been dumped over the highest ridge, to pour down the slope and through the trees, to cover lawns and long-lost driveways.

Our destination—the spilling end of another lava tube—is marked by a steam plume rising high against the evening sky. When we left the car it was white and feathery at the top, two miles down the coast. After the sun has set and the light begins to dim, the plume turns pink and red. Spatter thrown up from the collision of lava and surf has formed a littoral cone now outlined against the steam. As we approach, tiny figures can be seen standing at the edge of this cone, like cutouts against the fiery backdrop.

On one side of the cone, flat spreads of lava ooze toward the cliff. On the other side, an orange gusher is arcing 30 feet above the water, while a mound slowly rises beneath it. Beyond this tube, another spill obscured by steam sends lava straight into the water at about sea level. Black and crimson floating gobs spew out from the steam, or sometimes fly into the air, breaking into fiery spatter that is gradually building the littoral cone.

These fires light the billowing plume from below. As it churns away toward the west, it sends a pinkish glow back down onto the marbled surf, which makes me think of the Royal Hawaiian Hotel, where they spend a lot of money on lightbulbs and filters trying to tint the offshore waters a Waikīkī pink that can never come close to Pele's cosmetic kit.

A video cameraman is out here, perched at the cliff edge, filming the buildup on the mound below the arching orange tube. His tripod legs are spindly black against the glow. Nearby, a couple of dozen people stand gazing at the spectacle, from Volcano Observatory and the University of Hawai'i. They are out here in numbers, Jack tells me later, because this is a rare night. Spills like this are usually closer to the surf, and the lava will pour until the mound builds from below to seal off its opening. But this littoral cone is unstable, and part of it has fallen away, to behead the end of the tube, so the lava spills free from high up the cliff, making an endless column of liquid orange.

If you can take your eyes off its mesmerizing arc and turn inland, you can see another glow in the night. It hangs above the nearest ridge, light from the lake called Kūpaianaha, the source of the lava moving around us. It's a new lake, inside a new shield cone. From there the lava snakes seaward via a channel that loops wide to the east, then back toward where we stand. You can see evidence of its twisting, subterranean path about halfway down the mountain, where tiny fires seem to be burning, four or five eyes of flame against the black.

We linger for an hour, maybe more, chatting, bearing witness, sharing our wonder with the others lucky enough to be out here on such a night, at the cutting edge of destruction and creation. We are about to start back when Lockwood says this is probably as good a time as any for me to add my name to the "one thousandth of one percent of the human population who have stuck their ax in hot lava." And with that he begins to prowl around a couple of oozing streams to see how close we can get.

I watch him step out onto some hot stuff that has barely stopped moving, and see the surface give under his boot. With a grin he jumps back. "That's probably a little too soft."

We move around to the far side, 40 feet away, and approach the fiery mush from another angle. With ax in hand, he hops across the one-inch crust and digs into the front edge of a narrow strip, but it's already cooling and a little too thick to lift. He can only pull it up an inch or so, the front lip already in that halfway zone between liquid and solid stone.

He's pulling so hard he loses his footing and half falls toward the crust. His gloved hand reaches out to take the fall, and for a moment his crouching body is silhouetted against the molten stream, while behind him the red and orange steam plume surges like a backdrop curtain for his dance. He comes rolling and hopping toward me with a wild grin and a rascal eye.

"That's a little too viscous. It's surprising. It's cooler than it looks."

So we move on, heading back the way we've come, under a black sky with its infinity of stars, our flashlight beams bobbing across the rocks, while the plume grows smaller behind us.

We drop down to a new beach of dark volcanic sand, then climb out of the sand onto that day's fresh lava, where the red slits once again glow around us. As we pick our way, in the furnace heat, we come upon a flow that wasn't here when we crossed the first time.

"Pele is being good to you," says Jack, grinning, his beard red tinted underneath. He hands me his ax. "This is perfect. Just keep your back to the heat, and move in quickly."

Which is what I do.

The stream is maybe twenty feet wide, crackling, creeping toward the sea. I back-pedal up next to it, reaching with the flat chisel-end of the metal blade, dip and scoop into the burning lip. It is smoother than wet cement, thicker than honey, thicker than three-finger poi. Maybe the consistency of glazing compound, or the wet clay potters use. For the first minisecond it feels that way. As I dig in and pull, it is already harder. It clings to the flow, but I tug and finally come away with a chunk the size of a tennis ball, which holds to the blade as I leap back away from the heat.

Jack is excited. "Throw it down here, quickly!"

I plop it between us, on a black slab.

"Now press your heel in hard!"

I press my boot heel into the glob, flattening it with a boot-print. When the rubber begins to smoke, I pull my foot away.

"Now," he says, with a happy grin, "we'll put this on my shovel blade and carry it to the car while it cools, and this will be your souvenir."

By the time we reach the asphalt road, the heat has given way to balmy coastal air off the water. The slits and fissures and plumes and flows are all behind us, and that is the end of our expedition.

But it is not the end of my relationship with this flattened piece of rock. I live with it for another week, trying to decide what to do. After such a magical night, the idea of a souvenir appeals to me. It is mine, I suppose, because I have marked it with my boot. It is smooth, as shiny as black glass, and if I lived here I'd probably have it sitting on my desk for years. But I don't feel right about bringing this trophy back home. I keep thinking about the tug of the lava as I pulled the ax away. Through the handle I felt its texture, its consistency, and something else that haunts me. A reluctance. A protest. As if live flesh were being torn from a body.

Maybe this is what the Hawaiians mean when they say all the rocks belong to Pele and should not leave the Islands. Maybe the unwritten law that says be respectful of the rocks is another way of honoring that old yearning in the stone. Maybe I have finally understood something, through my hands, something I've heard about and read about and talked about and even tried to write about.

A couple of days later I drove down to the south shore again. Sighting from the new black sand beach, I think I got pretty close to where we'd been. I dropped the chunk of lava down into a jagged crevice and asked it to forgive me for any liberties I might have taken, and I thanked Pele for letting me carry this rock around for a while.

Back on the Mainland I probably won't tell anybody about this. You come home and tell someone you've been talking to rocks, they give you that certain kind of look. I've mentioned it to Jack Lockwood, of course. It's easier to talk about when you're here in the Islands. When you're in or near volcano country, it's easier to remember that each rock was once a moving, breathing thing, as red as blood and making eyes of fire in the night.

James D. Houston, author of five novels, including Continental Drift, Gig *and* Love Life, *was married on the beach at Waikīkī to Jeanne Wakatsuki Houston; together they wrote* Farewell to Manzanar, *an award-winning screenplay about the internment of California's Japanese during World War II. They live in Santa Cruz, California. His nonfiction works include* In the Ring of Fire: A Pacific Basin Journey *from which this story was excerpted, and* Californians: Searching for the Golden State.

*

For me, times and feelings of the old ones are best savored in what they made and used—for living, for beauty, and for the spirit—and above all the stones. The stones are a wonder. Molten stone stirred the Hawaiians' earth. Stone was everywhere: stone of sensual porosity and textures; stone that begged handling and shaping; beach and stream stones, tumbled and buffed to millions of satin-smooth moldings. There was soft stone, cindery stone, stone tiny and immense. Stones for building, for shrines, trails, household gods, sinkers, anchors, slings of war, and games of peace. Laboriously, bruisingly, the ancients chipped one against the other, forming precious adzes from densest basalt, quarried, sometimes in snow dustings, from the highest mountains, to be fashioned for farming, tree-felling, canoe- and god-carving. The great *heiau*, temples, were fashioned of hundreds of thousands of carefully placed stones. They stood, platforms of magnificence, in long ago suns—and many still stand, lost in thickets of today.

—Ed Sheehan, *The Hawaiians*

THOMAS FARBER

Coming Home

Sometimes you can go home, to a place you've never been.

I HAD A DISTURBING SENSE OF COMING HOME WHEN I FIRST arrived in Hawai'i as the sixties became the seventies, encountering not only the tropics and Polynesia but the architecture of my childhood in various nineteenth-century Hawaiian churches and homes. There was Red Sand Beach and its ironwood trees, there was Haleakalā and Kaupō Gap, there were the *māhū* in women's clothing singing in falsetto at a baby *lū'au* on Moloka'i—clearly here was another place, another people, another set of premises. With all this, however, there was the overlay of, the undertone of, a too-familiar reality and set of proprieties. Between them, the nineteenth-century New England missionaries and traders had powerfully influenced—had in time taken control of—the life of these Islands. Six thousand miles from the home I'd long since left behind, I was forced to remember what it was in my childhood I had bridled against, incorporated, sought to purge from my heart.

The period in which I first visited the outer Islands was the end of the plantation era, many of the country towns still sleepy backwaters, a period also marked by the arrival of a wave of young whites in search of Eden, migrants often uninterested in or actively determined to ignore the human history of the Islands, content simply to reach a farther California. If the hippie *haoles* could seem selfish or callous, narcissistic in their obsession with religious search or diet, on the other hand many of them lived close to the land or the water, simply and quietly, came to know the physical environment very well indeed. Had, in some cases, an extraordinary if occasionally self-destructive yearning to merge with it. At the least, their impulse to purity or pleasure or Nature forced one to define one's own mission in the Islands and, inevitably, to take stock of the white continuum that had begun with the traders and missionaries. I spent many mornings at the ocean, many afternoons in the Wailuku Public Library.

Years later, in Honolulu, I'd go down to the beach each day for an hour. Often I'd see the same very tan young woman in a folding chair listening to a Sony Walkman, bounding with the beat, smearing herself with another round of oil. Always she'd be wearing the barest of bikinis, her breasts pneumatic to a degree not in all likelihood envisioned by the Almighty. Thus exposed, she nonetheless radiated the desire to be left alone, and so I did my best. Occasionally, she'd take out a joint and light up, and I'd smell the sweet smoke, watch her legs moving hard to the invisible drummer's tempos. One day, after weeks of seeing me there, perhaps appreciating that I'd done no more than nod hello, she offered to share a joint with me. Subsequently, we'd exchanged a few words, and finally, had a conversation.

Her name was Rose, I learned, which I might have guessed from the tattoo on her left bicep. It turned out Rose was a "dancer," and before I could stop myself I asked, "What kind of dancer?" though I nearly bit my tongue trying to keep the words from coming out of my mouth. Too late: Rose seemed disappointed—I'd shown such admirable restraint thus far—but nonetheless continued the conversation. She'd been a coke freak, it turned out, down to 90 pounds, (a girlfriend died from an overdose). She worked as a stripper only a few months at a time; could get a job anywhere she wanted, and...she was from Boston. From East Boston, actually, Italian-Irish; raised on the third floor of one of the old three-deckers near Logan Airport. Her father was a fireman who often knocked her around, particularly when she began to get interested in boys; her father had recently remarried a woman younger than Rose.

Now this may seem odd, but on that beach in Honolulu that day, Pacific stretching out before us, Rose well-oiled, toking her joint—it may seem odd, but of everything about Rose—from tattoo to bikini to Sony Walkman—what engaged me most was that she was from Boston. I felt a special connection, being able as I thought to read what had shaped her; what she'd emerged from; what she carried in her heart; knowing the streets she'd walked, schools she'd attended, faces she'd seen, the voices still in her ear. What she'd confronted, ducked, escaped, would be nostalgic for. Talking to Rose, I could see the North End of my college days, of Rose's childhood. Very close, the North End was, to East Boston, the other end of the Sumner Tunnel. Just twenty, I was going out with a woman who lived in the North End, on snowy evenings would ride my motorcycle down the narrow streets, tar glistening, past the old tight graveyards overlooking Boston Harbor—Paul Revere's house was down here, the church the famous lantern had hung in (one if by land/two if by sea)—and past the Italian markets with rabbits dangling in the window. I'd spend the night, radiator clanking, clanking, but then be very very careful not to hold her hand in public, not to put my arm around her as we made a slow progress through the neighborhood stopping for vegetables, bread, or pasta at each small shop, not to appear to be her lover lest her reputation be...shot.

Boston, Honolulu, on a beach with Rose, sun beating down, the healing waters close by, a lone frigate bird sailing high overhead. Willy-nilly, Rose and I took our place in the continuum of New Englanders who'd come to the Islands, people who would in time become either more or less New Englanders—asserting their distance from, or hunger to come closer to, an environment and a people so very unlike what had been left behind.

Thomas Farber is a recipient of Guggenheim and National Endowment for the Humanities fellowships for fiction. A frequent visitor to Hawai'i, Farber has been Visiting Distinguished Writer at the University of Hawai'i, a Fulbright Scholar for Pacific Island Studies, and Visiting Fellow at the East-West Center in Honolulu. His fiction and nonfiction works include Learning to Love It, Tales for the Son of My Unborn Child, Curves of Pursuit, Compared to What?, Who Wrote the Book of Love, *and* On Water, *from which this story was excerpted.*

✶

Think you know Hawai'i?

Answer all ten questions correctly and win an autographed photo of Don Ho. Okay, just answer the questions.

1. Hawai'i is located: a.) off the coast of Los Angeles; b.) in the North Pacific; c.) in the South Pacific.
   Answer: b.) in the North Pacific.
2. True or false: Honolulu is the most remote city and Hawai'i the farthest islands from any continent on the planet.
   Answer: true.
3. Hawai'i has: a.) four islands; b.) eight islands; c.) 132 islands.
   Answer: 132 islands.
4. The last monarch of Hawai'i was: a.) King Kamehameha the Great; b.) Queen Lili'uokalani; c.) King Kalākaua.
   Answer: b.) Queen Lili'uokalani.
5. The mai tai, the classic tropical cocktail of Hawai'i, was invented by Trader Vic Bergeron in: a.) Hawai'i; b.) Tahiti; c.) California.
   Answer: c.) California.
6. The official state bird of Hawai'i is: a.) a sea gull; b.) a goose; c.) a mynah.
   Answer: b.) a goose.
7. A Loco Moco is: a.) a crazy person; b.) something to eat; c.) a Hawaiian male.
   Answer: b.) something to eat.
8. Rainbows occur in Hawai'i: a.) only at sundown; b.) when it rains; c.) when they are turned on.
   Answer: b.) when it rains.
9. Is Honolulu closer to Tokyo or to Washington, D.C.?
   Answer: Tokyo.
10. Aloha means: a.) hello; b.) good-bye; c.) with love.
    Answer: all of the above.

—RC & MC

JAN MORRIS

Paradox in the Sun

The most isolated city under the sun is also the most worldly.

ALMOST OPPOSITE THE HYATT REGENCY WAIKĪKĪ, IN THE flashiest part of Honolulu, where the towering hotels jostle one another for supremacy along the sandy line of Waikīkī Beach—beneath some palm trees at this supremely brassy spot—four dark boulders unprepossessingly brood. Few people take much notice of them, except perhaps to throw their towels on them while rinsing the sand off their feet at a nearby faucet, and the stones seem to me to stand there in attitudes of perpetual reproach.

They are the Wizard Stones, immemorial totems of Hawaiian awe, and they were standing there, very much more honored then, in the days when Waikīkī was the power center of an independent Polynesian chiefdom. I interpret them as reminder that the city of Honolulu is far, far more than its popular legend allows; not just a glittery pleasure-haven, but a place of profound and remarkable consequence. It is a complete modern conurbation, a place in many ways prophetic of the way the world is going, and it is stunningly deposited in the most geographically isolated spot on earth, the island of O'ahu in the middle of the Pacific Ocean.

No other sea has ever given birth to such a place, unless you count the mythical lost city of Atlantis. It is as though a Lisbon were to exist on the Cape Verde Islands, or a Bombay in the Maldives. Honolulu is 2,400 miles from the nearest continental shore, and, except for neighboring Islands, nothing but open sea lies between O'ahu and California, Japan, Alaska, or South America. History could not have chosen a more improbable spot for the creation of a metropolis.

> The undertones of every day in Honolulu, the one fact that colors every other, is the place's absolute remove from the rest of the world. Many American cities began remote, but only Honolulu is fated to remain so, and only in Honolulu do the attitudes and institutions born of extreme isolation continue to set the tone of daily life. The edge of the available world is sharply defined: one turns a corner or glances out an office window and there it is, blue sea. There is no cheap freedom to be gained by getting in a car, since as far as one can go on the Island of O'ahu takes about an hour and fifteen minutes.
>
> ◆
>
> —Joan Didion, "Honolulu Days," *New West*

Honolulu is the capital of the 50th state of the Union, embracing all the Islands of the Hawaiian archipelago, but actually it is very like a city-state itself. With a population approaching 900,000, it has its own private hinterland in O'ahu, all 600 square miles of which fall within the city and county limits, like a gigantic civic park with Honolulu in its lee. From the sea, the blue-green highlands, wild and jagged on their summit ridges, gently sloping below, seem to descend directly into the city's back gardens; and silhouetted astonishingly against them, bustled about by tumultuous traffic, topped by radio masts, with vessels moving constantly offshore and aircraft flinging themselves ceaselessly into the sky, Honolulu's serried tower blocks stand like a living logo—a declaration of wealth and energy at the remotest spot on the planet.

If it looks from the sea like an exhibition city, its ground plan too suggests to me a planner's theorem. All is rational. There is the original commercial and industrial quarter, around the old docks. There is a university district on the hill slopes behind. There is Waikīkī, the famous pleasure quarter, populated chiefly by vacationists. To the west is the naval base of Pearl Harbor, and in a swath all around, reaching up into the mountains and along the shore, are Honolulu's residential districts, whose housing prices are among the highest of any city in the United States, whose citizens are said to possess more cars than any other citizenry, and whose residents range from reclusive billionaires in barricaded mansions to diligent corporation men in ties and striped suits to destitute beachcombers with straw hats and tangled gray beards, representing between them almost every race and condition under the sun.

No wonder the Wizard Stones seem resentful. This is not just an overhyped tourist destination, as the world generally supposed, but a great contemporary working city.

It happened while I was in Honolulu last time (I have been going there on and off for more than 30 years) that the city was honoring the birthday of Kalākaua, nicknamed the Merrie Monarch, the last Hawaiian king to rule these Islands before the United States annexed them in 1898. I went to a celebratory parade of the Royal Guard at the 'Iolani Palace, the endearingly ornate mansion the royal family built for itself in downtown Honolulu; the building is now no more than a museum, but the occasion movingly illustrated for me the historical compulsion of this city.

A century ago, Honolulu was hardly more than a village; yet it is inescapably impregnated with a sense of history. The Royal Guard that day was dressed in liveries (white pith helmets, bandoliers) that looked like uniforms from the Zulu War, and was given its orders in the Hawaiian language. Its music was provided by the Royal Hawaiian Band, founded in 1836, and appropriately conducted by a magnificently bearded bandmaster. Before the Palace steps was placed a huge eagle-topped trophy presented to the king in 1881 by his colleague the emperor of Germany. The march-past was to music composed by the king himself. The national anthem was the anthem of the Hawaiian Kingdom, whose lyrics were written by the king. And the parade was inspired by Prince Edward Kawānanakoa, the man who would, if the monarchy still existed, now himself be ruler of Hawai'i. All this, in the capital of the 50th state! Flags flew everywhere that day, and the place was draped in bunting, but there was not a Stars and Stripes in sight.

> The Merrie Monarch was indeed the last king to rule Hawai'i before the kingdom fell victim to a power struggle orchestrated by American sugar interests, ending with annexation in 1898. But he was not the last monarch; that sad page in history belonged to his sister, Lili'uokalani, the tragic queen who was forced to give over her Islands to imperialistic Westerners—and subsequently was imprisoned in her own palace.
>
> ◆
>
> —RC & MC

Only some 9,000 people, I am told, now speak the Hawaiian language fluently. Only 12 percent of this population can claim Hawaiian, or even half-Hawaiian, blood; the original Islanders have long ago been swamped by the Caucasians, Japanese, Chinese, and all the others who have come here since Captain Cook first revealed the existence of Hawai'i to the world in 1778. Yet there is no forgetting the society that was here before, and the figure of Prince Edward on the steps of the Palace, unmistakably Hawaiian despite his elegant European suit, descended from chieftains who dressed in feathers of the *'ō'ō* bird and appeased their gods with human sacrifice—Edward's dignified presence there, as his guard marched by, seemed to me inexpressibly poignant. Indelibly, the Hawaiian civilization has been debased by generations of occupation and tourism. Its ancient music has been vulgarized. Its ritual dances have been trivialized. Its language has been ignorantly plundered or patronized as a tourist gimmick.

Half-submerged, the culture does live on—passionate enthusiasts keep the language going, and at almost any of the old Hawaiian temples, dedicated to the gods of long ago, you may still see offerings of flower and fruit laid in gratitude or supplication. It is a ghost of itself, though. The illusion of the old society is promoted boisterously everywhere, but its reality loiters wraithlike through the city, wistfully reaching out to susceptible travelers in the rustle of the palms, or through the sickly mooning of guitars beneath the stars of happy hour.

One characteristic of the indigenous, however, lives on more robustly in Honolulu. The old Hawaiians had a supreme capacity for enjoying themselves, when they were not being sacrificed to deities. They were the original surfers, the original Waikīkī escapists, and old pictures show them besporting themselves along their beaches just like the package tourists of today. Honolulu has inherited from them a genuinely rollicking talent for having a good time, exploited of course by the tourist industry, but perfectly organic still.

The Wizard Stones may grumble to find the mystique of their environment reduced to Waikīkī's cheap publicity, but actually this two-and-a-half-mile-long enclave of hedonism is a model of its kind. You might not think so, if you found yourself allotted one of the many Waikīkī hotel rooms that look desperately out on a blank wall across a noisy alley, but actually your bedroom is the last thing to worry about here. This is an uninhibitedly public, cheerfully democratic resort. Jam-packed indescribably into its narrow limits, climbing always higher above the long-dwarfed palms and banyans, it often suggests to me a kind of neo-Oriental pleasure bazaar. Seen, for instance, across the artificial waterfall of the Halekulani, an oasis of green, luxurious calm amid the general hubbub, Waikīkī at night looks remarkably like a richer Calcutta, all movement, lights, noises, smells, with an all-night restaurant gaudy on the corner, and the dazzle of Kalākaua Avenue, Waikīkī's strip, casting everything into a bilious glow beyond.

Nothing clashes in Waikīkī. Anything goes, and you can make your own combinations. You can sleep in a back-street boardinghouse and breakfast at the Halekulani. You can breakfast on a Big

Mac and swim at the Royal Hawaiian Hotel beach—all beaches are public on O'ahu, and all are equally clean. You can buy dreadful mementos at honky-tonk stores, or spend a bit more at Tiffany's, Cartier, or Alfred Dunhill. At the Sheraton Moana Surfrider Hotel, you can even sit on a real open veranda beneath a banyan tree, in a miraculously restored retreat of South Seas clapboard. Every degree of squalor or refinement informs these remarkable few city blocks—eager prostitutes and chichi restaurateurs, five-star suites and sleeping bags in Kapi'olani Park.

Well, almost every refinement. Hard though the posher hoteliers try to give the resort exclusivity, this is decidedly not an upmarket Elysium. It is too populist to be exclusive; too easygoing: not since the Hawaiian kings maintained this particular stretch of sand and surf as their royal preserve has Waikīkī managed to be snooty.

Many citizens scarcely go to Waikīkī from one year to the next. It is no more than one city quarter of several, and the fulcrum of their Honolulu is a different quarter altogether—downtown, the original port and business district, where the Palace is, and the modernistic State Capitol, and the City Hall and the portentous offices of the corporations that have made their money down the years from Hawai'i's sugar and pineapple plantations. There is heavy Japanese investment down there, too, and real estate fortunes are frequently made or lost, and enormous tourist developments are plotted.

It is a handsome downtown—one of the best looking in America, I think—yet here, history agreeably blurs the edges. Honolulu is not one of your flash-in-the-pan business cities. It was a whaling station 150 years ago, and even now it has its schooner-port echoes, its Conradian moments: when you look down a steel-and-glass business thoroughfare, say, to see the piers of the old port, where the Nantucket ships used to dock for their provisions, and where the interisland freighters still set sail for Kaua'i, Moloka'i, Maui, and the Big Island. On the corner of Merchant Street is Murphy's Bar & Grill, formerly the Royal Saloon, a splendidly plush-and-mahogany kind of tavern where the Merrie Monarch used to amuse himself by mingling with the seagoing classes. The little Catholic cathedral of Our Lady of Peace stands magically hushed even now in its secluded close at the end of a shopping mall, while Chinatown bravely resists the inroads of gentrification with a proper mix of the homey and the raffish, food market beside art gallery, pool hall and nude video show along the road from modish boutique.

> Boys with skins like expensive luggage lounged in the cross-legged way of true superiority as I paddled out through the tiny surf. Cowboy and I turned and waited for the wave. At the critical moment he pushed me and the board shoreward. "You're a good boy, Adam." The push momentum merged into the wave momentum, a sudden acceleration, a self-sufficient feeling of all-rightness, the surf gushing around my feet as if electric pump driven. My giant plank was away, I was up, buoyant, standing, cruising in on the organized chaos of surf, toward the shining towers of Waikīkī.
>
> ◆
>
> —Adam Nicolson, "O'ahu," *Islands*

Downtown Honolulu as a whole, though, is not at all a quaint or nostalgic place. It has a recognizable power to it, as the heart of a great city should, expressed not just in the buildings of consequence, old and new, but in an articulated sense of purpose. You can hardly have a serious conversation in Honolulu, can hardly pick up one of its newspapers, without realizing that this city now thinks of itself not at all as an isolated speck on the map, but as a Pacific fulcrum where the world meets, and Honolulu already sees its destiny as a prime point of contact for all the countries of the Pacific Rim—the Geneva, as one visionary lately put it, of the Pacific.

It is almost happening already. This hardly feels like an American city nowadays, even of the most exotic kind. It is multinational to a degree unknown even in the most teeming immigrant cities of Mainland USA, and it looks to its Pacific neighbors, Japan, California, Australia, British Columbia, far more naturally than it looks to the distant authority of Washington, D.C. All the Pacific faces, all the Pacific tongues and influences are here: much of Honolulu is Japanese owned; Chinatown is largely Filipino and Vietnamese; many of the best restaurants are Thai; and you can hardly walk down Kalākaua Avenue without hearing Australian accents.

In short, Honolulu, capital of the 50th state, officially an American city for 90 years, is turning itself into something else—just as the world, too, while we watch, is becoming another kind of community. If Honolulu really were what people generally suppose it to be, the city might well be bewildered by such momentous progressions. In fact, it is very well equipped to assume the special status its situation seems to demand for it. It is not a shallow city at all, as its popular reputation suggests, but a city truly in the round.

It is well acquainted, for a start, with power. Much of central O'ahu is one big military base, with helicopters massed on airfields and rambling military townships, while the landlocked inlet of Pearl Harbor, almost within sight of Waikīkī, has been for half a century and more one of the great power factors of the world. From its bunkers, the commander of United States fleets throughout the Pacific exerts his vast authority, maintains his hundreds of ships and thousands of men; there are gray masts and rigging everywhere, and mighty satellite dishes, and submarines steal in from the sea past the wreck of USS *Arizona*, sunk by the Japanese in 1941 and still leaking, even now, a gallon of oil to color the harbor water every day.

For better or worse, this is a city of mature experience. It has had direct experience of war, such as no other American city can claim, and it knows of all the problems that contemporary cities are heir to. It is no mere tropical paradise. Drug abuse is chronic, crime is all too familiar, traffic congestion is terrible, there are thousands of homeless people and many hungry ones. At the same time it has at hand all the resources of a highly developed modern metropolis. I do not mean, of course, just money—any tomfool American beach resort has that. I mean the intellectual and cultural strengths that alone enable a city to take a distinguished place in history. Honolulu is well aware of its historical potential, and possesses the institutions to handle it.

The University of Hawai'i, for example, housed in a leafy meander of a campus, has powerful departments of linguistics, marine science, tropical agriculture, and other specialties relevant to the new Pacific. The East-West Center is one of the world's chief exchanges of Occidental and Oriental thought, working in 40 different languages, and attracting scholars, diplomats, and business people from all over the Pacific. The Bishop Museum is an unrivaled repository of Pacific knowledge; Honolulu's international film festival is an exuberantly pan-Pacific affair; and even in the performing arts this city plays a symbiotic role: when I was there last, the Honolulu Symphony Orchestra was preparing a performance of Fauré's *Requiem,* accompanied by specially choreographed hula dancing.

Do not be deceived, then, if you arrive in Waikīkī one balmy evening, straight off your flight from the Mainland, and see the city apparently seized by the perpetual pursuit of fun and money. Take note of the Wizard Stones!

Those strange vessels you see offshore may be sunset cruise ships, but they may be experimental warships of the Pacific fleet. The sound of electrified ukulele will doubtless fill the twilight air, but the Ballet Hawai'i may well be performing later in the evening.

For myself, I sense in Honolulu not just the balanced modern city that I have been trying to describe, but an archetypal city of the future, empowered by the new mingling of all our races, liberated by the abolition of distance, given an altogether new significance by its extraordinary place on the map. History was right, after all, and 21°19' N, 157°50' W, which used to seem so quixotic a location, now seems perfectly logical.

Few cities speak so clearly of shifting national meanings and ethnic conceptions. I am sure, however, that Honolulu's original loyalties will never be eradicated. Bashed, guyed, and degraded as it has been, its native Hawaiianness may well be strengthened rather than weakened by the city's new place in the world—the wider the outlook, the tougher the root. A century from now, I do not doubt, a Hawaiian prince will still be reviewing his guard on Kalākaua's birthday, while the royal band oompah-pahs, as always, beneath the palm trees, the commands ring out in the tongue of the Islands, and the old memories stir sweet and sad among the skyscrapers.

Jan Morris has been wandering the world and writing about her experiences for more than 40 years. She is the author of numerous books and her essays on travel are among the classics of the genre. She lives in Wales, the only person in her postal code.

*

I had intended to swim in the pool here, but when I went to inspect it from the balcony, it was in deep shadow, quite deserted, and somehow uninviting. So I put on a pair of bathing trunks under my shorts and drove down to the beach that fronts Kapi'olani Park, which begins where the hotels of Waikīkī end.

I found a place for my car under the trees of the park without difficulty, for the hour was late and the beach relatively empty. The holidaymakers who jostle for sunbathing space here during the day had rolled up their towels and straw mats and flip-flopped back to their tower-block hatcheries to feed. The scattering of people still on the beach mostly looked like locals who had come down at the end of a working day, with a few beers or Cokes, to take a swim, relax, and watch the sun go down.

It was a perfect hour for a swim. The sun was low in the sky and had lost its fierce daytime heat, but the sea was warm and the air balmy. I swam vigorously for about a hundred yards in the general direction of Australia, then floated on my back and gazed up at the overarching sky. Long shreds of mauve-tinted cloud, edged with gold, streamed like banners from the west. A jet droned overhead, but could not disturb the peace and beauty of the evening. The hum of the city seemed muted and distant. I emptied my mind and let the waves rock me as if I were a piece of flotsam. Occasionally, a bigger wave surged past, swamping me or lifting me in the air like a matchstick, leaving me spluttering in its wake, laughing like a boy. I decided I would do this more often.

—David Lodge, *Paradise News*

MAXINE HONG KINGSTON

A Sea Worry

Why surf?—a mother searches Sandy's for the answer.

THIS SUMMER OUR SON BODY SURFS. HE SAYS IT'S HIS "JOB" AND rises each morning at 5:30 to catch the bus to Sandy Beach. I hope that by September he will have had enough of the ocean. Tall waves throw surfers against the shallow bottom. Undertows have snatched them away, sharks prowl Sandy's. Joseph told me that once he got out of the water because he saw an enormous shark.

"Did you tell the lifeguard?" I asked.

"No."

"Why not?"

"I didn't want to spoil the surfing."

The ocean pulls at the boys who turn into surfing addicts. At sunset you can see surfers waiting for the last golden wave.

"Why do you go surfing so often?" I ask my students.

"It feels so good," they say. "Inside the tube. I can't describe it. There are no words for it."

"You can describe it," I scold, and I am very angry. "Everything can be described. Find the words for it, you lazy boy. Why don't you stay home and read?" I am afraid that the boys give themselves up to the ocean's mindlessness.

In the summer of 1976, I watched the U.S. Navy bomb Kaho'olawe, the red dirt island off the coast of Maui. I could see bombs falling nightly from Ben Keau's green plantation-style house in Kula on the slopes of Haleakalā. The air raids lit up the night like the Fourth of July. I told people in California about bombs falling on Hawai'i but nobody believed me. Nobody in Hawai'i seemed too upset even after a 500-pound Navy bomb landed in a West Maui sugarcane field.

That summer, though, nine native Hawaiians, led by Dr. Emmit Aluli, a Moloka'i physician, made the first of many sea landings on Kaho'olawe to protest the Navy's abuses—and they filed a federal lawsuit charging the Navy with violating the environment, historic preservation, and religious freedom.

In 1990, President George Bush halted the bombing and ordered the Navy to spend $400 million to clean up Kaho'olawe. In 1993, Congress returned the 45-square-mile island to native Hawaiians.

◆

—RC

When the waves are up, surfers all over Hawai'i don't do their homework. They cut school. They know how the surf is breaking at any moment because every fifteen minutes the reports come over the radio; in fact, one of my former students is the surf reporter.

Some boys leave for Mainland colleges and write their parents heart-rending letters. They beg to come home for Thanksgiving. "If I can just touch the ocean," they write from Missouri and Kansas, "I'll last for the rest of the semester." Some come home for Christmas and don't go back.

Even when the assignment is about something else, the students write about surfing. They try to describe what it is to be inside the wave as it curls over them, making a tube or "chamber" or "green room" or "pipeline" or "time warp." They write about the silence, the peace, "no hassles," the feeling of being reborn as they shoot out the end. They've written about the voice of God. The "commandments" they hear. In the margins, they draw the perfect wave. Their writing is full of clichés. "The endless summer," they say. "Unreal."

Surfing is like a religion. Among the martyrs are George Helm, Kimo Mitchell, and Eddie Aikau. Helm and Mitchell were lost at sea riding their surfboards from Kaho'olawe, where they had gone to protest the Navy's bombing of that island. Eddie Aikau was a champion surfer and lifeguard. A storm had capsized the *Hōkūle'a*, the ship that traced the route that the Polynesian ancestors sailed from Tahiti, and Eddie Aikau had set out on his board to get help.

Since the ocean captivates our son, we decided to go with him to see Sandy's.

We got up before dawn, picked up his friend Marty, and drove out of Honolulu. Almost all the traffic was going in the opposite direction, the freeway coned to make more lanes into the city. We came to a place where raw mountains rose on our left and the sea fell on our right, smashing against the cliffs. The strip of cliff pulverized into sand is Sandy's. "Dangerous Current Exist," said the ungrammatical sign.

Earll and I sat on the shore with our blankets and thermos of coffee. Joseph and Marty put on their fins and stood at the edge of the sea for a moment, touching the water with their fingers and crossing their hearts before going in. There were fifteen boys out there, all about the same age, fourteen to twenty, all with the same kind of lean, V-shaped build, most of them with black hair that made their wet heads look like sea lions. It was hard to tell whether our kid was one of those who popped up after a big wave. A few had surfboards, which are against the rules at a body-surfing beach, but the lifeguard wasn't on duty that early.

As they watched for the next wave, the boys turned toward the ocean. They gazed slightly upward; I thought of altar boys before a great god. When a good wave arrived, they turned, faced shore, and came shooting in, some taking the wave to the right and some to the left, their bodies fishlike, one arm out in front, the hand and fingers pointed before them, like a swordfish's beak. A few held credit card trays, and some slid in on trays from McDonald's.

"That is no country for middle-aged women," I said. We had on bathing suits underneath our clothes in case we felt moved to participate. There were no older men either.

Even from the shore, we could see inside the tubes sometimes, when they came at an angle, we saw into them a long way. When the wave dug into the sand, it formed a brown tube or gold one. The magic ones, though, were made out of just water, green and turquoise rooms, translucent walls and ceilings. I saw one that was powder-blue, perfect, thin; the sun filled it with sky blue and water light. The best thing, the kids say, is when you are in the middle of the tube, and there is water all around you but you're dry.

The waves came in sets; the boys passed up the smaller ones. Inside a big one, you could see their bodies hanging upright, knees bent, duckfeet fins paddling, bodies dangling there in the wave.

Once in a while, we heard a boy yell, "Aa-whoo!" "Poontah!" "Aaroo!" And then we noticed how rare human voice was here; the surfers did not talk, but silently, silently rode the waves.

Since Joseph and Marty were considerate of us, they stopped after two hours, and we took them out for breakfast. We kept asking them how it felt, so that they would not lose language.

"Like a stairwell in an apartment building," said Joseph, which I liked immensely. He hasn't been in very many apartment buildings, so had to reach a bit to get the simile. "I saw somebody I knew coming toward me in the tube, and I shouted, 'Jeff. Hey, Jeff,' and my voice echoed like a stairwell in an apartment building. Jeff and I came straight at each other—mirror tube."

"Are there ever girls out there?" Earll asked.

"There's a few women who come at about eleven," said Marty.

"How old are they?"

"About twenty."

"Why do you cross your heart with water?"

"So the ocean doesn't kill us."

I described the powder-blue tube I had seen. "That part of Sandy's is called Chambers," they said.

I have gotten some surfing magazines, the ones kids steal from the school library, to see if the professionals try to describe the tube.

Bradford Baker writes:

..Round and pregnant in Emptiness
I slide,
laughing,
into the sun,
into the night.

Frank Miller calls the surfer:

...mother's fumbling
curly-haired
tubey-laired
son.

"Ooh, offshores," writes Reno Abbellira, "where wind and wave most often form that terminal rendezvous of love—when the wave can reveal her deepest longings, her crest caressed, cannily covered to form those peeling concavities we know, perhaps a bit irreverently, as tubes. Here we strive to spend every second—enclosed, encased, sometimes fatefully entombed, and hopefully, gleefully, ejected—Whoosh!"

"An iridescent ride through the entrails of God," says Gary L. Crandall.

I am relieved that the surfers keep asking one another for descriptions. I also find some comfort in the stream of commuter traffic, cars filled with men over twenty, passing Sandy Beach on their way to work.

Maxine Hong Kingston, born in Stockton, California, and educated at University of California, Berkeley, taught high school in California and Hawai'i for twelve years. She lives in Oakland. She is the author of The Woman Warrior, *winner of the National Book Critics Circle Award,* China Men, *winner of the American Book Award, and* Tripmaster Monkey, *winner of the 1989 International PEN West Award in Fiction. A Living Treasure of Hawai'i, she received the National Humanities Medal in 1998. She and her husband, actor Earll Kingston, have a son Joseph, a musician, who is of course the young surfer in this story.*

⋆

Wealth can be measured in many ways. I consider myself blessed and a wealthy person. I have a vigorous and dynamic family and enjoy good health. Men and women of diverse backgrounds enrich my life.

I live in Hawai'i.

From the crest of Mauna Kea the cold of the snow goddess Poli'ahu has chilled my soul. My heart has pounded the rhythm of a chanting drum while running across the blistering lava fields of Kona. Upon the peak of Haleakalā, I have felt the golden rays of the dawn's sun caress these Islands.

In the dark loneliness of Pāpalaua Valley on Moloka'i, I have heard the wind whisper of ancient Hawai'i. My back has ached from countless strokes while racing a koa canoe across the Ka'iwi channel. In the shadow of Kōnāhuanui, I have seen the warrior's ghosts. I have danced with the waves in the soft light of a full moon night. I have glided across the face of azure walls of water while surfing the mystical waves of these Islands of Hawai'i.

I am a surfer.

All of this is my wealth.

—Fred Hemmings, *The Soul of Surfing is Hawai'i*

BARBARA KINGSOLVER

* * *

Infernal Paradise

In Haleakalā's great crater, the author finds remnants of a disappearing Hawai'i.

IN THE DARKNESS BEFORE DAWN I STOOD ON THE PRECIPICE OF A wilderness. Inches in front of my toes, a lava cliff dropped away into the mammoth bowl of Haleakalā, the world's largest dormant volcano. Behind me lay a long green slope where clouds rolled up from the sea, great tumbleweeds of vapor, passing through the pastures and eucalyptus forests of upland Maui to the volcano's crest, then spilling over its edge into the abyss.

Above the rim rock and roiling vapor, the sun was about to break. Far from the world where *"Aloha 'Oe"* whines through hotel lobbies, I stood in a remote place at an impossibly silent hour.

But pandemonium had an appointment. Grunting, hissing, a dozen buses pulled up behind me and threw open their doors. Tourists swarmed like ants over the tiny visitors' center at the crater's edge. Loading cameras, dancing from foot to foot in the cold, they positioned for the spectacle. "Darn," a man griped through his viewfinder. "I can't get it all in."

"Take two shots then," his wife advised.

In the throng, I lost and then relocated Steven, my fellow traveler. In his hiking boots, sturdy fedora, and backpack, he apparently struck such a picturesque silhouette against the dawn he'd been cornered by a pro and enlisted as foreground. "Perfect for a wilderness catalog," the photographer testified, while his camera whirred meaningfully.

Sunrise over Haleakalā is a packaged Maui tradition: tourists in the beachfront hotels can catch a bus at 3 a.m., ride the winding road to the summit, witness the daybreak moment, and return in time for a late breakfast. As religious experiences go, this one is succinct. In fifteen minutes the crowd was gone.

I wandered 100 yards back to the parking lot, where a second troop was assembling. For about $120, intrepid sightseers can get a one-way bus ride to the summit for a different thrill: outfitted with helmets, Day-Glo safety vests, and rental bikes, they speed back down to the coast in a huge mob, apparently risking life and limb for a 38-mile exercise in hand braking. The group leaders, who presumably knew the score, were padded from head to toe like hockey goalies. As they lined up their herds of cyclers, they delivered flat monologues about hand signals and road conditions. "Ready to go play in traffic?" demanded a guide, straddling his mount. "Okay, let's go play in traffic." With the hiss of 100 thin tires on a ribbon of asphalt, this crowd vanished too.

> What draws everyone to Maui, besides its natural diversity, great beaches, and endless summer weather, is its location—smack dab in the middle of the inhabited Hawaiian chain with clear views of five nearby Islands. Many people—continental people, Mainland people, people who live landlocked lives—somehow feel comforted by the presence of other Islands in plain sight. I don't know why this is. I only know that to be all alone on the vast Pacific is an isolation only solo sailors crave. In the empty ocean, even migratory whales seek out Maui.
>
> ◆
>
> —RC

I blinked in the quiet light, feeling passed over by a raucous visitation. Now the crater lay deserted, in the howling wind, by all but one pair of picturesque stragglers. The toes of our boots turned toward the rim and found purchase on a rough cinder trail called Sliding Sands, which would lead us down into the belly of Haleakalā. The price: a $6.95 waterproof trail map and whatever else it might take to haul ourselves down and back again.

Entering the crater at dawn seemed unearthly, though Haleakalā is entirely of the earth, and nothing of human artifice. The cliffs absorbed and enclosed us in a mounting horizon of bleak obsidian crags. A lake of cloud slid over the rim, wave by wave, and fell into the crater's separate atmosphere, dispersing in vapor trails. The sharp perimeter of cliffs contains a volcanic bowl 3,000 feet deep and 8 miles across as the crow flies (or twice that far as the hiker hikes). The depression would hold Manhattan, though fortunately it doesn't.

We walked and slid down miles of gravelly slope toward the crater floor, where the earth had repeatedly disgorged its contents. Black swirls of bubbling lava had once flowed around red cinder cones, then cooled to a tortured standstill. I stood still myself, allowing my eye a minute to take in the lunatic landscape. In the absence of any human construction or familiar vegetation like, say, trees, it was impossible to judge distances. An irregular dot on the trail ahead might be a person or a house-size boulder. Down below, sections of the trail were sketched across the valley, crossing dark lava flows and green fields, disappearing into a velvet fog that hid the crater's eastern half.

The strange topography of Haleakalā Crater makes its own weather. Some areas are parched as the Sahara, while others harbor fern forests under a permanent veil of cloud. Any part of the high-altitude crater can scorch in searing sun, or be lashed by freezing rain, or both, on just about any day of the year. Altogether it is one of the most difficult landscapes ever to host natural life. It is also one of the few places in Hawai'i that looks as it did 200 years ago—or for that matter, 2,000. Haleakalā is a tiny, threatened ark.

To learn about the natural history of Hawai'i is to understand a story of unceasing invasion. These Islands, when they first lifted their heads out of the waves a million years ago, were naked, defiant rock—the most isolated archipelago in the world. Life, when it landed here, arrived only through powerful stamina or spectacular accident: a fern's spore drifting on the trade wind, a seed in the craw of a bird, the bird itself. If it survived, that was an accident all the more spectacular. Natural selection led these survivors to become new species unique in the world: the silversword, for example, a plant that lives in lava beds and dies in a giant flowery star burst; or the *nēnē,* a crater-dwelling goose that has lost the need for webbed feet because it shuns the sea, foraging instead in foggy meadows, grown languid and tame in the absence of predators. Over the course of a million years, hundreds of creatures like these evolved from the few stray immigrants. Now they are endemic species, living nowhere on earth but here. For many quiet eons they thrived in their sequestered home.

And why are we the only ones enjoying this incomparable grandeur? Why aren't there thousands of people climbing over one another to hang all around the rim of "the greatest extinct crater in the world?" Such a reputation ought to be irresistible. Why, there's nothing on earth so wonderful as this!

◆

—Jack London, quoted in *Our Hawai'i: Islands and Islanders* by Charmian K. London

Then humans arrived, also through stamina and spectacular accident. The Polynesians came first, bringing along some 30 plants and animals they considered indispensable, including bananas, taro, sugarcane, pigs, dogs, chickens. And also a few stowaways: rats, snails, and lizards. All of these went forth and multiplied throughout the Islands. Each subsequent wave of human immigration brought fresh invasions. Sugarcane and pineapples filled the valleys, crowding out native herbs. Logging operations decimated the endemic rainforests. Pigs, goats, and cattle uprooted and ate whatever was left. Without a native carnivore to stop them, rats flourished like the Pied Piper's dream. Mongooses were imported in a harebrained plan to control them but the mongoose forages by day and the rat by night, so these creatures rarely encounter one another. Both, though, are happy to feast on the eggs of native birds.

More species have now become extinct in Hawai'i than in all of North America. At least 200 of the Islands' endemic plant species are gone from the Earth for good, and 800 more are endangered. Of the original cornucopia of native birds, many were never classified, including 50 species that were all flightless, like the dodo—and now, like the dodo, all gone. A total of only 30 endemic bird species still survives.

It's quite possible now to visit the Hawaiian Islands without ever laying eyes on a single animal or plant that is actually Hawaiian—from the plumeria *lei* at the airport (this beloved flower is a Southeast Asian import) to the farewell bouquet of ginger (also Asian). African flame trees, Brazilian jacarandas, mangoes and banyans from India, coffee from Africa, macadamia nuts from Australia—these are beautiful impostors all, but to enjoy them is to dance on a graveyard. Exotics are costing native Hawai'i its life.

Haleakalā Crater is fortified against invasion, because of its protected status as a national park, and because its landscape is hostile ground for pineapples and orchids. The endemic had millennia to adapt to their difficult niche, but the balance of such a fine-tuned ecosystem is precarious, easily thrown into chaos; the plants fall prey to feral pigs and rats and are rendered infertile by insect invaders like Argentine ants and yellow jacket wasps, which destroy the native pollinators.

Humans have sated their strange appetites in Haleakalā too, and while a pig can hardly be blamed for filling its belly, people, it would seem, might know better. The dazzling silverswords, which grow nowhere else on earth, have been collected for souvenirs, *lei*, scientific study, Oriental medicine, and—of all things—parade floats. These magical plants once covered the ground so thickly a visitor in 1873 wrote that Haleakalā's slopes glowed silvery white "like winter in moonlight." But in 1911, a frustrated collector named Dr. Aiken complained that "wild cattle had eaten most of the plants in places of easy access." However, after much hard work he "obtained gunnysacks full." By 1930, it was possible to count the surviving members of this species.

The *nēnē* suffered an even more dire decline, nearly following the dodo. Since it had evolved in the absence of predators, nothing in this gentle little goose's ground dwelling habits prepared it for egg-eating rodents, or a creature that walked upright and killed whenever it found an easy mark. By 1951, there were 33 *nēnē* geese left living in the world, half of them in zoos.

Midway through the century, Hawaiians began to protect their Islands' biodiversity. Today, a tourist caught with a gunnysack of silverswords would find them pricey souvenirs—there's a $10,000 fine. The Park Service and The Nature Conservancy, which owns adjacent land, are trying to exclude wild pigs from the crater and native forests by means of a fence, though in such rugged ground it's a task akin to dividing needles from haystacks. Under this fierce protection, the silverswords are making a gradual comeback. *Nēnē* geese have been bred in captivity and reintroduced to the crater as well, but their population, numbered at 200 and declining, is not yet considered saved. Meanwhile, the invasion creeps forward: even within the protected boundaries of a national park, 47 percent of the plant species growing in Haleakalā are aliens. The whole ecosystem is endangered. If the silverswords, *nēnē* geese, and other colorful endemics of Hawai'i survive this century, it will be by the skin of their teeth. It will only happen because we decided to notice, and hold on tight.

Like a child anticipating sleigh bells at Christmas, I saw illusory silverswords everywhere, I fixed my binoculars on every shining dot in the distance and located a lot of roundish rocks in the noonday sun. Finally I saw the real thing. I was not prepared for how they would appear to glow from within, against the dark ground. They are actually silver. For all the world, they looked like huge spherical bouquets of curved silver swords. Cautiously, I leaned out and touched one that grew near the path. The knives were soft as bunnies' ears. Unlike the spiny inhabitants of other deserts, the arid-adapted silverswords evolved without the danger of being eaten. Defenseless, they became a delicacy for wild pigs. Such bad luck. This landscape was so unready for what has come to pass.

I never saw "winter in moonlight," but as we trudged deep into the crater we saw silverswords by twos and threes, then clumps of a dozen. Finally, we saw them in bloom. Just once before dying, the knee-high plant throws up a six-foot flower spike—a monstrous, phallic bouquet of purple asters. If a florist delivered this, you would hide it in a closet. Like a torrid sunset or a rousing thunderstorm, it's the kind of excess that only nature can pull off, to rave reviews.

The sun blazed ferociously. My pack was stuffed with a wool sweater, sleeping bag, and rain gear—ludicrous baggage I'd brought at the insistence of Park Service brochures. The gallon of water, on the other hand, was a brilliant idea. The trail leveled out on the valley floor, and dusty cinders gave way to fields of delicate-looking ferns, which felt to the touch like plastic. Under a white-hot sky, blue-back cinder cones rose above the fern fields. From the cliffs came the gossipy chatter of petrels, rare endemic gull-like birds that hunt at sea and nest in Haleakalā. I envied them their shady holes.

When we topped a small rise, a tin-roofed cabin and water tank greeted us like a mirage. The Park Service maintains a primitive cabin in each of three remote areas of the crater where hikers, with advance permission, can avail themselves of bunks, a wood stove, and water (there are no other water sources within Haleakalā). We had a permit for a cabin, but not this one—we would spend the night at Palikū, six miles down the trail. The next day we would backtrack across the crater by a different path and exit Haleakalā via a formidable set of switchbacks known as the Halemau'u Trail. Even on the level, the trail was hard, skulking over knife-edge rocks, requiring exhaustive attention; I could hardly imagine doing this up the side of a cliff. I decided I'd think about that tomorrow.

Meanwhile, we flopped on a grassy knoll at the Kapaloa Cabin, devouring our lunchtime ration and most of our water. Steven, my ornithologist companion, observed that we were sitting on a litter of excrement whose source could only be the *nēnē*. He was very excited about this. I lay down on the endangered goose poop and fell asleep.

I woke up groggy, weary of the sun, and grateful to be more than halfway to Palikū. We marched through a transition zone of low scrub that softened the lava fields. Ahead of us hung the perpetual mystery of fog that had obscured the crater's eastern end all day, hiding our destination.

Suddenly we walked through that curtain into another world: cool, gray air, a grassy meadow where mist dappled our faces and dripped from bright berries that hung in tall briar thickets. We had passed from the mouth of hell to the gates of heaven—presuming heaven looks like the Smoky Mountains or Ireland. Awestruck and possessed of aching feet, we sat down on the ground. Immediately, we heard a quiet honking call. A little zebra-striped goose materialized out of mist and flew very low, circling over our heads. It landed a stone's throw away, cocked its head, and watched us. "Perfect for a wilderness catalog," it might have been thinking. In the past, I have scoffed at anthropomorphic descriptions of Hawai'i's state bird, which people like to call "friendly"and "curious." Now you can scoff at mine.

Soaked to the bone and suddenly shivering, we walked through miles of deep mist, surrounded by the honking of invisible *nēnē*. The world grew quiet, white, punctuated with vermilion berries. The trail ended in Palikū meadow. Beyond the field, a wall of cliffs rose straight up like a Japanese carving of a mountainside in jade. The vertical rock faces were crisscrossed with switchback crevices where gnarled trees and giant ferns sprang out in a sidesaddle forest. On these impossible ledges dwell the last traces of native rain forest. They survive there for only one reason: pigs can't fly.

Palikū Cabin, nestled among giant ferns, was a sight for sore muscles. Its iron stove was an antique giant, slow to warm up but ultimately unstoppable. Rain roared on the tin roof of our haven. In the thickening dark, we lit candles and boiled water for coffee. I hugged the sleeping bag and heavy wool sweater which, at lunch time, I'd secretly longed to bury under a rock. It was impossible now to recall the intensity of the morning's heat. And tomorrow I would have trouble believing I'd stood tonight fogging the windowpane with my breath, looking out on the wet tangle of a Hawaiian rainforest. Where does it go when it leaves us, the memory of beautiful strange things?

At dawn the sun broke over the cliffs and parted the pink mantle of clouds, reaching down like a torch to light the tops of red cinder cones in the crater, one at a time. For half a minute, sunlight twinkled starlike against what must have been the glass front of the visitors' center, all those miles away. I pictured the rowdy scene that must have been playing there. I found I couldn't really believe in any other world but the perfect calm of where I stood.

The mist cleared. Fern trees dripped. *Nēnē* flew across the cliff face by twos and threes, in heartbreaking imitation of a Japanese pen-and-ink drawing. Birds called from the trees, leading us on a goose chase through soggy vegetation. We spotted the red *'apapane,* the yellow Maui creeper, and the *'i'iwi,* an odd crimson creature with a down-curved bill—all three gravely threatened species.

I would happily have turned over rocks in search of endangered worms—anything to postpone packing up and striking out. But we had eleven miles to go, all uphill, and the sun was gaining ground. I groaned as I shouldered my pack. "We can still do everything we could when we were twenty," Steven pointed out companionably, "except now it hurts."

We backtracked through the meadows on a trail that grew steadily less muddy. We rested under a crooked acacia, the last tree in an increasingly arid landscape, before taking a new, more northerly trail that would lead us back up and out. Like an old-fashioned hologram, the crater offered two views of itself that were impossible to integrate. All day yesterday, we'd walked toward white mist and green cliffs at the crater's wet eastern side; today we did the opposite, facing the drought-stricken western slopes.

Planting one boot carefully in front of the other, we crossed acres of black lava flow, where the ground seemed to hula-dance in the heat. We skirted tall cinder cones whose sides were striped yellow and orange like paint pots. Several times I stopped and took note of the fact that there was not, in my whole field of vision, anything living. It might well have been the moon.

The trail graduated from rugged to punishing, and in the afternoon the mists returned. The landscape flowed from lava field to meadow and back again, until we were tossed up at last on the Halemau'u switchbacks. We spent the next two hours scaling the cliff face. With each turn the panorama broadened. We ascended through layers of cloud and emerged on top—nearly two miles above sea level. I invented new names for the Halemau'u Trail, which I will keep to myself.

Back home again, still nursing a few aches, I found myself deflecting odd looks from friends who seemed to think a trek through a scorched desert and freezing rain in Hawai'i was evidence of poor vacation skills.

I would do it all again, in a heartbeat. There are few enough places in the world that belong entirely to themselves. The human passion to carry all things everywhere, so that every place is home, seems well on its way to homogenizing our planet, save for the odd unreachable corner. Haleakalā Crater is one of those corners.

The casualties are the species trampled and lost, extinguished forever, at the rate of tens of thousand per year.... The first tragedy I remember having really understood in my life was the extinction of the dodo. I was four years old. I'd found its picture in the dictionary and asked my mother if we could see a bird like that. I was dismayed by her answer. Not "Yes, at the zoo," or "When you grow up, if you travel to a faraway country." Just: No. The idea that such a fabulous creature had existed, and then simply stopped being—this is the kind of bad news that children refuse to accept. I hauled the dictionary off to bed with me and prayed for the restoration of the dodo to this earth. I vowed that if I could only see such a creature in my lifetime, I would throw myself in front of its demise.

Haleakalā Crater is such a creature in our lifetime. In its great cupped hand it holds a bygone Hawai'i, a vision of curled fern leaves, a held-back breath of bird song, things that mostly lie buried now under fields of brighter flowers. The memory of beautiful, strange things slips so far beyond reach, when it goes. If I hadn't seen it, I couldn't care half well enough.

Barbara Kingsolver is the author of several best-selling books, including High Tide in Tucson, *from which this story was excerpted.*

*

I am nearly flattened on the long drive down from Hawai'i Volcanoes National Park. I suppose that I have been riding the brake too much. I've been pumping it, but still, 38 miles is a long way to pump. I am enjoying the scenery so much that I fail to realize my brakes have burned up. It is when I attempt to stop at one of the protea nurseries in Kula that I get into trouble. I wheel into the crowded parking lot (a bus full of camera-bearing tourists is offloading with exquisite leisure), and when I brake slightly to pull into a parking spot, the pedal goes all the way to the floor with a dull, useless, metallic clink. It is as if my foot has punched through a weak spot in lake ice, so sudden and complete is the terror. The chill of fright is everywhere in me all at once—my fingertips, in my chest, high in my throat.

I jerk the wheel to swerve away from the parked cars and wandering tourists, like a shark trying to turn and head back to open sea. Instead of plowing through the head-high, gorgeous protea, doing about a million dollars worth of damage (though I'd be able to bring my wife one hell of a nice bouquet), I make a wide circle, jump the curb, and drive across the grass, hoping to coast to a stop uphill. Pedestrians stare, rather than running like *nēnē*, and right before I am set to jump the curb, I pull the emergency brake and throw the gearshift into park. There is an explosion of grinding sprocket teeth being spun off, lovely music to the ears of any nearby transmission mechanic, and the car bucks as if lassoed and pitches nose down to a stop. As I get out, I'm aware of how goofy I look, moving in that rare and heightened super-saturated air of mortification where every move is observed, and robbed of grace.

—Rick Bass, "Paradise Rising," *Condé Nast Traveler*

WALT NOVAK

* * *

The Last Wave

Bravery isn't always a matter of choice.
Sometimes the alternative is scarier.

THE BEST WAVE AT WAIMEA IS A TWO-FOOT PIECE OF CHOP. IT'S located at the exact pinnacle of the biggest peaks. It comes from behind (on onshore days) and propels you into a fabulous takeoff. This isn't something someone told me. This is something I found out for myself.

I'm not certain of the year or the month, but I'll never forget the day I surfed Waimea, real Waimea. It was a weekday in the mid-1970s, and it was the first time I ever rode a twenty-foot wave. It was also the last. One twenty-footer in my lifetime is enough.

My college friend Jerry and I had surfed Sunset and Pipeline on numerous occasions. We were two teenagers living in the same dormitory at UH. We used to carpool to the surf spots after class. I had a beat-up Fiat. He had a rusty Datsun. We both thought we were kinda brave.

That day Sunset was closed out. The National Weather Service was calling it "fifteen to twenty feet with occasional higher sets." At around 4 p.m., we paddled our eight-foot-six-inch guns out at Waimea. I would never have done it, except Jerry did. He would never have done it except I did. Our big-wave experience was lacking, and our surfboards were about a foot too short. But we had testosterone aplenty, and we had each other.

It was overcast, slightly onshore with only ten guys out. Jerry caught an eighteen-footer right off the bat. When he paddled back out, his eyes were the size of baseballs. Before I knew it, he scored another one. I paddled for a whopper wave on the shoulder, but couldn't get in. It felt like I was just getting jacked up to the top for a preparatory launch.

> When surfing Waimea, it is essential to have the proper crazed attitude that implies a certain reckless disregard for personal safety.
>
> —Greg Ambrose, *Surfer's Guide to Hawai'i*

I backed out of three waves that way. After twenty blustery strokes, I would pull back at the last possible second and watch that monstrosity heave from behind. By itself. Without me.

I know that sounds cowardly, but what the heck, no one knows what a relief it is to let an eighteen-foot wave break without your measly attempt to harvest its weighty energy. One guy that day didn't back off when he should have. He went over Niagara without a barrel. It didn't look too pleasant. I would have preferred the heaving tackles of a hundred NFL linemen. That poor dude looked vacuum-sealed, hydraulically pinioned in the suctioned cylindricality of that hideous ogre. He couldn't move his arms or legs. He probably couldn't even move his face muscles.

I didn't see him again, but presumably he lived. I was fidgety. I felt geekish, like I couldn't surf and didn't even know the basics of paddling into a wave and standing up.

A couple of the gray mountains lurched into enormous tubes of water. I felt like a paddling insect in dinosaur-land, waiting for my puny spine to get snapped. I like my spine, having grown quite accustomed to it and all. So I hung around the safety zone, avoiding the takeoff zone and thereby not catching a thing. The safety zone is exactly that—safe. It's the sloppy side of those whopper peaks, a deep channel region where cowards may sit without fear of participation. Waves don't break there because it's so deep and over to the side.

Just then I noticed something terrible: Jerry had vanished. Gone, traceless. I couldn't see him anywhere. Then I noticed that the other ten guys had vanished too. The difference between them and me was that they were actually surfing, they had all caught a wave to shore.

It was getting dark. I was eighteen years old and I was terrified. To get stuck out after dark at fifteen-to-twenty-foot Waimea was as bad as it got. Nowadays, there are lifeguards and jet skis and helicopters. Back then, there was fear and more fear. I would have loved to be rescued. But, of course, lifeguards were like cops—never there when you needed them.

> I tried...once, but made a failure of it. I got the board placed right, and at the right moment, too; but missed the connection myself. The board struck the shore in three-quarters of a second, without any cargo, and I struck the bottom about the same time, with a couple of barrels of water in me.
>
> —Mark Twain

There was a lull. My heart was brutalizing my chest-plate with uncontrolled fluttering. My innards were taking a beating. I sat fidgety on my board, scanning the darkening shoreline more than 200 yards distant. I couldn't see any approaching saviors. I couldn't see shit. But I spent a lot of energy trying. Unwittingly, I drifted from the safety zone deeper and deeper into "the pit" where men are turned to mincemeat, where strong wills become bleary narcoleptic aneurysms. Where humans don't belong.

All of a sudden, a huge set bullied the horizon. The first hydraulic dinosaur charging straight for my puny spine was gigantic! I paddled up that ogre in a frenzy. I had to get over the unbroken top before it crested and flung me beachward with a force that would pulverize plutonium. My arms were a cartoon blur. Halfway to the top I realized I wouldn't make it. I slid off, and pushed my board up with every drop of adrenaline in my right arm. I dove through the back like a demented dolphin. When I resurfaced, I couldn't find my board. Then it crashed down next to me. Apparently, it had been fluttering like a whirling dervish up there in the spray zone.

I paddled up the second mountain the same way. And the third. These gray, muscular monstrosities seemed at least 100 yards wide, and their heights could only be measured in increments of terror.

Although I barely made it over the top of the fourth wave, I didn't need to dismount and sling my board. I made it over the fifth and sixth waves with frenzied ease. There it was: the seventh wave.

Beyond gray, it was black.

Beyond huge, it was humonstrous.

Beyond scared, I was paralyzed.

But I was perfectly positioned at the exact pinnacle of a twenty-foot-plus peak. And it was getting dark, really fast. Only one thing in the whole wide world was scarier than this wave—the prospect of spending the night on my eight-foot-six, dodging sets in blubbering insanity.

I was way outside. I paddled like a maniac, a good 20 to 25 strokes. All of a sudden I felt myself accelerate. But it wasn't the monstrosity that was propelling me, it was a two-foot piece of chop that materialized from behind and shot me into a fabulous takeoff. I got into that twenty-footer early. My lithe butt was squatting. My feet were planted. My concentration was focused. I was on it.

I crouched with tendoned elasticity at the top, middle, and bottom of that drop. I wasn't going to blow this, no way.

And it was easy! There was no jacking to the top, no sticking in the lip, just a long, almost sloppy drop straight down. I owed everything to that two-foot chop.

The rest of my ride was a piece of cake—continual conservative cutbacks, again and again, all the way through Pinballs and practically on to the sand. I kicked out over the six-foot shore break, grabbed my board, and careened not so gently on the beach. I was on land! I was alive! It was cool.

And except for a few stars and half a moon, it was black. I found Jerry standing alone with his board. "That was a good wave," he said. "It's about time you caught one."

Walt Novak, aging surfer and eighth-grade English teacher, lives in a coastal penthouse on O'ahu's North Shore, thanks to his first novel, The Haole Substitute, *and two other manuscripts which earned large Hollywood film contracts. A native of North Carolina, Novak enrolled at University of Hawai'i because of "its excellent wave department," earned three degrees, and began teaching at rough, tough Wai'anae Intermediate School while writing for surfing magazines. In 1983–1984, he was named "top surfing writer in the world." A decade later, his autobiographical novel received critical acclaim. "I used to surf Pipeline, and I teach in Wai'anae; now that's a dangerous life, and I've survived both," Novak says. "All I had to do was write it down."*

★

I saw it coming, turned my back on it, and paddled for dear life. Faster and faster my board went, till it seemed my arms would drop off.

What was happening behind me I could not tell. One cannot look behind and paddle the windmill stroke. I heard the crest of the wave hissing and churning, and then my board was lifted and flung forward.

I scarcely knew what happened the first half minute. Though I kept my eyes open, I could not see anything, for I was buried in the rushing white of the crest. But I did not mind. I was chiefly conscious of ecstatic bliss at having caught the wave.

At the end of the half minute, however, I began to see things, and to breathe. I saw that three feet of the nose of my board was clear out of water and riding in the air. I shifted my weight forward and made the nose come down. Then I lay, quite at rest in the midst of the wild movement, and watched the shore and the bathers on the beach grow distinct.

—Jack London, *Stories of Hawai'i*

GARRETT HONGO

Kapu Tube

A forbidden puka *(hole) leads to a mysterious underworld.*

FROM NEIGHBORS AND FRIENDS AROUND THE VILLAGE I KEPT hearing about a gigantic tube that ran from one of the old Kīlauea flows, down under the land behind Hongo Store, and onward through Mauna Loa Estates on the other side of the highway. Geologist friends said it was thought to be a continuation of Nāhuku, the Thurston Lava Tube, which ran downslope from Kīlauea Iki. You were supposed to be able to walk it, to fit a moving van inside of it, and you were supposed to find another world down there. I'd heard of cave petroglyphs and burial bones, about huge *'ōhi'a* root systems that hung down from the surface like bristly Spanish moss, teeming with hissing beetles—an underworld Shangri-la, alive with shadows made into flesh, fed by what drained from this one.

I told myself I'd find that tube and asked around about it. Someone in the village would say, "You could drop down into it and walk all the way to a papaya patch back of Mountain View." That was ten miles downslope from Volcano.

Geologists would say, "Oh, yeah, this tube is probably some major conduit off Kīlauea—but I never heard anything about walking to Kea'au or Mountain View—where'd you hear that one?"

Finally, a neighbor admitted he knew where an entrance was.

"Get one *beeg* skylight in dah lot next to mine," he said one day. We were hanging out at Hongo Store, drinking bad coffee from plastic, cone-shaped cups. "Get dog skeleton in dere. I t'ink one family of pigs use to live inside too."

He described a hole in the earth behind a stand of fire trees and brush, rimmed with sword ferns and a few bamboo orchids, the kind of collapsed tube you were supposed to stay away from if you were buying property to build a house on.

But a scientist had bought this lot—a Stanford biologist living in the village—and was using it for a special study on evolution inside lava tubes.

My neighbor had trespassed. He told me he'd gone exploring there one Halloween with his wife and child, taking a picnic dinner and flashlights.

"Evening time aftah dah sun go down, we juss drop insighe, eh? Dat was dah easy part. We went scamble ch'rough sword fern patch down to where not so deep, grab and hol' on to one tree limb den juhlike skeed down to dah tube floor, yeah? Juss a few fee' chyeah? We just poot on slippah, hop dah realtor streeng on dah property line, a slighe down onna long grass until we wass insighe dah tube. No problem. Wass easy."

Villagers like to make events for themselves this way. A family might take in a night out on the lava flow to be under the stars, camping on the beach from where lava emptied into the sea, taking box lunches and beach chairs and ice coolers filled with beer down to the spot where the road was covered by the latest flow, laughing it up, listening to the radio and the pidgin patter of a "local boy" deejay. The dread skylight became, in this same way, an occasion for a family outing, transforming a small piece of science and regional lore into part of a Halloween memory.

I got him to take me there one afternoon. It was a formation about twenty feet across and from six to fifteen feet deep under the opening. Part of the old skylight was like a little hummocked lip or awning over the old bed, which had a multilayered surface that was cut and channeled and terraced up its sides partway. It was old.

The rock had turned soft gray and lost all trace of the metallic sheen of freshly hardened lava. Its deepest black seemed the product of mosses and the accumulated dankness of time. Epiphytes hung down over the rim, and water dripped over them, splashing in a coppery pool on the bottom of the hole. The tube undulated where it opened to the light of day, then plunged away like a tree root down into depths and darkness beyond my seeing.

Enter not prayerless the house of Pele.

—Hawaiian proverb

My neighbor had been quiet as we walked over, and there was a zombie's look in his green eyes as we stood over the opening to the tube. He was part Hawaiian—the term of someone with a little Hawaiian blood. But he was part *haole* (Caucasian) and part Filipino, too, a mix of races, like so many of my neighbors. He had tanned skin and a large frame, his brown hair was wavy, and his eyes seem to have sunk back into their deep sockets.

"Hear dat?" he said.

"Hear what?" I answered.

"Dat *howling.*"

I shook my head, my mind changing cast with his remark.

"Ju' lissen more careful," he said, "like you went cross bot' ears or somet'ing. Try listen in 3-D."

I paid attention to him for things like that, for teaching me these little local tricks, taking the techniques of one of our senses and applying them in another. He was *evolved,* as good dreamers used to say back in the Sixties. I listened in 3-D and heard my heart first, then I heard the wind through the tops of the *'ōhi'a* trees around us, and then a lot of miscellaneous white noise of the forest. And then nothing for a while.

I looked at him out of the corner of my eye.

"No move," he said, placing his palm on my belly, steadying my pose.

I noticed the rhythm of my own breathing then. A bird twittered. It was an *'amakihi*, a little green piper of the lower forest giving off a chirruping whistle somewhere close by. I heard the heavy heads of the broom grass brushing against themselves, and I heard, or thought I heard, drops of water falling into the pool at the bottom of the tube.

"No breathe hard," he said, touching my chest lightly with his index finger.

I sighed, mind racing to thoughts, when I picked something up. It was a low moan. It was a sob and a light chuffing. It was like the low note of an end-blown flute, a faint, harmonic warble on the edge of human hearing. I picked it up through the skin around my testicles first, and then my anus clenched. I felt something on my breastbone where a ghost might have stood cold against it.

It was the wind, of course, atmosphere moving across the opening of a cave, vibrating, sending out a note like a shaman singing into the mouth of a body recently dead, summoning its wisdom from the other world. It was the afterlife speaking, and we felt it.

"See?" my neighbor said, not looking at me but gazing at his feet. He was watching a beetle track its way over the brown grasses by the sloping earth we stood upon. Its black antennae worked like digital filaments, trying to pick up signals, listening in 3-D. I cleared my throat.

"Hey, man," I said. "Maybe this is *kapu*. We don't have to go down."

He nodded. We stood there silently for a while, waiting for the moment to trail out. Then we walked away. Traipsing through the forest, I bowed my head, and neither of us spoke until we got to the road. My neighbor had brought me to the brink again, to a feeling I recognized, a sense of belonging to the land known to me at five but not twenty. I'd fallen back to a spot of consciousness, a belief in the power of the land.

Kapu was a gambit I had used as a child sometimes when I was afraid and needed to save pride among playmates. If I feared crossing a private beach, if I didn't want to swim in the cold springs at night in the dark end of a particular lagoon, if I balked at the notion that a bunch of us neighborhood kids had to pass through the trestle ribs of a WPA bridge and over a shallow, mossy-rocked creek on a night of the Turkish moon, I said it was *kapu*—forbidden by sacred law. It was a reference to the old Hawaiian system of prohibitions, creating differences between rulers, the *ali'i,* and commoners, the *maka'āinana.* When you said something was *kapu,* it meant a line had been drawn that couldn't be crossed. It meant a border between one world and another. *Kapu.* It meant a body that could not be held.

Garrett Hongo, born in the Hawaiian town of Volcano, is a professor at the University of Oregon where he was director of the program in creative writing from 1989 to 1993. He is the author of Volcano: A Memoir of Hawai'i *from which this story was excerpted, and two books of poetry,* Yellow Light *and* The River of Heaven. *He lives in Eugene, Oregon, with his wife and their two sons.*

*

I walk into the black tunnel of the lava tube. The walls curve gently to the right, ridged horizontally like striations of muscles, marking the levels of the molten lava as it diminished and narrowed. The tube must once have been filled to the brim with a fiery river; as it drained, it cascaded and cooled, creating intricate, molded patterns on the floor. When the molten rock subsided, the residue on the ceiling hardened into smooth conical drips, teat-shaped, like some vast statuary of a many-breasted mother goddess.

For a few hundred paces, the smooth musculature of the cave makes walking easy, but then the ceiling narrows to a crawl space. I shut off the light and lean against the laminated wall.

Absolute night surrounds me, warm, moist, palpable—the pressure of amniotic fluid, or of the eyelid on the eye. It is a nonhuman presence so overwhelming that it threatens to dissolve the fragile boundaries of self. Nothing in it seems benign or disposed toward humans. Nor indisposed. Simply there, a vast mystery behind every element of this landscape. I switch the flashlight back on quickly. Some great current seems to flow from the inner recesses, propelling me back toward the entrance.

And into an astoundingly noisy outer world, where the darkness fractures into a million forms. The wind is hissing through grass, and for the first time I hear in its lower register the base note of waves pounding the coast. I glance at the crowd of human figures (petroglyphs) at the north mouth of the lava tube. Midway between the light and the darkness, arms akimbo, some point up, some pointing down, guarding the passage, or pointing the way.

—Pamela Frierson, "In the Heart of Volcano Country," *The Burning Island*

LEI-ANN STENDER DURANT

For the Love of Hula

A devoted dancer is part of the rebirth of Hawaiian culture.

HULA: THIS ONE LITTLE WORD CAN CONJURE UP A VARIETY OF images, engage individuals in long discussions, and sometimes cause controversy among Hawaiians and non-Hawaiians alike. I love to talk about hula. I love to watch hula. I love to dance. I am a *Kumu Hula*, but I do not profess to be an expert. With hula and things Hawaiian, there is always something to learn; and I believe that learning goes on for a lifetime.

My story is a personal account about my hula life and how it has, in a very big way, contributed to who I am today.

Like my grandmother, mother, aunts, and cousins, I grew up dancing hula. Perhaps I was born with the desire to dance or perhaps I wanted to reach out to those watching the hula like my relatives did. While I was growing up, there were always stories about "Boat Days" in Hawai'i—those magical times when the SS *Lurline* and other Matson liners would bring visitors to Hawai'i from somewhere across the Pacific Ocean. Upon arrival at the Aloha Tower, the visitors were greeted with fresh flower *lei* and entertained by musicians singing Hawaiian melodies and beautiful hula dancers.

My grandmother told stories about performances for the troops during World War II (my grandmother would sing and play music while my mother and her sisters would dance the hula). I marveled at the black-and-white photos in family scrapbooks and loved to hear the stories that went along with them. I dreamed of being a hula dancer.

Hula lessons began at age five and continued until I left for college in Oregon. Except for the chance to dance at our Hawaiian Club *lū'au* every year, my hula life virtually came to a halt. In the late 1970s, college degree in hand, I returned home.

I discovered there was a renaissance going on. Hawaiian culture, Hawaiian language, and hula were at the forefront of a very exciting time in Hawaiian history. Hawaiians were beginning to bring back all that was lost when the missionaries arrived, and they were ready to reestablish what was lost for a very long time. Things Hawaiian were fast becoming a very big deal.

> The hula was a religious service in which poetry, music, pantomime, and the dance lent themselves, under the form of dramatic art, to the refreshment of men's minds. Its view of life was idyllic, it gave itself to the celebration of those mythical times when gods and goddesses moved on the earth, and men and women were as gods.
>
> ◆
>
> —Nathaniel Emerson, *Unwritten Literature of Hawai'i: The Sacred Songs of the Hula*

The Hawaiian baby boomers embarked on a journey to learn all they could about their roots, and hula was essential to that. Hula was changing—no longer were classes being taught only in the modern style of hula called *'auana. Hula kahiko* (ancient or traditional hula) was the focus in most *hālau,* and the Hawaiian language was fast becoming a second language for many. Chants emerged from the archives; there was no stopping now.

Not since the dance was performed for King David Kalākaua in 1883 was traditional hula given so much attention. The king is beloved even today for allowing the dance to be performed in public at his coronation—for the first time in the half century or so since the missionaries banned it. The stories of Hōpoe teaching the hula to her friend, Hi'iaka (Pele's sister), were known by all, and Laka was recognized by hula dancers everywhere as the goddess of hula.

Since childhood I had been taught *hula 'auana* and loved it. It was fun, light, and carefree. When I was introduced to *hula kahiko*, I was impressed with the chanting, drumming, *lei,* and costumes. Traditional hula was beautiful in a different way, and I wanted so much to be a part of the renaissance. It was not enough for me to simply be a witness to the revival of this classic style of dance and the excitement that surrounded it; I had to participate. My search for the *hālau* that would nourish my Hawaiian soul ended when I met my *Kumu Hula*, Māpuana de Silva, known to us as Māpu. My journey with Hālau Mōhala 'Ilima would take me places I never imagined. Every encounter would teach me something about my culture, my fellow human beings, and myself.

Hālau Mōhala 'Ilima was a new school in 1979, but we possessed boundless energy, and our desire to learn matched our *kumu*'s desire to teach. Māpu tended her garden of young shoots and watched us blossom into beautiful flowers. The name of the *hālau* means to gather up the *'ilima* flowers, the flowers of our Island, O'ahu.

A dancer makes a great commitment when joining a *hālau.* She (or he) not only gives her time, but also her talents and herself. Personal lives are sometimes put on hold, and activities revolve around a dancer's practice and performance schedule. Two hours a week is an average commitment time to learn language, chant, and dance. If a *hālau* enters one of the many competitions that are familiar to hula enthusiasts, fund-raising is another ongoing activity which requires more time and stamina. Prior to a competition, practice hours increase, and hours of preparation are added to make costumes and *lei*. Hula can be serious business.

I made the commitment, and I received so much back from my commitment to hula. My whole family became involved in supporting the *hālau*. The knowledge I gained in the areas of Hawaiian history, culture, and language was a given; I also learned to make hula instruments and costumes; I learned to appreciate all of it. These gifts, however, were not the most valuable. I belonged to a special group known as hula sisters. My hula sisters were my life, my strength, my courage, my playmates. My hula sisters were there when I was happy and when things were at their best; my hula sisters gave me strength when I was sad and thought I just couldn't endure one more crisis in life. In this close sisterhood, we all grew up together.

> Hāna is perfection to many lovers of the Islands, and that week I came to agree. My family and I happened to be staying at the Hotel Hāna-Maui during the Haku Mele festival, and over the next few days a deep impression was made on us by hula, the likes of which must be danced in Heaven, singing and storytelling that so impressed my daughters they requested Hawaiian be the second language of choice in their school back home, and a calling-up-the-sun ceremony at dawn that convinced me that not only have we lost our way in the modern world, but that Hawai'i, no matter how overrun it becomes, is forever blessed.
>
> ◆
>
> —James O'Reilly, "Haku Mele"

Now I am no longer active in the *hālau* and am busy being a wife and mother of two little boys. But I often reflect on the ten years I spent studying the hula and always I smile. The memories are so fresh in my mind, and most of what happened during that time is always so clear to me. I had a few struggles along the way and hurdles to conquer, but I learned from each situation and grew up a little each time.

I like to remember most the fun times, and there were many. In those days when I started as a new dancer, I felt like I had two left feet and no memory in my brain—how awkward I was. I remember long hours of practice when I thought my legs would surely fall off when the day was done. I remember struggling to get a costume sewn correctly, making my first *haku* (braided) *lei* and praying neither would fall apart when I was on stage. I remember making mistakes at a competition and my crossing fingers that the television cameras were not pointed at me when I made them. I remember all the fun, the laughter, and the practical jokes. Most of all, I remember my love for the hula family I shared the stage with—my hula sisters, my *kumu,* her husband and two daughters. I remember my love for those who supported me and helped me through it all—my own family and my friends.

Hula...one little word that can bring about so many images. What image do you see when you hear the word? Perhaps you picture a Hawaiian sunset with the silhouette of a dancer wearing flowers and a grass skirt or a young man in a *malo* (loincloth) dancing to the beat of a drum Whatever you see, enjoy the moment and know that hula always tells a story.

Hula...one little word that means so much to me. As I end my story, let me share one last thing that is very important: to share the hula is to share being Hawaiian; and to be proud to be Hawaiian. We have just begun to discover where this pride will take us. To love the hula is to love life in our Islands. I love hula, I love life, and I am proud to be Hawaiian.

Lei-Ann Stender Durant was one of the Best of the Best dancers, a select group who performed every year at the Merrie Monarch Festival in Hilo, the "Super Bowl of hula." Frequently they won awards and accolades for Hālau Mōhala 'Ilima, respected for its strictly traditional approach to the dance. From expert she went to teacher, undergoing the special training reserved for those who would carry the flame, then to mother, helping write the Hawaiian future for her sons.

*

Māpuana and Kīhei de Silva searched the records and photos of the past to research costumes and chants and hula steps long lost to modern Hawaiians. The school grew to more than 300 students, representing all ages and flavors in Hawai'i's cultural stew. Kīhei wrote songs and chants and treatises on ancient hula; Māpuana had a special gift for inspiring her students to do their best, no matter what their abilities. *Hālau* sprang up everywhere in the Islands, and men and women flocked to join the schools and learn the dance of Hawai'i, the most sophisticated native dance in Polynesia.

They all help preserve the dance. Today you don't have to be a devotee to see the real thing; visitors can see it everywhere in Hawai'i, including the hotels of Waikīkī and other resort areas which have "adopted" *hālau* that perform often for their guests. If you are interested, ask the dancers about the dance, and you will instantly break through all the barriers that keep the "real Hawai'i" at arms length.

The dance in turn has inspired participants to learn Hawaiian language, to send their children to schools that teach in Hawaiian, and to recapture other lost skills of their ancient forebears, such as creating drums from chunks of palm trunk or printing costumes with tapa designs, or making *lei* of feathers (partly to spare vanishing native flowers and ferns). These days, many hula schools on all Islands continue to educate Hawai'i's children in the cultural skills revolving around this sacred dance.

—MC & RC

NILES B. SZWED

David and the Mango Tree

Hurricane 'Iwa changed lives forever on Kaua'i.

TWO WEEKS AFTER THE STORM, I WAS STAYING IN A DOORLESS TIN shed with Karen. We were about to retire beneath the mosquito netting for the night when the phone rang. The electricity was still out in our neck of the woods, and we slept each night on the platform bed in the only corner of the shack where the hurricane hadn't ripped any leaks in the roof.

We had helped Roger and Janet board the place up before Hurricane 'Iwa struck. Now they had moved into a one-story suburban house down the road, leaving the shed to us while we figured out what to do next. Though they had not yet disconnected their phone service, we were still surprised to hear the phone ring that full-moon night in December. I think it was the only time we ever heard the phone ring in that house. That familiar jangling sound was incongruous with the sounds of the night: the leaking roof, the rats scurrying behind the unhooked stove, the fluttering of banana leaves in the wet, laden air.

Hurricane 'Iwa (pronounced like "Eva") left a trail of mojo stories in its wake. The rumor of God's Hand within the storm buzzed all over the Island of Kaua'i. Everyone had their story. Everyone always does in an ordeal like that. My own story had begun three days before the storm struck. I had landed on Kaua'i with two dollars in my pocket and prospects of a job trimming buds for the dope harvest. Karen, who had flown out a few months before, and I were planning to work the harvest, then travel to Bali and onward around the world. Our gypsy fortunes seemed assured.

But then, just as I began to settle into the heady, lush atmosphere of Kaua'i and the routines of the dope harvest, a little-urgent official voice came over the radio one morning. 'Iwa was just around the bend and headed our way.

"I think we better hitch down to Kīlauea and help Janet board up the house," Karen said, concerned. "Roger's still over on the Big Island checking out land, and she's too pregnant to do everything herself."

"I don't see what's the big deal about a hurricane," I said. "I've been in big wind storms before." And I had, though nothing with winds of more than about 50 miles per hour. 'Iwa was to hit 90 to 110 mph, supposedly mild by comparison to other hurricanes. Still, I had no concept of what that kind of power could do.

So we hitched to their shack in Kīlauea all the same. Karen helped Janet to jam-pack her station wagon with all of her family's belongings while I scrounged up pieces of wood and nailed them down all over the tin shed. At one point I told Karen and Janet that I still thought all this hurricane stuff was exaggerated, and that nailing everything down like this was probably overkill.

No sooner had the words left my mouth when a sudden gust of wind blew so hard that the corrugated roof buzzed loudly, screeching at us, like when you blow between two tightly drawn sheets of paper, but about twenty times louder. It was not just the sound. There was a stirring of the elements like I had never felt before, a mighty and troublesome spirit looming near. The sudden presence of that kind of power rattled me, made me uneasy under my skin.

We finished sealing up the shack as quickly as we could. Janet had no room left to drive us, so we hitched back to Princeville through the brewing storm. Along the way, a Java plum tree snapped free from a windrow and crashed across the highway in front of us. This was clearly not a safe place to get stuck, as any other tree in the windrow could land on us at any minute. About a dozen of us got out of our cars, walked up to the downed tree, and, wordlessly, in perfect unison gave one heave-ho after another. The tree swung round just enough to let the stranded line of cars through.

Back at the harvest house, everyone was putting big Xs of masking tape on the windows to impede the shattering glass, and dancing around the living room to a tape of the reggae band Third World. I stepped out briefly in the lee of the house just in time to see the roof blow off the house next door. It ripped loose in slow motion, screeching and wheeling, and went crashing on the lip of the bluff before tumbling into the ocean. I knew this was no laughing matter, and dashed inside just as our own roof tore loose.

When the storm turned serious, we all crowded downstairs listening to the windows shatter on the next floor. The floor beneath us heaved visibly upward in waves, as if it would at any moment burst loose and flatten us against the ceiling. We huddled arm in arm, shivering and crying out prayers to every saint we could think of, as loudly as we could. But nothing was louder than that wind. It was a throaty old spirit, with a deep and hideous growl, trying to fit its long lower jaw down under us as it scraped its teeth over the earth.

Somehow the lull in the storm arrived, and we had not been crushed inside our own box. We ran out to the truck through the 70 mph winds before the storm could resume in earnest. Careening around fallen eucalyptus and detouring across the soggy golf course, we beat it to the Red Cross shelter at the fire station, the only stone building in the area, where we rode out the remainder of the storm.

No sooner had we returned to our neighborhood that same night than the stories began to pour in. Wandering through moonlit streets strewn with splintered wreckage, we heard the strains of a party going on. Some neighbors, a bunch of Rajneeshers, had smoked and drank, danced and banged drums and guitars all through the storm.

"Yeah," one of the guys said, "when the roof blew off we knew everything would be all right."

My jaw dropped at their cavalier attitude. Had we just been through the same storm or not? Then he added that he and a friend had been upstairs lying on the bed, listening to loud rock on the headphones, staring up at the ceiling when it had suddenly snapped off above them like the cap of a Coke bottle.

Somehow they had already gotten the latest dope grower gossip too. Seems there was a man stranded in the storm, who knocked on the door of some house at random to get out of that terrifying wind. It happened to be another dope trimming house, not far away, and of course it was full of huge marijuana stalks hanging to dry. The dope grower in residence had refused to let the stranded man come in, for fear of exposing his crop. No sooner had he told the stranded man to go away, though, than the roof tore off the house and crushed the grower's brand-new uninsured four-wheel drive.

During the days to come, everyone shared some story of mysteries they had witnessed or heard of close by. For instance, in our neighborhood, which was composed of pole houses perched on the edge of a gulch, almost every house lost its roof. Rumor had it that the contractor who had built that subdivision had told his crews to use greased nails to finish the job faster. Only three houses still had their lids on, and they all belonged to a devout church-going woman.

Then there was the story of the sailboat, named *'Iwa II*, which was caught off the south shore of Kaua'i when the storm hit. First, the mast broke, then the rudder broke, and the boat was set adrift, helplessly wandering past the jagged volcanic cliffs east of Po'ipū. But despite the powerful winds blowing out of the south, the boat was not wrecked there, or even blown ashore. Instead, it drifted east along the shore of the Island as the crew watched, unable to do anything. When the boat rounded the corner of the Island it drifted north, past Līhu'e's Nāwiliwili Harbor. If the boat were to drift much farther north, driven by the relentless winds, it would soon end up lost in the trackless expanse of the North Pacific.

Instead, when *'Iwa II* reached the middle of the eastern shore, she mysteriously drifted west, through the narrow channel in the reef, into Anahola Bay and safety. Anahola, by the way, was the home port of *'Iwa II.*

Perhaps the greatest miracle of all was that nobody on Kaua'i was killed, or even injured too seriously during the storm. The only injury I knew of happened the next day when a falling two-by-four broke our friend Darby's arm as she poked through the wreckage of her home. We had heard that a couple of sailors were lost, blown from the deck of a naval vessel stationed at Pearl Harbor on O'ahu, but no such losses occurred on Kaua'i.

In fact, as devastating as Hurricane 'Iwa was, it brought new life to us all. It reaffirmed our belief in magic, it doubled wages on the Island overnight, and it brought people out of their shells to help each other. On the hard-hit south shore, it was even rumored that the hotels were paying $15-$20 per hour for workers just to carry debris away—more than the dope harvesters, processing the dregs of the ruined crop, could make. Unfortunately, it was hard to get through the police roadblocks just then, as they didn't want wholesale looting to occur.

In the surrealistic air of the storm's passing, though, life seemed lighter, easier to bear. Everyone was starting from zero together. Between the federal government and various insurance companies, millions of dollars poured into the devastated economy of the tiny Island. Donations of clothing and food from church groups around the country poured in too. There was plenty of aboveboard work at a time of year when there was usually none. There was free food and clothing. People helped each other, read by candle light, shared whatever they had and talked face to face as long as the lines were down and the roofs remained to be fixed.

It was in this atmosphere, a couple weeks after the storm, when I learned of David and the mango tree. He was calling for Karen, to invite her out to some small, spiritual full-moon gathering. Apparently, the last time they had seen each other was before I came out to the Islands. I did not talk to him; I only met him through conversations with others. He had been hiking the Nā Pali

Coast when the storm struck and had tied himself to a huge old mango tree at Hanakāpī'ai to keep from flying off the cliffs into the ocean. This may have been foolhardy in hindsight, considering the number of huge old trees at Hanakāpī'ai which blew down, criss-crossing each other's trunks with what must have been thunderous impact. But it probably seemed like the only option at the time, and in any case it worked.

> Just about the time recovery from 'Iwa was fairly complete on Kaua'i, Hurricane 'Iniki came along and smashed the Island even worse, this time leaving scars that persist even today, on the landscape, the economy, and the psyches of the residents. Many people, faced with no job and no home, had to leave, at least for a couple of years. Some stuck it out through a lot of hard times. Promises of federal aid were only partly fulfilled. Today, however, Kaua'i is as green and magical as ever, most of the hotels have reopened and business is brisk. But the memories are still there, and everyone in Hawai'i pays more attention when hurricanes are passing by in the tropical Pacific.
>
> —MC & RC

It had been a religious experience for him, being tied to the tree amidst the howling winds, like some modern-day Odysseus resisting the sirens, and his life hadn't been the same since. Hell, it was a religious experience going through that storm even inside a house. Sure, it would rearrange your neurons, facing the storm with no more shelter than a tree trunk. Besides, if you're going to have a religious experience, it may as well be under the august shelter of a mango tree. Mango, who gives divine nectar fruit; mango, whose shade lets only a few soft ferns grow within its circle; under whose limbs peace is more restful, the breath more hushed. Seeing this old tree, you might expect it to reach down, wrapping its protective arms around you. It would not have been the same if he'd been tied to a *kukui* or a guava tree.

Now he felt like this full-moon night was a turning point in his life, an unspecified sort of culmination. Karen chose not to go to the gathering because that would have meant hitching to Līhu'e at night. She was just glad that David was okay and glad to hear another amazing tale of the hurricane. We thought that was the end of the story.

On the spur of the moment, we hiked out to the grassy knoll by the lighthouse and made love under the stars. At one moment, we looked up and saw a bright light flying past a hole in the clouds.

"Wow! Is that a UFO?" I said, sitting bolt upright.

"Hey, wait a second," said Karen, "there's another…and another!"

Before we knew it, there were five bright lights whizzing by in formation. Just when we were certain we were having a major visitation, we suddenly saw the full moon chasing after the smaller lights at the same speed.

"What the...," I began to say, then we broke out cackling. It had, of course, been the clouds that were moving all that time, blowing by hurriedly in the other direction. Somehow for a moment, we had lost our awareness of illusion and relativity.

The next morning I hitched into Kapa'a to work. I always met my boss Ted at the 'Ohana Family Restaurant so I could have pancakes with coconut syrup if I got there early enough. Together, we would go around cutting and hauling fallen trees and foliage, blowdown from 'Iwa, from people's yards.

Ted and his sidekick Bill were both Jehovah's Witnesses. So it surprised me that morning when Bill told me this strange story. He had been up late the night before, sitting on a hillside watching the moon over Līhu'e with a friend, involved in some intense religious discussion.

Suddenly his friend had gotten up, staring at the moon and said "I'm going to swim for it."

"What do you mean?"

"I'm going to swim for the moon."

"What d'you mean?"

"I'm going to swim to God."

"Don't go out there, man," Bill had warned, "That's a shark breeding ground."

This, of course, was even more dangerous because sharks feed largely at night. But Bill's friend wouldn't listen. He just peeled off his clothes and vanished into the moonlit water. Bill was shaken, certain that his friend was swimming to his death in pursuit of some delusional vision. Bill brought his friend's clothes and belongings to the police and reported it as a possible suicide.

"And he had just survived the hurricane tied to a mango tree."

My brain clicked. "Was his name David?"

"Yeah, how did you know?"

"He called up my ladyfriend Karen last night to invite her out for some full-moon gathering."

We both agreed this was "too weird," but, in its own way, typical of life on the Island. In between trips to the dump with loads of lichee branches and torch ginger, I thought a lot—about God and delusion, life and death, beauty and tragedy, about the police searching for David's shark-mauled body at that moment.

Word of David's death spread quickly. A lot of our friends in Kīlauea also knew David. A few nights later, Karen and I were visiting Roger and Janet in their new home, partly as a respite from life in the tin shed. They were Tibetan Buddhists. Janet commented with concern about where suicidal souls end up after death, and that sometimes people who really want to commit suicide have a way of disguising that fact from themselves, but it's still the same as killing yourself.

"The Lama says that people like that still end up stuck in one of the lower *bardos* even if they think they're killing themselves for spiritual reasons."

"But what if he's really not dead," I mused. I thought it would be terribly ironic if, after all the worry over which *bardo* he would land in, he were still walking around the Island. Perhaps, as a visionary, he didn't feel compelled to go back to his former friends and former life after this major initiation. A death in the eye of the beholder.

"Oh cut it out! You know he's dead!" said Karen in a disapproving voice. My musings were deemed in poor taste right then. But something inside said to keep my mind open, not to rest with the obvious.

The next day at work, still hauling brush in Wailua, Bill had another story. He had indeed seen David just the day before. David had not gone out of his way, after all, to tell people he was back from the dead, perhaps because he didn't even know he was considered missing in the first place.

Sure enough, though, he had swum across the bay in a trail of moonlight. In his state of exaltation, he barely noticed the startled locals who were night-fishing on the breakwater where he emerged, as if from the very deep. He wandered naked, mindlessly back toward town. Eventually, David realized he was naked. He knocked on some random door. An old man came out, took one look and laughed, then gave David some old clothes which barely fit. It was not until days later that David bumped into Bill again, when Bill told him that his clothes and all were at the police station, and that he had been reported missing and possibly dead. Apparently, everyone was so convinced that he was dead that nobody thought to stop by his home and check it out.

David told Bill that he was planning to start some sort of "spiritual center" on the Island, that maybe his dad would put up the money for the project. I don't know if he ever was able to live that part of his vision or not. In years to come, it became a stock joke, people who would come to the Islands, wanting to establish a "spiritual center" or a "healing center," when in fact Hawai'i already is such a spiritual and healing nexus, just as it is. These plans always seemed to dissolve into thin air, no matter how solid they looked at the outset. But that is another story.

That day in Wailua, though, there was a rainbow across the face of the mountain, west across the plateau from the temporary dump, as Bill finished his story. It was the first of many rainbows which I would read as a message from God: "Pay attention to this moment," or "Remember I am with you." And sure enough, even when swimming among the sharks, this is still so.

Niles B. Szwed lives in Marin County, California, where he teaches and does massage. His idea of travel in the 1980s was either to hitchhike or buy a one-way ticket, which is how he reached Hawai'i. He only intended to use the Islands as a stepping stone but stayed five years. He takes "short" vacations now but continues to have an eye for the magic in everyday life.

✶

In September 11, 1992, the highest recorded wind speed from Hurricane 'Iniki, the most powerful storm in the Pacific, was 227 mph, a reading from the U.S. Navy's Mākaha Ridge radar station on Kaua'i. Geologists said the storm aged the island 100 years in a single day.

—Jan TenBruggencate, *Honolulu Advertiser*

PART TWO

Some Things to Do

SALLY-JO KEALA-O-ĀNUENUE BOWMAN

Travels with Bird

Every Hawai'i adventurer should travel with Bird in hand.

HILO. THERE IS A SAYING AMONG SAILORS: "FOLLOW A PACIFIC shower and it will lead you to Hilo," Isabella Bird wrote.

> In 1873, Isabella Bird, a 41-year-old British spinster, hoped to restore her ailing health by traveling in the Pacific. She sent letters home to England that would become the still-popular classic *Six Months in the Sandwich Islands*. In one adventure, Bird set out from Hilo to explore the Big Island on horseback. This writer and photographer followed her trail.
>
> ◆
>
> —RC & MC

'Tis still true. This February day, winter rain drums on tarps covering the Farmer's Market, located in sight of the spot near Coconut Island where Isabella alighted from a whale boat to stay two days before venturing on to Kīlauea. Hilo, she noted, "*is the paradise of Hawai'i...such a lively place for such a mere village....*"

'Tis still true. This morning, customers crowd the market's makeshift aisles, fingering and pondering: Limes, oranges, lemons. Lettuces, radishes, purple sweet potatoes. Roses, variegated anthuriums, yellow *kāhili* ginger. Everything costs a dollar—except a dozen roses, which go for eight bucks. Men and women cradle long-stemmed flowers, or babies, in their arms and dangle plastic grocery bags of potatoes and papayas from their fingers, timing their dash from the market to their car to coincide with a gap in the rain.

My photographer companion, Brad—yes, Isabella, I know, I should call him "Mr. Lewis"—comes here often. "The beauty of the rain in Hilo," he tells me, "is that it keeps Hilo real. People don't come all the way to Hawai'i to sit in their hotel rooms and watch it rain."

We breakfast on *'ahi* and eggs for three bucks. I think about buying *kūlolo* roadside at Kimo's Lau Lau Stand. Mr. Lewis thinks the post office lawn is where, in Isabella's time, the city fathers passed their mornings playing croquet.

Volcano of Kīlauea, January 31, 1873. The track, on the whole, is a perpetual upward scramble...nearly 4,000 feet in 30 miles. Only strong, surefooted, well-shod horses can undertake this journey...Often, I only knew that my companions were ahead by the sparks struck from their horses' shoes....We reached the crater house at eight, clouds of red vapour mixed with flame were curling ceaselessly out of a huge invisible pit of blackness.

Brad, I mean Mr. Lewis, zips along the track, scrambling smoothly upward toward Kīlauea at the wheel of a Thunderbird. Surely Isabella would have chosen a Thunderbird over a horse, had the option been available. After all, it took her only a few miserable hours of galloping to forsake sidesaddle for riding astride.

At Kīlauea, something akin to Isabella's crater house still stands—a rustic, weathered 1877 hotel that is now the Volcano Art Center. Isabella slept not a hundred feet from here, in this building's grass-and-bamboo predecessor.

This morning is wet and murky as many mornings here are...so far, nothing has changed. I warm myself at the art center's rock fireplace, along with a Mainland visitor who is as resourceful as Isabella: she is wearing her large but damp hotel bath towel as a shawl.

Isabella's guide, Upa, was a Hawaiian *who boasts a little English...*

and was got up in the native style with garlands of flowers round his hat and throat. Our guide is Jim Kau'ahikaua, a Hawai'i Volcanoes Observatory geologist who boasts a little Hawaiian and who is "got up" in the geologist style of camouflage pants and Teva sandals.

Upa and his party climbed down into Kīlauea, the lava *so hot a shower of rain hissed as it fell upon it...I fell through several times, and always into holes full of sulphurous steam...*Halema'uma'u appeared as a *fiery sea whose waves are never weary.*

I look across the crater, knowing the tilt meters recently showed a possibility of a summit eruption. I squint until I imagine fountains of fire. I open my eyes and see plumes of sulfur steam. The promise of Pele.

Today we trundle out onto Kīlauea's 1790 flow in Kau'ahikaua's government-issued four-wheel drive. He talks about geology. And then he speaks of Pele legends. I perk up. For Isabella, *Pele was undoubtedly one of the grandest of heathen mythical creations.* For our Hawaiian geologist, stories of Pele are clues.

"You can read legends and figure out which flow they pertain to, look at features and identify them in the legends," Kau'ahikaua says. He discards from the legends what he calls the "moralistic aspects," and is left with information. "We record information differently now," he muses, "but is it better?"

I sort out the moralistic bits from Isabella's letters—her references to the "heathens" and her commentary on the Christian influence—and in the remaining narrative, as in the legends, lie verifiable facts.

For our departure, Mr. Lewis and I are right with Isabella: *the drip, drip, of vertical, earnest, tepid, tropical rain accompanies us nearly to Hilo.*

At Rainbow Falls, we pad 100 feet along a paved walkway from the parking lot to the vantage point over the Wailuku River, instead of spending all afternoon slaloming by horse around rocks and holes as Isabella did. Tourists snap pictures with throwaway cameras and pan with camcorders. Above us, buds are forming on enormous old mango trees. Did Isabella know them as saplings?

Isabella loved Onomea, *600 feet high...exquisite ferns and trailers which mantle the cliffs down to the water's edge...women in rose and green* holokū...*a whole cluster of grass houses under* lau hala *and bananas.... The distracting beauty of this coast is what are called gulches...we came through eleven, fording all but two. The descent into some of them is quite alarming. You go down almost standing in your stirrups...grasping (your horse's) mane to prevent the saddle (from) slipping.*

Today, Mr. Lewis grasps the steering wheel to prevent the auto from a head-on collision on a narrow, old bridge. "Old" is 1922, built 50 years after Isabella stood in her stirrups to cross the gulch streams, which still tumble and rush past banks jungled with palms and mangoes and ferns. And here we discover another bond with Isabella: our first mosquito. She also found in the lowlands *ants that assemble in legions as if by magic* and *monstrous cockroaches really the size of mice.* I take a perverse comfort in the familiarity of these pests.

In Waipi'o Valley, Isabella wrote, *I am in a native house in which not a word of English is spoken...this beautiful valley was once very populous, and even 40 years ago...there were 1,300 people here. Now probably there are not more than 200.*

Today in Waipi'o, Hawaiian language is gone. Taro struggles in a few *lo'i*. But the streams still braid themselves from the falls to the sea, and the rose-crimson mountain apples and golden balls of guava that Isabella wrote of still hang ripe for the picking. We come to horse tracks in the mud. Isabella? We follow, and find day travelers on an hour's trail ride.

After Waipi'o, Mr. Lewis and I belt ourselves into our six-cylinder steed. In moments, it seems, we pop over a rise.

Mauna Kea's pristine snow mantle gleams sharply against a perfectly blue and cloudless sky. Like Mauna Loa and Kīlauea, this mountain has changed since Isabella's time, but not by act of God—or of Pele, if you prefer. Even at this distance, the round heads of astronomers' observatories appear as pimples on the White Mountain's profile.

Like Isabella, we head for the mountain from Waimea. But not before breakfast. Through the window of the Paniolo Country Inn, I see pickups pulling horse trailers. Is this as close as we'll get to horses? Mr. Lewis, who has purchased a *Hawai'i Tribune Herald*, says, "Your horse is now reading the sports page."

We hit the road, a reasonable lane through Parker Ranch land. Gone are the sheep of Isabella's time. *The afternoon fog, which serves instead of rain, rolled up in dense masses.* The fog appears, on cue, for we have Bird in hand. The red dirt washboard road grows ever less distinct, and we slow to Isabella's pace. We stop, for photos: The Kohala Mountains behind us, the mass of Mauna Kea ahead. And that is all. No cows, no horses, no cowboys. Just rolling green with a lone *koa* tree bent to the wind on the horizon.

And then, suddenly, a *pueo*, a Hawaiian owl, hovers not 30 feet from us. He lights on a grassy knoll, his round, white face quizzical on his swiveling neck. We spot wild turkeys, and a China pheasant rooster with two hens. At 8,500 feet, my ears pop. The radio gives a small craft advisory and flash flood warnings for all Islands. Too late. Washouts from yesterday cross our path. Yahoo! This is nature at its wildest—just like Isabella experienced!

By midafternoon, we wind up Mauna Kea's observatory road. And then around the fateful bend, those horizon pimples pop. Mr. Lewis exclaims, "Science Central!"

Skiers emerge from a red Isuzu Amigo, buckle their stiff boots into their high-tech skis, bail over a guardrail and disappear into blowing fog. The wind gusts and buffets the car while we eat tortilla chips, waiting for the fog to blow away. I get out and discover I can barely walk, I'm so dizzy from the altitude—almost 14,000 feet.

After riding steadily for six hours, our horses, snorting and panting, and plunging up to their knees in fine volcanic ash, and halting, trembling, and exhausted, every few feet, carried us up the great tufa cone which crowns the summit of this vast fire-flushed, fire-created mountain.... This summit is a group of six red tufa cones...the clouds...lay in glistening masses all round the mountain about halfway up, shutting out the smiling Earth....

No kidding. In the fog, the cones appear and disappear, as if by some trick of smoke and mirrors. When the sun breaks through, Mr. Lewis is eating a banana. By the time he swallows, the cones have disappeared again. He sets up a camera with a lens the size of a telescope. A five-second blast of sun hits the cones. And then all we can see is immediately next to us: ten-foot wide letters made in a snowbank with cherry shave ice—

HAWAI'I
Aloha
2/26/96

The fog turns to snow. We abandon our plan to camp near the visitor center. Instead, I call my Aunty Betty in Kohala to beg for a bunk for the night. Isabella toughed it out in a hut at a sheep station, though she woke at three from the hopeless cold. Are Brad and I wandering wimps? The Milquetoasts of Mauna Kea?

At Aunty Betty's house, my cousin Lani has a good suggestion: "Make the story 'Where Isabella Didn't Go: Mauna Lani Resort.'"

The next morning, Mr. Lewis and I scan the skies and decide to try climbing Mauna Loa from the Saddle Road. Isabella ascended from the Kīlauea side, but hey, this is better than nothing. Besides, we can make a stop at the U.S. weather station at about 11,000 feet.

Isabella began on horseback at 7 a.m. with a Mr. Gandle and *two natives who knew not a word of English,* after a night in a cabin at 'Āinapō with swarms of fleas. Ahead was 7,000 vertical feet of lava. *I put on all my warm clothes…which gave me the squat, padded look of a puffin or Esquimaux. At timberline began the vastness of this mountain. The whole south of this large island, down to and below the water's edge, is composed of its slopes. Its height is nearly 3 miles, its base is 180 miles in circumference, so that Wales might be packed away within it, leaving room to spare…For 24 hours the lower world, "works and ways of busy men" were entirely shut out, and we were alone with this trackless and inanimate region of horror.*

In our first view, Mauna Loa's purple, snow-frosted summit appears as a sky-island floating on a frothing sea of clouds. The one-lane roller-coaster road to the weather observatory is marked down the middle by a wavering white stripe, not to divide the pavement but as a guide in fog. In the oceans of *'a'ā, 'ōhelo* bushes cling in crevices protected from the wind. I hear the whinny of horses. I'm so sure, I look for riders to come over a rise. In a moment I realize I'm hearing wind-ghosts.

We begin hiking from the observatory. An Isabellian description of the sound of *'a'ā* clinkers crunching underfoot eludes me. Our steps sound just like chewing dry Cheerios. When I stop, I hear Mr. Lewis's shutter cheeping like a small lost bird.

We pick our way from cairn to cairn 50 yards at a time, over ropes of *pāhoehoe*, up coils of black lava that cascade in steps. I stop often, breathing hard in the thin air. We are alone in vastness. The horizon on all sides is the mountain—blue-black, yellow ocher and sienna patched with the white of snow. There is no vista here, no coastline to be seen, no other peaks. Mauna Loa is the world.

We lunch in a cave, a cinder-floored lava tube with a skylight entrance. Someone has left bottled water. Half-melted candles perch on a lava shelf. The ceiling is frescoed in calcified white. My thermometer says 40 degrees. Refrigerator temperature.

Our guide took us a little wrong once… "Wrong" on Mauna Loa means being arrested by an impassable 'a'ā *stream.* Mr. Lewis takes us a "little wrong" right after the last smoked oyster and tidbit of

---

Mauna Loa has erupted, on the average, every three and a half years, and in that short time has poured out four billion cubic yards of lava; enough to pave Iceland.

Mauna Loa has coated and recoated itself so often that it has never had time to erode. Whatever the rain may have taken away has quickly been replaced.

The mountain is 50 miles long. Viewed from the edge of the ocean, it is an astonishing trompe l'oeil, because it is so smoothly constructed that it appears in two dimensions and presents a deceptive depth of field. It looks like a low, friendly hill, a singing dune, at worst at bald Scottish brae.

You think, I'll run up there and have a look around before lunch. The long mountain is as high as the Alps. If it were dissected by streams—given promontories and reentrants, serrated by canyons, invaded by shadows—it might look something like the Alps.

◆

—John McPhee, "Cooling the Lava," *The Control of Nature*

---

cheese. I step immediately up to mid-shin into a snow-bridged *'a'ā* hole. "Holy *'a'ā*!" he declares. We survey the expanse of snow-covered *'a'ā* ahead. We confer, mentioning prospective broken ankles and a helicopter rescue. In 30 seconds, we turn downhill.

Oh, Isabella, forgive us for giving up on Moku'āweoweo, the summit crater. It's still another 1,500 lung-busting feet up, and, unlike your day, it's not erupting. Call us quitters. Call us sissies. Call us smart.

In a condo kitchen in Kailua-Kona, Mr. Lewis sautés *'ahi* while I sip chardonnay on the *lānai.* Have we totally taken leave of our heroine? Maybe not, for just beyond the hotel grounds, the eternal sea pounds the same black lava shore, coconut palms dance in silhouettes against the twilight, and geckos cluck in the trees.

At Kealakekua, Isabella stayed at a boarding house near Christ Church, a small Episcopal chapel still perched *mauka* of the road. But after a few days of the languid life and stifling heat of Kona, she had a relapse of itchy feet. The cure was her last Big Island adventure. And ours: Hualālai.

While at the boarding house, Isabella met a Mr. Greenwell, who ran a store and had orange and coffee plantations, though *he has a disagreeably embittered sarcastic tone and has a bad temper....*

Today we meet our guide at Mr. Greenwell's stone-and-mortar store, now the Kona Historical Society Museum in Kealakekua. Sherwood Greenwell is the merchant-farmer's grandson and president of the historical society. This younger Greenwell, now a man of years himself, is as charming as his forebear was severe. Sherwood and his cousin-in-law, society historian Jean Greenwell, speak of Isabella as if she is a friend who visited just last year. Sherwood stashes *bento* boxes and a cooler of beverages in the rear of his four-wheel drive, and up we go, climbing steadily from 1,500 feet through cattle country into grass and shrubby *pūkiawe* at 5,200 feet. In Isabella's time, before cattle, this area was densely forested in *'ōhi'a, koa,* and tree ferns.

Above timberline, she found *no permanent track, and on the occasions when I have ridden up here alone, the directions given me have been to steer for an ox bone, and from that to a dwarf* 'ōhi'a...

The slopes of this ranch land are laced with jeep trails that are barely better than nothing. Sherwood may well be steering from ox bone to a bonsai *'ōhi'a*. By lunchtime he has turned and backtracked so many times that all I can tell for sure is that Hualālai's 9,000-foot summit is over yonder, because I can see it.

At Kealapu'ali, I sit on a fallen eucalyptus balancing the *bento* box on my knees. We joke about getting home, given Sherwood's circuitous navigation. He says, "Maybe it's not a good idea to eat both your rice balls now."

Isabella stayed with Hawaiians in this wild country, at a sheep station, in a woolshed, and in a "wigwam" of grass, eating boiled jerked beef or mutton, sour *poi* and pilot biscuits soaked in coffee. She was reduced to a single chemise for underclothing. It seems she washed her only spare garment and hung it out the window to dry, but, as she would put it, alas, some hogs or calves destroyed it.

At Kealapu'ali, the air is customarily still, and the trees grow straight. The silence, Sherwood says, drives some people mad. Hualālai's slopes feel gentle, perhaps hospitable, compared with the other worlds of Mauna Kea and Mauna Loa. This mountain beckons rather than challenges. Come live on my slopes and in my forests.

We dine at the ruins of a dairy that occupied this place in the 1880s after the sheep business was doomed by lamb-killing wild dogs and pigs. I step gingerly into the remnants of the main house, hoping not to fall through the rotting floorboards. It's hard to be sure whether this is one of the places Isabella stayed. All that's left of her other Hualālai stops is a wool press at a sheep station some eight miles away.

"I want so much for her to have stayed here," Jean Greenwell says. Me too. I want to step in her actual footsteps, not just imitate her itinerary.

In midafternoon we turn downslope, though Isabella twice ascended to Hualālai's summit. For me, it's enough for now.

I left Hualālai yesterday morning, and dined with my kind host and hostess in the wigwam. It was the last taste of the wild Hawaiian life I have learned to love so well, the last meal on a mat, the last exercise of skill in eating "two-fingered" poi.... It is best to leave the Islands now. I love them better every day, and dreams of the Fatherland are growing fainter in this perfumed air and under this glittering sky.

It is best to leave Isabella's trail now. I love it better every day, and dreams of doing this properly, of riding these mountains on horseback, of sleeping in huts and dining on jerked beef and black coffee—these dreams grow ever larger in this perfumed air and under this glittering sky.

After her travels in Hawai'i, Isabella Bird was never able to settle down to ordinary existence again. She went on to the Rocky Mountains, to Japan, to Malaysia, Persia, Kurdistan, Manchuria.

And after my travels with Mr. Lewis? I shall never come to the Big Island again without wanting to travel its shores and slopes with Bird in hand.

Native Hawaiian freelance writer Sally-Jo Keala-o-Ānuenue Bowman grew up in Kailua, O'ahu, and spent childhood summers in the rain forest of Volcano, not realizing she was already retracing the travels of Isabella Bird. Bowman's Hawaiian name, Keala-o-Ānuenue means "The Path of the Rainbow." In 1996, she won a Hawai'i Publishers' Association "Best Editorial Feature" award for "Rage, Bones and Hope." Her essays on native topics have won three first prizes at the Pacific Northwest Writers Conference. An adjunct professor of journalism at University of Oregon, she is finishing Nā Koa: The Warriors, *a novel about the overthrow of the Hawaiian monarchy. She divides her time between Hawai'i and Oregon.*

⋆

The long uphill grind to the summit of Mauna Loa Volcano is the Mount Everest of Hawai'i hikes—a grueling eighteen miles over crunching lava with a steady elevation gain from 7,000 feet to nearly 14,000 feet. This is made more exhausting by the necessity of hauling a heavy backpack, the effects of altitude which seem to multiply each mile into three, chilling winds and the possibility of freezing temperatures even in the summer.

I made the ascent with seven other members of the Sierra Club mainly because I wanted to explore the steaming caldera on top and also as a kind of personal challenge—to see if I was strong enough to make it all the way there.

Machismo is a big reason many people make the climb. In a group of bragging hikers, it's still a conversation stopper to mention the top of Mauna Loa.

For others, the trip to the top is a chance to join company with an eccentric group of oddballs chronicled in Hawaiian history, such as Lt. Charles Wilkes, commander of the U.S. Exploring Expedition, who set out for the snowy summit in the winter of 1841, riding in a sedan chair carried by four Hawaiians clad only in *malo* and ti-leaf sandals. So painful was this journey, that, during the rest breaks, the native bearers reportedly hid in the bushes along the way, hoping to escape their duties.

Or there was Isabella Bird, the 40-year-old English traveler, who made it to the top of an erupting Mauna Loa in 1873, in a difficult horseback journey that left the horses' hooves drenched in blood. Frustrated because water for her tea would not boil at the summit, she wrote: "In spite of my objection to stimulants and in defiance of the law against giving liquor to natives, I made a great tin of brandy today, of which all partook, along with tinned salmon and doughnuts."

—Denby Fawcett, *Mauna Loa—A Source Book, Historical Eruptions & Exploration*

TONY PERROTTET

Cliffhanger in Kaua'i

Some say you haven't seen Kaua'i until you've walked the Kalalau Trail.

SOMEWHERE BEYOND THOSE MISTY RIDGE TOPS WAS A LOST VALLEY, a place of giant waterfalls and primal souls oblivious to urban dreads, living off the neon-green bounty of the land. Those who entered there would find a realm devoid of Benetton, telemarketers, and even Larry King. And no passports were required, because this Lost Horizon, once a sacred retreat for ancient Hawaiians, slumbered within the boundaries of the USA on Kaua'i's dramatic Nā Pali Coast. There was just one problem—like all lost valleys, the Promised Land of Kalalau was in no hurry to be visited.

My Hawaiian Happy Valley remained bruisingly out of reach, and at mile ten, I was losing faith. Staggering beneath my pack and ravaged by the tropical sun, I struggled to keep whipping winds from launching me off 2,000-foot cliffs like a gum wrapper. My feet were blistered; my throat was parched. The fluted cliffs went on and on to the salty horizon. A magnificent sight, without a doubt—one of the most stunning vistas of the Pacific, even. But by this stage, all I wanted to do was fling myself onto a nice hammock and drink a half-dozen chilled mai tai in quick succession.

And then I stumbled around a corner and into a burbling, forest-shrouded creek that looked like some Keatsian elfin grotto. That's when a sign, a messenger from this lost territory—sun-bleached, blue-eyed, wild-haired, a Natural Man in all his priapic glory—stepped out of the surrounding foliage.

His only accessory was a white plastic bucket full of fresh drinking water. He smiled a beatific smile, his eyes focused somewhere in the distance, and conveyed the greeting of his exotic realm. "Aloha!"

My quest had begun one dismal winter day in my New York City apartment, surrounded by seven million stir-crazy shut-ins. I discovered that the farthest tourist-accommodating warm place from Manhattan still within the 50 states was the Island of Kaua'i—the oldest and greenest rock in the Hawaiian archipelago.

"When you think of Hawai'i," a friend had said, "you're actually picturing Kaua'i." But just getting to the Garden Island wasn't good enough. Not only would I go to Kaua'i, I would head for its remotest shore—the Nā Pali Coast, where a thousand-year-old walking trail would lead me from Hell's Kitchen to Xanadu; the Kalalau Valley.

The Līhu'e Airport was already a good start, a tiny, low-slung facility that felt more like a patio than an arrival center, no shoving mobs or squawking taxis. I was suddenly hit with bracing lungfuls of something sweet and fragrant and foreign to my urban lungs: fresh air.

After picking up a camping permit from the Nā Pali State Park Office, I headed north on Route 56, also called the Kaumuali'i Highway in honor of Kaua'i's last king, the only Island leader able to fend off conquest by King Kamehameha the Great. The road gets around the Island the only way possible, hugging the coast and avoiding the jagged peaks of the interior until it gets to the fifteen-mile stretch of Nā Pali cliffs, one of the most effective roadblocks this side of the Himalayas.

My friend was right. These were the scenes I'd filed in my Hawai'i image bank. Near the town of Wailua, the ancient residence of Kaua'i's kings, stood the Coco Palms Hotel, wedding site of another King—Elvis—in *Blue Hawai'i.* Harrison Ford leapt into the Hulē'ia River on the southern part of the Island in *Raiders of the Lost Ark.* The 80-foot Wailua Falls upstaged Ricardo Montalban at the beginning of every episode of *Fantasy Island.*

The farther north I drove, the more lush and twisted the terrain became. Deep folds gouged the mountainsides, the creases cut like landslides by centuries of wind and water.

Back along the shore, I passed Kaua'i's most famous scene, one that embodied forbidden paradise for millions of postwar moviegoers: Lumaha'i Beach and its misty mountain known as Bali Hai. Here, on the sandy set of *South Pacific*, the island paradise myth was born.

But plate tectonics and Noah-style rainfall, not Rodgers and Hammerstein, own the copyright on Eden here. The Island is one gigantic dormant shield, with a volume of about 1,000 cubic miles. As a result, Kaua'i's interior is nearly all parkland or forest reserve, dominated by Wai'ale'ale mountain and Mount Kawaikini which rise 5,148 feet (1,569 meters) and 5,243 feet (1,598 meters) respectively.

In lieu of a caldera, Wai'ale'ale's summit is a wind-lashed, rain-slick, cloud-shrouded plateau, home to Kāne, the ancient Hawaiians' greatest god. The mountain also serves as the Island's divining rod—and it's a good one, collecting more that 466 inches of rain a year, enough to make it the wettest place on earth. Together, Wai'ale'ale and the great Alaka'i Swamp on its northwest flank water the garden of Kaua'i, producing a florist's Valhalla that inspired Hawaiians to chant its praises:

> Beautiful is Kaua'i beyond compare,
> She sends forth a bud in the summit of Wai'ale'ale
> She flowers in the heights of Kawaikini
> Her strength radiates in awful splendor from the Alaka'i;
> Though I weary, though I faint, she renews my
>   strength in her soft petals.

At the trailhead, the path led straight up through a tropical forest. For the first two miles, cheery day-trippers bounded past, eyeing my heavy pack and saying witty things like, "Gee I'm glad I'm not you." You can do anything you like on the road to Nirvana. I smiled and pretended to speak only Russian.

I soon paid for my flippancy. The track turned ominously onto Nā Pali cliffs, a billowing curtain of rock pulverized by the Pacific. A million years ago this coast fell in gentle slope to the sea, geologists theorize. Today, it looks as if it's been savaged by a giant claw, the work of storms and eroding rivers. Far below, layers of coral reef poked through the crystal waters of Kē'ē Beach at Hā'ena State Park, a snorkelers' haven. Wedged between sand and cliff lay the stone ruins of an ancient Hawaiian hula school.

Trainees were sequestered here for months learning the sacred art of hula, the keeper of tales and traditions. For the duration of their studies they couldn't cut their fingernails or hair, or have sexual intercourse. The graduation party was a ten-day orgy of feasting, chanting, dancing, even homemade fireworks.

The ban on sex must have been particularly trying for the dancers. The ancient Hawaiians were free spirits who could have made Margaret Mead blush. Early European sailors were amazed to find their ships surrounded by canoes full of beautiful women. "In a moment our decks were crowded with young, good-natured girls...uncivilized brunette(s) in a state of nature," wrote Captain George Vancouver's first mate in what must have been a shaky hand. "The surface of the water around us was covered with some hundreds soliciting admittance. Our bark instantly became a scene of jollity and all was pleasure and delight."

But not for long. When Vancouver's former Captain James Cook became the first European to sail into Kaua'i's Waimea Bay in 1778, at least half of his 112-man crew had "the venereal distemper," a disease unknown to the Hawaiians. He refused to let infected sailors leave the ship under threat of flogging. But a small supply party looking for yams on the nearby Island of Ni'ihau was trapped by heavy seas for three days. By the time Cook returned a year later, the disease had spread throughout the entire Hawaiian chain. "The very thing happened that I had above all others wished to prevent," he later wrote in his log.

*

From the overlook of Kē'ē, the path descended to Hanakāpī'ai Beach, the first designated camping area on the route. It had all the essentials of paradise. From a balmy, palm-lined shore, I watched the sun sink in glory, and when the full moon slipped from behind the mountaintops, it was as if someone had flicked on a giant floodlight, bathing the beach with its glow.

The next morning I began scrambling up the cliff again. About 100 yards up, a signpost announced that this was how high you should be if a tsunami, or tidal wave, hit. The Honolulu newspapers had been warning that a monster wave was long overdue. A Chilean earthquake in 1960 unleashed a wall of water that killed 61 people on the Island of Hawai'i.

On the Kalalau Trail, tsunami were the least of my worries. The path stayed far above apocalyptic waves, zigzagging around sheer headlands, crossing tiny creeks, and passing through natural tunnels of hibiscus and plumeria. Around noon I found Hanakoa, a deserted village surrounded by overgrown coffee terraces. The place was so high that a cloud seemed to have permanently settled on it. Every few seconds a fine spray of water descended from above, like a lettuce display at the grocery store. According to a cheap guidebook I'd found in Līhu'e, the hardest part of the trail was over. Why not knock over the last leg in the afternoon, I confidently thought, and be in Kalalau for dinner?

The moral here is: don't trust cheap guidebooks. Beyond Hanakoa, the cliff sides dried out, the earth turned volcanic red, trees disappeared, and the landscape became almost arid. I felt like an intruder in the Valley of the Giants, surrounded by huge spiked plants like the heads of mutant pineapples. But things really got serious when the cliffs began to show the scars of Hurricane 'Iniki, the devastating 1992 storm that hit the Island with winds up to 175 mph. About half the structures on the Island were seriously damaged, with an estimated cost of $2 billion.

'Iniki and the general overuse had torn out and eroded entire sections of the Kalalau Trail, leaving only a vague outline of a path on a 45-degree slope. The cliffs below looked like a giant ski jump, and I could picture myself sliding off the craggy lip with all the grace and aplomb of the "agony of defeat" guy from *Wide World of Sports*. Later I learned that several people do just that every year, never to be heard from again. To add to the excitement, the ground was covered with ball-bearing-like pebbles, while a howling wind mashed my body to the cliff. I slid my way across, clutching the few assorted roots and clumps of grass that hadn't been clawed to shreds by other desperate hikers. Tiny boats full of sightseers passed below, those with good eyesight no doubt gazing up and thinking, "Gee, I'm glad I'm not him!" This time I saw their point.

Which is why, when I finally met the naked, aloha-hailed ambassador from Kalalau, I could have kissed him. He politely explained that, yes, I had reached the Kalalau Valley, the last redoubt of shell-shocked urbanites. All I had to do was walk another mile along the beach. There I could camp among the groves, drink from fresh flowing streams, shed my twentieth-century inhibitions and restrictive garb and return to idyllic Polynesia. His actual words were "Just head down that-a-way," but you get the idea.

When I crawled out of my tent the next morning, a half dozen dolphins cavorted in the waves offshore. Scarlet cardinals chirped in the bush. Perhaps this wouldn't be such a bad new home, I thought. After all, nothing short of a tsunami could force me back up that trail. This was it for me, forever.

In the happy valley of Kalalau, I found that everything you need is a stone's throw from your tent. The mile-long beach lies right outside the flap. A waterfall plummets from the cliff behind the beach, where everyone comes to shower, wash dishes, and get drinking water (which, rather unromantically, has to be treated or boiled to prevent leptospirosis, a sometimes fatal bug-borne illness similar to hepatitis).

The waterfall serves as Kalalau's town square and meeting place, where the newcomers and old-timers gather. The main topics of conversation seemed to center around the difficulty of the trail, the weather (nearly perfect every day despite fierce winds), and the many trials of nudity. I overheard one freckled woman from

Virginia announce, "I stripped all day yesterday, and now mah butt's as purple as a little plum."

The basic social division in Kalalau was between the Naked and the Clothed. Nobody seems to have heard of the ozone hole here. The pecking order was determined by how tan one is all over, the highest caste being those who looked as if they'd been turned on a spit. These were the regulars who almost never left Kalalau.

The lowest of the low on the social order were those who had fallen from grace and hid their nakedness with swimming suits. Naturally, I was one of the wretched Clothed. But an odd thing happens to people in Kalalau: If everyone else is naked, then you actually feel foolish wearing a swimsuit. Pretty soon, I wanted to strip just to stop people from staring.

The main adventure of any Kalalau day was having a swim. The waves looked about the size of the Matterhorn, but I went in anyway and got pounded, tossed, and spit out. The violence of it all was strangely therapeutic, as if I were sacrificing myself to the sea gods.

After a few days, I felt steady enough to explore the Kalalau Valley. The trail followed a river into the mountains above, passing taro and sweet potato terraces that once sustained a thriving population of Hawaiians. Mango and guava trees filled the forest; the air smelled like the essence of passion fruit. Soon the waterfalls began, tumbling into swimming holes in spectacular scenes. Off in the distance, the blue Pacific stretched uninterrupted to Japan.

The only dampers on my Arcadian sojourn were (1) having to leave and (2) the nagging certainty of miles of Nā Pali precipices on the way back. As the waves pounded in front, I considered water transit options. Giant surf. No docks. A long swim. Then I ran into a couple of French backpackers limping down to the waterfall. They mentioned that they'd seen a motorized rubber raft pull up to the beach that morning. They'd negotiated with the captain to take them back to Hanalei, a small town a few miles from the trailhead, for $60 each the next morning. I scoffed at this craven cop-out—and then immediately resolved to join them.

By the time I reached the landing spot, the swells were still massive, a sandbar blocked the way, and the captain could only get the smaller of his two dinghies to the beach. The only thing left to do was dump the packs in one boat and swim for the other which floated just outside the breakers. Several sets pounded me, sending me to the ocean floor. A rip current dueled with me at each stroke.

Finally hauling myself over the side of the Zodiac, I came face-to-face with a half-dozen passengers who'd come out on a comfortable morning cruise. They greeted me with stares more appropriate for feral pigs or some other grungy, mildly dangerous form of wildlife. But within a few hours I'd be back in Hanalei with them, knocking back cold beers and chowing down on shrimp salad. That night I'd crawl into a real bed in the Princeville Hotel, once described as "the place people in heaven go after they die."

It's amazing how worthy you can feel when you've earned it by the sweat of your brow, the blood of your heels, and the purple skin of your butt.

Tony Perrottet is an Australian-born writer who lives in New York City. After graduating with a degree in history from Sydney University, he headed off to South America to work as a newspaper correspondent, and lived in Buenos Aires for two years. His travel writing has appeared in Esquire, Outside, Escape, Islands, Civilization, *most Australian magazines, and the* London Sunday Times. *His collection of travel stories,* Off The Deep End: Travels in Forgotten Frontiers, *was published in 1997.*

*

My family is the quintessential tourist family. Look up "tourist" in *Webster's,* and you'll find a picture of my kinfolk. God love 'em, they showed up in Hawai'i in a small pack recently to do a production number for my sister Vicki's wedding at the Fern Grotto on Kaua'i. It was Vicki's third, and as for the groom, Tony, well, he described himself as a member of the "marriage of the month club."

If the Fern Grotto isn't the most touristy place in the state, I don't know what is. Boatloads of people going up the river to view a little trickle of water issuing from a cliffside seems a little suspect as a premise to charge a guy ten bucks, anyway, but the whole scenario gets pretty weird. First of all, if you're getting married, doesn't the symbolism of "going up the river" seem a little out of place? It does to me.

There was Vicki in her wedding gown, her intended by her side, sitting in the back of a twenty-person launch complete with a captain, a guide who does a little comedy spiel, a photographer, and a singer.

That little spiel—do they have a school to teach people how to do that? I've been in helicopters, scuba dive classes, on buses to lū'au—they all have the same rhythm: "Hey...how many grandmothers from Omaha are here today?"

The video was rolling, of course, with brother David providing the voice-over and uncle Joel shooting away. As we were just about to leave the dock, one of the other boats was pulling in, and it happened to be loaded with Japanese tourists.

When they caught sight of Vicki, they all moved to our side of their boat. They were smiling broadly and chattering gaily among themselves. Then, Vicki made the critical mistake: she waved. Just a simple hello, but as soon as she did, every single one of them whipped out a camera and started taking pictures of her waving.

The more she waved, the more pictures they took, until they disembarked their craft and lined up next to ours to get her and Tony—overwhelmed, weary-armed, and in stitches—waving in their wedding attire, about to head up the river.

It's a fine family, we all agree. Perhaps Cousin Roger put it best when he remarked, "We'll all have to get together again...maybe the next time Vicki gets married!"

Stitches, I'm telling you, we all end up in stitches.

—George Fuller, *"Bobby and Lou! Bobby and Lou! Go Over by the Plant. OK, Now, Smile!"*

ROBB WALSH

The Tropic of Spam

Don't knock it until you've tried it, maybe with some sushi rice or poi.

THERE IS A LONG LINE AT THE CONVENIENCE STORE IN KAILUA-Kona and I am in a hurry. When it is my turn to pay, I rattle off my purchases: "Ten bucks worth of gas, a large cup of coffee, and..." My eyes dart around, looking for a quick breakfast. There is a large display case on the counter, the kind usually stocked with croissants and breakfast tacos, but this one is filled with a different kind of morning treat. "And one of those," I blurt out. "And one Spam *musubi*," says the clerk, handing me the thick, warm square of rice topped with Spam and wrapped in a strip of seaweed.

As I zoom up the highway, trying to make my tee time, I sip my coffee and consider the Spam-covered chunk of rice. In the pink light of a Hawaiian sunrise, it doesn't look half bad. Besides, I am hungry. So I bite in. The spices and grease of the fried Spam have soaked into the sticky rice, giving it a sweet, oily tang. I wash the Spam sushi down with the rest of my coffee and make it to the golf course with time to spare.

The people of the Hawaiian Islands consume 4.3 million cans of Spam a year, more than any other state in the Union. Hawaiians snack on Spam *musubi* for breakfast, pack their *bento* boxes with Spam and rice for lunch, and dine on grilled Spam with pineapple for dinner. One of Hawai'i's most famous chefs, Sam Choy, even serves Spam dishes in his popular restaurants. And, like a lot of Hawaiians, he gets a little touchy if you needle him about it.

For the rest of the world, Spam is an icon of absurdity. The can, with its huge yellow letters on a dark-blue background and the photo of the pink pressed-meat loaf, looks like a Warhol-inspired parody of itself. Just the word *Spam* can provoke giggles. In a Monty Python restaurant skit, waiters in Viking helmets sing "Spam, Spam, Spam, Spam" over and over as hapless customers try to order something else. At Spam-carving contests, Spam-eating contests, and Spam-cooking contests across the country, contestants ham it up with Spam slapstick.

Luckily, the people at Hormel, the makers of Spam, have a sense of humor. They have even authorized a mail-order catalog selling Spam neckties, Spam boxer shorts, and Spam t-shirts. And why not? In 1994, the company sold its five billionth can of Spam. As long as Americans continue to consume the stuff at an average of 3.6 cans per second, Hormel can afford to keep laughing.

But as the world's second largest per capita consumers of Spam (after Guam), Hawaiians don't get the joke. They, too, have Spam-cooking contests, but there's a difference. In Hawai'i, the contestants take it quite seriously.

"I'm proud to serve Spam in my restaurants, and I don't care what Mainlanders think about it," says Sam Choy when I stop by his eponymous restaurant on the Big Island. "In fact, I hope to do a Spam cookbook someday."

"Isn't there already a Spam cookbook?" I ask.

"Yes, but I want to take it to the gourmet level," Choy says without a trace of irony.

Spam became a part of Sam Choy's repertoire through his involvement in the Hawai'i Regional Cuisine movement. The chefs who started the trend were trying to incorporate indigenous foods into their cooking, including the delicious local fishes and exotic fruits. But Choy, the only native Hawaiian in the group, argued that Spam was a Hawaiian food tradition, too. Like most Hawaiians, he grew up with Spam, and he isn't willing to abandon it just because Mainlanders may snicker at it. As incongruous as it seems, the canned luncheon meat from Austin, Minnesota, is deeply embedded in Hawaiian culture.

There are several explanations for Spam's popularity on the Islands. Most trace the beginnings of the phenomenon to World War II, when the American military served it to soldiers, sailors, and base personnel stationed there. Others note that Spam kept well in the tropical climate at a time when refrigerators were scarce. And then there's the livestock theory, that since sugar and pineapple had always dominated Hawaiian agriculture, there was never a large supply of meat.

All of these explanations make a certain amount of sense. But the war has been over for more than 50 years now, Hawaiians have plenty of refrigerators, and meat is now readily available. So why does Spam persist as a Hawaiian favorite?

I gain some insight when I return to Choy's restaurant to taste a few of his Spam specialties. He is off on O'ahu, but his sister, Claire Wai Sun Choy, who manages the place, is ready for me. She serves me Spam in creamed corn, Spam with homemade papaya marmalade, and Spam *musubi*. When she joins me at my table, I confess that none of the Spam dishes are really winning me over.

Claire gets up, walks over to a cooler, and comes back with a small dish of lavender goop.

"Have you ever eaten poi?" she asks.

"No." I admit I know that poi, a starch made from ground taro root, has been Hawai'i's most important staple throughout history, but I have also been warned that it tastes like wallpaper paste.

"Poi is like yogurt," Claire says philosophically. "It tastes bad by itself." I sample a little of the sour, ice-cold paste and agree, with a grimace. "But when you combine poi with other flavors, something happens," Claire continues as she hands me a plate of slow-cooked *laulau* pork. The pork is excellent, but when I try it with the poi, the poi tastes good, too. What once seemed sour, now seems sweet. In fact, the combination of pork and poi is much more interesting than the pork alone. At Claire's direction, I also try poi with fried *poke* fish.

"Now, eat some of this," Claire says, shoving the Spam and some papaya toward me. I cut off a big hunk of Spam and start to chew. As usual, it tastes too salty, too greasy, and too sweet.

"Now, eat some poi," she urges. I shove a huge spoonful of poi into my mouth with the Spam and continue to chew. The salty, sweet greasiness of the hot Spam is perfectly offset by the thick, starchy sourness of the cold poi. It is much better than poi with pork or poi with fish. When I get over my disbelief, I gobble another mouthful of the culinary odd couple. I smile as I realize what Hawaiians figured out long ago. Claire sums it up with a shrug. "Nothing tastes better with poi than hot, crispy Spam."

Robb Walsh of Austin, Texas, writes about food and golf for American Way Magazine *where he is a contributing editor. A commentator for National Public Radio's Weekend Edition, Walsh is coauthor of three cookbooks:* Traveling Jamaica with Knife, Fork & Spoon, Nuevo Tex-Mex, *and* A Cowboy in the Kitchen. *Founder and head judge of the* Austin Chronicle *Hot Sauce Festival, reputedly the world's largest hot sauce cook-off, Walsh once set out on a Caribbean trek in search of hot sauces—and won the 1996 James Beard Journalism Award for feature magazine writing.*

⋆

Easter is a spectacular time in Hawai'i, an explosion of flowers and beautiful spring weather that calls for even more special measures than usual for that happy season. Every year, our friends Jerry and Debby added their own special touch to Easter festivities with a waffle brunch, *"kōkua style,"* meaning guests bring potluck toppings for the waffles that are mixed by the gallon and served steaming from an army of waffle irons. Everyone wore *lei* and wandered in and out from the sunny *lānai* to the breezy dining room shaded by a huge banyan.

The brunch buffet was arranged on an antique wooden surfboard, and like all potlucks, there was a bit of competitiveness involved in which guest cook brought the most *'ono* concoction. Plenty of strawberries and whipped cream, homemade mango jam, fresh papaya fluffs, sweet butters, and the like crowded the surfboard each year. This was a health-conscious crowd, but it was Easter brunch and we figured anything goes.

We were the newcomers and decided left field was a good place from which to launch our entries. The first year, we got good reviews for creating a *lomilomi* cheese spread, kind of a Hawaiian lox and cream cheese. But then we had to best it the next year, and there was only one solution. We presented our dish, a creamy blend of mystery ingredients, white stuff with bits of pink and green inside. "Wow! What is that?" demanded our hostess. "Try some first," we responded. Everyone did. We had stumbled on a perfect offset of flavors and textures—it was a hit. So we could confess the ingredients: crème fraîche, slivers of fresh basil picked from our deck garden…and the secret touch that made it special, pureed SPAM!

—MC

BETTY FULLARD-LEO

Kalaupapa, an Inspirational Outpost

This Moloka'i trail leads to a never-never-again land, lest we forget.

BUZZY SPROAT HAD THE LOOK OF A REAL MULE SKINNER: Grizzled gray whiskers, weather-beaten leather chaps. He smiled at his favorite mule more than he smiled at me.

"Relax," he said, blurred pidgin unmistakably marking him as a local guy. "Dis mule so sure-foot you can take notes when you ride the trail to Kalaupapa. Lots a time, I like carve racing cars when we go down the trail."

Perched on Black Jack's broad back five feet up in the air, I looked down the cliff side, trying to count the 26 switchbacks along the narrow path clinging to the hillside like a skinny string stuck on a curtain of green velvet. Kalaupapa lay 1,664 feet below, a five-square-mile peninsula, splendid in its windswept isolation, dappled greens against the brilliant blue of the ocean.

Were it not for Buzzy Sproat, the quiet colony that still houses 63 former victims of leprosy (euphemistically called Hansen's disease), would have been nearly as inaccessible as it was in Father Damien's day—except for the planes that occasionally fly tourists down from Moloka'i's tiny airport topside. Hardier souls than I do hike down, and locals still talk about the Swede who ran up the three-and-one-eighth-mile trail in 38 minutes.

The mule ride to Kalaupapa was always Moloka'i's most thrilling adventure, so when the former owner closed it in the early 1990s, a trip to the "Friendly Isle" seemed to have lost some of its zing.

Sproat, who shod and generally took care of the mules, ended up with them. He comes by his love for the recalcitrant animals naturally, he says.

"My dad and my grandfather were always hors'n around mules," Sproat says. "Granddad used mules to put the (irrigation) ditch in the Kohala mountains (a historic feat of engineering on the Big Island) in 1905."

In 1994–1995, the National Parks system hired Sproat and a few others to rebuild the trail to Kalaupapa—"It was a lot rougher, rockier before," Sproat insists. When the peninsula was ready to be reopened to visitors, he went to Roy Horner, a Moloka'i businessman for financial advice. The two became partners, and the mule ride was back in business under their management in 1995, after a two-year closure. It continues to be Moloka'i's most moving experience—literally and figuratively.

We were a pack of about fifteen descending the trail, a guide at the head and one at the tail. The mules plodded along at their own speed, never once crushing our legs against the inside cliff or stumbling over the edge even at the tightest, most precarious of switchbacks. Within half an hour, my legs felt locked into position from the constant instinctive braking, and by the time we hit level land, most of us midlife adventurers had spaghetti limbs when we tried to stand.

Jimmy Brede, our guide and a patient-resident for 54 years who came to Kalaupapa when he was fourteen, ushered us aboard an old school bus before we had time to wonder how we could possibly survive the ride up the cliff again.

The peninsula is flat with only a few semipaved roads wending through *kiawe*, pandanus, and scaviola, giving way here and there to vistas of blue sea and frothing white surf. We stopped at monuments to Father Damien, the famous Belgian priest who cared for the lepers until he caught the disease himself and died, and Mother Marianne Cope, a Franciscan nun who arrived at Kalaupapa the year before Damien died.

Father Damien, the Reverend Damien de Veuster, was assigned at his own request to tend the outcast lepers of Moloka'i in 1873. By the time he arrived, 797 lepers had been sent to Kalaupapa; almost half of them had died. The Board of Health had chosen Kalaupapa as a leper colony because it was a natural prison, surrounded by cliffs and sea.

> I have met up with some visitors who, as soon as they got into the van, would say, "Where are the lepers?" I've tried my best to explain to them in a nice way that we're not called "lepers" anymore but that we would accept the term "Hansen's disease." Many of the patients don't mind if we use the word "leprosy" but to be called a "leper"—many of us don't feel so good when we hear that word.
>
> —Helen Keao, Kalaupapa resident since 1942

In the beginning, Damien took care to protect himself. One of his first distressing visits was to see a young girl. He found that worms were eating away one side of her body. "Many times," he wrote, "I have been obliged, not only to close my nostrils, but to remain outside to breathe fresh air. To counteract the bad smell, I got myself accustomed to the use of (pipe) tobacco."

In December 1884, he was soaking his feet in some hot water, but noticed he had no sense of heat or pain. After eleven years of working and caring for his flock, teaching them to farm, to sing, to play instruments, building churches and tending the stricken, Damien had caught the disease. He died on April 15, 1889, and was laid to rest under a pandanus tree in the little cemetery by St. Philomena Church, where he had preached so many times.

In 1936 his remains were exhumed and sent to his birthplace in Belgium. In 1995, he was beatified by Pope John Paul II and declared "blessed," the second step toward sainthood.

Guide Jimmy Brede pointed out holes in the floor of St. Philomena Church. "At Father Damien's first Mass," he said, "patients stood outside listening, because they were so ashamed. They had no control of saliva running from their mouth, because some were partially paralyzed, and they had to walk outside to spit. So Damien had holes put in the floor for people's comfort. The second Sunday, Father Damien had a pile of *'ape* leaves. He gave one to each person. They folded the leaf like a funnel and stuck it in the hole. So as not to disturb the Mass with going in and out, they could spit into the tube."

You could have heard a pin drop in the church, where beautiful pastel scenes and statues of religious figures decorated the walls. Through the window, the cross on Father Damien's grave was visible, hung with a fresh plumeria *lei*. Beyond, the knife-edge cliffs of Moloka'i and the tiny islands of Mōkapu and 'Ōkala jutted from the sea in lonely isolation.

The stories of the elderly people who have chosen to live out their days at Kalaupapa pull at the heartstrings nearly as much as the tales of Father Damien.

"I landed at the harbor May 15, 1942, when I was fourteen," Brede reminisced. There were fathers and mothers and 33 kids, all strangers, all with leprosy. We were so afraid of what we saw. We cried our hearts out. It took us time to be accustomed to the sight of the afflicted, but they wanted to share their love. Babies that were born on Kalaupapa were taken to Honolulu and *hānai'd* (adopted). When we came, the patients went crazy over my six-year-old brother, but I told them, 'You take him, you got to take me,' so we could stay together.

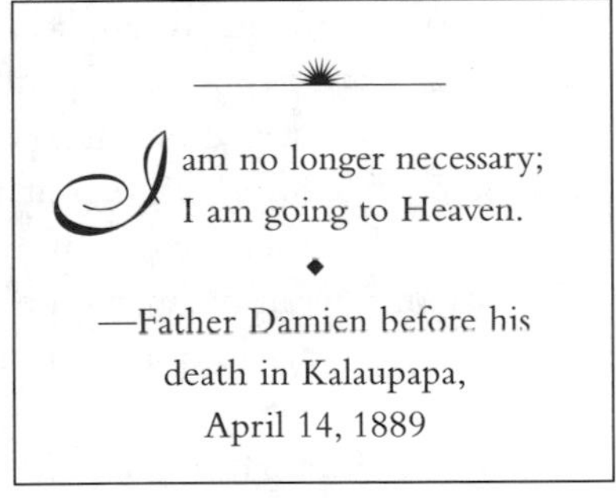
I am no longer necessary;
I am going to Heaven.

—Father Damien before his death in Kalaupapa, April 14, 1889

"In 1946 we became human guinea pigs when doctors discovered sulfur drugs. They gave us 36 pills a day. Many died from the overdoses, but they felt they would die anyway.

"I married my wife here, and after we were cured, we had a son and a daughter. We were afraid. There was no guarantee, so our kids were raised by their grandparents on O'ahu. When they were infants, we didn't dare touch them."

Today Brede's children are success stories. His daughter graduated with a master's degree in sociology, and his son, whose wife recently had their first baby, lives in Utah. The elder Bredes, like many other former patients with telltale deformities from the cruel disease, choose to stay at Kalaupapa.

Quietly, we boarded the old yellow school bus, disembarking again at what is perhaps the most beautiful scenic spot on Moloka'i, Kūka'iwa'a Point, a promontory looking across the ocean to those steep, jagged cliffs that made Kalaupapa such a secure prison. We were a somber, reflective group of mule riders.

By the time Brede dropped us off at Kalaupapa's arts and crafts gallery and museum, the mood had lightened. Literature and crafts made by residents—paintings of the peninsula, Christmas ornaments made of local materials, a monkey pod lamp, coconut shell vases—were for sale. The little museum's displays were poignant—spoons and forks with modified looped handles so deformed hands could hold them, historic photos of patients, nuns, and Father Damien.

The settlement is little more than a crossroads that ends at the harbor. There's a fire station, but there are few fires. There's a police station, but there's no crime. There is no bank, but it's not a problem on a peninsula where people do not own their homes and most exist on a ration of five pounds of beef and $45 a week. The biggest excitement of the year is not Christmas, but the day the barge arrives from Honolulu with all the really big things that people have ordered. Brede said, "Everyone comes even if they have to crawl, or hobble on crutches. They want to see who gets a new car or new furniture."

Ironically, our ride up the cliff didn't seem to produce nearly as much pain as it had on the way down. We rode silently onto the plateau topside, survivors of a trip into the past that left us awed, inspired, and maybe a little more compassionate to our fellow man.

Betty Fullard-Leo came to Hawai'i from the Pacific Northwest 35 years ago. She found work as a restaurant hostess at Honolulu Airport and met a dashing kama'āina. *They married and raised two sons; he retired and she returned to school, graduating from University of Hawai'i with a journalism degree. A freelance travel writer, she is contributing editor for* Hawai'i Magazine. *Her articles have appeared in the* Los Angeles Times, Fodor's Hawai'i Guides, *and* Coffee Times.

*

They were strangers to each other, collected by common calamity, disfigured, mortally sick, banished without sin from home and friends. Few would understand the principle on which they were thus forfeited in all that makes life dear; many must have conceived their ostracism to be grounded in malevolent caprice; all came with sorrow at heart, many with despair and rage. In the chronicle of man there is perhaps no more melancholy landing than this....

—Robert Louis Stevenson, *Travels in Hawai'i*

JIM NOLLMAN

Swimming with Dolphins

An interspecies musician prompts a natural performance.

TODAY, A PERSON FLOATING QUIETLY A QUARTER MILE FROM shore interacting with the sleek spinner dolphins of Kealakekua Bay on the Big Island of Hawai'i stands a good chance of getting fined by federal agents.

The dolphin cops actually climb into the palm trees lining the beach, at taxpayers' expense, to videotape swimmers breaking the marine mammal laws by attracting curious dolphins to their side. It doesn't seem to matter that the dolphins approach at their own volition. Nor does it matter that spinners swim at 25 miles per hour and can easily avoid hanky-panky with the slightest flip of their flukes.

I first met those same dolphins in 1976, years before the practice of swimming with them became an issue of contention. I swam 200 yards from shore on a becalmed, coral-studded, blue-green bay.

I wasn't much of a swimmer at that time, so I was happy to support my weight by cradling a musical instrument known as a waterphone, constructed from a stainless steel salad bowl welded to a pizza plate to form a hemisphere, with a vacuum cleaner tube projecting from the bowl to serve as a handle and as a mouthpiece. All around the lip of the instrument projected tuned brass prongs. Rubbing the prongs with a cello bow produced a sound like a violin immersed in a bowl of jello.

Because it was 1976, I had not yet heard of anyone else ever swimming with dolphins, so a part of my media-cluttered brain imagined shark-infested movie-set oceans.

Directly in front, twenty spinner dolphin dorsal fins rolled over the ocean surface in close formation. I had read John Lilly's accounts of communicating with captive dolphins and, as a budding interspecies musician, I wondered if dolphins might be attracted to a person making music in their midst. I stroked the main tube of the waterphone with the cello bow. Cradling the instrument, the vibration coursed clear through my body. As the spinners continued about their business of exploring the outer edge of the bay, I stopped bowing long enough to plunge my head into the water to listen. There was no sound beside the low, fading bellow of the waterphone. I altered my technique; produced shorter, more rhythmical sounds, tapping a palm directly on the prongs that rim the equator of the sphere. The beat issued clear and simple, five seconds of sound, followed by five of silence. Once

---

If you want to see spinner dolphins from land, drive Maui's northwest coast to Nākālele Bay overlook. One early morning, bound for Kahakuloa, several of us talked about Hawai'i's wonderful elusive sights—the green flash, moonlight rainbows, and spinners in motion. I confessed that in fifteen years in Hawai'i, I had never seen dolphins spinning. We rounded a curve and stopped to look at Nākālele Bay. Suddenly they came, hundreds of shiny gray chorus girls in a follies revue, twirling and dancing on wave tops, splashing and spinning clockwise and counterclockwise and end to end, flipping for sheer joy. We screamed with delight. They danced all the more.

◆

—RC & MC

---

again I stuck my head in the water. The sphere was vibrating so sharply it hurt my ears. The spinners kept their distance, so I tried something else, struck the center tube with a mallet while simultaneously immersing various sections of the sphere. A ringing tone was produced, the pitch modulated by the immersions. It sounded a bit like cartoon music accompanying the throbbing of Wile E. Coyote's heart.

This time the dolphins responded by swimming toward me. At 50 meters they formed a circle, turning on an axis like Israeli folk dancers doing the Have Negila. One at a time they broke from the circle, drew closer. It was difficult to judge distance accurately with my eyes six inches off the water's surface. Their eyes became visible. That smile! Several lifted their heads high above the water's surface to examine the source of the vibrations. I looked upon them as human beings dressed in dolphin suits. The image vanished when they blew, like champagne corks popping all over the surface of the ocean. I continued to draw long sliding notes from the throat of the waterphone. The sphere sounded like a church organ, then an Oriental gong. I dunked my head, opened my eyes. Seven blurry figures scooted past the edge of my vision.

Spinner dolphins vocalize at frequencies at or above the limit of our audible range, like the highest tones on a hearing test, but with the perceived gravity of intrigues whispered at the opposite end of a cathedral. So suddenly as to make my blood rush, one of the dolphins jumped six feet clear of the water. They were all jumping, spinning, somersaulting. And from the shore, so far away, the audience of human beings gathered to watch started laughing, clapping, slapping each other on the backs.

Someone on shore blared out a "charge" on a trumpet. The dolphins jumped higher. At that moment, I understood why captive dolphins attract large audiences. They are born performers. If musicians, acrobats, and clowns had a totem animal, it would be a dolphin. Yet, we reward their joyous talent by trying to own it, capturing them, placing them in concrete pools, and then making them do insipid tricks for dead fish and shortened life spans.

The spinners frolicked about for ten minutes, then moved off, formed their circle a second time. Gone. I suddenly felt cold, my arms sore from treading water, feeling much too far from shore.

Jim Nollman is a pioneer in the field of communication between species and is the author of Spiritual Ecology. *He lives in Friday Harbor, Washington. He is founder of Interspecies Communication, an organization dedicated to promoting dialogue between humans and wild animals. This story was excerpted from his book* The Charged Border: Where Whales and Humans Meet.

*

I had thought that nothing [on Kaua'i] could equal the thrill of seeing those cliffs from a kayak. I was wrong, for the next day, headed back to Nu'alolo Kai to look at ruins, we were diverted by some splashing out to sea—probably dolphins—and we paddled in that direction.

I was totally unprepared for what now appeared: 60 or 70 dolphins—a variety called spinners, four or five feet long, and some babies—swimming in an irregular circle about a quarter of a mile in diameter. They were jumping clear of the water, swimming upside down, frolicking in groups. And they were gasping. I had always seen dolphins from bigger, noisier craft, so I had not known anything about the sounds they make—how they breathe and sigh and blow. Every time they break the surface they gasp, like swimmers sucking air. Hearing this laboring breath, an affecting and lovable human noise, I was struck by how much we miss when we can't hear the creature we are looking at.

—Paul Theroux, "Sea Spell," *Travel Holiday*

MARCIE CARROLL

Birdland: Lullaby of Midway

This Hawaiian island is like none of the others.

It's midday at Midway. A thin winter sun warms the parade green by the stone war monuments that honor the past heroes of this tiny far-flung islet. But my thoughts are on the future of an egg, a granddaddy of a gooney egg, about five inches long, perfectly shaped, khaki colored. It has rolled away from the place it belongs, which is inside a bowl-shaped indentation on a small hummock where it can be properly sat on by a white-breasted, nine-pound Laysan albatross, aka gooney bird, *moli* (in Hawaiian) and *Diomedea immutabilis*.

I want desperately to pick it up and put it back, but this intervention would not be divine. You don't want to mess with Nature here—this is the Midway Islands National Wildlife Refuge, former off-limits Navy base turned ecotourism destination. Still, I touch the egg gingerly. Only one egg per mother bird per year, and if there's a chance...but it's cold. One of about 30,000 eggs here that won't make it. Like a giant Easter egg roll gone awry, abandoned eggs litter the lawns and gardens and dunes and pine-needle carpets.

But so many other eggs are lifebound, tucked safely underneath some 400,000 plump white breasts snugged into their nests,

800,000 if you count the albatross mates who are out in search of food. Those nesting pairs are the most prominent among an estimated two million birds here. The Midway gooneys include most of the world population of Laysan albatross, as well as 44,000 dusky black-footed albatross—and one rare short-tailed albatross or "golden gooney."

The birds are drawn by pelagic magic back to the nests in which they were born on the three sandy pinpricks of this very remote Hawaiian Islands atoll, some 1,200 miles northwest of Honolulu and roughly halfway between San Francisco and Tokyo. And I am drawn to see them, mostly because the U.S. Navy has opened the gates at last. Midway came to be a Navy post because of the birds, and it seems only right that the Navy relinquished the islets to the albatross and their admirers in a "Guns for Gooneys" transaction in 1997.

> Midway Islands are some of the oldest in the Hawaiian Islands chain of 132 islands, atolls, and seamounts strewn across the North Pacific, past the Tropic of Cancer, all the way to Kure Atoll. Midway is a possession of the United States and not officially a part of the state or the City and County of Honolulu as the others are.
>
> —RC & MC

Discovered (by Western accounting) in 1859 by Capt. Nick Brooks and annexed to the U.S. in 1867, Midway attracted the attention of Japanese sailors, who came to kill the gooneys for feathers and rob the nests of eggs, each big enough for a substantial *donburi*. This incensed a small outpost of Commercial Pacific Cable Co. employees living on Midway at the turn of the century, who helped lay the last link in the first trans-Pacific cable and thus enabled President Teddy Roosevelt to send a cable message round the world in a mere nine minutes. The cable enclave petitioned the president to put a stop to the Japanese pilfering, and he ordered U.S. Navy protection, decrying the "wanton destruction of birds that breed on Midway." Roosevelt also created the National

Wildlife Refuge system in 1909, but it didn't happen on Midway until 1988.

In 1935, Midway became a fueling stop in the ambitious plans of Pan American World Airways to fly its Clipper seaplanes across the Pacific, but the Clipper was soon outpaced by other aviation. American military presence came and went, resuming prior to World War II—in time for the heroic tide-turning Battle of Midway in 1942 and the Cold War days along the DEW line. Midway's war history includes the first Congressional Medal of Honor winner, young Marine Lt. George Cannon, who did his best to save his men before he died December 7, 1941, victim of an air strike by Japanese warriors on their way home from Pearl Harbor.

Landing at Midway at night to minimize conflict with birds, our Midway Phoenix flight is greeted by a friendly human contingent. We are welcomed with warm smiles and waves as we walk past the decorative blue, red, and white torpedo in the lobby of the cavernous hangar, brightened up with some potted plants. My husband, son of an Air Force pilot and dependent veteran of many a base, flashes nostalgic. "Look at the stenciled signs, 'Billeting.' And the green and black linoleum tile, they all had that." I've seldom set foot on a base—Midway reminds me of a campus, except for the military architecture and war souvenirs.

We wind down lanes past trim officers' homes to Charley Building, a revamped BOQ, clean and shipshape, that has been made comfortable and almost cheery. It has the most reasonable minibar I've even seen, good news when you arrive after the restaurants close.

We passed gooneys in the dark; saw the hummocky nests, watched and heard 50 or so dancing their famous elaborate courtship reel under the window, and a few terns and petrels, but I didn't begin to grasp the magnitude of the bird presence until the next day. You shoulda been here, Alfred Hitchcock.

Birds overwhelm the landscape. They are everywhere on the ground, nesting three or four feet apart on the lawns, by the doors, lanes, bike racks, and walkways; in the lee of buildings, under ironwood trees and hibiscus bushes; in the sand dunes, any place they can scrape up a nest. Fortunately they eschew nesting on road asphalt, the substance for which they aim when relieving themselves. They do roost or saunter onto the street, necessitating a roving path around them when in transit on foot or via bike, golf cart, or the rare motor vehicle, as well as a warning on the cable TV channel:

"REMEMBER TO PREFLIGHT YOUR VEHICLE FOR ALBATROSS PRIOR TO MOVING, BY CHECKING UNDER TIRES."

When I walk by, nesting gooneys lean away from me without getting up and clack their bills in benign disapproval. As I pass by on my bike, the indignant clacking sounds like rounds of polite applause. The birds are droll, serene, vulnerable, beautiful, and not at all scary, dignified in their gooneyness. I snap off a roll of film at the green, so crowded with nesting and dancing birds that it looks like a rock concert, then sit down in the grass myself. Pretty soon a gooney bird sashays up to take my measure, looks at me with curious black eyes in a handsome masked face, and tentatively pecks my knee before wandering off. I think he was asking me to dance.

The gooneys share the refuge with thirteen other species of breeding seabirds and vacationing shorebirds and passing loners, a sizable pod of spinner dolphins, a couple hundred green sea turtles, an ocean of fish (with a 200-mile fishing limit all around), 50 endangered Hawaiian monk seals, and about 130 people who operate the former base as a cooperative federal/private ecotourism venture. Up to 100 tour guests at any one time can come to see the gooney birds nesting in winter and to dive and fish in summer, when the gooneys are gone but unusual bird encounters persist, including a face-to-face with an inquisitive, angelic white tern. Birds of one sort or another are nesting or raising chicks most of the time on Midway Islands.

The pact between the U.S. Fish and Wildlife Service and Midway Phoenix Corp., an airline spinoff owned by one of those civilian shadow pilots who flew missions for the government, is a first in the federal refuge system. Midway Phoenix, which manages the place and runs the air service to Midway, in turn works with

Oceanic Society Expeditions, a research and ecotourism organization based in San Francisco, and Midway Sport Fishing, a fishing/diving tour operation that explores the virgin seas, to bring people in. Midway Phoenix also handles independent travelers and tours.

> White fairy terns, the Tinkerbells of Midway, are too busy flying around to make nests, so they lay their eggs just anywhere. Ranger James Aliberti recounts how a friend left an awning window open one day and returned to find a precarious tern egg balanced in the angle of the window. "He couldn't close it until after they had the chick on the window," he adds. In addition to tree branches, terns have also selected bike racks and fire hydrants. Their chicks have large feet with sharp claws, so that they can hang on until they're big enough to fly.
>
> —MC

"We love this place," declares Mike Gautreaux, Midway Phoenix manager, retired Marine fighter pilot and, in a way, mayor of the "town" of Midway. The RIFed Navy left, and a $82 million cleanup is complete. Leaky fuel tanks were removed and the ground scoured, excess buildings torn down to make room for more birds, military secrets transported elsewhere. The priority now is on wildlife and visitors.

Young albatross which pecked their way out of those big eggs and were raised by devoted parents on Midway return after three to seven airborne years at sea, the biologists report—never having touched land, probably never having thought about land since that fateful day when as fluffy fledglings, they made a clumsy liftoff over the crystalline coral-sand beach and sailed up over the brilliant blue lagoon, past the barrage of hungry tiger sharks eagerly awaiting their mistakes. What a glorious discovery, the freedom of flight. Then, driven by an undeniable urge, they flew back last fall, crash-landing into trees and golf carts and buildings and runways and at best, into sand. What a surprise, solid earth, powerful wings suddenly useless. Awkward on land with big webbed feet and far from their food source, the birds are truly grounded. These eggs everywhere are the cause, and the result.

The gooneys responded to the Navy's departure with a joyous increase in population. Now in mid-January, near the end of the 65-day tour of nest duty, the birds sit patiently on a bumper crop of fertile eggs, dozing or picking with long hooked bills at bits of dirt or grass and flinging them over their shoulders to pile up the mound around them. A nester periodically rises and points that bill down between its legs to tap the egg gently, as if to make sure it's still there. Both adults make cooing noises, baby-talk, to the egg so that when it hatches, the chick will know who they are. These birds pair for life, which can be 40 or more years. Wildlife officials speculate some gooneys might have witnessed the Battle of Midway in 1942. The pairs cuddle like honeymooners, covering each other's faces with bill kisses. It's just about hatching time. A few black-footed albatross babies have already appeared, all gray fuzz and appetite. A sense of anticipation seizes the researchers, biologists and volunteers of Midway, soon to become a giant nursery.

Lost in their own subplot, those birds who didn't raise fertile eggs are raising hell, dancing their feathers off, stuck in ballet mode like the girl in the Red Shoes. They are "practicing for next time," as the wildlife guides put it. Which is to say that long past mating time, the birds continue to dance their aerobic ritual.

Here is the dance: Usually two birds, but up to five or six and, ideally, including a male and female—face one another and begin to bob up and down and boogie around on those big feet. They stretch their long necks up and point their bills toward the sky, up, up on their webbed tiptoes. One draws back and develops an immediate itch under one wing. A couple of honks and back to the "skypoint." They fence with their bills. They gabble. They moan, like cows. They whine. They rattle. They pop. They clack, under the wing, at each other, at me, at any moving object. They clatter those bills like WWII machine guns. Then a culmination—one rapidly turns its head side to side, screaming with glee. (Nothing happened—it's just the dance). The birds dance night and day, with only short bird-nap timeouts. I laugh the first dozen times I watch them; then I wonder what music they hear.

Over on the dazzling white beach, whipped by gusty winds on this particular day, the albatross line up for takeoffs like Navy pilots on a carrier deck, one by one running off the edge of a dune into the wind, stretching their wings, seven feet from tip to tip, and swooping gracefully and effortlessly above the frothy waves.

"These are birds of the wind," says Robert Dieli, outdoor recreation planner for the U.S. Fish and Wildlife Service at Midway. Their flight prowess is legendary, as demonstrated by an experiment some years back. Midway biologists flew banded and blindfolded gooneys to California, Australia and Alaska and other points around the Pacific, and released them. The birds were back on Midway within 10 days, having averaged 60 mph on the way. It takes humans five or six days by sea to get there from Honolulu; two to three hours by charter jet.

Until Midway became an official refuge, few people saw this much of the gentle gooney, considered around the world to be the sailor's friend and celebrated in the literary classic, "Rime of the Ancient Mariner" by English poet Samuel Taylor Coleridge. Modern men could do well to heed the warning in Coleridge's poem, that witless harm to albatross will come back to haunt them. On Midway, men are protectors of the albatross, killing off rats by the heaps, trying to restore the natural environment and remove obstacles.

But elsewhere man can be a very effective enemy, including those who have never heard of a gooney. This is revealed one day when we board a relic amphibious landing craft and head for Eastern Island, across the big blue lagoon. No structures remain on this bleak island, once a busy wartime airstrip, except a rusty old gun emplacement. Eastern is now devoted solely to those albatross, great frigate birds, terns, noddies, tropic birds, and red-footed boobies that prefer to nest without humans around. Eastern's albatross react to a small tour much more aggressively than do the mellow birds on the main islet, Sand Island. A black-footed mom nips me on the back of the leg when I stand close enough for her to reach me. Worse, we have upset a gooney that stepped on her egg, now a mess of yolk and blood, and confused, she tries to sit back down on it. Weeds grow through the concrete runway where the WWII veteran in our group, 84-year-old Cy Gillette, flew in and out in 1941 and 1942. His pilot's eyes look far away as he tries to adjust memory to reality.

Despite the wild emptiness, man's effects are still terribly evident. Fish and Wildlife ranger James Aliberti demonstrates by gently kicking apart the desiccated carcasses of several young gooneys. Inside is a shameful array of plastic trash—bottle caps, colorful shards, and the signature culprit, plastic throwaway cigarette lighters, one in almost every dead bird. Gooneys scoop food from the ocean surface, mistake a floating Bic for a squid, then take it home to the nest and feed it to their chick. Grown birds can throw up plastic trash; young birds cannot, and they die slowly. Back in the Oceanic Society offices, Garv Hoefler has a (plastic) "Bic Bag" filled with hundreds of lighters people have picked up off the beach. He'll cheerfully issue you a large (plastic) trash bag to fill with plastic debris during your stay on Midway. I fill one in an hour on the beach.

Everyone is anxious for the fledgling Midway eco-resort to succeed, including guests like me who go home full-hearted and empty-handed (you can't take anything at all, beachcombers and bird-watchers, not even a feather; fishermen, it's tag and release except for food fish for island consumption), wondering how to help. This feeling lingers even after a long, expensive flight and a slightly spartan resort experience on a remote atoll that bears little resemblance to the famous tropical Edens to the south. Midway is a pearl of an experience, but it's not Maui. No hula, no room service, no Evian spritzers by the pool, and in fact, no sign of a pool.

Nonetheless, a visit to Midway is somehow very fulfilling. I'm not what one wry host called a "psycho-birder," checking species methodically off a list, never mind that there are a million of them at once. I'm not a birder at all, but I love wild things and admire the aerial artists of Hawaiian seas—the great frigate bird (*'iwa*) pirates that commute over my seaside home on O'ahu, the wheeling and soaring gooneys and boobies offshore and the red-tailed tropic birds that hang-glide off seacliffs and show up as white dots on my photos. I've never seen any of them up close, never steered a bike around them or looked them in the eye or held my breath while they fed a chick, nor tiptoed away from an empty beach because a big blob of a monk seal was snoozing there, until Midway.

After many years of grieving for Hawai'i's vanishing species, I am reassured just to see a thriving, healthy native population of wildlife. The birds give me a sense of well-being, fellow creatures doing all right in a changing world, room enough for both of us as we get ready for the new millennium. *Immutabilis.* It has an enduring ring. Life goes on, for the good eggs.

Marcie Carroll, former news journalist, is a freelance travel writer whose beat is Hawai'i and the Pacific. She also contributed "Beauty and the Beach" to Part Five.

⋆

Lying on my back in the sand, staring up at the birds, I tried to work out a profile of the traveler best suited for a stay on Midway. The ideal visitor would be a diver, but not a rabid diver. A fisherman, but not a trophy fisherman. An ex-soldier with a complicated fondness for the ambiance of the military base. A birder uninterested in all the countless little thrushes and finches of land, but impressed, since early childhood, by seabirds and all the Coleridgean symbolism they seem to bear so easily on those trim white wings. The ideal Midway visitor, in other words, would be someone very much like me.

A certain immaturity is desirable. My epiphanies on Midway came not in any Gibbon-like ruminations on the Pacific War, nor in Dawinesque insights into problems of island biogeography. Mine came on my bike, after sojourns at Frigate Point, racing back down the long runway with the wind behind me before an audience of noddy terns nesting in the sparse weeds along the runway. All beaks turned to follow me.

I can't explain what a thrill it was, the giant hand of the west wind on my back, the admiration of the terns, the fat, white, intermittent centerline speeding under my tires on a dark plain of tarmac.

So, a visitor to Midway should be childlike enough to take simple pleasure in residence on a remote island, yet old enough to find resonance in the Pacific War. The visitor should be war-buff enough to find poignancy in the old gun emplacements, bunkers, and bullet holes, yet pacifist enough to appreciate the miracle of the atoll's ongoing transformation.

After more than a half century as a landing field for warplanes, Midway is reverting to feathery, unarmed aircraft. The Navy is surrendering its sword to albatrosses, frigates, boobies, and terns. The meek are inheriting the atoll.

—Kenneth Brower, "The Last Pacific Isle, Return to Midway," *Islands*

JO BROYLES YOHAY

Doing Battle with One Tough Plant

Spirited "weed warriors" fight against difficult odds.

A FLIGHT ATTENDANT, HARRIED BY TOO MANY HOURS OF cheerful service, passed through the cabin carrying a fistful of Hawai'i Department of Agriculture forms and thrust them down the rows for us to fill out.

My son Jacob and I were headed for Hawai'i on the spur of the moment to hike and camp with friends on the Islands of Maui and Moloka'i for two weeks over college break. A first-timer, I secretly worried that the once-pristine Islands, with their lush vegetation, had been gobbled up by pineapple barons and developers, leaving nothing but condos and t-shirt shops.

I glanced down the form. "State of Hawai'i. Department of Agriculture. Aloha!" I groaned inwardly and unpacked my already packed pen. Was I carrying fresh fruits or vegetables, algae, plant cuttings? Algae? Plant cuttings? If I'd visited any farms lately, I was supposed to "wash all clothing, footwear, and persons thoroughly before entering Hawai'i." Yeah, right. In the plane's two-inch lavatory with folding door. I signed my name and sent the form back.

A few days later, on Maui, I hung onto the door handle of a jeep pitching sharply to avoid a mud hole. We had left the macadam miles back to lurch along a deeply rutted back road made almost impassable by recent storms. Could this be Hawai'i, aloha paradise?

The car radio crackled. A song ended and the DJ began what he called his daily rant. "A gorgeous ornamental plant from Latin America has leapt the garden wall and is threatening Hawai'i's rain forests," he said. "*Miconia* has already destroyed 70 percent of Tahiti's wilderness." He described mammoth leaves that cast dense shade, killing native plants and spongy mosses, promoting erosion and water runoff. He urged every citizen to join "Operation *Miconia*" to help eradicate the pest. "If you see its pretty, velvety leaves with purple undersides, call the hot line."

Hawai'i was at war with a plant.

Listening to him, I remembered the Little Prince, in Saint Exupery's famous children's book. He diligently pulled up every shoot of the baobab tree because it was "something you will never, never be able to get rid of if you attend to it too late. It spreads over the entire planet."

Enlivened by the DJ's passion, our locally born driver took up the cry. *Miconia* is only one horror on a long list of so-called "alien species" that plague Hawai'i. Feral pigs, imported long ago for food, roam the tropical forests, digging up roots and clearing the way for foreign plants. Mongooses, brought in to kill rats, have eaten native birds' eggs instead. Mosquitoes, once unknown to the Islands, brought avian malaria, wiping out many birds. Ginger, raspberry—all fine in their countries of origin—devastate the fragile island ecology.

The driver pointed to the scrubby forest we were going through. "All imports," he said. "Eucalyptus from Australia, strawberry guava from Central America." Faster growing than the endemic species, the invaders have dominated the landscape.

He described a frailty that took my breath away. More than 2,000 miles from the nearest continent, Hawai'i is the most remote island chain in the world. Ninety percent of its native species grow nowhere else on earth. Plants and animals evolved in isolation with few diseases or predators, so they had scant need of natural defenses. Shrubs developed neither thorns nor poisons to defend against hungry browsers, since the only land mammal was a bat. Several birds were flightless. This gentle Eden had an innocence that left it especially vulnerable.

> Everywhere else the crow is a common pest. In Hawai'i, *Crovus hawaiiensess* is nearly extinct. Hunters shot them, developers spoiled their habitat; the birds were plagued by disease and reproductive disorder. Hawaiians, who considered the crow "Alumakua," or family guardian, denied Captain James Cook a specimen. Only eleven captive birds remain in the Big Island's Endangered Species Facility, last stand of the Hawaiian Crow.
>
> —RC

We parked at the head of the trail, grabbed our day packs and set out. After another hundred yards of eucalyptus, we passed through a gate designed to keep the pigs out. On the other side, a major effort had been made to destroy non-native plants, such as gorse, to give the original dwellers a chance to come back.

Here everything changed. The forest was soft and delicate. Deep moss covered the damp ground; ferns of a dozen shades of green mingled with the vermilion blossoms of *'ōhi'a lehua* trees; sprays of silver lilies hung from branches; a red honeycreeper with curved beak sipped nectar from a flower. Even the air was different, fragrant as when the first raindrops moisten the earth.

This was the wild Hawai'i we'd been afraid to hope for. The t-shirt shops and developers hadn't yet swallowed it all. But seeing it, and knowing it could vanish, now filled us with a keen sense of dread.

During the next days, hiking through several preserves that are still paradisiacal, we came upon other people who care deeply what happens to the land.

On a trail through Mo'omomi Dunes Preserve on Moloka'i, a

safe haven where indigenous plants have begun to reemerge, we met Joan, a powerful, tanned woman of 70 or more, exactly the sort I'd like to be at her age. On a previous hike there, Joan told me, she spotted sprigs of *pōpolo,* just beginning to recover a stronghold at ocean's edge. She leapt ahead when she spied the patch.

"Look how they've spread since the rain!" she exclaimed. Her joy was contagious. I bent to inspect the pale yellow leaves and fragile purple flowers as if they were a national treasure. They are.

We spoke with Maui High School volunteers, self-dubbed the "Weed Warriors," who give up free Saturdays to slog through dense underbrush to search and destroy alien plants that are choking out natives. Two 70-something brothers stopped to chat. Great walkers, they travel the back roads and woodlands of Hāna and report *miconia* sightings to weed specialists. We saw a newspaper with "The Ten Most Unwanted" list, a poster for "*Miconia*: Wanted Dead or Alive."

One morning on the trail a ten-year-old boy appeared carrying a *miconia* by the roots, oval leaves dangling. "I've got one, roots and all," he announced. He was headed for a phone to call the hot line.

A thought had been brewing in us. Why not enlist? We phoned the Maui office of The Nature Conservancy to volunteer. Our job: to help the weed specialist Pat Bily search out reported *miconia* and destroy as many plants as possible.

By morning's light, we traded our hiking boots for tall rubber Wellies, gloves, and day packs boldly labeled "*miconia* only." Pat explained that the tiny seeds attach easily to footwear and clothing, spreading pestilence to new areas. Now I understood those agriculture forms.

Carrying machetes, we headed off, single file, up a streambed framed by steep slopes of thick vegetation. The boulders underfoot were slithery with mossy damp, and I tried to steady myself by digging fingernails into rocks. I inched my way along. A farm, perched on a cliff, appeared. Four furiously barking dogs stood stiff-legged, sentinels demanding our retreat. Trying to look nonchalant, I crept on. Mercifully, they didn't come after us, and I started to breathe again.

I caught Jacob's eye and we both laughed, I in relief at being alive, he at the irony. Were we crazy? Here we were in the land of *lū'au* and pounding surf, hula dancers and beckoning sands. And we were struggling upstream in tropical heat, warriors in the front lines against a weed that two weeks earlier we'd never even heard of.

Pat's shout alerted us that we'd reached an infestation of *miconia*: two sturdy trees, breathtakingly graceful. Scattered about the steep bank were its babies. Pat started to hack at a tree. I searched for toeholds in the slippery red earth and pulled myself alongside a two-foot seedling; its intricately veined leaves nodded in the breeze. I grasped the machete, ready to do battle.

On such a lovely plant? My raised arm slumped. Suddenly, I realized what I was up against. I was engaged in hand-to-hand combat, not with the horrors of tourism as I had expected, but with Nature herself. It was not a stance I felt comfortable with.

I remembered the baobab. Then I flashed on Veronica Lake, beautiful and pernicious, in a 1940s film noir. A tempting mantrap, a *miconia* woman, poised to eat Alan Ladd alive. I recalled the image of a destroyed Tahitian rain forest, acres of ground laid bare by *miconia*. A high school Weed Warrior's words echoed in my head: "The native forest is an extension to our house; if you're going to let some part of it decay, what's the use of living there?"

What use, indeed? I grasped the sapling with my seed-free glove and ripped it out of the ground, roots and all. "I've got one!" I yelled, moving on to the next. All's fair in love and war, and this was both.

New Yorker Jo Broyles Yohay specializes in stories of personal adventure and vacations spent as a volunteer. She writes for the New York Times, Travel & Leisure Magazine, *and* International Wildlife. *In addition to her trip to Hawai'i to fight* miconia, *some of her all-time favorite journeys include a solo trip to India, a botanical expedition to the French Guiana rainforest, a stint as a volunteer restorer of a twelfth-century building in the south of France, and a jaunt to Grenada as a primate researcher.*

⋆

I once learned from a conchologist in Hawai'i that the Islands were home to thousands of colorful tree snails, known as *pūpū kani oe*. How they reached the Islands can only be imagined, but they did and they flourished. Jewels of the forest, they came in many colors—yellow, red, orange, green, and white—and thrived in such abundance in 1912, that Hawaiian poet George Kane described "the songs of the land shells, that have a sound as sweet as that of a dove on a clear night." When a single shell sold in Europe for $10, it sparked a shell rush. Hundreds of thousands were collected. Today, of the 41 species in this genus, 22 are extinct and 19 are endangered. They cling to survival primarily in Moloka'i rain forests. A few specimens may be seen in glass cases at O'ahu's Bishop Museum.

—RC

RICK CARROLL

At the Bishop

Antiquities with Hawaiian soul enliven the venerable museum.

THE BISHOP MUSEUM IS AN IMPOSING EDIFICE, FORBIDDING LIKE A mortuary, solid as a small-town bank. Few seeing it for the first time doubt the 1889 Victorian building could be anything but a grand old museum. There are, I am told, twenty million acquisitions from Hawai'i and the Pacific—ancestral relics, religious figures, spirit idols, feather capes, war clubs, skulls and bones of dearly departed Hawaiians, the inevitable dust of a once proud Polynesian kingdom.

Sometimes I think of the gray stone building as a kind of mausoleum of *mana*, chock-full of captive spirits. When I see all the fishhooks carved out of the human bones of defeated warriors, I can't help but wonder if their spirits still haunt this place. As I long suspected, when the doors close and night starts to fall, strange things begin to happen.

I found her in Archives, a tiny Asian woman who sat at a desk covered with manuscripts, surrounded by volumes of history, translating what appeared to be Hawaiian words heavy with *'okina* and *kahakō* (Hawaiian diacritical marks) into plain English.

I had come to the Bishop suspecting that the repository of the greatest collection of Hawai'i and Pacific artifacts in the world must teem with ghostly stories. Who has not gazed upon the royal capes of King Kalākaua and imagined the monarchy coming to life in Hawaiian Hall at the stroke of midnight?

To confirm my suspicions I sought out this Japanese woman with the unlikely *haole* name of Pat Bacon who is something of an artifact herself. She is a child of the museum, the *hānai* (adopted) daughter of Mary Kawena Pukui, the famed Hawaiian translator and author of the *Hawaiian Dictionary*, *Place Names of Hawai'i*, and thousands of other manuscripts.

"I practically grew up at the museum," Mrs. Bacon told me, and, in fact, she had first arrived as a small child to sit at her mother's side. "My first job here was in 1939; then I got married and quit. I came back in 1959 and," she said with a laugh, "I'm still here." She seemed both proud of and surprised at her tenure. I figured her time at the Bishop amounted to seven of the eleven decades the museum has been in business. If there were skeletons in the closet, this woman would know where they were, but she seemed reluctant. She wanted to know more about my project. I told her it was to be a collection of true, inexplicable stories of events experienced by skeptics.

"What do you mean by 'skeptics'?" she asked in her precise, library-soft voice, one eyebrow arched.

"Those who doubt or do not believe," I replied.

"I believe," she said evenly. "I am not a skeptic. I was raised in a Hawaiian household. We learned to deal with both today and yesterday. We were raised Christian, but we were told we could not doubt those kinds of things. They did exist."

What kinds of things, I asked. And who are "they?"

"Those things." She laughed nervously. "You know, whoever or whomever, or whatever. It's hard to explain," she said. I think I knew what she meant.

"We grew up showing respect to things we couldn't understand or explain," she said. "The older Hawaiians knew all the rituals and *kapu*, but we were not taught. We were taught to respect the old ways, but they were not for us at this time."

Had she ever been frightened by strange events in the museum?

I had in mind a desolate wandering ghost hovering over a skull on a shelf in Anthropology searching for lost kin. Before she could answer, a thin man with a beard dropped a tray of slides behind her. The clatter startled us. We laughed and she continued. "My encounters have not been such that I have been afraid of anything. I feel quite safe. But there are others who have had scary things happen. A botanist here during the 1930s, who came to work at night with her dog, heard footsteps going into the room next door. She knew her dog could see something, because its hackles would rise. But nobody was there.

"Sometimes you hear noises but you can't prove what it is. I've never been here at midnight, but I've been here at 10 p.m., and I never saw anything, but there are others who have had experiences, who have been frightened.

"Years ago, in the 1960s," she said, in a voice so soft I had to draw my chair closer, "a night watchman used to see this Hawaiian woman in a white gown with silvery hair walk across the courtyard to climb up and sit in Queen Lili'uokalani's carriage," she said, and paused. "And her feet did not touch the ground.

"She never said anything to him, and he never said anything to this apparition. He saw her a few times at certain times of the year, but I don't remember when."

He quit to work elsewhere. The royal carriage later was moved inside and placed on the second floor of Hawaiian Hall. The night visitor has not been seen since. Maybe she was only trying to get the queen's carriage moved indoors for safekeeping.

"In the late 1950s, in Anthropology," she said, "I would double lock the door at night and go home, and in the morning, one lock would be open. But nothing was moved or disturbed."

She smiled.

I told her that Dr. Yosihiko Sinoto, the museum's own legendary Pacific archaeologist, had told me that some nights when researchers would stay late working all alone in Anthropology, they would hear typing in the room next door, get up, go and look and, of course, nobody was there.

She smiled again.

"Sometimes when I worked late I would open the windows and sit down again and they would be closed. Okay, I'd say, and I'd close up and go home but I wasn't frightened. I always feel quite safe here. That's how they were talking to me. They wanted me to go home," she said. "So I did."

There are signs, you know, warnings, to heed. She told me about one old, almost forgotten *kapu*:

"If you are out at night and all alone and come upon a sweet smell like *pīkake* [jasmine] or gardenia, and there's nothing there, it's a warning. Get out, get away from the area. Leave it alone and go away. You leave it alone and they leave you alone."

I've never thought gardenias, a flower I usually associate with Billie Holliday or Polynesian women with a certain style, could be capable of issuing *kapu* warnings in Hawai'i, but Mary Kawena Pukui's *hānai* daughter spoke with such conviction it was difficult not to believe her.

Of all the incidents at the Bishop, the most spectacular, she said, involved a bloody death on the stones of Waha'ula *heiau* "shrine," which archaeologist John F. G. Stokes brought back from the Big Island of Hawai'i in the 1930s for a museum exhibit.

For those unfamiliar with Waha'ula *heiau*, it was built in 1250 A.D. and was in use until the early nineteenth century. It was the last temple destroyed by chiefs who banned ancient rites the year before Christian missionaries arrived in 1820.

One of the bloodiest sacrificial temples in all of Hawai'i (its name means "red or sore mouth"), the *heiau* had many ghosts, including one made famous in the 1915 edition of William D. Westervelt's *Hawaiian Legends of Ghosts and Ghost Gods*. "The Ghost of Waha'ula Temple" tells the story of the son of the high chief of Ka'ū, who was killed by the Mū, or body-catchers, and sacrificed on the altar. His ghost managed to return, recover his bones, and flee to the spirit world.

Not so lucky was a young Hawaiian man who worked at the Bishop in the 1930s, when the Waha'ula *heiau* model went on public exhibit.

"His mother had a dream that warned of danger to her son,

and she asked him not to go to work because something would happen. He didn't believe her, but those who were working up there on the roof saw something, they don't know what," Mrs. Bacon recalled.

He fell through the skylight to his death on the *heiau* exhibit made from the stones of Waha'ula.

"Old people at that time said the *heiau* had been consecrated by claiming its first sacrifice," she said.

"Mr. Stokes was the one who cleaned up all the blood there," she said, leaving the implication that he never should have removed the stones from the *heiau* in the first place.

The intrinsic power of the Big Island *heiau* stones was further demonstrated in 1989 when red-hot molten lava from Kīlauea volcano destroyed the $1.2 million National Park Visitor Center, ran up to the very edge of the Waha'ula sacred stones—and stopped. I made a note to take a look at those stones from the *heiau*, which she thought might still be in the garden of the museum courtyard.

Since many objects in the museum hail from all over the Pacific, I wondered if perhaps a Papua New Guinea spirit mask, or maybe a *moai kava kava* (wood carving from Rapa Nui) ever got out of line and stirred excitement. I imagined an anarchy of artifacts, a revolt of relics hissing and spewing ancient curses.

"Oh, there have been a few things," she said, "but by and large, I think they—whatever it is that is in and around here—have really liked being here, because nothing sinister has happened. So we must be okay."

The bones of two old Hawaiian chiefs, however, did walk out of the museum one night not too long ago, probably on the shoulders of burglars who looted the museum of what is known as the *kā'ai*, two woven sennit caskets that contained the 500-year-old bones of Hawaiian chiefs Līloa and his great-grandson, Lonoikamakahiki. The bones had been held in trust by the museum for 76 years and, despite double locks and round-the-clock security, vanished without a clue on the night of February 24, 1994.

Considered sacred by Hawaiians and obviously priceless, they are, or were, historically significant, because in and among the human remains were cloth and metal objects that may have predated Captain James Cook's 1778 arrival in Hawai'i. And since the weave of the sennit is like no other found in Polynesia, their origin has always posed a mystery to archaeologists.

"They were so beautiful," she said. "You know those are the only ones that exist in the world. The workmanship was really beautiful."

The *kā'ai* were brought to the museum by Prince Jonah Kūhiō Kalaniana'ole in 1918 for safekeeping until a suitable burial chamber could be erected at the Royal Mausoleum in O'ahu's Nu'uanu Valley. Held in a locked cabinet in the collection storage area of Anthropology, the *kā'ai* were last seen at the museum February 17, 1994, when the museum was fumigated for termites. To this day the burglary remains one of Hawai'i's great unsolved mysteries.

Did she have any clue to their disappearance? "I haven't the foggiest," she said, folding her arms across her chest. "I don't even want to know where they are."

I could tell she knew many other stories, but it was time to go, so we said good-bye. She returned to her manuscripts. I went to find the stones that long ago claimed a life at the museum. All I found in the shadowy courtyard was a stone fish idol and the perfectly hewn stone slabs from Kīkīa Ola, Kaua'i's so-called Menehune Ditch. As I searched deeper, the cloying, telltale fragrance of gardenias began to fill the moist still air. At first I thought it was some cheap perfume worn by a tourist, but I was all alone in the courtyard.

I looked around expecting to see a forgotten *lei*, perhaps, but there was none, and I knew even as the skin on my arms turned to a fine pebble grain that this could only be a sign. I left the museum before doors and windows started opening and closing. I would see the sacrificial stones of Waha'ula another day.

Later, as I thought about my floral caveat and the stories I heard at the Bishop that afternoon, I tried to make sense of it all. Each story, it seemed, could be explained by logic. Doors and windows closing can be the work of the wind. Footfalls and clacking typewriters are often the product of an overheated imagination. The botanist's dog with raised hackles? A common occurrence. Dogs hear things we don't. I had heard, too, of other sightings of a silver-haired Hawaiian woman in a long flowing white gown whose feet never touch the ground. (Jocelyn Fujii told me her sister saw the woman walking *above* the beach at Hanalei one night.) As for the Hawaiian fellow who slipped and fell to his death on the Waha'ula stones? A mere coincidence, don't you think? Or, maybe, power of suggestion.

While the disappearance of the *kā'ai* remains a great mystery, from a detective's point of view it was a textbook case of first-degree burglary. Probably an inside job. I mean, 500-year-old bones just don't get up one night and walk out of the museum, do they? Many people I talked to believe the *kā'ai* were spirited out of the museum (you don't suppose by night marchers, do you?) for a proper burial in Waipi'o Valley. Nobody knows, or is saying, where the last earthly remains of the chiefs and a small clue to Hawai'i's own mysterious past now repose.

Bones and stones and old ghosts. The unknown and fear of the unknown almost always cause chicken skin even for skeptics like me. I'm still not altogether comfortable with the idea of invisible gardenias issuing *kapu* warnings. What I do know for sure is this: when I smelled gardenias at the Bishop after hours and my skin began to crawl, I knew that they—whoever *they* might be—wanted me to go, and I did and I was not afraid. In the end, it's all in who and what you believe.

Rick Carroll is the author of numerous books, including Chicken Skin: True Spooky Stories of Hawai'i, *a best-seller in the Islands, from which this story was excerpted. He also contributed* "Last Dance at the Palace" *in Part Four.*

⋆

Almost every child raised in the Hawaiian Islands has participated in circles of storytelling. The most requested and awe-inspiring stories are those dealing with the supernatural, commonly called *kahuna* in Hawaiian, *obake* in Japanese, and "chicken skin," or ghost stories, in English. Various ethnic groups in Hawai'i have contributed their own motifs, resulting in creolized tales that are the legends of twentieth-century Hawai'i.

One of the motifs of Hawaiian supernatural tales is *akualele*, the "flying god" or fireball. *Akualele* seems to be a supernatural phenomenon and not a physical manifestation. It cannot or has not been associated with natural phenomena.

The Hawaiian fireball...is generally described as an elongated ball which in flight resembles a tadpole with a long tail leaving sparks as it flies. The fireball can be stopped in flight and destroyed simply by swearing at it. Its destruction always starts with a brilliant explosion which does not harm people standing nearby; neither does it cause secondary fires. Upon explosion, each piece moves about on the ground; and these according to one informant, are the *'e'epa* people, who scamper about to do their missions of mischief.

A most complex and interesting story was told to me by a young Japanese insurance salesman who resided at Hakipu'u on the Island of O'ahu.

The head of the Japanese household went to use the outdoor toilet one night and was astonished when the area lit up as if a bright meteor had just flashed by. When he returned to his house, his wife and his father said they saw a fireball fly by and disappear into a thicket of *hau* trees. It seems that the fireball was frequently seen at night flying into the same location. The family decided to investigate the next day, and, after a considerable tedious search, they found a decapitated skeleton. The family then consulted a local priest of Hawaiian ancestry and were told that the skeleton belonged to a murdered man whose body had never been found. The priest's advice was for the family to seek the direction from which the fireball originated and that its source would be the location of the head. The family then followed the priest's advice and soon after found the skull. The skull and the body were brought together and buried. After this the fireball was no longer seen flying in the area. The spirit had not been able to rest as long as its body and the misdeed had not been discovered, and so in its nightly flights, the spirit had been trying to attract the attention of someone who might help.

—William K. Kikuchi, *The Fireball in Hawaiian Folklore*

LARRY HABEGGER

Going to Hānā

Cruising through the Islands on the S.S. Constitution, *they docked at Kahului and set out for Maui's most Hawaiian place—Hāna.*

ONCE WE LEFT KAHULUI, WE WERE DRIVING ALONG A COUNTRY road with the deep blue sea on our left. Windsurfers raced across the whitecaps at Ho'okipa Beach Park, and a few miles on, we entered the rain forest on the Hāna Road, perhaps the most picturesque stretch of tarmac on earth.

> The SS *Constitution,* sold for scrap by American Hawai'i Cruises, sank in heavy seas 700 miles north of Hawai'i in 1997, while being towed to India.
>
> —RC & MC

The Hāna Road makes some 600 elbow bends and crosses 54 one-lane bridges as it burrows through jungle and winds along cliffs above the sea. Just about every time you look to your right, you see streams and waterfalls; to your left, the sea pops out of the greenery in dramatic vistas or quick winks of azure.

The scenery demands that you stop, park the car, get out and idle away the day. We did it over and over, sometimes at obvious places where other cars were parked, sometimes at our own whim. Parked cars usually meant it was one of the major sites along the way—a dramatic waterfall, a deep pool.

At one breathtakingly beautiful waterfall, we hiked up a trail along the creek and over boulders above the falls. Soon we left all of our fellow tourists behind with the cars and the road and the clicking cameras. We didn't go far, maybe a half mile at most, when we found another waterfall, a deep green pool, sunlight filtering through the trees. Could this be true? we wondered. Our own private waterfall? Not likely, but we decided to take a swim and enjoy it before someone else arrived.

No one else did. We swam. We lay like lizards on the rocks in the sun. We swam again. We took snapshots. We lingered longer than we'd planned, then headed back to the car so we could reach Hāna before dark.

The drive was pure joy. Just a few years ago the road was a rocky challenge to all but the most hardy vehicles, but now it's smooth black tarmac all the way, perfect for convertibles or sports cars. No doubt Nature will have its say, though. At countless bends along the way, we saw the double yellow center lines break and swerve off as if painted by a drunken sailor, and it took us a while to realize that the stripes laid down on the tarmac had been melted by the sun. How long would it take before the rain forest roots thrust their way up and started the road on its journey back to rubble?

We stopped again and again, inspired by the tranquility of a place more beautiful than seemed possible in this time of cynical media hype and tourism come-ons. The Ke'anae Arboretum was a quiet retreat with magnificent specimens of indigenous and other tropical plants. The bamboo forest was the biggest I'd ever seen. Farther up the trail we reached taro fields in the embrace of surrounding rain forest, and it was a scene you could imagine getting lost in.

We moved on reluctantly, only to stop again at the Ke'anae Peninsula, a flat piece of land that pokes out into the sea on feet of black lava. An old man sat under a tree with jewelry for sale while the sea pounded and frothed behind him, black lava formations hammered by white surf, blue sky above, taro fields iridescent green in the distance. Our senses were getting overloaded.

> It didn't seem that much different, fifteen years later, except for the fact that instead of being Adam and Eve on our honeymoon, my wife and I were now swimming in the roadside grottos en route to Hāna with three young daughters. We were still amazed at the number of people who didn't get in the water. They came, they looked, they took pictures, they left.
>
> ◆
>
> —James O'Reilly, "Unifinished Hawai'i"

Finally we rolled into Hāna, a town so small you'd be through it without knowing it if you weren't paying attention. The Hotel Hāna-Maui sits inconspicuously by the main road, and we did in fact drive past it. When we checked in, we found out we'd arrived on the night of their weekly *lū'au*. Would we come? How much time did we have? About 45 minutes before the van would depart for the beach a few miles away. What the heck?

We signed up, then got a ride on a golf cart through manicured gardens with a huge Hawaiian who went on and on about how welcome we were and how friendly Hāna was and how much he hoped we'd enjoy our stay. He was disarming in a completely casual way, a genuine fellow who enjoyed his life and was happy to be in Hāna.

He showed us to our cottage, which was about twice the size of our flat in San Francisco, had a hot tub and deck outside, a huge walk-in shower and a kitchenette we could use if we wanted. The garden rolled from our window down to the sea a short distance away, and horse pastures ran along the beach into the distance. Looking around I was astounded. Our friends had insisted we spend at least three nights here. We planned only one. Now I wondered how we could have done such a thing. One night here would be agony. I wanted to stay a week, a month! How could we spend just one night? And why had we arrived so late in the evening? I wanted to absorb everything.

What to do? Take a hot tub? Make some fresh Kona coffee? There was cold beer in the fridge, a mini-bar of fine whisky, the first one I'd ever seen whose prices were no higher than the local saloon. What a treasure. But we had barely half an hour.

We sat on the bed feeling virtually helpless. Every option was appealing. Finally we chose the hot tub, then a shower, a quick change, and a rush to catch the van for the *lu'au*.

We didn't notice till we'd got out of the shower that there were no towels in the bath. Dripping wet, we tracked water all over the place searching in every nook and cranny for bath towels, hand towels, wash cloths, sterile pads, anything to dry ourselves, but the only option was toilet paper. A warm breeze blew in through the windows, and I stood in the center of the room like a drowned rat, dripping onto the polished wood floor.

A phone call brought a housekeeper on a cart piled with towels. She made her way up to our cottage with mountains of terry cloth and knocked. The smile on her face disarmed me again. How could I care about missing towels in a place so beautiful? She was in no hurry, perhaps I should slow down a little too. Or maybe her smile was for my ridiculous predicament: stark naked and dripping wet, taking towels in the doorway from a stranger.

The van took us out of town, along the horse pastures, and down into trees shading a hidden beach. Tiki torches lined a stairway down to the sand and a roofed pavilion where the party was already underway. We arrived just in time to see the pig—our main course—being dug out of his fire pit where he'd slowly cooked all day. Behind the scenes he went, only to reappear a few moments later looking truly succulent on a platter.

We milled around with the other guests, maybe as many as 50 people, drinking punch and nibbling sushi. As often happens, we met people from San Francisco and sat looking out over the Pacific on the eastern edge of Maui and talked of familiar places just beyond the horizon. We ate well, perhaps too well, and then the music began.

Lū'au, in my experience, have always been corny. You eat the pig, maybe some poi, then sit around and listen to insipid local music from people who derive little joy from performing for tourists. This one had all the same signs—the Hawaiian shirts, the ukulele, the large men with big smiles. But it was clear that this one was different. As soon as the band leader opened his mouth to sing, it was obvious he was delighted to be here. He began to strum his ukulele affectionately, the guitars started up, and lilting Island rhythms wafted over us all. Before long children of various ages joined in singing and dancing, and we learned that the hula girls and the band leader were from one large family from Hāna.

Somehow the girls persuaded us all to get up on stage to learn to dance the hula. It was the sort of thing that usually sent me shuffling toward the exit, but this time it was pure fun. After all, those kids were enjoying themselves so much, how could we not join in?

> One day I remember we had a terrific shower. It came down like a big waterfall on the side of the hills. That morning the old Hawaiian man who brought milk up to the house in a little tin bucket appeared in the kitchen without a stitch of clothing on, just as naked as the day he was born, with the exception of wearing a hat. Water dripped from his brown body and, laughing and chatting to me, he finally took off his hat to show me that his pants and shirt were stuffed inside, so that when the rain stopped he would have dry clothes to put on.
>
> ◆
>
> —Meta Hedemann, *A Photographer in the Kingdom: Christian J. Hedemann's Early Images of Hawai'i* edited by Lynn Ann Davis with Nelson Foster

Two hours later we got back to town, still swaying with the music. There were lights aglow in the distance and we took a walk to investigate. What we found was pure fantasy. An emerald ballfield gleamed beneath lights rimmed by the darkness of trees. A game was underway, a player racing around the bases as the ball was thrown back to the infield. Other teams in uniforms hung out in the shadows. Mothers cradled infants and children chased each other in their own invented games.

Insects buzzed around the lights, and encroaching on left field were a tennis court and basketball court. Once upon a time, not so long ago, the whole park had been built for baseball, by Paul Fagan, owner of the Pacific Coast League's San Francisco Seals. He wanted to bring baseball to Hawai'i so he built a park and had his players train here, and for a glorious time the crack of the bat rang out over this cattle ranch on the edge of the sea. Today it's a softball field, but the magic is still here, as romantic and nostalgic a place as I've ever seen.

We settled into the mood and watched for a long time. The whole community was here, and doubtless those from other communities as well, united by a balmy night, children, friends, and softball.

When the last game ended and the lights dimmed, we walked home. We were drawn to the swimming pool overlooking the sea. As we were about to get in, dark shadows in the grass started to move. We couldn't see what they were because the illumination from the pool was too bright, but when one jumped on Paula's foot and she leaped even higher, we saw that they were frogs, big as Calaveras County bullfrogs. Paula did a hilarious dance to the pool's edge until the frogs jumped in, and we all swam together, Paula, me, and the frogs. What effect the chlorine had on them we couldn't imagine, but they hung around the edge of the pool as if it were a pond full of lily pads.

Moments later, without warning, the wind kicked up and rain began to fall in a torrent. We swam in the rain, wind lashing the Island with close to a gale force, till we felt we'd better get out and back to our cottage. It sounded like a hurricane, but 30 minutes later the wind died, the rain stopped, the sky cleared, and we were alone with the tropical night sounds in a cottage that felt like our own.

The morning came too soon, and with it, checkout time, which was about a week early. We immediately began plotting our return, knowing we had to get back here to this quiet town on the edge of the sea. We even decided not to bother going down to the Seven Sacred Pools or the bamboo forest we'd heard so much about so we could enjoy what little time we had in Hāna.

Before departing we took a last walk, this time up the hill behind the town to the memorial called Fagan's Cross. It was a pleasant walk through tall grass whose burrs ultimately forced us to throw away our socks, but the view over the village was inspiring. The wind was brisk, the grass bent with it like Kansas wheat, and the spirit of Hāna filled our vision. Clearly Paul Fagan had loved this place, and been loved in return. It looked as if it hadn't changed a bit since he'd arrived in the 1930s, and we could only hope that it would remain unchanged until we returned.

We'd been told about a place we shouldn't miss on the way back to Kahului called the Blue Pool. A few miles out of town we found the turnoff, followed the road till it turned to gravel, then to rock, then to pot holes, then to hardly a road at all. We crossed two streams, wondering at each whether we should risk it without four-wheel drive, and silently wishing we'd rented a jeep.

But we pressed on and parked when we reached the mouth of a creek where it met the sea.

As we scampered across the creek when the surge of surf receded, we discovered that we were alone. What we found was beyond our dreams.

It was the kind of tropical setting you assume could only exist in fairy tales. A triple waterfall tumbled from flower-bedecked cliffs, clear freshwater dropping out of the rain forest, out of the clouds above. The pool was broad and deep enough for swimming, both under the falls and in calm reaches. Grasses and flowers grew out of the rocks, embracing the pool in a mantle of green. At our backs, just over a ridge of rocks and sand not more than twenty feet away, the sea pounded in. Look one way, a tropical waterfall. Look the other way, the Pacific Ocean. Look around, pure heaven. And we had it all to ourselves for as long as we dared stay.

Many questions ran through our minds as we soaked in the most amazing confluence of natural wonders we'd ever encountered. What would happen if we missed the boat? In the end we knew we had to leave.

Larry Habegger is executive editor of Travelers Tales *and coauthor of* "World Travel Watch," *a syndicated newspaper travel column. He was born in Minnesota and lives with his family on Telegraph Hill in San Francisco.*

*

Another morning, my last in Hāna, I follow a narrow trail carved into a cliff just above the sea at Kauiki Head, a red cinder-cone reminder of Haleakalā's volcanic reach. The trail, which I have walked several times before, winds around a headland to a tiny cove backed by an amphitheater of sheer red cliffs, sheltered from the sea by a toothy outcrop of jagged rocks. During my days in Hāna, I have swum in the cove, calm even when the surf was running, as a scattering of beachgoers, some clothed, some not, from toddlers to one white-haired couple with dark tans, arrived and spread out their towels.

But today I have come just to see the sun's early light flood into the cove. As I edge around the headland, I see I am not alone. Below me, at the water's edge, a graceful young woman rehearses a hula, her feet moving across the dark red sand.

—Dewey Schurman, "Hawai'i On Foot," *Islands*

ELGY GILLESPIE

Where the Whales Play

The Big Ones are dating, and singing
their love songs under the sea.

COZILY HAMMOCKED BY GIANT BILLOWS, THE CRUISE SHIP STEERED between furry, whale-shaped Moloka'i and Kaho'olawe flanking the narrow straits of the protected waters where humpbacks migrate from Alaska, following their blowholes. Big chunks of Maui's volcanoes slipped past my pillow as I dreamt on, half-waking with every nudge from a giant lover.

According to the Hawaiians, whales come to the Islands for their honeymoons because the Islands resemble their own selves: vast benign hummocks. Kindly in their cloud-sized immensity, whales suckle their young, pitch their woo, behave amorously in Hawaiian seas. And are as curious about us as we are about them.

Saxon seafarers of the eighth century used to call such waters the *hranrad*, the "whales' road," where whales meet, mate, and calve in winter: hundreds of them, as long as 45 feet and weighing up to 40 tons, so that my white liner is forced to stop often. Protected by Hawaiian state law from any kind of harassment and by international law from hunting, humpbacks are now increasing in number. And we are on a mission to observe them, *Megaptera noveangliae* (Great-Winged New Englanders, the old name), in the name of "eco-tourism."

This is just about as near to heaven as I'd ever been. More than a hundred years ago, Robert Louis Stevenson wrote, "I am never well but at sea." As he looked for southern constellations, the skinny Scot began a love affair with the southern seas: "The moon beaconed, the stars paraded their lustrous regiment—I was aware of a molecular change or perhaps of a molecular reconstruction. My bones were sweeter to me."

A giant sneezing just below the surface, a delicate *a-tishoo*, heralded one humpback in the dawn, checking out our big white ship. Man has lived with whales for over 30 million years; but they are still as surprising to us as they were to Jonah.

On the first day after mango and papaya for breakfast, we listened to marine biologist Richard Roshen from Kaua'i, who spends weeks alone in his kayak every season, sleeping and eating afloat as he follows migrating whale cows. Bearded, spectacled, intense, Richard has tracked breeding patterns for over a decade, retaining a gallant infatuation for his leviathans that's charmingly sentimental.

In response to Richard's efforts to play whale songs for us, the nearby water churned into "footprints," and a smaller sneeze (say, fountain-sized) showed the presence of a baby humpback, a mere fifteen feet long. Then a sharp, shiny dorsal fin rolled above the eerily neon-green water, followed by a smaller fin. The mummy fluke rose, followed by a baby fluke. The skin looked as soft and shiny as black chamois, except upon the cow's old barnacle- and sea lice-encrusted head.

One cow, whom he recognized as Daisy by her "fluke" (tail markings are how humpbacks are identified) is so fond of him that she floats beside his kayak, flopping her fifteen-foot flipper over the prow to be stroked, he said, and even swims below his kayak putting huge flippers around it. He thinks she mistakes him for a calf.

Although Daisy's flipper could wallop him into the back of beyond or smash him to a pulp, Richard has no fear. Seasoned divers are careful of whale flukes, but whales are equally careful of humans. At this time of year, males are congregating to fight in competition or swarm lone females, singing them love songs of courtship, arias of long trembling bass notes with bedspring groans: oo-s, ee-s, yips, yups, ai-ees and abrupt changes to falsetto warblings.

Mysteriously, each bull whale repeats the song, which changes slightly each season, note-perfect. Imagine a pod of siren Pavarottis rehearsing together in the Pacific to perfect their song, then singing it for three months to passing females, like 600 Walthers in *Die Meistersinger von Nürnberg.* Who knows what they are singing, how they decide on the song, or how they sing, since they emit no air and have no vocal cords: only fancy plumbing? We do know they breathe at the same pauses, and sing facing downwards. What I'm learning comes mainly from Diane Ackerman's beautiful book *The Moon By Whale Light*, but many questions remain unanswered.

But next day I saw only whitecaps and gray billows as I staggered to my cabin bathroom. At four-foot square, it was a miracle of ship design with a circular mini-shower, basin, and toilet, with which I was becoming horribly intimate. After forcing down more mango and papaya, we took a kayaking jaunt from which we hoped to interview Kauaian whales. We set off in convoy, as I prayed for an Eskimo roll to cover my losing battle with breakfast. "Do you have a hangover?" asks our guide Kimo very tenderly. Kauaians are no strangers to hangovers.

Later, we listen to Mark and Debbie Ferrari from the Institute of Whale Studies; they've been following whales for fifteen years, checking on some whales year after year. It was Debbie who discovered how to tell a female from a male and who discovered that some females calved every winter before migrating to krill-rich Alaskan waters to feed themselves fat again.

Next day, we'd neared Lahaina, Maui, in order to scramble into a Zodiac raft. A woman of 85 called Eda Merrin was lifted in. She's a former Boston actress who played Bessie in O'Casey's *The Plough and the Stars* in the 1930s and whose dear wish it was to see a whale. In the bow, I got drenched: a mother humpback and her calf circled us, swimming below and showing their flukes as they dove anew, first big mummy flukes and then little baby flukes, an Olympic synchronized bathing display on a vast scale.

Of course, what we hoped for was the romance of a "breach"—the sudden, shocking leap of a humpback hurling its weight into the air before crashing down or smacking its flukes against the waves. Whale watching is becoming an addiction; it's easy to understand the Ferraris' passion.

Cased in yellow PVC, Eda wore an ecstatic smile and said she would die happy. "You know," she remarks, "There are many other kinds of romance when the first kind has worn off. Many more."

Transplanted Dublin journalist Elgy Gillespie lives in San Francisco's Mission District. Her travel writing highlights the food, film, and music of European, Latin American, Asian, and North American destinations. She helps put out a community newspaper, the Irish Herald, *as well as aiding the Irish Arts Foundation in hosting Irish events.*

*

The fastest whale ever recorded in the annual migration from Alaska to Hawai'i was a humpback whale sighted in Sitka Bay, Alaska, which traveled to Kohala, Hawai'i, a distance of 3,000 miles, in 39 days—76.92 miles a day or 3.2 miles an hour. The whale, identified by tail markings, was sighted January 3, 1988, then showed up off Kohala on February 11.

—RC & MC

SIMON WINCHESTER

Searching for ʻŌʻō

An Englishman looking for endangered birds finds other oddities along the trail.

TOWARD THE BACK OF THE PITT-RIVERS MUSEUM IN OXFORD, past the collection of shrunken heads from Borneo, across from the Transylvanian bagpipes and beside the British Colombian totem pole—in a glass case fitted with curtains which you must pull back in order to see its contents—is a Hawaiian ceremonial cape made of about 20,000 of the tiny, bright-yellow thigh feathers of the *ʻōʻō* bird. Dating from the eighteenth century and said to be of incalculable value, it is certainly one of the most remarkably lovely things in any museum in England—and its beauty enhanced by the knowledge that no birds had to die for it, since Hawaiian tradition required that they be caught on sticky poles, relieved of their choicest plumage and then allowed to fly away.

The *ʻōʻō* bird—which is actually jet black, save for its Technicolored thighs—may not have suffered from King Kamehameha the Great's predatory court cape-makers, but it declined savagely at the hand of other nameless foes. It is mentioned in all today's ornithological literature (notable, Pratt's *The Birds of the Tropical Pacific*) as being extinct—except, importantly, for one species that clings on in the most northerly (major) Island in the Hawaiian chain. (I am advised to discount "the event that amazed the birding world"—the discovery of a Bishop's *ʻōʻō* on Maui in 1981—as an aberration.) No. The single species of this extraordinary bird which remains is *Moho braccatus*, the Kauaian *o'o*, and it lives, elusive but extant, in a dismally wet mountaintop slough called the Alakaʻi Swamp.

The Island of Kauaʻi, which has many distinctions, is a sanctuary for many survivors, avian and otherwise, perhaps in part because of its physical isolation. For many years Kauaʻi has been an island reliquary, a place were many of the people, the flora and fauna, the traditions, much of the charm of the old Pacific, have come to rest and look like staying on. It was the first of the Sandwich Islands on which James Cook landed; the last of the Hawaiian Islands to relinquish its regal independence and accept the suzerainty of King Kamehameha. In consequence it is an Island with a certain sense of pride and a place that is fighting hard not to be ruined.

> Their eyes were continually flying from object to object, the wildness of their looks and actions fully expressed their surprise and astonishment at the several new objects before them and evinced that they never had been on board of a ship before.
>
> ◆
>
> —Capt. James Cook, on the day Hawaiians discovered the British at Kauaʻi, 1778

But thousands of visitors stream in daily through Līhuʻe airport, quite careless of all this. Jets arrive every 30 minutes, their passengers bound from the chill of the American continent (and increasingly, from the big cities of Japan and the prosperous states of East Asia, just a dateline away) for the beaches and resort hotels of the Kauaʻi shores. Watching this mass daily immigrating—though it is far larger and more disagreeable in Waikīkī, or the more celebrated parts of Maui—it is tempting to suppose that the old Hawaiian charm has already been submerged, even in Kauaʻi, under the contemporary myth of the Styrofoam aloha and all its horrid trappings.

"You had a leg reading yet?" asked the girl beside me on the plane, that brief parabolic excursion constituting the excuse for a flight between Honolulu and Līhu'e. Sue-Anne was from the South, from Mississippi, and this was her third vacation in Hawai'i. She always came with her girlfriends Cindy and Tammy, and they all thought the place was really neat, the beaches were neat, the food was neat, the guys were neat, and they have those really neat cliffs where these old fellows used to throw each other off and git fed to the sharks. The trio giggled horribly, then Sue-Anne repeated her curious, twanging query, "You had a leg reading yet?"

I knew a little of the geomantic reputation of Kaua'i and assumed that this was the connection. In fact, one of the people I was hoping to see was a woman from Pittsburgh who had settled in the old Kauaian sugar town of Hanapēpē because she believed in the presence of a "vortex" nearby. On arrival, she had changed her name from Ann Merrit to Roberleigh Hale because, she explained, "numerologically speaking, Ann Merrit sucks," and she was a woman deeply impressed by the strange "magic" of numbers. She was also very anxious about her health—hers and that of those around her. So she bought a tiny hotel and now offers her visitors a somber regime of massages, strenuous bouts of colonic irrigation, meals purged of all free oil and dairy products, also phrenology, iris diagnosis, aromatheraphy, and palm readings.

As with palm readings, so with leg readings—and thus I assumed (foolishly, it turned out) that Sue-Anne was a friend or at least a client of this celebrated Dr. Hale of Hanapēpē, purveyor of healthy vacations, astrological readings, and interior irrigations. But before I could ask her, the plane had shuddered to a halt on the Līhu'e runway and we were all rushing for the exit. I came across her later waiting for her bags; a pretty Hawaiian girl had just put a massive *lei* of frangipani around her neck, and she was smiling broadly. "See here!" she cried, pointing at the rope of blossoms. "I got one again," she twanged. "I got a leg reading." So that was it. Her accent. She had never met Dr. Hale, nor ever heard of her, in her life.

The thousands of duly *lei*-greeted arrivals like Sue-Anne make only the most limited of forays into the Island. Kauaʻi is more or less circular, being the cone of an enormous volcano called Waiʻaleʻale, and a narrow road runs along most of its circumference at sea level. Wherever the road meets a beach, or more particularly (if the beach is on the windward side of the island, where the northeast trades bend the palms and stir up the surf) a stretch of sand protected by an offshore reef, some developer will have slapped down a hotel—and it is to scores of these dire establishments that the thousands all repair. The more affluent take trips by helicopter or Zodiac boat; the secretaries from Scranton, Pennsylvania, and the Chevrolet dealers from Cedar Rapids, Iowa—and Sue-Anne and her friends, no doubt—just bake in the sun, squeal at the colors of the tropical fish, take half-day excursions with "Cap'n Andy's Sailing Adventures" or frolic at endless and wholly artificial *lūʻau*, where the pig is put in an oven (rather than in a traditional *imu* pit) and its carcass is swabbed down with a ghastly Ohio-made synthetic called Likwid Smoke instead of being roasted above a fire of *kiawe* wood and hot chunks of basalt.

Tourists of whatever nationality sometimes have a special knack of ruining anywhere and anything that's perfectly good—and in Hawaiʻi, it is often tempting to think that they've done it in spades.

But not quite...not on Kauaʻi. A map will show that the Island peripherique does not circle the Island in its entirety. In the south, it runs across the lower plains, where the old sugar barons—the Sinclairs, Robinsons, McBrydes, and the heirs of the legendary Gaylord P. Wilcox—tend to their canefields still. (But there is no refining these days; no delicious smell of boiling molasses and cane straw. Kauaian sugar is exported as a liquid in what look like oil tankers and goes thus unromantically to California.) In the west, the road wanders idly through sleepy, run-down, rather pleasant old mill towns, places like Hanapēpē and Kekaha and Waimea town, where Captain Cook first came ashore and where there is a statue (a replica of the one that stands on the seafront back in Whitby in the United Kingdom). On the eastern side, the road is much busier, taking the rental car crowd from resorts to beaches, from sight ("Where Mitzi Gaynor washed that man right out of her hair") to sight ("Kīlauea Lighthouse—the most northerly point in the [major] Hawaiian Islands").

But on the northern side, there is no road at all. From the triple chain-link electrified fence around the Barking Sands Pacific missile range—where technicians track rockets rushing between Vandenberg Air Force Base in California and Kwajalein Island in the far Pacific, and where others fire torpedoes into the sea and play complicated war games with them—to a cluster of caves and Hawaiian holy sites and a tiny cove at Hā'ena State Park, there is a fifteen-mile arc of Kauaian coast around which not even the world's greatest highway engineer could ever imagine building a road.

The thick basalt layers have been lifted up and eroded into immense hanging valleys separated from each other by vast, almost sheer—but still green-jungle-covered–walls thousands of feet high, with columns capped by elegant entablatures of iron-black lava.

The Nā Pali Coast, as these cliffs and valleys are known where they plunged suddenly into the raging ocean, is a wilderness of spectacular, almost frightening remoteness. It is well-nigh impossible to trek in it: the basalt is old and well eroded, and the rock faces which from a distance look so sturdy and knitted together by the liana and ferns of the rainforest are in fact quite rotten; given any applied pressure, they will crumble like Demerara sugar, robbing any walker of footholds and handholds and plunging him—like scores before him who have died and whose bodies have lain unrecovered for years—into the canyon below. There is a slippery, evil trail from Hā'ena State Park running west along the coast for eleven miles into the mystically reputed Kalalau Valley; but in places this is only a few inches wide, and is no more than a thin stain of red mud on rocks that rise vertically on the landward side and on the other drop 1,000 feet, quite sheer, into the bottomless Pacific. The awesome cliffs and the potential for dizzying falls remain an ever-present warning to anyone who tries to pass along to Kalalau and its legendary valley.

The state of Hawai'i now forbids strangers to stay in the Valley for more than five days. This ordinance—which seems extraordinarily mean to anyone who makes it along the trail and reaches this deep green valley with its waterfalls, old taro plantations, orange groves, and long gold sand beach—was enacted because (as with so many of the world's most beautifully remote places) the Valley was once a magnet for those refugees from modernism who were known as hippies.

Back in the sixties, the secluded caves of Nā Pali became temporary grottoes for their alternative living. The valleys—Kalalau was the most celebrated, but Hanakapi'ai, Honopū, and Po'opo'oiki became briefly fashionable too—had mystic associations with long-vanished Hawaiian cultures, with men and women whose ghosts still drifted around their ruined *heiau* and tumble down villages, and gave out the alluring siren call of...Polynesia! So small hippie villages sprang up, little communities of white Americans in ragged clothes, with their grubby children and their dogs—and official Hawai'i became briefly outraged and passed the law. Most of the hippies had gone within a year, but Kaua'i is a reliquary: some, like the *'ō'ō* bird, cling on.

The "barking sands" phenomenon was described in 1875 by a Mr. W. R. Frink of Honolulu in a letter to the California Academy of Sciences. "If you slap two handfuls of sand together," he wrote, "a sound is produced like the hooting of an owl. If a person kneels on the steep incline (on the dunes) and then, with the two hands extended and grasping as much sand as possible, slides rapidly down carrying all the sand he can, the sound accumulates till it is like distant thunder."

I attempted to repeat the experiments single handed. I slapped sand together, slithered on it, jumped on it, and rolled on it. No sound emerged. At some personal risk, I launched myself head first down the dunes exactly as Frink had specified. Still no sound. By now I was covered head to toe with sand, feeling rather foolish, and attracting strange looks from people on the beach.

◆

—Ron Hall, "Best Beaches of Hawai'i," *Condé Nast Traveler*

Nā Pali is difficult to reach and equally difficult to police. And while the state still occasionally drops rangers and gangs of henchmen by helicopter, to check that no one outstays his welcome, the odd reclusive pair from the Mainland can still be found eking out a living in the jungle. I found a couple in a corner of the beach one evening; they were quite naked and had come down from their cave-home to bathe in the sea. They had lived wild for ten years and saw few outsiders, save for a grocer who bartered their marijuana plants for cigarettes and a few bottles of beer. They grew corn, oranges, guavas, and taro (which they pounded into purple poi paste; the thicker it was, the fewer fingers required to eat it, thus two-finger poi is a hippie favorite). They kept goats and pigs and chickens and insisted they were perfectly happy. The man—shaggy, deeply tanned, and something of a sentimentalist—quoted a line from one Bernard Wheatley, a Negro doctor, who disappeared in Kalalau twenty years ago after having lived off the land for ten. "There is more here than just quietness. There is a big peace. There is music in the wind and the surf. I like sundown best, and the moonlight on the ripples in the sand. I like to sit in my cave and watch Venus in the night sky." But this man didn't want to tell me his name, and once he had loped off back into the woods it was as though he had never been at all.

It is said to be impossible to climb up the head of Kalalau to the rim of the Valley, and to the huge forested wilderness of the Koke'e State Park. However, the lip is reachable from the other side of the Island: the 4,000 unclimbably vertical feet that separate the head of the Kalalau Valley from the Koke'e lookout above can be bridged by walking back along the treacherous trail and then driving 70 miles around the circumference of Kaua'i; then up the side of the immense Waimea Canyon (canyon connoisseurs say it is as deep and magnificent as the Grand Canyon of the Colorado, though the dark cindery rock make it a lot less colorful) and along deep forest roads to Koke'e Lodge and to the lookout itself.

It takes three hours if you have a decent car and the tourists are not bunched up looking at the Mitzi Gaynor site, or outside the Paradise Thrift Shop in Kapa'a where second-hand ("pre-worn")

Hawaiian shirts are on sale at—being "collector's items"—up to $150 apiece. After these three hours of walking and driving you reach a point high up on the mountain rim where you can see down into Kalalau and watch tropic birds soaring half a mile below, almost halfway to where you stood at sea level in the heat, gazing up at this inaccessible ridge.

The rim is Kaua'i's most dramatic borderline. Below is the lushly dangerous valley—land where the human species goes—ancient Hawaiian, modern hippie, the legions of helicopter-borne travelers; above the rim is a wilderness inhabited only by nature, a watery plain of foggy immensity, a place of primeval strangeness.

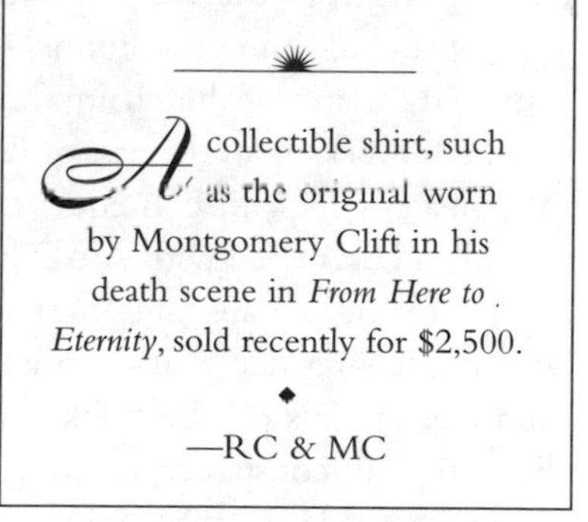

A collectible shirt, such as the original worn by Montgomery Clift in his death scene in *From Here to Eternity*, sold recently for $2,500.

—RC & MC

A walker can approach the Alaka'i Swamp, as it is known, along a footpath from the Koke'e Lookout. At first, the path is well-traveled, and has the look of permanency, and you will meet an occasional hiker well wrapped against the increasing cool. But farther along the path—the farther inland—where the trail begins to thin and vanish into puddles of black mud, so blankets of thick gray fog snake down from the sky, eddies of the trade winds bring down smothering slabs of wetness which make everything invisible and coat every branch and leaf with huge drops of freshwater. Thick coats of sphagnum moss cover the branches here. Ferns, some as tall as trees, others of cobweblike delicacy, grow everywhere. Black-feathered birds stand gloomily in the rain and mist, waiting for a brief glimpse of the sky and the chance to flutter on before the next shower.

The mud gets thicker, such paths as there are seem built on sliding rafts of decaying vegetation from which bubbles of gas rise ominously, like the belches of a sleeping god. People who slip off the pathways and into the swamp can be trapped for hours, held waist-deep in thick black mud. Some plants would drown if their roots went too deep into the quagmire, so natural selection has determined that the roots float beside them on the boggy surface and the plant, a stunted, blackened-looking thing, tries its best to tower above but looks sheepishly unable to do so.

The Alaka'i is a very odd place. It is also the wettest in the world. A rain gauge at the summit of Mount Wai'ale'ale has recorded 50 feet of rain in some years, and an average of very nearly 500 inches annually. The damp, warm trade winds which seep down from the landless ocean to the northeast of Kaua'i are caught in an immense funnel when they arrive at this most northerly Island of the chain; the Anahola range in the north and the Hā'upu range in the east of Kaua'i direct them all on to Mount Wai'ale'ale, which in consequence is nearly always shrouded with cloud and drenched with rain. The rain falls almost as continuously on the twenty square miles of the Alaka'i—a tepid, wettening, rusting, mildewing rain that encourages everything to grow furiously and falls endless on the thick carpet of black mud and green foliage that it constantly creates. I came to love the rain of the Alaka'i: it made the place seem primeval, the mud like some comfortable Proterozoic ooze. (A not wholly inappropriate metaphor, a state geologist later remarked: the volcanoes of Hawai'i ranged along the suture-line that is the birthplace of the new Pacific—if the new ocean is being created in Hawai'i, he said, why not new life to go along with it?)

And it is in the Alaka'i, that the Kauaian *'ō'ō* is said to live. I went hunting for one; indeed, the glum-looking black birds which waited on dripping perches for the skies to clear could well have been *'ō'ō*, but each time one flew off it did so when I was looking elsewhere and thus denied me the sight of its flashing ocher thighs. My guide, however, said she had spent a year looking for one, but in vain: sea eagles, yes, and a bewildering variety of frogs, insect-eating plants, and honeycreepers. But not an *'ō'ō*, nary a one.

Down below me on the ring road were thousands of ordinary Americans, performing the unchanging Coppertone-and-Coors rituals of the perpetual summertime of this mid-Pacific American possession. Up here, on this wedge-shaped piece of swampy mountainside, and on the cliffs and in the valleys which drained the rains from it and took them back into the sea from which they had come...up here, all was so very, very different. "It is swampy and dangerous," wrote Isabella Bird when she visited Kauaʻi a century ago and looked up to Waʻaleʻale and the misty acres of the Alakaʻi. "It is very little explored, and little seems to be known of the area."

And it is much the same today. Bypassed by the millions, loved by the few, a refuge for curious people, a homeland for strange plants and beasts, and, it is said, the nesting place and the resting place for a tiny black bird; a bird that was once a symbol—known as far away as the University of Oxford—of the very essence of Hawaiʻi, but which now, like so much of the essence of Hawaiʻi itself, has almost vanished clear away.

Simon Winchester writes about the Pacific for Manchester Guardian Weekly *and* Condé Nast Traveler. *This story was excerpted from his book,* Pacific Rising: The Emergence of New World Order. *He is also the author of the bestseller,* The Professor and the Madman: A Tale of Murder, Insanity, and the Making of the Oxford English Dictionary.

*

It was, I think, the aloha shirt featuring bikini-clad women cavorting with striped beach balls that finally convinced my wife I'd taken utter leave of whatever fashion sense I had. She fixed me with her finest what-a-bozo stare the minute I put it on. It is a withering look she usually reserves for far more felonious lapses.

Admittedly, there was nothing subtle about that shirt. Three lissome beach bunnies bracketed by palm trees prance on the sand across its front. Two more identical blondes joined the line on the back. Each kicked up her left heel in frisky abandon. What was clearly meant to be the beach at Waikīkī curved off in the background.

Couldn't my wife recognize it was surely intended as wearable art? What about the parody implicit in the tacky design? If not the humor, how about the intricate work or the bright colors? She was a stone wall.

In retrospect, maybe it was my fault for admitting that I'd given all five beach bunnies names ending in *i*.

I've been collecting and wearing alohas for years, much to the chagrin of my wife. To me, at least, aloha shirts make perfect sense. We live in Los Angeles and since I can never figure out what to wear anyway, I consider alohas the ultimate in usefully ambivalent fashion. After all, how many shirts can you wear barefoot and in shorts, as well as with shoes and a linen jacket, on more formal occasions? (For those of you now cringing, remember—I live in Los Angeles.)

Senseless dedication to aloha shirts is a kind of low caliber mania, and I'll admit that I'm driven by it. My collection numbers more than two dozen and I continue to prowl for more. Still, as these things go, it's a fairly harmless obsession. I don't collect ceramic owls, shake-before-viewing snow scenes, or paintings that require black light.

—Richard J. Pietschmann, "What do Tom Selleck, Patrick Swayze and Elvis Have in Common?" *Travel & Leisure*

STEVE HELLER

Valley of Ghosts

Ancient Hawai'i was governed by spirits of every kind. But only one island was known as the Island of Ghosts: Lāna'i.

ACCORDING TO MANY A LEGEND AND STORY, LĀNA'I'S ONLY humanoid inhabitants were man-eating spirits controlled by the sorceress Pahulu. Hawaiians avoided Lāna'i until the nineteenth century A.D., when Kaululā'au, the mischievous son of Ka'akalaneo, the King of Maui, was banished to Lāna'i for a series of destructive pranks. The banishment was regarded as a death sentence because for more than 500 years, no human being had stayed overnight on Lāna'i—and lived until the following dawn. Nevertheless, with the help of his *'aumakua* (guardian spirit) the brave and clever prince of Maui was able to trick and kill all of the ghosts of Lāna'i and make the Island safe for human habitation.

Today it is said that the only ghosts on Lāna'i are those the visitor brings with him. I discovered the truth of this saying a few summers ago when the Hawaiian Literary Arts Council invited me to read my fiction at the old Hotel Lāna'i lodge, at that time the only hotel on the Island. As a frequent visitor to Lāna'i and long-time student of its history, I had previously visited most of the Island's sacred and culturally significant sites, such as Kaunolū (the God's Landing and the favorite summer residence of Kamehameha the Great), the ancient fishponds at Naha on the leeward coast, and

Polihua Beach, where the fishing god 'Ai'ai introduced the green sea turtle to Hawai'i by dropping a small stone on the white sand and chanting a prayer to his parents Kū'ulakai and Hinapukui'a. But there was one place on Lāna'i I had never been: the sacred, forbidden valley of Maunalei.

Maunalei is actually a deep green gulch carved into the windward side of 3,000-foot Mount Lāna'ihale. Narrower and not quite as steep as Waipi'o on the Big Island and Kalalau on Kaua'i, the valley of Maunalei is nevertheless perhaps even more dramatic. According to legend, the volcano goddess Pele often visited Maunalei to gather *le'ie* vines, whose roots were perfect for weaving baskets. The steep sides of the valley are still marked by stone terraces built by taro farmers. At the mouth of the valley, a Hawaiian village once thrived, supported by the fresh clean water of Maunalei Stream, which once flowed all the way to the sea.

Today the valley is fenced off near its mouth to keep the curious from disturbing traces of native Hawaiian culture, as

---

In Hawai'i where land is rare, finite, and costly, it may seem odd that anyone could own an island. It would be like Donald Trump owning Manhattan.

Yet, it is possible because Hawai'i once was a kingdom and the king sold islands when he needed cash.

Charles Gay, grandson of Eliza Sinclair of New Zealand, who bought the island of Ni'ihau from King Kalākaua for $10,000 in gold and her grand piano in 1864, paid $200,000 for Lāna'i several years later. He sold the island to James Dole who turned Lāna'i into the world's biggest pineapple patch.

In the 1980s, Los Angeles entrepreneur David Murdock gained control of Dole Food Corp., and discovered he owned Lāna'i. He closed the pineapple plantation, recycled Filipino field hands into chambermaids, opened two ritzy resorts, created a suburb of million dollar houses, and began cultivating well-heeled tourists on the red dirt island.

—RC & MC

well as from contaminating the Island's primary source of freshwater. On my third and final day on Lāna'i I received permission from the Lāna'i Company to enter the forbidden valley and hike up it as far as my weary legs would carry me.

Using the key the Company gave me, I unlocked the chain fence at the mouth of the valley and drove my rented jeep up a sandy rutted path through *kiawe* and ironwood trees. After a minute or two, the trail began to rise, and suddenly I emerged from the *kiawe*. The sky opened blue above me between the walls of the gulch. Maunalei is more than half a mile wide at this point near its mouth, and the stony gray-green walls slope at 45-degree angles on each side. As I drove inland, the walls rose higher and more steeply until they became sheer green cliffs, cutting a deeper and narrower groove in the massive mountain. Maunalei and all its tributaries are marked by narrow waterfalls that send moisture raked from passing clouds cascading down cliffs hundreds of feet high into the stream that flows at times all the way to the sea. Maunalei literally means "Wreath Mountain," and from the floor of the valley one can easily see why. Clouds are snared by the jagged head peaks of the gulch, creating mist. When the light is right, rainbows arc from cliff to cliff above the waterfalls. The head of the valley is almost always in shadow; clouds and the steep mountainsides block the sun. The hidden head of the valley, the most remote and mysterious place on the Island, was my destination.

"Maunalei is a place of great *kapu*," a Lāna'i man once told me. "*Kapu*," like many Hawaiian words, is a complex term. It can mean many things: forbidden, sacred, consecrated, special, filled with spirits. Maunalei is all these things, and more—a place of history and legend. Somewhere up on the cliffs near the head of the gulch is Ho'okio Ridge, a fortification where in 1778 Kahekili, the king of both Maui and Lāna'i, was defeated in battle by Kalaniōpu'u, King of Hawai'i. Fighting on the side of Kalaniōpu'u was Kamehameha, who would one day unite all the Islands under his rule. The invaders hurled sling stones at the warriors defending the ridge and cut off their water supply. In the end the defenders were slaughtered. After the Island fell to Kalaniōpu'u, his troops remained for a time. The Island had too little food to support both the army and the residents, and in the famine that followed many more perished. Although the evil cannibalistic ghosts of Lāna'i had been destroyed by Kaululā'au centuries earlier, the spirits of all who died on Lāna'i as a result of Kalaniopu'u's invasion are said to dwell in the upper forest and the even higher, shadowed mossy cliffs of the gulch. Maunalei is consecrated with the blood of the dead.

After about a mile and a half of twisting ruts, I rounded a hillside curve. Through the V-shaped opening before me loomed the tall jagged cliffs of the valley's head, its serrated green peaks rising like the spires of a giant natural cathedral. But I was still more than a mile from my ultimate destination. I parked at the pumping station at the edge of the green wall of the upper forest. With only an improvised walking stick to protect me, I found a narrow trail and pushed into the forest.

Inside was another world: a forest cavern with a ceiling of green and a floor of black volcanic stone and mashed leaves. The first thing I noticed was the hush. The caressing breeze, the salty breath of the sea I had taken for granted in the open areas of the valley did not penetrate the wood, and the sounds it brought to my ears moment by moment—birds warbling, leaves rustling—vanished with the sky. But the forest was not silent. Inside the wooded cavern, every noise was sharp and distinct: the crunch of stones, the snap of twigs beneath my feet, the pitter and shush of water over rock. Each sound carried through the trees. Not an echo: a lingering resonance, like a lone note held on a piano. The depth and weight of my movements were amplified; instinctively I fell into a reverent silence, proceeding in slow, almost mincing steps. The valley narrowed noticeably as I advanced, crossing and recrossing the narrow stream. Tiny fruit balls crunched beneath my feet, and ferns clutched at my pant legs. I paused a moment beside a 60-foot waterfall on the side of the gulch, then pressed ahead until the encroaching flora forced me to crawl over slick stones in the center of the stream.

Then all at once the roof opened. I emerged from the upper

forest and found myself in the bottom of a giant ravine, ten times as high as it was wide: the deepest cleft in the mountain. On each side of me, slick green mossy walls rose a thousand feet or more. Somewhere above the mountain, thunder rumbled, and I shivered as the air grew suddenly colder. As gray clouds gathered overhead, forming a roof above the ravine, I felt stifled, edgy, as if the sides of the ravine might collapse on me at any moment.

I remember feeling this way only once before, in 1978: the morning my wife Mary and I drove our VW campmobile up the Big Thompson Canyon in Colorado, the day of the tragic flash flood. At the canyon's narrowest points, the winding walls of the Big Thompson are almost vertical and cannot be climbed by anyone but a professional. Nevertheless, log cabins dotted the banks of every other bend in the river. On the morning Mary and I snaked our way up toward Estes Park, a rolling ceiling of gray cloud poured down the canyon, shutting off the sun. I remember thinking that if the clouds opened and spilled their contents, there would be no way out, no way to escape the resulting flood. The water would simply sweep away everything in its path. Don't be a worrier, I chided myself as I drove. And besides, there was nothing I could do.

We drove all the way to Gunnison that day, and didn't learn of the flood until we turned on the TV in our room at the Best Western that evening. It turned out we had missed the storm and flood by one hour. I no longer remember how many people perished in a matter of minutes that day. I remember only the images of destruction: cars twisted and smashed like toys against sheer cliffs; rectangular-shaped grooves in bare slick earth, marking the spots where log cabins had once stood; bodies half-buried in ripples of mud. In one shot, a single hand reached up out of smooth brown glaze and stretched upward, as if there were something in the empty air above to grab onto.

I was lost in this memory when all at once the ceiling of clouds above me collapsed. For an instant, I didn't know where I was: in Maunalei or the Big Thompson. In seconds, the steep walls around me vanished, and I stood enveloped in billowing gray. Then it began to rain. The stream, merely a trickle moments earlier, began to surge around my ankles, then my calves. There was no escape. Whatever spirits inhabited this place would claim me now, if they wished. I could do nothing but stand and wait.

Then, as swiftly as it had come, the gray cloud passed. On each side of me, vertical cliffs sparkled green in a thinning mist. I stood, soaked and shivering in the returning light, and drew a deep breath.

Ahead of me, at the head of the gulch, a distant waterfall, created by the cloudburst, tumbled in a spindly white ribbon from a notch in the cliffs. For a few moments I just stood there and stared at it. Somewhere above and beyond the waterfall lay Ho'okio Ridge, and the final mysteries of Maunalei. Someday I may hike the final steps up the valley and confront them.

But not this day. On this day, I turned back.

Steve Heller is Professor of English and Chair of the Creative Writing Program at Kansas State University. He recently served as Distinguished Visiting Professor of Creative Writing at the University of Hawai'i-Mānoa, during which time he began work on a novel tracing the history of Lāna'i.

⋆

Kaunolū has been deserted for 50 years. The last man to reside in the vicinity was Ohua, elder brother of Keli'ihananui, now living at Lelehaka, on the top-lands. Ohua occupied a grass house in a detached bluff at the head of Mamaki Bay until his death about 1900.

The father of these two men was overseer (*konohiki*) for the district of Kaunolū under the old feudal system. Ohua was one of the men instructed by Kamehameha V in 1868 to hide the stone fish god Kunihi, which stood on the stone altar in the gulch directly below the temple of refuge. His death is attributed to a mishandling of this image.

I have heard various descriptions of the idol. All agree that it was not over three feet high and that it showed only crudely carved face and arms. Mrs. Awili Shaw, a blind native living at Lahaina, is accredited with knowing the hiding place and D. K. Kaenaokalani of Lahaina told me after I had left Lāna'i that Kunihi was lying face down not more than a hundred yards up the gulch from the altar and against the west bank.

—Kenneth P. Emory, *Island of Lāna'i: A Survey of Native Culture*

PART THREE

Going Your Own Way

JOHN FLINN

Pretending to be Rich

A penny-pinching traveler discovers the decadent way to do Hawai'i.

MY BUTLER HAS JUST ARRIVED WITH A FRESH MAI TAI, GARNISHED with a perfect little orchid and the straw pre-bent to the proper angle. I take a contented sip and gaze out beyond my private swimming pool and Jacuzzi, out beyond my private fishpond, out beyond the white-sand beach and coconut palm trees to the azure Pacific, where a humpback whale is leaping and slapping about, apparently for my sole amusement.

On my lap, the latest *Vanity Fair* is open to a story about the wedding at Versailles between His Serene Highness the Prince and Duke Pierre d'Arenberg and the aristocratic beauty Silvia de Castellane. The whole gang was there: Princess Caroline of Monaco, Prince Michael of Bourbon-Parma, the Duchess of Seville and what one wag called the "Concorde Frequent Fliers' Club"—Nan Kempner, Georgette Mosbacher, Lynn Wyatt. Could my invitation possibly have been lost in the mail?

Then I remember: I'm not one of those people, not even close. But for one brief moment—one sadistically, cruelly, inhumanely brief moment—I am living as they live when they come to Hawai'i. I am padding around on Italian marble floors in a cuddly soft terrycloth robe and admiring the fresh-cut bird of paradise in the crystal vases and wondering whether I should summon my butler to make me another of those invigorating mai tai or crack open the chilled champagne.

The Mauna Lani Bay Bungalows, on the arid Kohala Coast of the Big Island, are where royalty, Hollywood celebrities, and garden-variety billionaires check in when they come to Hawai'i. Bill Gates stays here. So do Rod Stewart, Steven Spielberg, Roseanne, Dustin Hoffman, Tom Cruise and Nicole Kidman. Kevin Costner moved in for six months during the filming of *Waterworld* (which might help explain why the movie was tens of millions of dollars over budget.) Princess Diana and Dodi Fayed had reservations for the week after Paris.

There are five bungalows, each decorated in the theme of a Hawaiian flower: Orchid, Hibiscus, Plumeria, Heliconia, and Bird of Paradise. Each is 2,700 square feet, with a 1,300-square-foot *lānai* with its own pool and Jacuzzi. Each cost $2 million to build and $175,000 to furnish. Each comes with its own butler and maid, and the five share a concierge. They're gated off, apparently to keep out the riffraff from the $575-a-night rooms at the adjacent Mauna Lani Bay Hotel.

Before you arrive they send you a questionnaire: Cotton or satin sheets? Down, feather, or foam pillows? Favorite booze, snacks, CDs? Will you be requiring a private secretary? Check it off on the questionnaire, and it's waiting for you when you arrive.

Oh, did I forget to mention the cost? It's between $3,500 and $4,400 a night. Let's just say they attract the kind of people for whom five nights in a bungalow and their daughter's annual tuition at Stanford are not an either/or proposition. (They're about the same price.) And as Paul Theroux once pointed out about a stay here: that price does include a Continental breakfast.

The Kohala Coast of the Big Island is an otherworldly landscape. Driving north from the Keahole Kona Airport, my wife Jeri and I passed through miles and miles of nothing but lava beds—the result of molten rock oozing out of volcanic vents and drying into chunky, brown-black rocks for as far as you can see. The effect is strikingly similar to the pictures brought back by the Mars

Pathfinder. Along the highway, the lava was festooned with a uniquely local form of graffiti: messages spelled out in contrasting white rocks, hauled up from the beach. Or at least some were. Some graffiti artists merely take apart existing messages and rearrange the stones to form new ones. At the turnoff to the Mauna Lani Resort there was a brief splash of color—an entranceway enlivened with bright purple bougainvillea. Then more black lava, a mile or two of it, before we arrived at an oasis of flowers, palm trees, and fairways and pulled up at the entrance to the Mauna Lani Bay Hotel.

We announced we had come to check into our bungalow, and I watched the bell captain's face closely for signs of utter disbelief, or a discreetly swallowed guffaw. But he never so much as arched an eyebrow. He picked up the phone and summoned our butler to come fetch us. (Most guests are picked up by chauffeured limousine at the airport, but we had a rental car.)

> William (age seven) and I were in Hawai'i last November. We took the tent and sleeping bags and camped at the beachside places and at Hawai'i Volcanoes National Park and Haleakalā and did not drink a single drink with a parasol in it nor did we eat a macadamia nut.
>
> We snuck into a couple of the expensive Shangri-la joints for the day, to check them out and splash in the pools. William noticed the odd part at the Hilton Waikaloa on the Big Island, which has a zillion pools, a monorail, slides, Disneyland boat rides through the lobby but which somehow does not have a beach.
>
> Where's the beach, Dad?
>
> —Steve Rubenstein, "Shangri-la for Tourists"

My knowledge of butlers comes almost entirely from Jeeves, the omniscient gentleman's gentleman in the P. G. Wodehouse novels, and so I was expecting a jowly, balding, 60ish Englishman in the manner of Sir John Gielgud or John Houseman. You could have knocked me over with a hibiscus flower when a Lincoln Towne Car pulled up and the person who stepped out looked like a Hawaiian aerobics instructor. "Hello, I'm Michelle," she said. "I'll be your butler." Struggling for something to say, I wondered: What does one call a female butler? A butless? A butress?

"'Butler' is fine, sir," said Michelle as she drove us around the corner, through the gate, and up the blue-tiled driveway to Orchid Bungalow.

The walkway up to the front door was lined with bougainvillea, gardenias, and jasmine. Michelle held open the door, and we stepped into an Italian marble entryway as big as my first apartment. Under a vaulted cathedral ceiling, the main living room was half the size of a basketball court and floored with native *koa* wood. In one corner stood a Jumbotron-sized television with a VCR, stereo sound system, and karaoke machine. On top was a list of available CDs, everything from the Brandenburg Concertos to Nat King Cole and Hawaiian slack-key guitar. The coffee table was covered with the latest issues of *Architectural Digest, Vogue, Vanity Fair, GQ, Gourmet, National Geographic,* and *Senior Golfer*. On a marble table behind the couch were that day's edition of the *Honolulu Advertiser,* a faxed digest of *The New York Times* and the *San Francisco Examiner.*

"We try to have the hometown paper for each guest," said Michelle. "If there are any other papers you'd like, just let me know." Another table held big bowls of Maui-style potato chips and macadamia nuts. I couldn't help grabbing a handful of the latter every time I passed by, and noticed that the bowl was always magically topped off before my next raid.

There was no mini-bar. Instead, one wall of the room contained a real bar: a marble countertop lined with full-sized, unopened bottles of just about every alcoholic libation one could desire: Chivas Regal, Jack Daniels, and Crown Royal whiskies; Tanqueray gin; Cuervo Especial tequila; Hennessy V.S. cognac; Myer's rum; Absolut vodka and Noilly Prat vermouth (both sweet and dry.) A refrigerator held Roederer Estate champagne; Buehler

Chardonnay; Heineken, Budweiser, and Bud Light beers; Coke; Diet Coke; Sprite; Schweppes tonic, club soda, ginger ale; and Evian water.

"Anything you want from the bar is included with the bungalow," said Michelle. "I'd be glad to make you a drink any time you'd like."

Off the living room was the butler's pantry, with a full kitchen and shelves full of extra macadamia nuts and liquor, in the unlikely event we ran through the stock in the living room. The pantry has its own entrance, and it was through here that Michelle and Lani, the afternoon/evening butler, materialized and vanished without a sound. All I ever had to do was entertain the thought that I'd like a little privacy, and Michelle and Lani would shimmer out before I could even form the words to ask.

The master bedroom had a queen-sized bed and an armoire with another large TV, VCR, and Nintendo game station. Any pay-per-view movies we cared to watch were included, gratis. Next to the bed was the current *TV Guide* with a bookmark indicating that day's listings, in the entirely likely event I forgot what day it was. There were his-and-her walk-in closets, each with its own plump terrycloth robe, kimono, and slippers.

The bathroom was a vast expanse of Italian marble half as large as a tennis court, with sinks and vanities at either end. One vanity held one of those horrifying lighted magnifying mirrors that reveal every pore and can make even Gwyneth Paltrow's complexion look like Manuel Noriega's. A good sales pitch, Jeri suggested, for a complete facial treatment at the local spa.

There was a bathtub-for-two with jets, and a glassed-in shower/steam room capacious enough to accommodate the entire 49ers offensive line. On the shelf were Neutrogena shampoo, conditioner, and "Rain Bath Gel"—not those dinky bottles you usually get in hotels, but full-sized containers. On the opposite side of the bungalow there was another bedroom, bathroom, TV, VCR, Nintendo, etc.—a mirror image of ours in every detail, except that it had two double beds. I never set foot in these rooms, except to poke my nose in and confirm they existed. (It turns out there was another chamber—a large powder room off the entryway—that I didn't even discover until I was checking out.)

"Is there anything you'd like me to do for you, sir?" asked Michelle. Not having much experience being butlered, I didn't know what to say. I tried to recall what services Jeeves performed for his affable, dimwitted master Bertie Wooster, other than to bail him out of jail and romantic entanglements. Weren't butlers supposed to iron the wrinkles out of the newspapers or something? I glanced over at the *Examiner*; it was already neatly pressed.

"So...what exactly is it that you butlers do?"

"I could unpack for you," she said brightly. I eyed my dusty duffel bag stuffed full of twice-worn t-shirts, wrinkled khaki Gap shorts and the kind of threadbare underwear my mother always warned me not to wear in case I got into a car accident.

"Uh, no thanks, I can unpack myself."

"Very good, sir."

"Uh...Michelle?"

"Sir?"

"What kinds of things do you do for the other guests?"

"Somebody once asked us to fill the bathtub with roses, and someone else wanted it filled with champagne," she said. "People ask to have *leis* floating in the pool and flower petals on the bed and private hula performances."

"Do they always get what they want?"

"If we can possibly accommodate them, we will."

Later, Susy Chillingworth, the bungalow manager, told me about a guest who developed a sudden desire for a kind of lotion sold only at a certain hotel spa on Maui.

"We called over to the hotel, had the concierge go to the spa and buy a bottle, put it in a cab, send it to the airport and put it on a flight to Kona. At the Kona airport we had it picked up in a cab and delivered here. We had it in her hands less than two hours after she asked for it."

Another guest had a thirst for an extremely rare vintage of Cristal Rose champagne. After many phone calls, the resort's head sommelier managed to track down two bottles in a private cellar on the Mainland and had them flown immediately to Kona. The guest was presented with one bottle and a note that said, "There's more where that came from."

These little extravagances, however, are not included in the price of the bungalow. The two bottles of Cristal, for example, cost the guest $1,600 apiece. But if you have such refined tastes that you can't stomach rotgut Dom Perignon, and are preposterously, unspeakably wealthy, this is what your life's like.

In the master bedroom, sliding wooden louver doors opened onto our private *lānai*. I walked outside to take stock of my domain. There was a private pool, twenty feet long, five feet deep and maintained at a perfect 86 degrees. Next to it was the Jacuzzi, heated around the clock to 102 degrees.

Beyond the swimming pool, our own private fishpond was carved out of black lava. As I admired the yellow tang, parrot fish, angel fish, mullets, and the official Hawaiian state fish known as—take a deep breath—the Humuhumunukunukuāpu'a, Michelle materialized with a plastic cup of fish food. I tossed in a small handful and watched the water boil with thrashing fins.

Michelle draped thick terrycloth towels on the two chaise lounges and oriented them toward the sun. Then she went inside and made a mai tai from scratch, squeezing the limes by hand. As I plopped down on one of the chaise lounges, she set the drink down on a table next to me along with a cordless phone. She showed me the speed-dial button I could use to summon her at any time.

"If there's anything you need—another mai tai, some iced tea, suntan lotion, whatever—just let me know," she said.

As Jeri climbed into the pool, Michelle held an air mattress for her. I gazed out beyond the fishpond to the white-sand beach, one of relatively few on this part of the Big Island. Perfectly formed waves were rolling in, and local surfers were zigzagging back and forth on the curls.

Every so often someone would wander down the beach and gape at me, probably wondering whether I was an over-the-hill rock star or a poorly groomed CEO. There was nothing I could do about it. All Hawaiian beaches are open to the public, a policy I strongly support—except at this very moment.

Some bungalow guests develop what Chillingworth calls "bungalow fever"—becoming hermits who never care to venture out of their pampered fortresses. They cocoon themselves in luxury, basting all day next to their private pools, watching humpback whales through their telescopes and having their butlers fetch them their meals from one of the resort's restaurants.

That evening, as Lani was serving our champagne and complimentary *pūpū* on the *lānai*—lobster nachos and Korean-style fern shoot salad with shrimp and swordfish—I inhaled the fragrant tropical night air and looked past the silhouetted palm trees to the moonlight dancing on the ocean. I tried to imprint the scene on my memory forever, knowing that all too soon our rental car would turn into a pumpkin and this little Cinderella fantasy would end.

Perhaps I was feeling the first twinges of bungalow fever. I yearned to stay here forever in my terrycloth robe, to wallow 24 hours a day in upper-crust excess, to have Michelle and Lani anticipate my every need. I began to work out a plan: I could use one of those marble tables to barricade the front door and strap some roadway flares together and claim to have a bomb.

I knew Jack Nicklaus, arriving for the Senior Skins event, was supposed to be moving into my bungalow as soon as I vacated. Tough tacos, Jack. Go ahead and call the SWAT team if you must. I'm not leaving. Ever.

San Francisco Examiner *Travel Editor John Flinn wanted to telecommute permanently from the Big Island but was unable to work out the details with the Hearst Corporation. He lives now in the often foggy coastal town of Pacifica south of San Francisco.*

⋆

A cloud of silvery minnows dashes past my mask, and as I turn my head to follow them, there he is—the green sea turtle. Though he is toothless and harmless and no more than three feet in length, he is frightening as he emerges from the gloom. His ancestors go back 200 million years to the earliest days of the dinosaurs, and he looks it. From his downturned beak and tiny eyes to the tail of his armored carapace, he is ugly—beautifully ugly. In contrast to the flighty fish, he moves with the ponderous grace of a brontosaurus. His flippers slowly paddle him on his unhurried way like the oars of a trolling fisherman. He seems the very embodiment of eternal serenity.

I kick and twist to get out of his path, but he pays me no notice and cruises past with implacable dignity. As I fall in behind him, his calmness is contagious. My heart slows, my arms sweep me along with little effort, and now I am one with him and 200 million years.

—Art Hoppe, "Swimming with Turtles," *San Francisco Chronicle*

DUSTIN W. LEAVITT

Tropic Bird

Living for the wind.

SO THERE WE WERE, ON A BOAT IN THE PACIFIC OCEAN, WITH hundreds—literally hundreds—of spinner dolphins all around us, leaping and spinning or just swimming by, just swimming by. We were off the Kona Coast of the Big Island of Hawai'i, and it was a good time for me. Two nights later, fishing in the same waters, we saw Mauna Loa erupt into the clouds, the rising column of molten stone like the fiery trunk of the tree of Time, and its reflection on the cloud canopy spreading and falling like the leaves of our days.

In 1984 I quit my job and went to Hawai'i to help my friend Tim expand upon a grand idea. The idea was about fishing, for which I had a fascination, and it was about sailing, for which I had a passion.

Tim was a champion of what we used to call "appropriate technology," the right tool for the job. In this instance, the right tool was a 56-foot sailing trimaran called *Tropic Bird*, which Tim had designed and built for the Hawaiian longline tuna fishery, believing that she could succeed economically where local powerboats were failing.

In 1955, the year I was born, estimated catch rates for Hawaiian longliners were only 0.03 fish per hook per day. By the 1980s, although methods had improved somewhat, many fishermen were suffering foreclosure upon their boats due to rising overhead costs and a concomitant decline in local fish stocks.

Tropic Bird, according to Tim, had an advantage over her competitors in that failure was taken into consideration when she was designed. Indeed, the ability to fail was one of her great strengths. She could, in other words, go fishing and catch nothing without grievous consequences because in theory it cost next to nothing to work her. She was a sailboat. She lived off the wind.

In the early '80s I was a young man, just beginning to understand the profundity of such a strength. I was also in love with that boat, upon which I would unabashedly lay my gaze like a hand, feeling with my eyes the sheer of her deck, the broad strength of her *ama*, like arms, the points of her three bows, purposefully aligned. I wanted to be like her, strong and resolute yet graceful, freely pursuing life on a broad reach, living off the wind…and for a time it was so.

Over a period of months following my arrival in Hawai'i, we prepared *Tropic Bird* for sea. She required new fishing gear. We built a new aluminum mainmast and converted her old mainmast into a new main boom. We installed reduction gear to improve her steerability and to dampen feedback from her great rudder. When all was ready, we scheduled a cruise around the Island to explore the fishing grounds and to test the new outfit.

On the chosen day we negotiated the treacherous 'Alenuihāhā Channel, that narrow funnel between Maui and the Big Island through which the trade winds squeeze from North to South Pacific, in the early hours of the morning when the wind was spanking. The dawn's early grayness had come alight with hot pearl-pinks and sweet, sherbety yellows and, as we rounded 'Upolu Point, the sea became blue and flat. *Tropic Bird* found her groove, I steered her on the offshore tack, with my bare feet on the big steel wheel as I sat backwards atop the wheelhouse, in the shade of a floppy hat, with one eye monitoring the trueness of our wake and my nose buried in a moldering paperback book.

The bright sun burned my back and a cool breeze sent waves

of gooseflesh racing over the landscape of my body like cloud shadows on a summer's day. The boat's mast hummed and her bows bit the blue Pacific, which stretched away for a thousand miles and a thousand miles again. Soon, on our starboard side, we passed Waipi'o Valley, settled by ancient Hawaiians on the Big Island's north coast. It is steep-sided and verdant. A cool, freshwater stream flows from a waterfall at the valley head through taro patches and then empties over a black-sand beach into the Pacific where we sometimes surfed at dawn with our friends. I remember sitting on the black beach, staring out to sea at the deep blue line on the horizon that marks the boundary between a perfect island existence and the deep, unknown ocean. How often from the purgatories of my life have I longed for that perfect existence, and yet how often have I also found myself seated in paradise longing for that deep blue line?

Tropic Bird was no glamour-girl, a hefty boat with a towering rise that would ship no sea and a breadth of beam that, while accommodating, would brook no foolishness from unruly winds. Yet light she was, and fast, and responsive to the faintest intimations from her wheel. She was built of plywood and epoxy, with aluminum fittings and spars. A 70-horse Ford diesel would push her along at ten knots, but under sail she was a goer. When in passage, with outriggers spread, she could troll for fast jacks and *mahi*, and under her main and a big genny she plowed the sea like a tractor.

Her bows held the lazarette, the chain locker, the sail locker, and a small machine shop. Behind the machine shop were the crew's quarters, two bunks and a table, and, below, two dry holds. Directly aft was a seven-ton fish hold accessed through a deck hatch. Then came the engine room, followed by the galley and mess. Above these were the wheelhouse and skipper's bunk and, in the stern, her cockpit fitted out with winches for the foresail sheets. Above her rudder post rose the radar mast. The *ama*, her two stabilizing hulls port and starboard, held miscellaneous stowage. Built into the spaces between were the fishing stations accommodating line bins, hydraulic line-pullers, and related gear. On her starboard side she had a hydraulic crane and shooter's tabernacle with its holstered rifle (a precaution against bringing aboard live sharks) and, forward of her mast, an electric windlass for hoisting anchor.

She was painted in two shades of green that, it must be admitted, were not entirely becoming. The locals considered her to be a bit of a folly until the first time we fished her, and she came through for us in a big way. Suddenly she was a respected workboat, color notwithstanding.

Artisanal longlining has been pursued in Hawai'i for many years. Its target species are tuna, billfish, and sharks, though others (hooked inadvertently, but welcomed with no less enthusiasm), such as *ono* and *mahimahi,* are also captured. A longline consists of a main line suspended horizontally, deep beneath the surface of the water, with multiple hook-bearing lines, or gangions, hung at intervals from it. It resembles a huge string curtain with baited ends through which one expects fish to swim, the probability increasing with the span of the set.

In the Hawaiian fishery, gangions and the buoy lines (from which the mainline was suspended, anchoring it to the surface periodically along its length) were typically attached to the mainline with connectors that looked rather like big safety pins. This system allowed the intervals between hooks to be varied depending upon fishing conditions and the habits of the target prey. Too many hooks on a line could be inefficient, considering the cost of baiting each one. And, if the gangions lay too close together they would inevitably become entangled when a lively fish was hooked, making recovery difficult at best.

In the early '80s, (depending upon the state of the market on any given day) a big tuna might have been worth a couple of thousand dollars to the boat. The only thing worse than losing a fish that had been insecurely hooked (or poached by sharks or pirates) was losing the expensive gear. Typically longliners employed radar to track their gear. However, in Hawai'i, where most fishermen could not afford expensive electronic tracking equipment, flags attached to the tops of tall bamboo poles were used for visual tracking. Thus, in Hawai'i, longlining was colloquially known as flaglining.

As a cheaper alternative to the gear-intensive flagline fishery, some Hawaiian fishermen pursued the *ika-sibi* fishery. *Ika-sibi* is a nighttime hand-line fishery peculiar to the Big Island, believed to have been initiated early in the century by Okinawans who immigrated to work the sugarcane fields. This fishery pursued *'ahi,* or yellowfin tuna, bigeye tuna, albacore, and in the process, squid.

The basic premise of the *ika-sibi* fishery was that since tuna like to eat squid, by attacting squid one will also attract and catch tuna. Tuna, like billfish, however, are primarily diurnal feeders and should be fished during daylight hours. The key to nighttime *ika-sibi* fishing is light. Light is used to attract squid, which draw tuna. Light also is used to catch the squid, which are then used to bait the tuna hooks. And light, in the form of cyalume sticks lashed to the leaders near hook and bait, attracts deepwater fish, even from a considerable distance.

Hand-lining for squid (or other small baitfish) using artificial illumination is called jigging. In Hawai'i one lowers a waterproofed 50-watt light bulb into the water and hangs another over the side from a small boom. Squid congregate within the pool of light, looking like pasta on a rolling boil. A squid hook is made of material that stores and emits light, from which eight barbless prongs rakishly protrude in a radiant pattern. In theory, squid do not bite the hook, but bodily attack it and are subsequently pierced by the needles. Gravity and the pressure of water prevents them from escaping as the lines are pulled in.

Hand-lining for tuna was less complicated than jigging squid. One simply baited a hook, threw it over the side, and then waited, the boat rolling on a darkling sea, a cool, wet wind caressing the face, the bright blade of heaven swinging above. The line itself was coiled down in a tub on deck, and to it was attached a buoy that would serve as a drogue to tire a hooked fish before it could take all the line. A restraining lanyard was also made fast to the line and then to a deck cleat. When a fish bit, the lanyard set the hook before parting with a crack like a pistol shot, the sound of which was the fisherman's first and only warning that his line was already half gone, zizzing and smoking over the side at impossible speeds. Tuna are amazingly fast and strong.

Small *'ahi* of less than 100 pounds were known locally as "rats." Large ones, which could approach 300 pounds, were fittingly called "gorillas." The capture of any fish never failed to arouse excitement on the boat, but of course one always hoped for gorillas.

Whenever we returned to the Kona Coast, sailing its deep, blue waters past its shoreline of black lava that reached up into the green mountains, we rediscovered a sense of belonging, of homecoming. These were our home grounds. On one such return, as familiar landmarks hove into view, we discussed making a last set before delivering our catch to the broker. We decided to set the longline at first light and, as darkness began to fall, we threw out the sea anchor some miles off Kailua-Kona and stood our watches by turns with its lights reflected in our eyes.

As morning broke, we tossed our first flag over the side and began our run under sail, barely making steerage way over the breathless water. We sailed directly offshore, paying out line as we went, Tim at the helm, as I snapped on leaders and buoys. Soon we noticed that the water ahead was ruffled by stray breezes and, when one took us, our hearts surged with the boat. It required three hours to set five miles of line—half our total gear.

The line set, we wore around to patrol it. Tim remained at the wheel while I prepared breakfast of toast, fish, *miso*, and yogurt. We checked the mainline periodically by hauling up a section of it to hold between our hands, feeling for the faint tugs that might indicate a fish on one of the hooks. Even over a distance of miles and a depth of many, many fathoms, a 300-pound tuna can be felt struggling in its captivity.

Buoys riding deep in the water or a pair of buoys bobbing close to each can signify a hooked fish below. When we had returned half the distance to our first flag, we noticed one such. Dousing sail, we drifted up to the buoy and captured it with the boat hook. I hauled in line, hand over hand, until I was able to secure the mainline over a deck cleat. Tim came forward and, lying on his stomach with his arms hanging over the side, held the mainline tentatively, as if weighing it with his hands. He stared out to sea, lifting first one hand, then the other, seeking a sign.

Then, in a voice that was barely a whisper, Tim spoke the word: *'ahi*. There was nothing more to be said. In perfect concord, we fell too. Tim started the engine to facilitate maneuvering, and I braced my barefeet against the deck and began the long, solid work of hauling the fish in.

Taking our best guess, we worked our way down the mainline, in the direction we believed the fish to be hooked, until we encountered the gangion that was taut and quivering. Drawing on leather gloves, I commenced hauling it in as Tim maneuvered the boat to prevent the fish from dragging the line under it, where it might entangle the centerboard or the screw. As the fish rose toward the surface, its sporadic struggles gained in power until its sudden lunges threatened to take my arms out by the roots. Giving line and then taking it back, I coaxed the fish in until it was possible to make out the hint of a shadow in the water, which gradually gained in substance as the fish rose until the distinctive coloration and pattern of a yellowfin tuna, swooping in figures of eight and long ellipses, became apparent.

I alternately gripped the deck with my toes and dug my heels in, on the verge of being toppled. I braced a foot and by inches dragged the tuna up until, in a sudden charge, its great head broached the air. Tim abandoned the wheel and leapt forward with the heavy gaff to secure the fish. With every ounce of his strength, he managed to pull its head out of the water, which was exploding in white chaos all around. Dropping the leader, I secured the fish with another gaff and, as I held the two gaffs, frantic with fatigue, Tim took the rifle from the shooter's station to his shoulder and fired one shot into the tuna's head.

Suddenly, everything was still. The water was calm. Small wavelets popped against the hull, the motor puttered in neutral. Our ears rang as in a vacuum, as if everything had been drawn up and away by a cyclone, the dry sucking at the bottom of a straw. We rigged out the crane and brought the big fish aboard—280 pounds of marketable flesh that turned the icy brine in the fish hold red as raspberry slush.

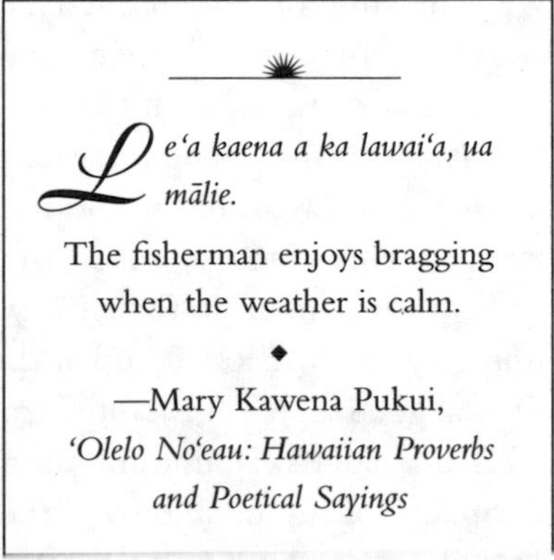

Le'a kaena a ka lawai'a, ua mālie.

The fisherman enjoys bragging when the weather is calm.

—Mary Kawena Pukui, *'Olelo No'eau: Hawaiian Proverbs and Poetical Sayings*

In the late afternoon we made port at Kailua-Kona, keeping company with Kona's sportfishing fleet of overpowered Fiberglas boats, all beer cans and Ray Bans, that roared through the approaches to the stone jetty, pushing mountains of water ahead of them like the chests of cock pigeons. With resounding farts from their engines, they sidled their backsides up to the dock and parked them, surrounded by crowds of onlookers waiting for billfish and tuna to be hoisted and weighed. Our approach, in the warm, low light of evening that illuminated the steep slope behind the town, was unassuming. Nevertheless, the big trimaran and its brown, salt-stained crewmen, orange buoys, armed shooter's tabernacle (we had forgotten to stow the rifle), crane, and hydraulic piping drew more than a few glances from the admirers of the marlin jockeys ashore.

Tim effected a perfect sideways docking, and I leapt ashore to tie up the boat. Looking up from our work, we found that an alarming number of the dock crowd had abandoned the sport boats to gather around *Tropic Bird.* The truck from our fish broker arrived, and we cracked the hatch and began to offload *'ahi*, marlin, *ono, mahimahi,* and enormous sharks. Fingers commenced to point and questions to fly. I believe the marlin boat skippers were livid.

Tim's girlfriend joined us with a picnic basket. We hung out for most of the evening, sitting on deck absorbed in the fisherman's preoccupation with untangling lines. We were briefly visited by the usual late-night denizens of the dock: drunk tourists, ex-professional triathletes, stoners, vague girls who wanted to join the crew, the police (we had overstayed our time limit at the dock). As we cast off and motored into the night, the crowd melted away with the aimlessness of amnesiacs.

A few miles offshore we threw out the sea anchor and slept through the rest of the night and into the morning. We rose to a bright, warm sun, a cool breeze, a blue sea, and hundreds of spinner dolphins cavorting around us for as far as the eye could see. We stripped and climbed down the stern ladder with skin-diving masks to join them in the clear water. Beneath the surface of that immense ocean, I looked up at the trimaran's three hulls, purposefully aligned. Small fish bolted from *ama* to *ama* in search of shelter and a bite to eat, nothing more. I turned my head and into the periphery of my mask moved the great, white blossom of the sea anchor, a parachute filled by the winds of the sea. Before it my friends swam, in dappled light, a man and a woman. And the same sea that embraced them embraced me.

Dustin Leavitt is a freelance writer and essayist who has most recently been researching indigenous boats in Southeast Asia.

⋆

In the absence of pottery, Hawaiian fishhooks exhibited sufficient temporal variation to render them as useful tools for seriation and relative dating, just as ceramics were used in other parts of the world.

Many distinctive features of the more elaborate forms can be tied to specific localities and to specific periods of time, which make them valuable in the tracing of ancient cultural movements and developments. Modern techniques of analysis endow prehistoric fishhooks with the power to draw knowledge from the past, much as the magic hooks of Polynesian demigods drew islands from the ocean depths.

—Patrick Vinton Kirch, *Feathered Gods and Fishhooks: An Introduction to Hawaiian Archaeology and Prehistory*

ROBERT STRAUSS

Honolulu Mamas

Who says you can't take your mothers to Hawai'i?

THEY SAID IT COULDN'T BE DONE. THAT GOING ON VACATION with my mother in Hawai'i would be a big mistake. Cooped up together there would be a good chance that the hard-fought calm between us would explode into corrosive flows of emotional lava.

I wasn't concerned. I didn't think we'd actually get to Hawai'i. For the last few years, as Mom closes in on 80, she has repeatedly voiced her interest in a series of improbable adventures that never came off.

"I'm thinking of studying Icelandic," she'll say to me on the phone from the East Coast. "Their epic storytelling fascinates me."

Or, she'll say, "You know what I'd like to do? I'd like to rent an RV and drive across the country."

I used to challenge her cruelly whenever she mentioned what I considered another preposterous notion. "What are you talking about?" I would have said. "You fall asleep behind the wheel on the way to the corner market. Now you're going to drive across the country in a Mini-Winnie?"

"Well, I'd like to," she'd say, her enthusiasm dampened. "If I could find someone to go with me."

Invariably, Mom begins our weekly telephone conversation

with, "Oh! You know who died?" It's her way of reminding me she's not going to be around forever, and that maybe I should pay more attention to her.

So when she said, for the sixth time, "You know what I'd really like to do?! I'd like to see Hawai'i," I realized that this was not another passing fancy.

Traveling anywhere with Mom is no carefree outing to the park. After 45 years in the frozen Northeast, she doesn't venture outside unless she has several layers of clothing, emergency food, and a snow shovel.

"What do you think the weather will be like in Hawai'i?" she asked. A decade ago I spent a summer in Hawai'i. That made me an expert on Island life.

"Snowy and cold," I told her, reverting to form.

"No, I'm serious," she said. "I want to know what clothes to bring."

"It'll be tropical and balmy," I told her.

"'Tropical and balmy?' What does that mean? Will I need a sweater?" she asked. "What about a raincoat?" As we discussed wardrobes, I saw storm clouds building off Waikīkī. I made a final attempt to discourage her.

"Mom," I said, "You don't like the sun. You don't like the beach. I can't see you taking up windsurfing. You don't even like swimming. I mean, you haven't gotten your hair wet since FDR was in office. Why do you want to go to Hawai'i?"

"I don't know why I want to go," she said, a tinge of anger rising in her voice. "I just know I want to see Hawai'i—while I'm alive!"

Cheap airline tickets and a free place to stay in Honolulu conspired to make Mom's dream a reality. After half a dozen telephone calls about the exact nature of "balmy and tropical weather," we were set to leave. "Guess what?" my wife said to me. "I mentioned the trip to my mother. She didn't exactly ask to be included, but I think she'd really like to go."

My wife and I had been married two years. Our mothers were conspiring to test our marriage.

"Would you like a peanut butter sandwich?" my mother asked

a few minutes after takeoff. She had been carrying them from the East Coast. "Just in case," as she likes to say. The jelly had already soaked through the bread and was clotting on the inside of the zip lock bag.

"No thanks," I told her. "They're going to be serving lunch in a few minutes." Besides, we had finished breakfast only 90 minutes earlier.

"I know," she said, "but I have to have something right now. I'm starved."

My mother has the metabolism of a lemming. If she doesn't eat continuously, she's likely to pass out. Her purse is always bursting with crackers, candy, gum, a few vintage sandwiches, and at least half a loaf of bread. In an ocean liner disaster, she will be the last one alive in the lifeboats.

Probably like everyone's mother, mine has a number of idiosyncrasies. To the outside world, they are endearing. "Your mother is just great," people say after having spent five minutes with Mom. But we were about to spend five days together. Five days of listening to Mom read all the street signs in Hawai'i out loud. Five days of watching her write mental notes in the air with her index finger and then erase them with a wipe of her hand. Five days of listening to her hum while she eats, watches television, and reads the paper.

I heard myself concocting justifiable homicide strategies to the judge. "Your Honor, I was becoming just like her," I would plead. But she was my mother. She wasn't getting any younger, as she often reminded me.

Five days. It was the least I could do.

I had no idea what we would do for five days. More importantly, I had no idea if our mothers would get along. My mother-in-law is a firebrand who marched through the streets of Berkeley in the sixties. At the slightest hint of any injustice done to anyone anywhere in the world, her first comment is likely to be, "The Bastards!" A piece of plastic litter blowing down the street will start her off on a crusade against the multinational petroleum companies ("The Bastards!"). On the plane to Hawai'i she insisted that we hang on to the sandwich bags and other plastic items for recycling on the Mainland. I still haven't found the courage to tell her that, on occasion, I have voted Republican.

My mother, on the other hand, can't stand confrontation. "It's a shame" or "Isn't that awful" or "Someone ought to look into that" are about the strongest comments she can muster about something like, for example, the Chernobyl disaster.

Mom has spent thousands of hours in the beauty salon. My wife's mother washes her own hair and leaves styling to the wind. She grew up eating spicy Middle-Eastern food. Anything more daring than a boiled chicken breast sends my mother to the gastroenterologist.

As the plane approached Honolulu, this family vacation in Hawai'i was looking more and more like a tsunami about to wash ashore.

The balmy and tropical weather I promised my mother turned out to be a tropical depression. Mom's hair was under assault before we left the airport. She quickly produced one of those hair protectors that begins about the size of a stick of gum and unfolds into a protective shield of hideously unattractive plastic. I'm told stores will not sell these to women under 65 years of age.

To escape the slashing, cold rain, we went to the IMAX theater in Waikīkī. *Circle of Fire,* a film about the movement of the tectonic plates of the Pacific Rim, was playing. On the enormous screen, mountaintops were exploding, earthquakes were reducing cities to rubble, rivers of lava flowed from red-hot fissures into the ocean which erupted into scalding columns of steam. The theater rumbled with Surround Sound. I looked over at Mom. Her head was thrown back. Her mouth was wide open. She was dead asleep.

"Wasn't that something?" she said as the credits came up. "I've never seen anything like that. That was great."

"You know why they let seniors into the movies two for one?" I said to my wife. "Because they figure that together two of them might see the entire movie."

The next day the weather at last turned balmy and tropical.

"What would you like to do?" I asked. I had told our mothers and my wife to get some travel books and research O'ahu's many sights. I didn't want to be responsible for everyone's entertainment. "I don't know," they each said. "What do you recommend?" We began our first of several circumnavigations of O'ahu.

Since our mothers come from the opposite ends of the political activism spectrum, spelling and pronunciation were items they could discuss right away without much potential for rancor. Every street sign, every advertisement, became a pronunciation challenge. It was a reverse spelling bee—in Hawaiian.

"K-a-l-a-k-a-u-a," Mom would spell out. "How do you say that?" she would ask from the back seat as though I were the Magnum P. I. of Hawaiian pronunciation.

"I think these names are very musical," my mother-in-law added. "Ka-me-ha-me-ha," she sang out with the trill of a tropical song bird.

"Kai-lu-ah-oo-ah," my mother chirped back.

My wife and I exchanged sideways glances of each other. This back and forth tweet-tweeting went on for the next four days.

Food was another area of noncontroversial common ground. One day we passed a store that had dried beans on sale. After spelling out and pronouncing the name of the shopping center ("Ha-wa-eee-Ka-ee" my mother-in-law yodeled), my mother commented, "We really don't have enough beans in our diet."

Reacting as though my Mom had just come up with the formula for world peace, my mother-in-law said, "You're right! And why not? They're delicious."

"And easy to fix."

"And inexpensive."

My mother then lowered her voice, as though she were about to reveal the details of a particularly sinister conspiracy, and said, "What I don't understand is why people don't eat more lentils. I love lentils."

"Yes, they have been ignored."

I looked at my wife. She was clenching her stomach, squeezing her eyes, her face frozen in a pained grimace beyond laughter. She either had to let go or we would have to come up with a good explanation for Avis.

"What about lima beans?" I asked of the back seat. "Why don't they get more attention? Or favas?"

"I've never understood that either," my mother said.

"There ought to be equal opportunity for beans," my mother-in-law said. A shriek sliced through the car. Tears streamed down my wife's face.

We did just about everything one could do in Hawai'i without getting wet or having one's hair blown out of place. Bit by bit Mom loosened up. At a roadside stand she tried some papaya. We went out for Japanese food. I ordered the chicken with *udon* noodles in *miso* for her, thinking that was about as close to boiled chicken breast as the Japanese got. It wasn't close enough. The next morning she was at our bedroom door. "Robert," she said, clutching her stomach with one hand and the door jamb with the other, "I need some bread."

"Now?" I asked. "It's quarter to seven."

"Now," she told me.

At Safeway she tore into a loaf of Italian white bread. The color came back to her face. She was restored.

As we drove around O'ahu, my mother-in-law exclaimed over every flowering shrub and tree. "Oh, look at that one," she said. "And that one. Oh my goodness, who can imagine such colors." Like a frenzied Hollywood fan at the Oscars, she tapped my mother on the shoulder at every new sighting. "Did you see that?" she would say having spotted another banyan or plumeria. "Did you see that?"—tap, tap, tap.

"Lovely," my mother answered. "Robert, can you find a store? I'd like to get some bread."

"Mom, what is it with you and bread? Are you worried that Hawai'i is going to run out of flour? We've got three loaves at the house."

"I'd just like to have some bread in the car," she would say, her voice a bit more forceful.

"But Mom," I'd begin again before feeling my wife poke me in the ribs, a reminder that it was easier to stop for bread than to uncover my mother's incessant need for it.

One day, driving along O'ahu's North Shore, I spotted a fisherman poised with his net on the rocks just above the surf. There is tremendous skill involved in tossing a net out in a perfect circle. I thought "the ladies," as we had begun to call our mothers, might like to see it.

For half an hour the fisherman didn't move. He peered into the surf and waited. And waited. And we waited. I don't exactly recall how the following conversation got started, but it went something like this.

"It's very sad," my twice-widowed mother said.

"What's that?" my divorced mother-in-law asked.

"When people are alone."

"Yes, it is sad."

"You know who it's particularly sad for? Gay men."

"Yes, you're right. And also for fishermen."

"That's true. Fishermen do have lonely lives."

"Do you suppose a lot of fishermen are gay?"

"Yes, I've heard that also."

"Isn't it terrible? They spend all that time by themselves, on the boat, and then they can't find anyone."

"It's sad to be alone. But to be a gay fisherman and alone, that is really very sad."

"You're right. Oh look!"

A pickup truck had pulled up on the side of the road. A single man got out. He went down on the rocks to confer with the fisherman. He stood there waiting, and watching, with the fisherman.

"Do you think that's his boyfriend?"

"I hope so. He looks very nice."

"And he's so patient. I think they're very happy together."

"Me too."

I looked at my wife. For the umpteenth time she was about to pee in her pants. I turned to the back seat.

"You know," I said, "I don't think that people really appreciate just how difficult life is for gay Hawaiian fishermen."

"No, they don't," the ladies chimed in from the back seat. There was a squeal from the seat next to me. The passenger door flew open and my wife raced out of the car holding her belly.

It took a bit of persuasion, but a day later I got the ladies out to Hanauma Bay, O'ahu's marine park and popular snorkeling spot. I don't think either had had her face in saltwater for many, many years.

"No way my Mom is going to do this," I told my wife.

"You're always underestimating her," she said.

"Well, she's not getting her hair wet, I'll tell you that."

"Wanna bet?"

We led the ladies out into the water by the hand.

"Now don't let go of my hand," Mom said. Although she was very careful not to get her hair wet she did stick her mask in the water to look around. We were lucky. Moorish idols, coronet fish, all kinds of wrasses and puffers swam right up to the ladies. It wasn't clear who was more enchanted: the ladies or the fish.

I was surprised by my mother's adventurousness. But after four days of wind, rain, and sun, her hair was a mess. The Aqua-Net force field that had protected her hair for as long as I can remember had failed her.

"I really should get a touch-up," she said looking in the car mirror.

"Don't worry, dear," my mother-in-law said, "We'll fix it at home." I sensed a smirk growing across my wife's face.

"You think so, dear?" my mother responded. On day four, the ladies had taken to calling each other "dear."

We dropped them at the house and went to the store for more bread. Mom wanted two loaves even though we had only 24 hours left in Hawai'i.

When we returned to the house, I heard light-hearted humming coming from the bathroom. "That looks lovely, dear," I heard my mother say.

"What's going on?" I asked.

"Nina's mom washed and set my hair," my mother said, her hair up in rollers.

"You washed your hair?!"

"Sure, why not?" my mother-in-law said. "You think she's allergic to shampoo?"

"HA!" my wife shrieked. "You owe me a hundred dollars."

"A hundred dollars? For what?" my mother asked.

"He bet me a hundred dollars you wouldn't wash your own hair."

"A hundred dollars! I don't believe it."

"Oh, yes," my wife said, her hand opening and closing in my direction. "Pay up."

Hearing about our wager, my mother broke up completely. She reached out for the sink, afraid she might topple off the toilet she was laughing so hard.

Tears began to fall. In my 40 years I had never seen this. "A hundred dollars. Oh my, oh my." The moment her hysteria began to fall to a girlish giggle she would look at me and break up again. "A hundred dollars." I couldn't believe it. She couldn't believe it.

The next day we set out for the airport three hours ahead of departure. Mom wanted to get there in plenty of time. Having spent most of her life traveling in and out of the Northeast, she must have been worried about a freak snowstorm.

"Well, I just want you all to know I had a wonderful time," she said.

"Thank you."

"Me too," my mother-in-law added. "This was great."

"I'm glad you enjoyed it," I told them. "Only two more hours till we leave."

The trip I had dreaded and now found myself enjoying was about to end. Neither of the ladies had learned to hula or surf but my wife and I had been hysterical most of the time. Turns out our aging mothers were stand-up comediennes. We were their straight men.

"Anyone hungry?" Mom asked as she puttered around in her purse. "I've still got a few peanut butter sandwiches. Let's not waste them."

We chewed our way through the week-old PB&Js in silence.

My mother-in-law gathered up the plastic sandwich bags for recycling on the Mainland.

"You know what I'm thinking, dear?" Mom finally said. "I've been thinking about a trip to Sicily next year."

"Ooohhh," my mother-in-law said, "That could be lovely, dear. You know the Italians have the most wonderful bread."

"I've heard that, too," my mother responded. "And some lovely trees."

My wife put her lips next to my ear. "Think they have any gay fishermen in Sicily?" she whispered.

"I don't know," I told her. "But it might be fun to find out."

Robert Strauss is the author of more than three dozen television documentaries and has worked as a management consultant in more than 50 countries. His articles have appeared in the Chicago Tribune *and* Saveur. *This Hawaiian piece recently won a Lowell Thomas award. He claims his favorite part of traveling is when the doors to the plane are closed for takeoff and everything is out of his hands.*

⋆

Two double-strength Tylenol at two o'clock in the morning, but my right cheek would not stop throbbing. The sound of the Pacific waves lapping a sandy shore and the splendid moonlit silhouette of Diamond Head on the eastern horizon didn't help a bit.

Who ya gonna call? I called the front desk. Call DOC, they said. The Doctors on Call van picked me up at the hotel door ten minutes later and whisked me five blocks away to their office. Armed with a diagnosis of an abcessed tooth, the phone number of a recommended dentist, and a fistful of pills, I was driven back to my hotel, then mercifully I fell asleep.

The next morning, I called the dentist. "Come over at eleven," he said. So I hopped aboard the Waikīkī Trolley to find his office. After about half an hour, the trolley driver came to tell me that we weren't going to make my dental appointment on time. If my face could have fallen further, it would have.

"So I'm going to abandon my regular route and take you directly there," he continued. Wait a minute! A random act of kindness here amid the crass commercialism of one of the busiest tourist areas on earth? The spirit of aloha lives on. I felt better already.

The dentist did a partial root canal to relieve the pressure and allow me to enjoy the rest of my week in Hawai'i. I felt so much better that I walked all the way back to my hotel.

I bounced down to the beach to the outrigger canoe in front of the Outrigger Hotel, and signed up for an hour's ride. Captain Eddy, an aging but fit bronzed beachboy, directed the paddling. "Paddle fast!" he yelled. "Now!" And the crest of a big wave picked up our big canoe and carried us swiftly shoreward. We paddled out again and rode two more waves back to shore.

What a fine day it was! Lunch on the terrace overlooking the ocean, a leisurely hike up to Diamond Head, a half-hour massage at poolside, and at sundown, double rainbows. Can life get much better than this? Toothache? What toothache?

—Carol Baker, "Hawai'i Calls"

HANK WESSELMAN

Spiritwalker

A visiting anthropologist learns firsthand that Hawai'i's mana *is real.*

ON THE DAY I FOUND THE *PŌHAKU* [STONE] AWASH IN THE WAVES, I had carried it into the old Hawaiian village and placed it under the tamarind tree just beyond the pond. There it remained for several months, visited daily by me and the children on our nature walk while I slowly established a relationship with it. I do not know why I did this. I just did.

One day the time seemed right, and I invoked the stone's spirit in my stone-moving ritual, asking its permission to bring it away from its beach and to my home. Its strong agreement flowed into me in response. I did not wish to be seen taking it from the site, so I arrived at the beach early the next morning before anyone was there and carried the stone to my car. When I got home, I placed it near my front door in the rock garden among the other beach stones. There it sat for a while, untouched. It had made its first voyage, however, from the wild place of its origin into the world of human beings in my Volkswagen van.

The curious bond between us continued to develop. The bond was not merely my thrill at possessing an object for which I felt attraction. The linkage involved a process between myself and the stone. My first hesitant attempts at dialogue were necessarily experimental, but I had an ongoing moment-to-moment awareness of presence. In the beginning I simply let my attention rest upon it meditatively while thoughts and feelings related to it moved through my mind. As the thoughts and feelings took on recurrent patterns, my personal awareness of it deepened.

One night the stone came to me in my dreaming, and upon awakening I saw it in my mind's eye in its completed form. I got up, went out to the stone, and asked its permission to sculpt it. I felt a strong, positive reaction, so that afternoon, I carried it to the tree stump I used as a base for sculpting. With bush hammers, I did a minimum of reducing of the "chin." A little chisel work brought out the "mouth," and it was done. Most of the stone remained untouched, just as I had found it.

I then replaced the *pōhaku* with its attendant sculptures in the rock garden, staring east toward the summit of the volcano of which it was a part. In my thoughts, I addressed it as Kapōhakuki'ihele—the stone that journeys. And as the stone's first custodian—or *kahu*-elect—I too would have ordinary and non-ordinary journeys and discoveries in everyday reality.

Soon after I rendered the stone, late in 1987, I attended a conference held at the Keauhou Beach Hotel, on the coast near Kailua-Kona, an insiders' affair put on by Hawaiians to honor the knowledge and achievements of their Polynesian ancestors. As an outsider, I was fortunate to have been invited—it was the efforts of a curator-photographer friend working at the Kona Historical Society Museum that got me an invitation. The conference was well attended by an interesting gathering of people, most of whom were of Polynesian descent. Professor Rubellite Kawena Johnson of the University of Hawai'i spoke about the *heiau* and about the Hawaiian gods and ceremonies. Hawaiian elders Papa Kala Nali'i'elua and David Mauna Roy spoke about the traditional Hawaiian world view and the intimate connection between Hawaiian culture and the land. They described the Hawaiians' respect for nature and how the Polynesians had taken care of the land, seeking harmony with it so that it would take care of them.

They spoke of the Hawaiian concept of spiritual unity with their *'aumakua*, their ancestral spirits, and how life and *mana* came out of everything in nature.

Another session was held by four crew members of the now-famous double-hulled voyaging canoe *Hōkūle'a*. This 60-foot re-creation of a traditional Hawaiian transoceanic sailing vessel has completed many round trips between Hawai'i and Tahiti, as well as a long voyage to New Zealand and back. The *haku* of the canoe, Captain Shorty Bertelmann, was there, as was the watch captain, Tava Taupu. Sam Ka'ai spoke strongly about the place of the sailing canoe in traditional Hawaiian society and revealed that the ancient Order of the Canoe was being reformed to "refill the bowl with what had been lost."…

A trim, handsome young man of Hawaiian descent was introduced. His name is Nainoa Thompson, the first Hawaiian in more than six centuries to navigate a great sailing canoe over the vast oceanic expanses of Polynesia without modern-day instruments. The respect and the awe in which this man is held is great. As navigator of the canoe, he is the most important crew member, the one into whose care the success of the voyage and the lives of all the voyagers are entrusted. He is the wayfinder. I had never heard him before that moment.

Partially trained by a traditional Micronesian navigator named Mau Piailug, Nainoa Thompson rediscovered the ancient Polynesian navigational system that used the stars, moon, clouds, winds, ocean swells, and currents. He re-created the way-finding method that had brought his ancestors to Hawai'i in several waves of migration, beginning around A.D. 300.

Nainoa Thompson spoke in a soft voice about his voyages and his ancestors and about harmony. He spoke with integrity, with power, and with humility—and he never mentioned himself. He talked about the canoe and the crew, the ocean and the heavens. All of these became one, he said, balanced and unified during the voyage. He suggested that this unity was the goal and the success of the journey—a goal in which each person was as important as everyone else.

The Hawaiians in the audience were misty-eyed with pride of him and, through him, for themselves. The *mana* generated by their collective emotion was palpable in the room.

After his talk I waited for an opportunity to approach him. We shook hands and exchanged pleasantries.... I wondered what moved through his mind and through his dreaming as he guided the double-hulled canoe across the vast expanses of the watery world. I wondered what it would be like to be out there with him. What would my own dreams produce under those circumstances?...

The last session at the conference was conducted by a Hawaiian healer, a *kahuna lapa'au* named Morrnah Nalamaku Simeona, who shared her knowledge and skill in *ho'opono'ono*, the traditional Hawaiian method of conflict resolution.

She spoke of the unity and balance of life and how everything in life begins with thought and intention. She discussed the three levels of being—the physical, the mental, and the spiritual—as they are conceived within traditional Hawaiian spiritual knowledge. She spoke of how these three aspects are

> Modern Hawaiians have continued to voyage in double-hulled canoes, including the *Hawai'i Loa*—a vessel made as much as possible of traditional materials, but also equipped with high-tech equipment, such as a satellite link that allowed the crew to talk with Hawaiian school classes daily.
>
> Over the years the voyagers have sailed not only to Tahiti but also to the Northwest and to the South Pacific: the Marquesas (believed the source of Hawai'i's original Polynesian settlers) and back, encountering the same sailing conditions the ancients would have faced, the Cook Islands, and elsewhere in Polynesia. In each place, the canoe and crew inspired a surge of efforts to recapture local culture, lost under the influence of conquering Westerners, and voyagers from other islands began to join the Hawaiians on their journeys.
>
> ◆
>
> —RC & MC

manifested within human beings: the spiritual as the superconscious mind or *'aumakua*, the mental as the conscious mind or *'uhane*, the physical as a material form, the body, and a nonmaterial form, the subconscious mind or *'unihipili*.

These concepts are not unique to Hawaiian culture and are well known to Western psychology, but hearing Morrnah Simeona's talk made me want to know more about Hawaiian shamanism and the body of knowledge called *Ho'omana*, or Hawaiian mysticism.

After her talk I politely asked her to clarify a point she had made about healing. She gave me a curious look and then reached out, took my hand in both of hers and closed her eyes. Long moments passed. Then she smiled and looked at me again, her alert gaze boring into mine and asked me if I knew what aloha really meant. "It means to be in the presence of the divinity," she explained. "*Alo* means 'to be in the presence of' and *ha* is 'the divine breath of life'—alo-haaa." She paused as if to see the effect of her words.

"Problems always begin in the mind, in the mental aspect," she continued. "Physical and psychological problems have their source in negative thought-forms. Illness is an effect of these distorted thoughts. Unfavorable thoughts arise in the conscious mind and are then held in the subconscious from which they can be transferred into the physical body. Because of this, true healing always has to begin at the spiritual level.

"One must ask the divinity for help. Then the divinity sends down its *ha* through one's *'aumakua* level of self. From one's spiritual aspect, it travels into the subconscious level of the physical. This deep level of the mind can then erase the negative thought-forms and emotions it holds, such as anger and fear, replacing them with light. This is how the cause of illness is dealt with and how all true healing is accomplished."

She smiled again and released my hand. Someone else asked her a question, but for long moments her gaze remained locked with mine as she looked into my soul. I do not know what she saw there, but she nodded slightly and beamed warmly at me before turning away.

I remained rooted to the spot while the crowd surged around me like water around a rock. I felt something within my body—something that had flowed from her to me during those brief moments. I recognized it as the sensation of power. I realized that I had received *mana* from her, transmitted through her touch. I felt something deep within me open in response. The sensation remained there, just below the surface, throughout the rest of the day.

This experience marked the beginning of my investigation into *Ho'omana.*

Hank Wesselman is a professional anthropologist who taught courses in anthropology for the University of California at San Diego and the University of Hawai'i at Hilo. He and his family divide their time between Northern California, where he teaches anthropology at American College and Sierra College, and Hawai'i, where they own and work a small farm. This article was excerpted from his book, Spiritwalker: Messages from the Future.

*

"Yes, the *kahu* exist," my friend told me. They are guardians, keepers of the sacred places, the burial caves of the *ali'i,* the temples of old. Almost always they are old people, in areas not easily reached. They may live as farmers or fishermen but they also live a greater responsibility."

"How can you tell who they are?" I asked him.

"Usually it is an old man sitting alone," he says. "He has finished his work of homage, cleaning the sacred place, and he is sitting by himself after his labor. He may even be chanting, but silently. Most times he will be neatly dressed, in respect—this old man sitting by himself in a field, a lonely place."

"How does one talk to him?" I wanted to know.

"Quietly, pleasantly, with no show, no anxiety," he answered. "And you must never fold arms or hold your hands behind your back or place them on your hips. These are signs of arrogance and disrespect, even if not meant to be. An old one speaks a great deal with his hands and his eyes. The movements of fingers will have meaning to him. It is best to stand with hands hung by the thighs. And you must never ask direct questions. Talk of other things, other places. One must deal in metaphors, it is the only way. When he talks you must be aware of the obliqueness of his reference. It is his nature to talk around, beneath, and over a theme. This must be interpreted. Mention of trees elsewhere means trees in his land. Stones, clouds, fish, people, objects become clues to other meanings. Subtleties will emerge and understandings will be reached. You will be allowed to glance through the door of being Hawaiian—if you are deemed worthy."

Many *haole* never have this experience. Their minds are too cluttered with tidiness, too well-ordered with education. They are too lacking in poetry and too obvious in such poverty, and the Hawaiian knows it and his mind is forever decisioned about you.

—Ed Sheehan, "The Kahu" *The Hawaiians*

SHIRLEY STRESHINSKY

In Praise of Lipstick Red Convertibles

Why rent a dull car when you can cruise the Big Island in style?

SOME PEOPLE DRIVE FOR THE FLAT-OUT FUN OF IT, OTHERS DRIVE to get from here to there. I fall into the latter category; a reliable machine that will not break down on the San Francisco-Oakland Bay Bridge is all I ask for, along with a radio with both AM and FM. The last car I can remember having a crush on was pink, had mini fins, and the Beach Boys sang a song about it ("Fun, Fun, Fun"). Some of us never forget that under all that sleek metal wrapping, beyond all the heavy-breathing advertisements, is a basic machine whose primary purpose is transportation.

Except: when I set foot on the Big Island of Hawai'i, where the preternatural happens more or less regularly, I undergo an astonishing transformation. Even before I collect my baggage at the Keāhole Kona airport, I march straight to the rental car hut to see if they have saved the lipstick red Mustang convertible I have requested. This past spring I had to make do with a Neon, its fluorescent red almost making up for the fact that the top doesn't come down.

Those first moments are a ritual. If the convertible cover is up, I put it down, or I roll down all the windows. Then I slip into the seat, wriggle a few times to make sure it fits properly. Move the seat forward. Position the mirror. Touch, ever so lightly, the steering wheel, run my fingertips around the rim of it, sigh. I turn off the radio, so it doesn't blast out at me and trash the mood. Then I snap on the seat belt. Turn on the engine, take one more test wiggle of the seat to make sure it's snug, hitch my skirt over my knees, and ease into gear. Together again after all these months, the red car and I slip slowly, as one, out of the parking lot and merge effortlessly onto the rim road that will carry us to the highway and north along the Kohala Coast.

My virgin exploration of the Big Island was in 1986. Afterwards I wrote that this largest in the Hawaiian chain is "big" in another, more oblique sense: "It is as if the Island has surged up from the sea bottom like some gigantic whale, breaking through to the surface rather gently, with you clinging to its broad flank, alone and altogether small in the grand scale of things. I felt it most while driving the two-lane blacktop that cuts straight and true through the lava beds that crust the Kohala Coast, with nothing in the rear view mirror and nothing ahead, mountains on one side and ocean on the other, all windows down and the trade winds blowing; it is a fine, swelling emptiness. Exhilarating. Big."

I remember my hair blowing in the warm wind, my sandaled foot on the gas pedal, the music echoing out over the volcanic wastelands; it was like floating on the rim of the world. On that first trip I drove all around the Island on the circle road—called, in various of its stretches, Queen Ka'ahumanu Highway, the Hawai'i Belt Road or Māmalahoa Highway.

Someone told me that if I should happen to come across an old woman carrying a child, I should be sure to offer her a ride because it almost certainly would be Pele, the goddess of the volcano and the most important and powerful goddess in Hawai'i. (Not so surprising, since she's the one who created all the volcanoes, and it was the volcanoes brewing up from the ocean bed that created the Islands.) Several people repeated riveting stories about Pele which they had heard from a cousin of a friend, or someone's uncle's brother-in-law. The stories were variations on a theme: An old woman would appear on the roadside, she would be offered a ride, and when the car or the truck broke down, the old woman would say "try again," and the engine would turn over right away and they would drive off.

I drove back roads, always with an eye out for Pele, debating what I really would do should I come upon an old woman walking alongside the empty road.

Happily ensconced in my bright red cars (even when they were gray or blue), I found another Hawai'i—open, empty, full of sky and unending ocean. With the windows down, I could hear the rustle of the trade winds whispering through the cane fields, or smell the freshest of air sweetened with *pīkake* or ginger. I fell into a rhythm with the car, moving with the lurching or changing of gears as we climbed, knowing that soon I would have a view from a thousand feet or so above the sea.

Every year I returned to the Big Island, and every time I tried out a new road. I remember certain stretches with perfect clarity. The Chain of Craters Road, south from the Kīlauea Caldera, cuts through a moonscape that is terrible and wondrous. The topographic map I always carry with me is marked with volcano notations (1969–1974 flows, 1986–1993 flows, etc.). For the past dozen years, Pele has played havoc in this area, cutting off the road. With an almost continuous display of fireworks, she has rearranged the landscape.

I might have been on another planet altogether when I drove up the Kohala Mountain Road in the middle of a perfect morning, blue skies up above filled with billowing clouds and the local Hilo station doing a Beatles retrospective. "Lucy in the Sky with Diamonds" blasted on; I sang along as I sailed under the lacy shade of the ironwood trees, feeling fine. No reason, just the car beneath me, the sky above, and the music.

Another day, another year, I came down the Belt Road from Waimea and at Saddle Road Junction, turned onto the Saddle Road, a two-lane blacktop which crosses the Island and gets rough as it reaches the center before heading down into Hilo. But I was only going about six miles to Waiki'i Ranch, a calm section of the road. It was a long, slow easy climb through open fields strewn

Hawaiians of the Big Island have a knack for the gracious gesture, the natural kindness. Recognizing that *haole*, or non-Hawaiiians, are plagued with a childlike inabilty to understand that time goes on forever, the Islanders combat the impatience of Mainland visitors with their own consummate patience and humor.

Even as I left Waipi'o, I was confronted by this. Flying down the road in my rental car, I rounded a bend and encountered a very slow cane truck. An older Hawaiian man sat in a comfortable half-doze in the rear. Through shuttered eyes, he watched my car weaving and bobbing, raring for an opportunity to pass. He smiled at my *haole*ness, gestured with his hands to slow down, be cool, then pointed right to indicate the truck would be turning anyway. I stopped weaving, smiled back, and waved at him. As the truck turned away, he blew me a farewell kiss. Friends forever. Aloha.

◆

—K. M. Kostyal,
"The Far Side of Paradise: Hawai'i's Big Island," *Islands*

with boulders, the detritus of old volcanoes and cacti; here and there cattle grazed. This is, still, ranch country. But it was the sweep of the land that transfixed me. I could imagine myself in the clouds above, watching a lone red automobile moving slowly up the rise of the land, rolling along in perfect sync with the empty road. On that trip I was staying in a bed and breakfast in the mountain town of Waimea; returning that day, the car and I sailed along in sunshine though I could see rain falling in wafting sheets over the town in the distance. Soon rainbows, one and then another, overarching, guided me home.

A couple of years ago, I realized that section of the Belt Road that runs from Kailua-Kona north along the Kohala Coast had become crowded at almost any time of the day, and I was never going to have it all to myself again. So I headed even farther north to check out Highway 270 (also called the Akoni Pule Highway) along the Kawaihae Coast. I went fairly early in the morning, and to my relief the road was as empty and as beckoning as it always had been. I was settling into the drive, thinking about nothing in particular, when I spotted it offshore—an island of sorts. But a crazy island, all patched and put together with what seemed to be metal plates, very weird. Enough to make me pull over to have a closer look. A small boat was nuzzling up to this apparition, otherwise there seemed to be no activity at all. I puzzled over it all the way to Hāwī, had a cup of coffee, then came back, down Highway 250 on the Kohala Mountain Road. I turned on the radio, remembering "Lucy in the Sky with Diamonds," but instead I got the Mākaha Sons—Moon, John, and Jerome—singing *Ke Alaula*. Hawaiian magic; on the road again, and all was still right.

When I returned to my hotel, I stopped to ask the concierge if she knew anything about the strange island I had spotted, and half expected her to offer some mystical explanation. She only laughed. "Hollywood," she said. "Kevin Costner built that island for his movie *Waterworld*." The last time I drove that road, it was gone.

Next time I go to the Big Island, I have designs on a route that has so far eluded me: the South Point Road leading to Ka Lae, the southernmost spot in the United States. I've been hesitating because nearby, at Mahana Bay, is a green-sand beach I ache to see, but to get there I will need a four-wheel-drive. This is a move that will take me into another realm, require a leap of faith. Still, I find myself wondering if four-wheel-drive vehicles come in lipstick red.

Shirley Streshinsky is the author of Gift of the Golden Mountain, *a historic novel set in Hawai'i, and* I Alone Survived, *which became a television movie. She lives in Northern California with her photojournalist husband Ted and frequently writes about Hawai'i for newspapers and magazines.*

*

The history of Hawai'i is condensed here, at the end of eleven miles of bad road that peters out at Kaulana Bay, in the lee of a jagged, black-lava promontory—the tail end of the United States.

This Plymouth Rock of Hawai'i, where the first Polynesians are believed to have arrived in seagoing canoes, probably from the Marquesas or

Tahiti, around A.D. 500, is a kind of open-faced midden, littered by layers of stuff left by successive conquerors. There are old Japanese truck farms, abandoned World War II military barracks, a deserted Pacific Missile Tracking site, a Mitsubishi wind farm (with 38 spinning propellers), rusty junk cars made in Detroit, and herds of fat cattle on leasehold land held by descendants of New England missionaries. Amid the debris on this windswept point stands a reminder of the lost kingdom, a poignant sculpture of a Hawaiian man bound in chains.

No historic marker marks the spot or gives any clue as to the significance of the place. If you walk out to the very tip, beware the big waves that lash the shore. The nearest continental landfall is Antarctica, 7,500 miles away. Bold 500-foot cliffs stand against the blue sea to the west and shelter the old fishing village of Wai'ahukini, which was born in A.D. 750 and lasted until the 1860s. Ancient canoe moorings, shelter caves, and *heiau* poke through wind-blown grass. The east coast curves inland to reveal a lonely green-sand beach, a world-famous anomaly that's accessible by foot or four-wheel drive. For most, the only reason to venture down to the southern tip of Hawai'i, of the United States, is to say you did.

—Rick Carroll, *Frommer's Hawai'i*

NYLA FUJII-BABB

Afternoon at Lake Waiau

Here's a malady you'd never expect to encounter in the tropics.

MAUNA KEA ON THE BIG ISLAND IS THE HOME OF POLI'AHU, THE snow goddess of Hawaiian mythology. Her white cloak of snow covers the summit at 13,786 feet, for more than four months of the year, from November through March. Certainly not the traditional picture of Hawai'i's tropical paradise.

More than 600 feet below the summit, nestled in the crater of Pu'u Waiau cinder cone, a scant half-mile hike from the Observatory Road, lies a small sacred lake, the highest freshwater lake in the United States. Its name, Waiau, means swirling waters. It is also the name of another Hawaiian snow goddess whose story is now lost in antiquity. The lake is 400 feet across and can be 15 to 40 feet deep depending on the amount of runoff from the rain and melting snows.

In late August, my husband and I, who live almost at sea level on the Island of O'ahu, parked our rental four-wheel drive at the 12.5 mile post on Observatory Road which marks the beginning of a trail. The dirt and cinder track winds between two cinder cones, sloping steeply upward on the flank of one cone and over fractured lava rocks that cooled and cracked against a wall of glacial ice, thousands of years ago. A few hundred yards below the crest of the trail, in the center of Pu'u Waiau cinder cone, is a placid lake—its water the color of coffee and cream.

We were experienced hikers, having trekked the mountain trails of O'ahu over the years. It took us only twenty minutes to reach the lake, though we did notice that we were panting and gasping for air as we climbed up the slope to the rim of Pu'u Waiau. We stood at the top of the rise for a moment, catching our breaths, before descending into the crater.

> *Poli'ahu, ka wahine kapa hau anu o Mauna Kea*
>
> Poli'ahu, the woman who wears the snow mantle of Mauna Kea.
>
> Poli'ahu is the goddess of snows; her home is on Mauna Kea.
>
> ◆
>
> —Mary Kawena Pukui, *'Ōlelo No'eau: Hawaiian Proverbs & Poetical Sayings*

Walled in by the sides of the cinder cone, we were the only people in this small, secluded hollow. The air at the edge of the lake was still and warm. No breeze rippled the surface. The only sound was the faint noise of tiny flying insects, soaring and banking, barely breaking the glassy stillness of the water.

The lake was rimmed with small, hardy plants and a few puff-ball weeds. There was no trail around the lake, and piles of large broken boulders formed a barrier on the left bank. My husband had decided to explore around the lake going off toward the right. I was feeling a little light-headed. Everything had a soft, dreamlike quality about it as if the air shimmered and was colored a muted yellow. I climbed the barrier of rocks to the left and found a large boulder shaped like a natural stone throne at the very edge of the water. I sat down to wait and fell deeply asleep.

I do not know how much time had passed. Perhaps 30 minutes to an hour later, my husband climbed over the rocks and sat down nearby to wake me. For a moment, I was disoriented and didn't remember where we were.

We sat for a while longer, blowing puff-ball weeds into the air, watching the snowlike seeds dot the calm surface of the lake. Then as the midafternoon sun began to sink and the air turn cold, we decided we'd best head back to the jeep.

I cannot remember much about the hike back, except that it felt as if we were in slow-motion. Confused and light-headed, I could not walk more than five or ten steps without gasping for air and stopping to rest. My husband kept pushing me along, telling me not to sit down but to keep moving, even if only a few steps at a time. What should have been a fifteen-minute downhill walk took well over an hour.

For a couple days afterward, we suffered headaches and frequent bouts of sleepiness. At the bed and breakfast where we were staying in Waimea, our host informed us that we were the victims of altitude sickness, the type of decompression illness suffered by explorers in the Himalayas. My husband's symptoms were less severe since his constant activity at the top of the mountain kept him breathing deeply and his blood well-oxygenated.

I had made the mistake of falling asleep. My breathing, while asleep, was too shallow to get enough oxygen to my bloodstream. I had slept beside the deceptively gentle and calm solitude of Lake Waiau and awakened to find that Hawaiian snow goddesses, like Pele, goddess of the volcano, require a price to be paid for ignorance and carelessness.

Nyla Fujii-Babb is one of Hawai'i's best known storytellers. She works as a librarian in Honolulu.

*

Hawai'i's waterfall pools are idyllic but freshwater lakes, ponds, or marshes are rare, curious delights if you can find them—and I have—in a Maui cloud forest, near Mauna Ke'a's snow-capped summit, and beside a trafficky O'ahu highway.

I can spit across Lake Violet, a heartache blue puddle dotted by red dragonflies in a jade green cloud forest. Anywhere else this dollop of a pond wouldn't rate a second look, but up on the boggy slopes of 5,871-foot-high Pu'u Kukui in the West Maui Mountains, it's a rare find.

Only a few hikers can visit Lake Violet on this still *kapu* mountain, which, according to legend, marked the intersection of heaven and earth. Now part of Kapalua Nature Preserve, Pu'u Kukui is one of the last unspoiled upland forests and the second wettest spot on the planet. It rained 654.83 inches in 1982—that's 54 1/2 feet! You would think Lake Violet would be bigger.

High atop Mauna Ke'a, the highest mountain in the Pacific Ocean, Lake Waiau is the only glacial lake in the tropics—and a great mystery. Although it sits in porous lava, where there are no natural springs, and only fifteen inches of rain a year, the lake never dries up. Nobody quite knows why, although scientists suspect the lake may be replenished by melted snow trickling in via underground lava tubes.

My favorite freshwater hole, Kawai Nui, (Hawaiian for "the big water"), is slowly disappearing. Once a bay, now a marsh, soon to be a silted plain, Hawai'i's largest body of fresh water is now a congestion of cattails and water hyacinths hard by windward Oahu's Highway 61. Thousands of Honolulu-bound commuters pass by twice daily, little realizing that the 750-acre wetlands that separates Kailua from Kāne'ohe once was a prehistoric fishpond where Hawaiians raised mullet and grew taro.

—RC

BABS HARRISON

Spirit of the Lodge

If you lose yourself in Hawai'i,
you may find yourself.

PEOPLE ASK ME WHAT I FOUND IN THE TWO YEARS I LIVED IN Hawai'i, and I have to say I found myself. Those same people say you shouldn't run from something, but to something, and I know that now. But back then I was just running away.

I moved to Hawai'i, the most isolated archipelago in the world, when I was escaping a stagnant marriage and an ongoing estrangement from my family. The New Mexico desert, where I had lived practically in isolation the previous five years, had not been a form of meditation, but rather self-immolation in a harsh and dry terrain that mirrored my closed heart.

Raised on the traditional WASP track, I had found little meaning in that culture and steered away by breaking off an engagement to a Dallas lawyer three days before the wedding. Later I crossed the Sahara on a two-month, two-person expedition with a man I hardly knew, and married him.

For a while we lived only for good food and better wine, and passionate romance in ancient cities, and we roamed the globe with laptops in tow. But once we settled down, the reality was not the dream. I felt myself running away again.

Carl Jung thought the root of human evil was "the refusal to meet the shadow," the dark side we each know is lurking inside us but don't want to face. I had not become Satan incarnate, but I did have unresolved issues of loss and betrayal buried deep down, which I steadfastly refused to acknowledge. It was just easier to change the scenery.

I flew alone across the vast Pacific to Honolulu and settled into a new home, a new job, a new life. I traveled lightly, checking my mental baggage and carrying with me the few personal belongings that still mattered. The seductive isolation of a tropical island was not overrated.

By the time my husband came six weeks later, I knew the state of our marriage was terribly wrong. I knew it the day he arrived. I was at the quarantine facility visiting my Abyssinian cat (victim of a required quarantine to protect the state against rabies). I begrudgingly left the facility before visiting hours were over and sped to the airport. But I was still an hour late. He was sitting on the curb with all his luggage piled around him. I said hello, opened the trunk, and got back in the car.

We tried to make light of it—taking in the postcard-perfect scenery, looking at colorful surfers instead of each other, drinking potent mai tais among honeymooners on the beach. But we could not become close again. We slept, each facing our own wall of disillusionment.

He was unhappy in Hawai'i, unable to find a job at 53; I was approaching life's excruciating midpoint of 40, wondering who I was outside of a suffocating marriage, and just how it got this bad. Did I have enough guts to change it, end it, or would I remain encamped forever on the outskirts of my own marriage, a spectator to a losing battle?

Hawai'i became the battleground, but it was not the relationship I was fighting for, it was me. And I ended up running to the very thing I was running from—love.

As much as I tried to isolate myself in Hawai'i, I became enveloped by that terminally Hawaiian concept known as aloha. While the tourist aloha of plastic *lei* and forced *lū'au* frivolity is a marketing concept, the real spirit of aloha is a way of life in the

Islands. Aloha is the standard greeting for hello or good-bye, but it also means love. "Live aloha" is a popular bumper sticker in Hawai'i, and it means to love, be generous of spirit, and care for the land and each other. The concept is extended unconditionally to visitors such as myself.

In the spirit of aloha, I was hugged and kissed, often by people I did not know. With the slightest excuse for celebration, I was included as part of the *'ohana*, or family, and ornamented with flowers in my hair and garlands around my neck. At outdoor concerts where I would try to lose myself in a crowd on the lawn, whomever I was sitting next to would offer me some of their food, water, or a blanket to take the chill off the evening trade winds blowing in from the ocean. During mango season, I was offered more ripe fruit than I had eaten in my entire life. Often, I would never see these people again, and so their openness and gentle caring struck me all the more.

The Islanders also had a pride in their homeland, and delighted in sharing its beauty. We dove in gin-clear water to see a fan of black coral growing at a depth of 80 feet, rode horses into a rain forest to see rare ferns, and hiked up into the clouds to pick wild guava. Slowly, I began to let go of grief and celebrate life.

My work carried me frequently to Lāna'i, an Island with much aloha and one of the most remote islands in the world. There is no instrument landing system on Lāna'i, so if the pilot cannot see the airport runway, there is no chance of landing.

When the tiny plane does land—and you must sit on the port side for the best view incoming and starboard outgoing—it parallels the length of the Island, past steep cliffs that rush straight down to the pounding ocean; then it skims the brilliantly hued red dirt and green fields and glides onto the short runway. Lāna'i is the only place I've been where the airline worker welcomes me back with a hug each time he sees me walk from the tarmac into the small airport.

This 141-square-mile Island, once planted with 20,000 acres of pineapple, bears not a single traffic light nor fast-food franchise. The first ATM was recently installed in the ambitiously named village of Lāna'i City, whose town square is surrounded by shops supplied weekly by a barge that arrives from Honolulu. Everyone knows the Haägen-Dazs shipment arrives on Thursday, which gives it a shelf life of about two hours before being sold out.

Lāna'i City is home to 2,000 residents, most of whom are of Filipino descent. The older ones came to "pick pine" and work in the fields when pineapple was king. They live in brightly painted wooden plantation-style houses with tin roofs and riotous vegetation in their front yards. There is no need to lock doors. They have abundant family and fertile gardens, they "talk story" and lead simple lives. They have nothing. They have everything.

Once known as the Pineapple Island, Lāna'i now tends two luxury resorts, the Lodge at Kō'ele and Mānele Bay Hotel, lauded among the best in the world. I was headed to the former, an upcountry lodge exuding quiet elegance, gourmet food, and more orchids than Kew Gardens.

I would be leaving Hawai'i soon, and I had come to sleep with the ghosts.

It had been reported by several female guests that ghosts occupied a particular room at the Lodge. The guests claim to have felt their presence and one even saw the ghost's face. The general manager had also received reports from housekeeping—one maid said she had been bitten.

Skeptical, I demanded the

I always smile at the anxious faces of first-time visitors to Lāna'i who look about the Magritte-like landscape for palm trees, tropical flowers, or any of the usual island icons. Instead: pine trees, mud-spattered pickup trucks, cute Filipino girls in blue jeans, sweatshirts, and cowboy boots. I arrived once in hunting season to see a trophy deer, its red tongue hanging, splayed over a rusty Jeep hood.

Lāna'i sits in the middle of the inhabited Hawaiian chain, in sight of every major Island except Kaua'i, yet I always feel removed in time and place. Heartland. Iowa of the Pacific.

◆

—Rick Carroll,
Spirit of Aloha Magazine

---

very same room for my one night on the Island. It was empty and I was given the key. "You can't think about them, or they won't come," said Kurt Matsumoto, general manager. "And they come only at night."

No sweat. I enjoyed dinner—seared wild venison from the Island and some heady red wine, then returned to my room. Once under the sheets, I turned out the lights. A raging silence, then some small noises. I poked my head out from the covers and saw, somewhat to my relief, nothing. I hid farther down under the Belgian cotton sheets and realized I was scared. Even worse, I was wide awake.

I must have drifted off to sleep because I was jarred awake by the buzzing of the alarm clock. I had not set the alarm, so I assumed it must have been set by the previous guest. But it was midnight. The first plane off the Island leaves at 6 a.m., and the airport is a mere ten minutes away. Why would anyone set the alarm for 12:00? Goose bumps—what locals call "chicken skin"—began to appear.

I got out of bed, sheepishly looking around corners and behind doors on my way to the bathroom. I was cold as ice. This is Upcountry Hawai'i, and it is normal to have a chill in the air, but this was definitely polar. I crept back into bed, turned off the lights, and shut my eyes tight. What happened next, I don't know how to describe.

What I remember is this: There was something in bed with me, on either side of me, and whatever it was, it was pushing me from both sides, as if to move me out of the bed. Each time it pushed, I felt something, an energy, pass through my body. I recall being half-awakened each time it happened during the course of the early morning, and each time my consciousness said, "It's only the ghosts, they're passing through." Whether it was a reality or a dream, it's what happened that night.

Legend has it that the son of the god Māui had been banished to the Island of Lāna'i, a land filled with terrible spirits, for misbehaving. But he triumphed over the spirits and built a bonfire as a sign to the gods of his success, and he was welcomed back home.

I left Hawai'i for San Francisco a few days later. During the next month, a string of unexpected events occurred. Doors once shut tightly to me began to slowly crack open. I reconnected with my parents after a seven-year absence. A book contract was accepted. I was finally becoming myself.

It's as if the ghosts were crying, "Don't go back to sleep." After two years of living in Hawai'i, I had learned not only that I could love myself by giving love in the smallest of ways, and to complete strangers, but I also learned the Zen principle known as *Nori Koerui*—to ride out your problem rather than avoid it, because it is better to go through the pain than run from it.

Hawai'i did not teach me how to love, heal, or free the soul. Hawai'i simply taught me how to be.

Born in the city of Texarkana, Babs Harrison remembers wanting to travel virtually as soon as she figured out where she was. In the years since, she's called everywhere from Honolulu to Santa Fe home. She lives in San Francisco and claims she no longer sleeps with ghosts. Her recent books include Kitschy Cocktails: Lucious Libations for the Swinger Set *and* Kitschy Canapes: Finger Foods for the Swinger Set.

⋆

In the early 1940s, Pele was seen on Lāna'i by my husband, Roy Fujie. She was all in white and rode on a fiery horse with her white dog running beside it. She came down Ninth Avenue from the Hotel Lāna'i, crossed Lāna'i Avenue, and headed toward Fraser Avenue and the Catholic Church. Roy heard the clippity-clop of the horse's hooves, but the horse with Pele and her dog seemed to fly or float through the air. He had just finished his night shift at the powerhouse there, so he thought he was just imagining all this in the early morning moonlight.

In the late 1950s, Roy was the night shift supervisor (*luna*) for the pineapple pickers in the farthest fields to the southwest of Lāna'i Plantation when Pele again appeared. She was all in white, a little old lady with her white dog on the dirt road. Roy stopped his pickup truck to offer her a ride, but she only asked for a cigarette. So he reached into his glove compartment and got a fresh new cigarette and lit it with his own to give it to her. But she wasn't there when he offered it to her.

When there was a radio news report about the rumblings of an imminent eruption at Kīlauea Volcano, Roy went to visit his two brothers, Ken and Megu, in Hilo and went to Halema'uma'u Crater. There was a boatload of tourists off the *Lurline* that morning at 9:30. They were all very disappointed because nothing was happening.

So Roy took a fresh cigarette from his shirt pocket, lit it, and threw it into the caldera saying, "Here, Pele, you did not take the cigarette I offered you on Lāna'i, so now please puff on this today." Then in full confidence he told the tourists around him that Pele would surely erupt that night. To his great joy and luck, Pele did blow up that very evening at 9:30. The *Lurline* crowd came back to thank Roy, whom they recognized as the fellow in a *lauhala* hat with a *kolohala* feather *lei* who had offered Pele a cigarette and asked her to puff that day.

—Helen Fujie, "Roy & Pele"

MAXINE HONG KINGSTON

Chinaman's Hat

Little islands afford a special, private perspective.

LIVING ON AN ISLAND, I MISS DRIVING, SETTING OUT AT DAWN AND ending up five or six hundred miles away—Mexico—at nightfall. Instead, we spin around and around a perimeter like a racetrack.

On drives along the windward side of O'ahu, I like looking out at the ocean and seeing the pointed Island offshore, not much bigger than a couple of houses—Mokoli'i Island, but nobody calls it that. I had a shock when I first heard it called Chinaman's Hat. That's what it looks like, all right, a crown and a brim on the water.

I did not call it Chinaman's Hat, and no one else calls it Mokoli'i Island, so for a long time, I didn't call it anything. "Chinaman's Hat," people say to visitors, "because it looks just like a Chinaman's hat. See?"

Although I don't swim very well, I ventured out to Chinaman's Hat three times. The first time, we waited until low tide to walk as far as we could. The other times we snorkeled, which is like flying; the moment your face enters clear water, you become a flying creature.

Schools of fish—zebra fish, rainbow fish, red fish—curve with the currents, swim alongside and away. Balloon fish puff out their porcupine quills. We hovered in perfect suspension; flew over spring forests and winter forests. No sound but my own breathing. Sometimes we entered blind spots, darkness, where the sand churned up gray fog, the sun behind clouds. Then I had to lift my head out of the water to see and not be afraid.

Then we were walking among the palm trees and bushes that we had seen from O'ahu. Under those bushes, large white birds nest on the ground. We hurried to the unseen side of the Island, the other face of the moon.

The ocean side is less green but wonderful in its variety. We found a cave, a tiny pirate's cove with a lick of ocean going in and out of it; a strip of beach made of fine yellow sand; a blowhole; brown and lavender cowry shells; black live crabs and red dead crabs, a lava rock shelf with tide pools as warm as baths. Lying in a tide pool, I saw nothing but sky and black rock; the ocean spit cold now and again.

The air of Hawai'i breathes warm on the skin; when it blows, I seem to turn into wind, too, and start to blow away. Maybe I can swim because the water is so comfortable. I melt into it and let it carry me like the fish and the frigate birds that make the currents visible. There is a rending. The soul leaks out to mix with the air, the skin in an osmotic membrane.

These Islands fool human beings into thinking they are safe. On our second trip to Chinaman's Hat, there was a Hawaiian and his son camping under the ledge by the palm trees. They had a boat and meat hooks and liver for catching sharks.

The third time we rowed a boat out there, our children sitting on the outrigger to weigh it down on the water. A cleft in the hill-side made a shelter for building a fire to get warm after swimming; at sunset, we cooked and ate fish the men had speared. We were climbing down to the boat, holding on to the face of the land in the dark, when a howling like wolves, like ghosts, came rising out of the Island. "Birds," somebody said. "The wind," said someone else. But the air was still and the high, clear sound wound like a ribbon around the Island. It was, I know it, the Island, the voice of the Island.

We all heard it, the voice of our Island singing.

Maxine Hong Kingston also contributed "A Sea Worry" in Part One.

✶

You can see them from almost anywhere in the Islands, the *'iwa*, the frigate birds, sailing home at dusk. They pause and float over the town, harbors, quiet beaches—as if reluctant to leave the sea. And when I see them I must pause too, for they enrapture with a grace disguising banditry. Against an orange sky of twilight, they are sharp, ominous ink-scratches, thin, hard creatures with long-boned wings and forked tails.

For long days they sail under searing sun over far waters, hooked beaks dipped, yellow eyes staring. They watch for the flying *mālolo*, the darting tuna, diving to snatch them from above wave tops. And when this fails they are bullies and robbers, cruelly tearing the food from other seabirds. But they are a loveliness, going home—hovering in a slow-motion ballet, a reversed retribution. They return to nestings high on mountainsides to feed their screeching young and to rest.

All through the days their talons do not touch water. For if they do, the birds cannot escape, and will die.

—Gavin Daws and Ed Sheehan, *The Hawaiians*

LINDA KEPHART FLYNN

Sail of a Lifetime

Will you?

THE DAY BEFORE THE FOURTH OF JULY, MIKE DECIDED TO GIVE UP his independence. He boarded his 21-foot Newport sloop at the Ala Wai Boat Harbor, raised the sails aloft, and proceeded up the coast toward Honolulu Harbor. He sailed past the surfers on their glistening boards, past the rocky breakwater where fishermen hunkered down for the day's catch, until he was out in the rough ocean waters. His journey was a blustery one, as strong winds tossed the small craft in choppy seas. Mike pressed on, determined to make a rendezvous in Honolulu Harbor.

Since small boats weren't normally allowed in the busy shipping thoroughfare at Honolulu Harbor, Mike had called ahead for permission to enter. The officials there had instructed him to use a cellular phone, an unusual accoutrement in 1990, to notify them when he was at the harbor mouth. As the little green sailboat approached, oceangoing cargo ships transporting everything from automobiles to zippers churned the waters. Mike skirted the floating behemoths and hauled up a new sail he'd had made especially for this day. The sea spray dampened his hair, and he smiled to himself in the warm Hawai'i sun.

At the time, I was sitting in an open-air, harborfront restaurant, having lunch with my friend Elsa. We were deep in conversation, enjoying our crisp Caesar salads as the ocean breeze ruffled the towering palms in the café courtyard and blew in on our second-floor table. In midsentence, it seems, Elsa pointed out to the harbor, and exclaimed, "Look at that little boat!"

I glanced briefly in the direction she indicated, but turned back to our conversation. She was, after all, explaining how she planned to handle some enormous change in her personal life. I attempted to resume the conversation.

She tried to finish the topic, but finally gave it up entirely. "It's Mike!" she cried, imploring me with her eyes to look toward the tiny boat picking its way between the commercial vessels in the harbor.

It was indeed Mike, tacking through the turbulent waters, attempting to approach the restaurant where we were dining. As he came alongside the pier, the lettering on his sail grew visible. Finally, we could see that it read, "Linda, Will You Sail to the Aisle with Me?"

I sat and stared, not comprehending.

Mike tacked back in the opposite direction, holding up a small sign that read, "Yes?"

I still stared.

Then back again with a different sign, "No?"

Yet again, he tacked, with a third sign, "Maybe?"

The fourth time, he stood up in the boat and raised his arms, palms up, as if to say, "Well?"

Elsa couldn't stand it anymore. "Aren't you going to answer him?"

She was right; what was I thinking? My Prince Charming was proposing right here on a balmy Thursday in Honolulu, smitten by the tropical magic we'd openly acknowledged for years. So I stood up and hollered, "Yes!"

The entire aerie, both floors packed with downtown lunch-time diners, broke into applause. I ran down to greet Mike, who was finally landing his boat at the restaurant's dock. As he stepped out, he handed me a dozen red roses and kissed me, again to the accompanying whoops from the crowd behind us. We went back upstairs, where Elsa and her husband Clarence had ordered a bottle of champagne for the celebration.

After numerous toasts and retelling of the story with friends who gathered, we finally had to disband. It had been a heady afternoon, but Mike had to sail the boat back to Waikīkī, and I had to return to my fourth-floor office across the street. I was prepared to bask in the postproposal afterglow all afternoon.

A few minutes after I settled in at my desk, though, a co-worker came in and said, "Mike just called and said for you to go to the window."

I did as he'd requested and looked out toward the ocean. There, as the little boat made its way out of the mouth of Honolulu Harbor and into the ocean for its return voyage down the coast, Mike had hauled up a brand new sail. It simply read, "Yes!"

Linda Kephart Flynn married her creative sailor eight months later. The pair, now a writing team in Kansas City, Missouri, frequently travel back to Hawai'i to recapture the magic on that tiny green boat.

✶

Our friends Jim and Berit from Carmel Valley, California, came often to Hawai'i to see us, falling more in love with the place each time—and apparently with each other as well, because they decided to get married in the Islands.

It was to be a surprise to her parents, who long ago had given up any notion of a wedding between these two. The elders also loved Hawai'i, had a romantic Islands tie of their own dating to 1941—when he arrived for an architectural project in early December and she was to follow to be his bride, until Pearl Harbor intervened. They married later elsewhere, but our friends thought they would like to see their youngest daughter wed in Honolulu.

The four of them planned an October vacation visit, while we made the secret wedding plans—official papers, traditional *lei*, lunch for six at the Royal Hawaiian—and most important, an appointment with the right judge. We chose Judge Thomas Kaulukukui Jr., revered and Hawaiian with a wonderfully musical name for our nervous friends to conquer pronouncing.

The day arrived, and so did the jet from California. We could barely contain our excitement in the crowded pink restaurant. When Jim worked up the courage to blurt out the wedding plan and seek their blessing, both parents just sat there in disbelief.

Later, we were ushered into Judge's chambers. He was a slight dark-haired man who looked too young to be judicial. But he was wise beyond his years. He disarmed us all right away with an old Hawaiian saying:

"Marriage," he said, "is like a canoe in the ocean. In order to get anywhere, you must work together. Someone's got to paddle. Someone's got to bail. And sometimes it may seem like everyone's bailing."

We have a photo from that day a decade ago, our friends draped with *lei*, happily stunned. We know they exchanged vows and kisses as we and her parents stood witness—but all any of us remembers is the imaginary canoe, careening through the waves. We ask sometimes who's paddling.

"Everyone's still bailing," laughs the bride.

—RC & MC

EMILY ACKLES

Learning Curve

How (and when) a haole *becomes local.*

I WATCHED THE GECKOS SCURRY ACROSS HILO AIRPORT'S TILE floor. The airline had lost my luggage, so I was arriving without a change of clothes. Or a place to sleep. Not an ideal start to my year in paradise.

One afternoon five years before, I had looked through the Seattle Yellow Pages for tap dance lessons, but "hula," listed before "tap," had caught my eye first. One week later I met Likolani for my first lesson. She taught us more than how to wiggle our hips. We read Hawaiian legends and learned the stories of Kamehameha, Kalākaua, and Liliʻuokalani, the royalty about whom we danced.

During my senior year of high school, Liko took us to Hawaiʻi to watch the Merrie Monarch Festival hula competition, and I was entranced by the hours of chanting and dancing.

Back home, I began planning for a year-long stay in Hilo. Friends warned me not to expect a warm Islands welcome. ("They hate all *haole*.") But even if no one spoke to me, I figured I could always take Hawaiian studies classes at the university. And if no hula teacher would accept me, the Parks and Recreation Department had to offer lessons. Somehow, I would experience Hawaiʻi.

And now, after a couple of days in a Hilo hotel, here I was helping the friend of a friend of a friend load my newly found luggage in her Jeep.

Denise Kenoi's Boston accent surprised me, because I knew she had lived in Hilo since marrying a Hawaiian fifteen years ago. With her two young sons, Lopaki and Pikai, we headed for their Keaukaha home. On the way Lopaka practiced his ukulele, and Pikai sang a Hawaiian song. I felt as if I were driving straight into the heart of the Hawaiian community.

To own a lot in Keaukaha, Denise explained, you had to prove Hawaiian ancestry. Lopaka and Pikai were in the pioneering Hawaiian immersion program at the local elementary school taught entirely in Hawaiian. The Kenois took me in, and as the days passed, they quickly and completely immersed me in local Hawaiian culture.

And did I have culture shock! No one warned me they speak a different language in Hawai'i—not Hawaiian, but pidgin. One morning soon after I arrived, I answered the phone. Before I could finish: "Hello, Kenoi residence," I heard "Uncle Pusstay."

"Excuse me?"

"Uncle Pus stay home?" the voice said more slowly.

"No," I answered, still unsure of the question or if it even was a question.

"Tell him Sammy boy wen' phone." And the line went dead. I stood for a few moments, trying to figure out exactly what message I was responsible for relaying.

Although I couldn't manage a phone call yet, I was learning other things. I knew that "grinds" meant food, to *'au'au* was to bathe, and "da kine" could mean anything the speaker wanted it to. I asked for *shoyu*, not soy sauce, to top the sticky white rice served at every meal. I never, ever entered a house with my shoes on, but instead left my rubber slippers at the door.

I did commit some social faux pas—arriving at friends' homes without hostess gifts; forgetting to immediately offer a meal to visitors in our home. Look, listen, don't ask questions, Liko taught me, but often I just couldn't act carefully enough. I lay in bed at night, listening to the pounding rain and drowning in my failures of the day. No matter how intently I watched, I would always be a *malihini*, a stranger.

One morning Denise's husband Dennis woke me at 5:30 to help bring in some fishing nets set the night before. As we walked down to the water, I recognized black *'opihi* suctioned to the hard lava just where the waves hit. (Although my local friends loved *'opihi*, I could not bear to scrape the warm limpet out of its shell and eat it raw.) We waded knee-deep in the Pacific, Dennis, surefooted after years of balancing against the waves, me, slipping and scraping my knees as I tried to keep up. When he handed me the net, I held it far from my body, wary of the crab trapped in it. Dennis collected a second net, with another crab and a lobster, and we walked back to the shore.

At home Denise boiled the crabs and lobster for breakfast, as Dennis cleaned and rolled the net. The family and I ate the fresh seafood at a picnic table, while neighbor children walked to the school across the street. When Lopaka finished eating, I followed him to the edge of the road to hear him and his classmates chant in Hawaiian their daily request to enter the classroom. A friend of Lopaka's bicycled by, but he paused, startled, when he saw my blond hair and white skin.

"Who that?" he asked.

Lopaka looked at me, then answered. "She my sister."

Warm in the morning sun, I smiled at my Hawaiian brother.

Emily Ackles began studying hula while in high school near Seattle, Washington. She later found that a year studying in Hilo, Hawaii, was a great way to escape the southern white male ethos of Davidson College in North Carolina. She currently lives in the Bronx, New York, and with her roommates and neighbors from the Dominican Republic, dreams of moving again to warmer climes with beautiful beaches.

*

Fresh off the plane, ringed by a plumeria *lei*, heading for Baggage Claim, you overhear a conversation between two local girls:

"Da kine wuz *huhu* cuz he wen stay ovah deah li 'dat! Wot she tink? Da buggah nevah like go wit' her!"

"Fo real? Humbug da guy!"

Welcome to the colorful world of pidgin, the local style of speaking in da Islands, brah. It's the patois first invented by the Chinese to do business; in fact, pidgin is short for bidness, Chinese-style. It was polished with some Japanese syntax and sprinkled with Hawaiian words, although the vocabulary is mostly English. It's not unknown to other Americans, thanks to those Hawaiian World War II heroes known as the 442nd Battalion whose motto was: Go Fo' Broke! Only Hawai'i has made it a daily part of linguistics, a quick expressive mode of speech. It's da kine talk, li' dat. 'Eh, fo real, brah. (better believe it!).

Basic Pidgin Vocabulary

'owzit!: contraction for "How is it?"—a common greeting.

wen': verb, "I wen' go beach."

da kine: the good kind, the type most popular.

try wait: instead of "wait a minute."

laters: short for "see you later," or "good-bye."

shaka, brah: a form of agreement, accompanied by a single shake of the hand with thumb and little finger extended.

mo bettah: a comparative phrase, meaning best, i.e.: "da kine guide book mo bettah."

'ono: Hawaiian word meaning tasty or delicious, usually applied to food, i.e., "Dis Maui potato chip *'ono*."

chance 'um: take a chance, go for it.

stink eye: disapproval, a dirty look, i.e., "Da *wahine* wen' bump my car door, I geev her one stink eye."

—Rick Carroll, *Great Outdoor Adventures of Hawai'i.*

ANNA JOHNSON

Phallic Rock

Sleep here at your peril!

IT'S EASY TO MAKE LIGHT OF MOLOKA'I'S DARK LEGENDS, ITS sexual spells, its moonlight hula dances meant for the gods. After seeing the Phallic Rock, you'll take Moloka'i more seriously.

I went to Moloka'i on the strength of exotic rumors. I was told something about transsexual cabarets, ancient fertility rocks, spiritual power, Wild West architecture, and the consumption of dogs. Like Paul Gauguin, I suffered from a voyeuristic appetite for taboo in the tropics. Pale and overanxious to appear culturally sensitive, I arrived on Moloka'i without a clue.

Instead of hibiscus-scented humidity, the air was dry and fiercely hot under an electric blue sky. I took a taxi west and saw bright red earth sparsely dotted with thorny trees. A sign wedged into a levee of roadside mud read, ALOHA. SLOW DOWN! THIS IS MOLOKA'I.

Upon my arrival at the Kaluako'i Resort, the women behind the counter, the gardeners and even the guys driving the golf buggies across the windswept links appeared to be moving in a cloud of ether. The immediate atmosphere was laconic and secretive, as if every man, woman, and child were laughing inwardly at a joke

I didn't get. When my waitress Lorna forgot the salad dressing, she simply put one hand on her hip and one on my shoulder and smiled. When she brought it, she told me about Moloka'i and the media: "The BBC came to do this program *Rough Guide.* They did this story about the hula festival and teenage pregnancies, and they interviewed lots of girls I know. When I saw it, I thought, 'How embarrassing!'"

"To have a baby under age?" I wondered. "No, no," Lorna said, giggling. "Just to go on TV."

Almost in the same breath she told me to visit the Phallic Rock, the sacred stone known for fertility. "Sleep there and you got a baby, that's for sure!" Stupidly, I laughed.

I could absorb stories of spiritual emanations and pantheist faith as folklore, at least. I had read that the prayers of the *kahuna* were not to be trifled with. One government superintendent, I was told, took a sacred altar stone from near Kalawao in an attempt to install it as a patio table. The stone broke neatly in half, and the superintendent died shortly thereafter of an unspecified malady.

One of Moloka'i's poetic names is *Moloka'i, Pule O'o,* which means literally, "Moloka'i of the Powerful Prayer." Invaders were kept at bay for centuries on the strength of the *mana* exuding from every rock, tree, and shrub. Where a thick mango plantation now knots Mapulehu, a 300-foot-long *heiau* (a pre-Christian Hawaiian temple) was once visible from Maui. Before ironwood trees were planted around the Phallic Rock, it could be seen for miles. Before the *kiawe* trees were planted at the water's edge, locals would make love on the beach. Before the *mu'umu'u* covered the body neck to ankle, there was bare flesh.

The next day, while taking The Nature Conservancy's hike at Mo'omomi Preserve, I met a photographer from Kaua'i. She told me she was visiting Moloka'i to scout advertising locations for Toyota. She was tan, muscled, and hardened by the wind and sun. Surely she was immune to fertility spells? Her face went dark when I asked. "Last time I was in Moloka'i," she said, "I was pregnant within two days of visiting that rock, and I hadn't even ovulated."

Anna Johnson wrote this story for Condé Nast Traveler *and lives in Australia.*

*

I met the dead of Hālawa Valley in broad daylight. My first skeleton was huddled under a house platform a little way up the talus slope. As I brushed away loose dirt with a whisk broom, the shape sprang out at me: a child crouched in the earth like an ancient bird about to spread its bony, orange-stained wings and fly.

We recorded the pathetic remains and covered them with a flannel rag weighed down with lava rocks. When the whole platform had been excavated and photographed, the dirt would be filled in again with the bones remaining in situ. This was after all a new era of archaeology, geared to sensitivity to local feelings. Many people on Moloka'i had either lived in Hālawa Valley themselves or were related to those who had. The municipally illegal custom of burying deceased kin in the backyard was still widespread. Nobody wanted to think his grandfather's skull was going to spend all eternity labeled and numbered on a basement shelf in the Bishop Museum. To the Moloka'i people these remains were Subjects, recent ones, not Objects.

The first year of the Hālawa dig, the archaeologist Gil Hendron was sitting in Kane's Bar in Kaunakakai one night having a peaceful beer when a big Hawaiian man came up to him. At first Gill didn't understand what he was mad about.

The man said it again, louder, "You fuck with them bones?" He was enormous. Gil knew the answer. "No!"

"You fuck with them bones," the man went on in a voice laden with menace—and here the pronoun was the surprise. "They come back, bust you up!"

"Coming back" was fairly standard practice for the dead of Moloka'i. By all accounts its ghostly population was as large and vocal as the living one. Dead relations swarmed like bees around the households of the East End. You couldn't keep them away, it seemed; they pressed in all around you clamoring with requests trivial and profound. All day long in the trenches the kids regaled me with these stories; in the evening visitors like

Mrs. Akina and others picked up the thread. One boy's grandfather came back because the cows from Murphy's Pu'u O Hōku ranch were trampling his grave. A mother came back to her three daughters as a loud wind in the night, but they were never able to determine her wishes.

—Victoria Nelson, *My Time in Hawai'i: A Polynesian Memoir*

CAROLE TERWILLIGER MEYERS

In My Father's Footsteps

A Marine's daughter traces her Dad's World War II experience in Hawai'i.

ON THE 50TH ANNIVERSARY OF THE ATTACK ON PEARL HARBOR, President George Bush declared, "The war is over. It is history." But the war is not over. And it never will be over for those who fought in it, or for their children, who lived with the aftermath of human anguish.

As the SS *Independence* sails out of the harbor, soft, warm tropical air caresses my skin. I look out over the twinkling lights of Waikīkī—just as my dad did when he sailed off to surprise the Japanese in battle in the Marshall Islands on January 15, 1944. Except that my father's troopship, holding about 2,000 men, was completely dark, and the sailors weren't permitted even to whisper. Their exit had to be silent due to the secrecy of their mission.

Just a bunch of excited American kids waiting to test their teenage muscles, they believed they were sailing off to fight gloriously in retaliation for the December 7, 1941, attack on Pearl Harbor, in which more than 2,300 American military personnel were killed—1,177 of whom were sailors and Marines aboard the USS *Arizona*. But in reality they were sailing straight into hell, and they were still too young and too innocent to be suitably afraid. That night my dad found himself floating past the sunken

Arizona—a ship he had sailed on five times during his first enlistment. He has never put in words what that felt like.

My dad, Earl Walter Terwilliger, a three-stripe sergeant, was only 22 years old. He says that while he and his fellow Marines were waiting there in Honolulu Harbor to sail out to the unknown battle in the Pacific, he could hear the sounds of people partying on shore. It is fitting that the music I hear played by my cruise ship's send-off band over 50 years later is from that era and includes the nostalgic, upbeat "In the Mood." My father's destination turned out to be on Engebi Island in the Eniwetok Atoll, where he remembers landing under fire. He proudly recalls his unit set a world record for taking an island—eight hours and two minutes.

> The *Arizona* feels like a cemetery. There is a heavy silence broken only by the chug of a tour boat or ferry, and calm water surrounds it, flat and green, like a graveyard lawn. The white mooring blocks that once anchored the doomed battleship resemble old tombstones.
>
> Nearby are other buried remains; the wreck of a midget submarine, "crash sites" of planes, and urns containing the ashes of *Arizona* veterans, lowered over the years onto the wreckage in a stainless-steel cylinder the Navy has built for this purpose. And there is the *Arizona*'s oil, a droplet escaping every nine seconds, floating along passageways, up ladders, and through a small crack in the deck, spreading a rainbowed film on the water, a process the park rangers describe as bleeding, as if the ship were a carelessly embalmed cadaver.
>
> —Thurston Clarke, *Pearl Harbor Ghosts*

The ship I am sailing on, the SS *Independence,* operated by American Hawaii Cruises, was built in the 1950s and is currently the only ocean liner sailing under the American flag (no ocean liner has been built in the U.S. since 1951) and is also the only ship cruising exclusively among the Hawaiian

Islands year-round. She is a testament to what humankind can accomplish in peacetime, and also a testament to what my father and his buddies went to war for—to assure that a party ship full of happy people can sail out of this harbor for a peaceful pleasure cruise.

While I enjoy accommodations in a spacious stateroom with a porthole, my dad's lot was sleeping crammed into a bunk, or hanging from a hammock, or stuffed into a bedding roll on a crowded deck. While I dine on fresh fruit and the bounty of the Islands in a full-service dining room, he was chowing down on rations or eating in the mess hall (though he complains about none of this and remembers being well-fed). He sailed anticipating adventure, but instead found horror; I sail anticipating relaxation, but discover enlightenment.

I am taking this most American of cruises primarily for pleasure, but also with the intent of using shore excursions to check out some of the military sites in Hawai'i my dad has spoken of. I want to follow in his footsteps, to try to catch a glimpse of his stride through time, just like as a child I trailed behind him while trying to keep up with his fast-paced feet, usually shod in combat boots.

It wasn't until my dad was in his 70s that I got the real story of his military service. As a child, stories of "The War" held little interest for me. Periodically he would ceremoniously open his footlocker and take out his battlefield souvenirs, among them his dog tags, the ripped helmet chin strap that deflected shrapnel from his head and probably saved his life, and a torn white Japanese flag with a big red dot in the center. I and my siblings would look at these objects with limited understanding of their history and importance, and unfortunately he would tell us very little about how he acquired them. Then he carefully packed everything back into a past he kept stuffed securely in his trunk.

The full tragedy of his war experience did not come back to haunt him until he retired and finally had time to reflect. Then, when I was an adult with grown children of my own, just prior to my leaving on a vacation to Hawai'i, Dad mentioned that he had been stationed on Maui. He told me he trained there with the 22nd Marines (he later joined the 5th Amphibious Corps and previously fought with the 3rd Marine Raiders in the Wallis and Marshall Islands), doing drills on snow-covered Haleakalā to "thicken our blood" for the coming Pacific battles. Something finally clicked. I was intrigued. I wanted to know more.

Our first port is Nāwiliwili Harbor, near Līhu'e on Kaua'i, where I face some of my own demons by remaining in a kayak that I am sure will dump me in the drink. Instead of drowning, I get the hang of it and enjoy a peaceful float down the Hulē'ia River, the very river that Indiana Jones swung over on a rope while making his daring movie escape. In a fabulous ending to the excursion, we trample barefoot over a muddy path through a dense, jungle-like expanse, bringing to mind my dad's tale of contracting filariasis (an illness brought on by a particular kind of mosquito that deposits eggs in the bloodstream which then hatch into worms) in the violent circumstances of his very different jungle visit in the Wallis Islands. The parasitic worms blocked off the blood vessels in his arm, which swelled to three times its normal size as he developed elephantiasis. But Dad credits the mosquitoes that bit him, and luck, with saving his life. Because of his disability, he was sent home through New Caledonia and wound up missing some even nastier battles. And he also credits that training stint in Maui with actually thickening his blood and thus keeping him from bleeding to death from the wounds that earned him a Purple Heart.

Our next port is Wailuku on Maui, where my dad's unit R&R'd. Here my husband and I rent a car so we can go wherever our leads direct us. Wailuku is such a sleepy town that it requires a real stretch to imagine it jumping with Marines on their night off. It is so untouristy that I'm unable to find a promotional t-shirt or a baseball cap to send back to my dad. But while I'm searching for such a souvenir, I start chatting in the town music shop with a good-natured, spacey fellow who seems interested in my mission. He tells me that the World War II "jarheads," as he calls them (a slang term referring to their general stubbornness), trained out at Ha'ikū. He thinks the training grounds are a park now.

Dad never mentioned Ha'ikū, and he doesn't remember it when I describe it to him later, but we find the town on the map and set out. In hip Pā'ia we pick up a picnic lunch and drive on to Honomanū Bay. Here we are entertained by colorful windsurfers dancing on the turquoise surf while we eat, stretched out in the warm sand. I realize later that this fabulously beautiful spot must have been what my dad and his buddies saw, minus the windsurfers, as their buses and trucks rumbled down the zigzagging, then-unpaved mountain road into town.

When I ask the clerk in Ha'ikū's little town store where the Marine base was in World War II, she hasn't a clue. The only other person in the store pipes up that there is a memorial park just outside of town. A few minutes later we arrive at a large open field with a sign declaring it the Fourth Marine Division Memorial Park. As we walk over the expanse of grass, I picture the field filled with tents and 5,000 excited young men, all of whom were volunteers. (My dad says the Marine Corps is "a year older than the United States." It began as a group of sailors who knew how to fire guns and is the only branch of the armed services made up entirely of enlisted men who volunteer their lives for defense.)

Dad says they were told never to eat any fruit found on the ground, because it might be contaminated. So, while training in paradise, these young men devised a way to let off steam and practice their battle skills at the same time: One soldier would shoot down a coconut, aiming at the stem, while another caught it. Then they used their combat knives to cut the nuts open. (This was the same knife my daddy would later grab from his bedstead when I came to his room as a child, afraid of suspicious night noises outside my bedroom window. He then stomped right out into the night, as if on a skirmish, in search of the enemy. Once a Marine, always a Marine. However, he says he gave up his guns—among them two Colt 45 automatics that he once holstered cowboy-style on each hip—when he left the service. He says he discharged his last shot at the enemy and has never again fired a gun.) These soldiers also practiced playing dead as hairy black banana spiders crawled over their bodies.

It was probably also here that this young man, my father, transformed his childhood talent for pitching baseballs into a life-saving skill for lobbing grenades. Later, in combat, instead of throwing balls to help his team win a game, he would be tossing grenades to keep his buddies alive.

After the war, the people of Maui erected a simple memorial in the park. I cry as I read:

THIS PLAQUE MARKS THE SITE OF CAMP MAUI WORLD WAR II HOME OF THE 4TH MARINE DIVISION AFFECTIONATELY AND PROUDLY CALLED "MAUI'S OWN."

This gratitude surprises me. I have to tweak my memory to recall that at the time of World War II, Hawai'i was not a state. I had assumed the local residents might be annoyed by the Marines invading their town and island. Instead, the people of Maui very much appreciated what these young men were sacrificing for them.

Unlike so many other men in that brutal war, my dad came back alive. But like most men who survived, he was scarred, both on the outside and the inside. On the outside, he suffered a head injury from shrapnel that scarred his scalp and brain, causing him to have occasional epileptic seizures. (I have seen him suffer a seizure only once. It occurred recently while he was telling me the devastatingly emotional story of his innocence lost as a Marine in battle, "earning" his Purple Heart. He broke down as he told me about Corporal Snyder, who came to check on my dad's injuries after he was hit in the head by shrapnel. Part of the corporal's face was blown away as my horrified father watched. He never saw him again and doesn't know if he survived.) On the inside, he is an open wound. Like the Vietnam vets, he still has flashbacks and bad dreams. And like the Vietnam vets, he came home to a world where no one really wanted to hear the true story of what he had been through. So, like any Marine worth his salt, he kept all the horror, all the blood and guts, inside, where he thought it belonged. A few years ago when he joined a Vietnam vets therapy group, I found it surprising that these younger men welcomed him, that they had no problem accepting him. But I shouldn't have been surprised, because they all had fought, and are still fighting, the same battle. War, it turns out, is war. In light of this, what a shame it is that the Veterans Administration cancelled his group, and others like it, due to lack of funding. It is my opinion that all men who experience battle should be decompressed with group or individual counseling that addresses their trauma, and that it should be paid for by "we the people."

After strolling through the memorial park, watching happy children frolicking on the contemporary playground, we continue on up the mountain. I try to imagine what my father had been feeling when he went up-country on "blood-thickening" excursions to the snow. We are running late and have to get back to the ship, so we turn around before reaching the top, where, even with no snow, it is still quite chilly.

Our ship makes several more stops. On the Big Island we drop the search for the past and vacation for a while, touring the spectacular Hawai'i Tropical Botanical Garden in Hilo and diving in the Atlantis submarine off Kona. I have enough of this submarine in 45 minutes to last a lifetime and cannot help drifting into a daydream about the men who, more than 50 years ago, served their country squashed into such tight quarters during seemingly endless tours of duty. I find out later from my dad that he and his fellow Marines were often picked up after a battle, in the South Pacific night, by submarines. He says they would escape inside by sliding down the torpedo tube, which was only about a foot and a half in diameter, landing on mattresses.

Back in Honolulu, at the end of our voyage, we join a post-cruise shore excursion to the USS *Arizona* Memorial in Pearl Harbor. This is Hawai'i's second most popular visitor attraction. (Number one is the national Memorial Cemetery of the Pacific at Punchbowl.) On the bus ride, the mood is somber and not even the driver cracks a joke. We learn that one of our tour members is a rare survivor of the Japanese attack.

Emotions start heating up in the *Arizona* museum, where I view letters home from very young men, many just teenagers, and see images of baby-faced soldiers that look like my dad in his enlistment photo, like my son in his high school graduation picture. After a silent boat ride out to the memorial, which floats above the famous sunken ship without touching it, I place my fragrant orange flower *lei* among the many purple orchid and white plumeria *lei* already piled at the base of the marble wall engraved tightly with the names of all the men who died here. Though traditionally *lei* are left for the crew that went down on the *Arizona*, I leave mine in memory of all servicemen. As tinkling bells play "Amazing Grace" and then the "Marine's Hymn," I, and many others, weep. A very light rain seems to be saying that the heavens are mourning, too, for these precious lost lives. I am crying also for what my dad went through as a young man, as he says he cries for today's young soldiers.

> The facts are almost too familiar: On Sunday morning December 7, 1941, the battleships of the Pacific Fleet were tied up at Pearl. A wave of Japanese warplanes suddenly appeared. Dive-bombing, torpedoing, and strafing the American forces with virtually no opposition, the Japanese attackers sank or seriously damaged 18 ships, destroyed or damaged nearly 350 planes, and killed 2,335 American servicemen. It was the biggest single loss in United States Navy history.
>
> What the Pearl Harbor Visitors' Center accomplishes is to give these facts a human face. Some volunteers on duty are survivors of the attack, spinning out memories and answering questions. Even the exhibits seem personal, like the display case of servicemen's memorabilia—Betty Grable pin-up photos, packs of Lucky Strike Green, olive-drab training handbooks.
>
> —Jerry Camarillo Dunn Jr., *National Geographic Traveler*

Before leaving, I stop at the gift shop and get Dad some souvenirs of the *Arizona*. They are doing a booming business here, making me wonder how many other fathers out there have lived a similar story.

My father is finally getting better. His descent into despair has flattened out, and he seems to have his seizures under control. But he is stubborn and doesn't always take his medicine. He is also drinking less, and his lips, once loosened to me by liquor, have tightened up again as taut as a blanket on a military cot awaiting morning inspection.

And now that I am finally listening, now when I am in fact taking notes when he rattles on about "The War," my dad seems to have less interest in talking. Isn't that just like a jarhead? Back from my cruise now for almost a year, it took me this long to finish writing, to fit the pieces together into a pattern. But it has taken my dad a lifetime. Back now for over 50 years from his immersion trip into World War II, he still hasn't put all the pieces together. Perhaps he never will. The last time I visited him, this 79-year-old Ernest Hemingway look-alike said, "There is an old saying that Marines never die: they just fade away, and I'm fading."

Carole Terwilliger Meyers is the founding publisher at Carousel Press and the author of Weekend Adventures in Northern California. *She lives in Berkeley, California, where she keeps her father's well-worn combat compass on her desk pointing her in the right direction. Her father was born and raised in Poughkeepsie, New York, and lives now in Eugene, Oregon.*

*

Twenty U.S. vessels went down that day, but seventeen rose to fight again, largely because the Japanese, in their enthusiasm for blowing up ships, forgot to knock out the dry docks and shipyards that would breathe life back into them. The *Helena* returned to strike at Guadalcanal. The *Nevada* lived to settle its score with the Japanese at Iwo Jima and Okinawa.

But the *West Virginia*'s fate was the most sublime of all. After being salvaged and winning five battle stars in twelve months, it steamed into Tokyo Bay on September 1, 1945, and nested alongside the *Missouri*, where Douglas MacArthur waited to accept the Japanese surrender. There it saw the final interment of the enemy that had nearly ended its days four years before. Of all the ironies of December 7, 1941, the strangest may be this: Of the 33 Japanese ships that took part in the victorious attack, 32 would end up on the bottom of the ocean. Yet, of the 20 American ships sunk at Pearl Harbor, 17 would return to the sea and claim a total of 85 battle stars against their attackers.

Of the three that didn't return, the *Oklahoma* was scrapped in 1946; the *Utah* lies submerged on the western side of Ford Island, with 58 of its crew members still trapped inside; and the *Arizona*, which was commissioned in 1915 and never fired a shot against an enemy, has become one of the most famous war monuments on earth.

—John McDonough, *Pearl Harbor: From Here to Eternity*

JANE ALBRITTON

Pizza Night at the Pau Hana Inn

Take off your shoes and come dance.

"FELLINI," SAID KATE. SHE RAISED HER GLASS TO SIP HER GIN martini, ordered to honor Madame Pele, who created Moloka'i with two small volcanoes and an afterthought flow at Kalaupapa.

"Fellini?" I asked.

"Yes, Fellini. This is a scene directed by Fellini in love with the Hawaiian Islands."

It was Pizza Night at the Pau Hana Inn, a night when the local population came out in force to celebrate the best pizza in the Islands, maybe the world. We had taken a table outside near the terrace bar. And as we sat there watching the children from the local *hula hālau* (hula school) rehearse under the great spread of the 100-year-old banyan tree, we could feel ourselves being eased into the Island's sweet eccentricity.

Despite marketing attempts to rechristen it the "Friendly Isle," Moloka'i is still the "Lonely Isle," passed over by everyone from Captain Cook to Rockresorts. Lovely and lush, the Island endures the shame of the lepresorium at Kalaupapa, the stress of an economy flattened by the unceremonious departure of the pineapple growers, and the caprice of tourist resort success.

We had arrived via Maui very early that morning from three days on the Big Island where we had paid our respects to Madame Pele and detoxed our Mainland souls with walks over freshly minted earth. Flying out of Maui's Kahului Airport, transmogrified since our last visit into a modern crisscross of concourses, our *wahine* captain alerted us that she would be banking a bit off course to give us a seabird's sweep over Moloka'i's spectacular seacliffs, the tallest in the world.

By the time we settled into our pizza some twelve hours after shimmying to a halt at Moloka'i Airport, we had negotiated a large and aging Plymouth (the last rental car available on the entire island) from Maunaloa town on the arid west side to Hālawa Beach in the lush, green east. Up until Kate's Fellini epiphany, we had been debriefing the day, trying to sort out just what it was we had seen and what it all meant.

> In 1934, the late R. Alex Anderson, one of Hawai'i's most prolific song composers, wrote "The Cockeyed Mayor of Kaunakakai," which Hilo Hattie made famous in the 1940s. Anderson used the term, cockeyed "mainly because it combined nicely with the last two syllables of the word Kaunakakai," according to *Hawaiian Music and Musicians.* Anderson, who composed nearly 200 songs, including "Lovely Hula Hands," "I Will Remember You," and "I Had to Lova and Leva on the Lava," died in 1995. He was 101. Since Moloka'i is part of Maui County, there is no mayor in Kaunakakai.
>
> —RC & MC

Maunaloa, our first stop of the day, was not much to look at. Its dusty, tin-roofed plantation buildings hold no Makawao, Maui-style promise for conversion to yoga centers or herbal health shops. The Maunaloa General Store has never inspired a single song.

But we took the turn off Highway 460 not to visit what Libby and Dole had wrought, but to get close to the place where Laka (sometimes described as a god and sometimes as a goddess) brought the hula to

Hawaiians. Pele brought fire, and Laka's male and female taught us mortals to dance on its hearth. Who knows why gods pick such god-forsaken places to confer their best gifts. Compensation? Focus? There were certainly no distractions here for that first hula lesson.

Having thanked Laka for the gift of dance, we turned back to the east and pushed our Plymouth to the boiling point on a nonstop dash along the southern shore, laced with fishponds constructed by Hawaiians long ago. Outside of French Polynesia, there are no better examples of this simple and effective fishery technology.

Beyond the fishponds and until about twenty miles from Kaunakakai, Kamehemeha V Highway easily accommodates a wide-bodied car. But as the landscape turns a dazzling green and lifts the ribbon-thin road up and around the weathered edges of Kamakou volcano's shield, a Plymouth becomes decidedly un-Hawaiian. Our temperature gauge began to quiver; we stubbornly turned the heat on, watched the needle drop, and drove to the end of the road.

Beautiful Hālawa Beach, favorite among local surfers, was all but abandoned. We had seen all the boards heading back to Kaunakakai strapped on the tops of cars. It occurred to us that those surfers were after our pizza. We took in as much of the scene as we could and then turned our car back for the lonely ride home. For miles we were the only car on the road.

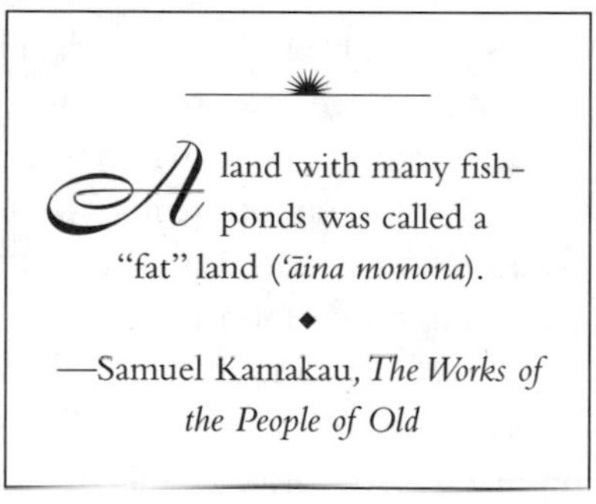

A land with many fishponds was called a "fat" land (*'āina momona*).

—Samuel Kamakau, *The Works of the People of Old*

Closing time comes early here on this sparsely settled Island, and it was only by begging that we prevailed on a gas station owner's better nature to open up and let us use his phone.

"Pau Hana? Save our pizza. We are coming."

Let no one doubt the power of a Pau Hana Pizza: a host with toppings. Having taken it, we could only hypothesize why these pizzas had not become a magnet for pizza pilgrims. Perhaps pizza does not fit into a marketing scheme that identifies Moloka'i as the "most Hawaiian of the Islands." That would require poi pizza with *lomi lomi* topping and some *laulau* on the side. No. This pizza is Hawai'i, Moloka'i style: Portagee-sweet-bread-tasting crust (hmmmm), layered with crushed local truck-garden tomatoes, garlic, herbs and spices, topped with succulent slivers of Maui onion, spun with cheese, and all cooked (according to the glowing pizza handler) "with love."

So there we were. Giddy on pizza at the open-air Pau Hana bar under the spreading banyan tree. "Pau Hana" means "Stop Work!" in Hawaiian. The term is emphatic: stop, already. And we were ready. Discovering an Island is hard work.

We settled in and began to see where we were. Anticipating the long Memorial Day weekend, the mood on the terrace was festive, elevated by the voices of the scores of women who had come to compete in the interisland softball tournament. Still in uniform, they leaned back in their chairs, told jokes, and drank beer out of the bottles. Through the clink and chatter, the sea breeze sent a sympathetic sigh through the banyan tree and turned our attention to the large concrete stage, where the children were being rehearsed for their upcoming performance by an unusually large woman. Her voice was just a shade too deep for contralto, her frame more like John Elway's than Hilo Hattie's. Obviously, there in the leaf-tossed light, Laka was among us.

As our waiter swept by in his short shorts and aloha shirt tied up in a midriff knot, we asked him: "Who is the hula teacher?" He arched a perfect eyebrow and replied, "She drives the school bus." She, understandably, had the children in perfect thrall. Accompanied by an impassive ukulele player of middle years, the towering *kumu hula* coaxed and praised and clapped the girls and boys through their motions in preparation for their formal performance the next night. Each group, composed by age, practiced steps and movements. In their shorts, with faces fixed in concentration, they looked less like the "most Hawaiian" of all the Islanders, than like an idiosyncratic blend of every immigrant group that ever sailed in to work, trade, or missionize the Islands. All of us in the audience—parents and friends, the entire Island population of women's softball, and random visitors—who had shared the rehearsal, tacitly vowed to return for the main performance the next night.

Kate and I looked forward to it especially, for we were not exactly sure how our mule trip over the *pali* to Kalaupapa the next day would go. Try as the marketers might to reframe loneliness into friendliness, Moloka'i's biggest attraction is the loneliest place in all Hawai'i and the most dazzling. I was prepared for the vertical mule ride and the 26 switchbacks down 1,600 feet to the place where lepers from all the Islands had been banished. I was prepared for the colony, no longer officially *kapu*. The site looks benign, like a derelict summer YMCA camp. What I was not prepared for was the rueful beauty of the place.

Our downward view of the sea cliffs from the little plane had inverted the perspective of nearly 100 years of looking up with no hope of flying away. It must have been with a profound sense of irony that Father Damien, the Belgian priest who ministered to the least of these, built his church at Kalawao. It stands a little distance from the colony against the impenetrable backdrop of sea cliffs that rise in grand succession and then recede like shades into the distance.

Sometimes the bitterness of this terrible isolation ate like bile through the veneer of our guide's measured exposition. Hyman Fujinaga, now a man in his 60s, had been taken away from his family in Honolulu when he was just a boy. His recitation of the history of Kalaupapa left me with no comfort. On the way back up the *pali,* we sought a little relief from the intensity of Hyman's witness in Moki, the young (mostly) Hawaiian muleteer. We used our praise of Pau Hana pizza as code for "We like it here, let's talk story."

Access granted. This Island's life is tough. Lots of Hawaiians, but not enough jobs. People take the ferry every day to go work in Lahaina. But we all come home. It's *'ohana*, family.

"You know why they can't keep police here on Moloka'i?" quizzed Moki.

"How come?"

"They won't arrest nobody. How you gonna arrest your family for growing a little *pakalolo*?"

"So what happens?"

"Oh, they send in the rookies. They send in the new guys to enforce the law. They are very good," he winked.

We returned that night to the terrace of the Pau Hana Inn for the Memorial Day weekend performance of the Moloka'i hula school. The easy joviality of the previous night had evolved into something more attentive. Our *kumu hula*, in a cloud of *pīkake lei* fragrance—majestic in her *mu'umu'u* and improbable white pumps—took the stage. Her fresh velvet contralto summoned each group, each member of which had been transfigured. Now wholly Hawaiian in their dress, in their movement and in the rapture of their eyes and smiles, the children moved flawlessly to both the old rhythms and the *hapa haole* beat. Every hula hand was perfect, at least it seemed perfect to those of us who had been enchanted.

Momentarily the link between the fullness of nature and the loneliness of the human condition held firm in a rhythmic bond of breezes, music, and motion: in what is "most Hawaiian." Then the moment passed, and the next morning had us on the plane to Kaua'i where the rough magic of Moloka'i melted into the many shades of green that a few days later we carried with us to Honolulu. There we settled into the familiar Moana Hotel, our bridge of choice back to the Mainland.

Now, some would argue that the Moana's tricked up, touristy Banyan Court on the beach at Waikīkī has nothing in common with the "real Hawai'i" that finds its repose at the Pau Hana Inn.

They're wrong, and here is how I know. Listen. Packed and ready to leave for our inconveniently late flight back to the Mainland, we settled ourselves under every tourists' banyan tree for a last mai tai. Jerry Santos and his group, brought to us courtesy of ITT Sheraton, proud owner of hotels worldwide, were singing easy Hawaiian tunes to the Pacific sunset. We had just become mellow and a little sad at leaving, when the breeze turned, gave the banyan leaves a shake, and blew us a little reminder from Moloka'i:

what happens, not where, makes a thing "most Hawaiian." Out from a wedding reception in the ballroom off the hotel *lānai* came Karen Keawehawai'i and her daughter, a dancer.

"Come dance," said Jerry. Old friends, *'ohana.* Caught in the moment, the daughter beckoned another friend who, by chance, was sitting on the terrace listening to his friends sing. "Come dance," she said. He left his sandals behind, and they danced, rapture in their eyes and smiles and in their hands and feet. The crowd, some fresh off the plane and crazed by jet lag and Mainland stress, yielded unaware to the net cast by the Moloka'i breeze and held in place with a song.

Jane DeHart Albritton (Jane II) was presented at age three by her mother to Madame Pele for her approval. Even from Texas, Jane Christman Albritton (Big Jane) made sure that her three children bonded with Hawai'i nei. Consequently, all can sing "Three Blind Mice" in Hawaiian, almost always say "I'm pau,*" when finished, and roll their eyes when someone calls a plumeria "frangipani." Mostly a Texan, Jane II lives in Fort Collins, Colorado, where she rides her horse, Paniolo, stalks elk with her camera, and writes.*

✶

When traveling from O'ahu to the Neighbor Islands, if you are observant, you will see a trickle of human traffic dressed in steel toe boots, chambray shirts with logos like Frigidaire and Au's Electric, picking up tool boxes at the luggage carousel. These are workers from Honolulu going out on jobs—carpenters, plumbers, electricians, masons. Come *pau hana* time, you will find many of them in the small bars, talking story.

As they travel the Islands, these workers learn about things that are special and take great pride in their depth of knowledge: the best beach in September, or where you can catch the illusive *moi*, or find the best *omiyage* (gifts). It's customary to bring *omiyage*—Maui potato chips, or Tasaka *guri-guri* (goody-goody) sherbet, dim sum or chow fun noodles from O'ahu, Macadamia nut cookies from Kaua'i, taro bread and *kamaboko* (fish cake) from Hilo.

That's how we found out about the Moloka'i "butt-bread" secret—in the bar of the Pau Hana Inn, listening to the workers talk story. Of course, everyone knows about Moloka'i butt-bread (potato bread from

Kanemitsu's Bakery). But only those in the know know about getting the special hot bread right out of the oven, long after closing time. The front of the bakery is locked up tight, and behind, it's pitch dark. But if you follow the alleyway on the east end around back, you'll see this door with light coming out underneath.

We are there, late at night, looking for the bread. We drive back and forth several times looking for the alley, missing it, and finally figuring out that it's not so much an alley, but a narrow passageway to a building with a corrugated roof. It's the smell that tells us. This is it!

It's dark as we cautiously walk toward the back, but soon we make out figures and voices. The top half of a small door creaks open, and reveals a man splattered with flour, a dish towel wrapped around his waist. One of his eyes is wildly askew. We make our request. He reaches in his back pocket for change and passes out the bread.

—George Fujita

JONATHAN RABAN

Hawai'i with Julia

A four-year-old optimist guides her papa through the Islands.

WHEN WE STEPPED OFF THE PLANE INTO THE SAUNA WEATHER OF a Honolulu evening in late December, my old friend Paul was waiting for us at the gate, carrying a brown paper bag, packed by his wife and full of gifts for my companion—a *lei*, a hula skirt, a straw sun hat, and a rainbow bikini. Everything, except for the bikini, which I nixed, was donned then and there, while our fellow passengers surged past us. Hatted, garlanded, hula skirt swirling, my companion strode off toward baggage claim. She looked like the tourist from hell.

Julia is four, and it was for her sake, mostly, that we were here. I like the sea, but not the seaside and Hawai'i has always struck me as too blatantly clichéd a destination. But four-year-olds have rigidly conventional tastes in travel, and for Julia there was still unsullied magic in the idea of sun, sand, sea, a "tropical paradise" with...

"Palm trees!" she yelled. "Look! Palm trees!" Joyfully incredulous at seeing the illustrations to *Curious George* and the *Enormous Crocodile* spring suddenly into 3-D all around her. "Why do they have those rings on them?" Each tree had a tin sleeve on its trunk fifteen feet above ground level.

"To stop the mice and rats from climbing up and eating the coconuts," Paul said. Julia stored this piece of information, her first serious nugget of Hawaiian lore. On the drive into town, she gazed perplexedly at the unfamiliar street signs, street lamps, traffic signals. "I keep thinking I'm in Seattle, but I know I'm in Hawai'i." To Paul she explained: "Hawai'i is always hot because it's nearer to the sun."

At the seafood restaurant where we were meeting Sheila, Paul's wife, Julia took the maitre d'hotel into her confidence: "I know I look like a Hawaiian girl, but I'm not really a Hawaiian girl. Actually, I'm from Seattle." The maitre d' did his best to appear astonished at this revelation.

The kid's menu yielded pizza. "They have pizza in Hawai'i!" Sometimes life just goes on getting better. But after one slice, and before the grown-ups were properly started on their hors d'oeuvres, Julia fell into a coma in Sheila's arms.

At dinner's end, I slung my unconscious daughter over my shoulder and carted her off to a room in the Sheraton Waikīkī where, a very few hours later, I was awakened by her announcement that it was "a beautiful morning." It wasn't beautiful. It wasn't morning. In the crepuscular light well short of dawn, Julia was out on the balcony, already dressed in hula skirt and *lei* watching pale explosions of surf on the black beach.

In 54 years of active fantasy life, I had never imagined that I might find myself on Waikīkī Beach at 7 a.m., in a thin and chilly drizzle, helping to dig burrows for nonexistent rabbits. Unsurprisingly, Julia and I had the place to ourselves.

"It's raining," I said reproachfully. "Just like Seattle."

"It isn't!" Julia was leaping to Hawai'i's defense. "It's hot rain. Hawai'i is always hot because it's closer to the sun."

"I wish I'd never told you that."

It was 9 a.m. before I persuaded her to hit the Rice Krispies.

Back at the airport, we found our flight to Lāna'i was delayed. Julia, unflappable and uncomplaining, crawled with her favorite bear in the space below the twin rows of back-to-back seats and took a nap. When the Dash 8 eventually began its sprint down the runway, she was enthralled by the takeoff, the sudden release from earth, the diminishing—and now sunlit—city. "We're higher even than the palm trees!"

But the weather worsened as we flew south over an increasingly sullen-looking sea. We came down low over a rocky shoreline, rimmed with white, no more tropical in its appearance than the Isle of Man. The landing gear plopped down, and we were almost on the ground, when with an abrupt snarl, the plane climbed steeply, and Lāna'i faded out as we lurched, bumping, into the clouds. The pilot's voice came over the intercom: he was going to make a second attempt to land at Lāna'i, but if the visibility defeated him again, we'd have to go on to Maui.

"I'm not scared anymore," Julia said, as we twisted and bounced through lumpy fog. "I like it now." I didn't. I held her hand, for my own comfort more than for hers. Red dirt materialized out of nowhere just beneath us, then the shuddering thump of the wheels on tarmac, and the voice of the pilot, rather too plainly registering his own adrenaline level, saying: "Welcome to Lāna'i." His passengers applauded him. Julia clapped the longest.

From the hotel bus, Lāna'i was unexpectedly forbidding. Patches of tawny rock showed through the mesquite scrub to which the abandoned pineapple fields were fast returning. Red mud sluiced along the roadside. We passed by the outskirts of Lāna'i City, a meager grid of dripping, tin-roofed bungalows with tangled yards. "Are we still in Hawai'i?" Julia asked. But as the bus started to corkscrew down the steep road to Mānele Bay, the rain stopped and there was a smear, at least, of sunshine on the gale-torn sea ahead.

All Julia's doubts fled when we stopped at the hotel, where a uniformed bell captain hung yet another *lei* round her neck—to which I added the *lei* he tried to drape on me. Bowed down by flowers and hugely, shyly grinning, Julia entered her paradise on earth.

Paradise—in the shape of the Mānele Bay Hotel—is where the taste of Ralph Lauren collides with that of the Tang dynasty: it has something of the English country house, something of the Venetian Lido and enough ostentatious chinoiserie to fill a container ship end to end. From the grand public rooms at the center of this marvelous confection, one is led out to a mass of beige-colored open cloisters, through gardens packed with jasmine, palms, bougainvillea, orchids, jacaranda, where a winding stream, full of ornamental carp, is fed by a succession of prettily constructed waterfalls. *In Xanadu....*

I woke up in my room at Mānele Bay early one morning and looked out over the gardens to see the dawn breaking on the bay. I hit the exercise spa, walked past the pool, and jogged along the beach toward the cliffs. Hulopo'e's beach is public—to the chagrin of a few company officials—and this morning it was empty. I ran along the hard wet crust, catching a path up an igneous cliff that climbed through dry grass until it circled up to a point where I was able to look down on a creamy blue half circle, a completely inaccessible cove on which the clouds were kaleidoscoping brief but dramatic little secret messages. I felt like I was in a Nike commercial.

—Robert Sullivan, "Hawaiian Highball," *Condé Nast Traveler*

The hotel's preferred term for its own architecture style is "Mediterranean"—but that's too modest. It is, rather, triumphantly American in its lavish capital investment, American in its lofty disregard for natural obstacles. The southern, leeward shore of Lāna'i is dry to the point of being arid; left to itself, it was a rust-colored cinder heap, nearly bereft of vegetation. When David H. Murdock, the Californian chairman and chief executive of Castle and Cooke and the Dole Food Company, the Kublai Khan of Lāna'i, took the Island out of pineapples and into up-market tourism, he built a new landscape with imported dirt, moistened by water piped down from the wet, forested uplands beyond Lāna'i City. The place is—in the eighteenth-century sense of the word—a folly; a monument to the wily artifice of the hydraulic engineer and the landscape gardener. In the can-do arrogance of its conception, it's in the spirit of Las Vegas or the Grand Coulee Dam.

Our room lay at the far end of the maze; backed by a waterfall, fronted by a lawn, a ha-ha, then the sea. Julia was enchanted—by the green at our doorstep ("We've got our own field!"), by the marbled splendor of the bathroom and its fittings, by the expensive collection of Chinese breakables. She expertly raided the minibar, changed into her bikini, and went visiting with the neighbors along the row of oceanfront patios.

She was instantly at home here. What I hadn't realized was how very closely the world of the resort hotel resembles that of the preschool. The young women who run the concierge desk are the controlling grown-ups; they set the curriculum and sort out squabbles. The indignant 55-year-old guest, in his beach romper wear, with bulging face and shrilling voice, is pure 200-pound toddler in a snit.

As at preschool, the hotel day is organized around mealtimes with, between meals, what Julia's Seattle school calls "sensory activities" centered on the pool, the spa, and the beach. For the adult guest, the trick is to adjust to being four years old again. You have to learn the school rules: *No swim wear in the public rooms...elegant resort attire is acceptable in the restaurant...* You have to slot yourself into the regimented spaces of the school day. I settled for the activities known to Julia as Quiet Time and Stories—lounging on our patio reading Trollope's *Bertrams* and trying to put names to the neighborhood birds.

The birds, as it turned out, exactly mirrored the human sociology of the Islands. Very few were native to Hawai'i. Most had been introduced within the last 150 years—foreigners that had thrived in the balmy climate with its easy pickings, just like the Chinese, the Scots, the Filipinos, the American Mainlanders, the Samoans. So the starlings, which roosted noisily each evening in the palms above our waterfall, had come from Britain by way of New York; the house sparrows had come from New Zealand; the black-hooded mynahs from India and the cardinals from the United

States. The many Japanese guests at the hotel could wake to the familiar dawn chorus of Japanese bush warblers, resident aliens in Hawai'i since 1929. Lāna'i was an Island of immigrants, more Filipino than Hawaiian native; a cultural salad of exotic birds and people. The imported bric-a-brac in our room, the German family from Munich staying two doors down, Julia's and my own presence here—we were all authentically part of the salad.

Meanwhile, Julia, in the care of the Children's Activity Center ("Let's pretend I'm going to school in Hawai'i") was conducting strenuous social life on her own behalf; she played bingo, went on epic scavenger hunts, watched movies, attended pool-side pizza parties, and fell in love with her swimming instructor.

I was walking to lunch, *The Bertrams* in hand, when I was hailed from the pool. "Daddy!" Julia, in rainbow bikini, was wetly reclining in the arms of a youthful, mahogany-tanned beach god. "This," she said, glowing with pride in her conquest, "is Kenji." "Hi Kenji," I said, reaching down with the fake bonhomie that, I guess, all fathers learn to exercise in this situation. Kenji, with Julia riding on his back, lapped the pool.

"I shall not forget this day in my entire life," said Julia.

Next morning, she awakened at 6:45, sitting bolt upright in her bed and announcing, "I love Kenji."

"I know," I said. "Go back to sleep."

Paul and Sheila were due to join us on Friday. But I woke that morning to the brush fire crackle of rain on the patio: our ocean view had gone, and from the radio I learned that Lāna'i Airport was closed to all traffic.

An intense *kona* storm, was dawdling through the Islands. Gleaming rods of rain were drilling holes in the lawn, and the dry creek bed just to the west of us (the favored haunt of the Japanese bush warbler) had become a foaming torrent of red water. It was tearing up small trees by the roots and flinging them into the ocean. The waterfalls were running red and so was the ornamental stream, which had burst its banks. The hybrid carp were nowhere to be seen. "Poor fish—I expect they're dead," said Julia. Our usual elevator was out of order: it had sprung a leak and red water was dripping through the shaft. At the top of the stairs, six maids were trying to staunch the flood by pushing at it with long brooms. I rolled up my trouser legs, hoisted Julia onto my shoulders and paddled the last twenty yards to the main body of the hotel. A brief lull in the rain revealed that the sea itself was stained red with runoff: a half-mile-wide band of water, the color of dark tomato soup, now encircled the Island.

We were marooned in our stately pleasure dome. Bands of would-be travelers were begging the concierge staff to make planes fly. The lobby was piled high with their luggage. "I have to be in New York tonight!" "I have to be in Tokyo tomorrow!" The only way off the island was by boat to Maui. "But it's rough and I get seasick!" wailed a toddler in her 60s.

Things were quieter below. Couples were bent over million-piece jigsaw puzzles. Single men were making tents of two-day-old copies of the *Wall Street Journal.* There were novels—John Grisham or Danielle Steele, depending on the reader's sex. People stared out into the gray yonder, then consulted their watches importantly, as if they expected their bomb to go off at any moment.

With Julia dispatched to the Children's Center, I finished *The Bertrams* and went off to browse through the hotel library where I encountered my daughter, who was on a scavenger hunt. "Have you seen Kenji?" she said.

Getting through to Honolulu on the phone was like trying to raise Bora Bora or Uttar Pradesh: Paul's voice was a whispery vibration in the wires. "Tomorrow!" it croaked, from another world.

So I got Julia as my dinner date. For my entertainment she juggled silverware. She conducted a physical experiment involving the horizontal flow of liquid (apple juice, in this case, and the experiment failed). She slid under the table. She waved at strangers and kept up a running commentary on their varying degrees of baldness, redness of face, girth, age, and fashion-victimhood.

The staff—pineapple pickers, retrained for the hotel trade—extended to both of us a smiling tolerance that went way beyond the call of duty. They indulged Julia; they talked to me of their children and grandchildren. Unaffected, with none of the solemn snootiness that tends to go with jobs at a $400-a-night hotel, these cheerful and elastic Islanders seemed the best possible advertisement for David Murdock's economic revolution.

On Saturday morning, it was still raining, with the cloud ceiling pegged to the ground. The weather system had stalled over Lāna'i and showed no sign of budging. No flights in or out. No Paul and Sheila. Our long-planned weekend was a bust. Julia splashed through the cloisters, clutching a fallen coconut that she'd found in the grass. She took in the thrashing palms, the rusty flood, the glum adults staring at the weather from their dripping patios. "I love Hawai'i," she said. She had an appointment with Kenji at the Children's Center.

I pride myself on meeting the ordinary happenstances of traveling with equanimity, but Julia was making me feel a rank amateur. "So do I," I said. We passed the concierge desks, with their throng of grown-ups throwing tantrums. Julia marched through them, full of happy purpose, while I bumbled in her wake. She was in command of the vacation now: she had the Mānele Bay world at her fingertips. "Come on! This way!" And I obeyed—glad to learn, at this late stage, how to travel gracefully from my daughter.

Jonathan Raban is the author of many books including Bad Land: An American Romance, Old Glory: A Voyage Down the Mississippi, *and* Hunting Mister Heartbreak: A Discovery of America. *He lives in Seattle.*

★

I think Lana'i is most interesting because of its history of defeating nearly all who set foot on the island—early Polynesians, fierce Hawaiian kings, European explorers, even Mormons, the most steadfast Pacific missionaries.

Ancient Hawaiians believed Lāna'i was haunted by "spirits so wily and vicious that no human who went there could survive," according to Ruth Tabrah, author of *Lāna'i*.

—RC

PAUL THEROUX

* * *

Eclipse

A primal event stirs peculiar feelings that affect the most jaded traveler.

TIME PASSED—MONTHS. I WAS STILL IN HAWAI'I, I HAD NOT LEFT Oceania. I was paddling my collapsible boat, marvelling at the way its canvas hull had faded in the punishing sun. Some days I paddled rented outriggers off Honolulu, and open hardshells off windward O'ahu. The places I had paddled to write about I was still paddling, for pleasure. There were more seacoasts I wanted to paddle: off Maui, to the bombsite of Kaho'olawe, and along the north coast of Moloka'i to Father Damien's old leper settlement of Kalaupapa, and eventually—in good weather—from one Island to another. Paddling had taken the place of writing. I thought about my book and then muttered, *Oh, never mind.*

Normally, at this point in the trip—in this chapter, say—the traveler is heading home. Or the traveler is already home, reflecting on the extraordinary trip, looking at slides, sorting notes, perhaps wishing the trip had not ended, or at least saying so. But that nostalgia can sound so insincere. You read it and think: *No, you're delighted to be home, dining out on your stories of megapode birds and muddy buttocks and what the king of Tonga told you!*

Isn't one of the greatest rewards of travel the return home—

the reassurance of family and old friends, familiar sights and homely comforts?

I used to go back home and be welcomed, and find months of mail stacked on my desk and spilling to the floor, and after I opened it all, I would answer some and pay bills and burn the letters and envelopes. It could take half a day at the incinerator in the garden, as I stirred the ashes of all the mail I had received. And when I was done and caught up, the routine of home would reassert itself. I would begin writing, spending the day at my desk reliving my trip, and when the pubs opened at 5:30 I would buy an evening newspaper and sit reading it with my elbows on the bar, drinking a pint of stout, thinking: *A month ago I was in a tent by a riverbank, swatting flies.*

Sitting there under the timbers of the cool musty pub, I would receive a clear recollection of someone like Tony the beachcomber on the Aboriginal coast of North Queensland—Tony saying, *I found some 'roo meat under a box once. Forgot I had it. Two years old it was. I ate it. Wonderful in soups, you know.* And, feeling blessed, I would give thanks that I had returned, that I had a home, that I was safe, that I had been missed, that I was loved.

A trip like that had a beginning and an end; it was an experience in parentheses, enclosed by my life. But this trip, paddling through Oceania, had turned into my life. Now I was in Hawai'i, living in a valley full of Honolulu rainbows, writing about the Trobriands and the Solomons and Australia, writing about Tony the beachcomber. I thought of the watchful Aboriginal Gladys as her grandson searched her hair for nits. The Kaisiga children singing *Weespa a frayer* in the darkness. The old man on Savo holding a big old radio to his ear, listening for news of the Gulf War. Mini in Morréa saying of her Marquesan child, "Someday she will be a Theroux." There were good people in the waterworld of Oceania. I thought often of Easter Island, the haunting stone faces, the scouring wind, and because I had seen so little hunger in Oceania, I thought of the hunger of little Roberto, muttering his thanks in Rapa Nui, as he clawed the shell from the hard-boiled egg I had not wanted, and wolfed it, his eyes bulging.

I spent a great deal of time wandering the beaches of Hawai'i. I kept paddling too. One morning, paddling off Kaua'i, I saw two humpback whales, and I slipped into the water and spent an hour or more with my ears submerged listening to this happy couple sing and grunt. I was still going, like the man who steps out for a paper and never comes back. I was that man. I had vanished. And there was no reason to go back now. No one missed me. Half my life had been eclipsed.

And then all of it was eclipsed. One morning in July, the Path of Totality lay over the Big Island. I woke at 5 a.m. and foraged around for my welder's mask. It had a density factor of fourteen—the most opaque obtainable. I put it on and was in darkness. If I stared at the sun (so I was told) I would see the same darkness, and a dim wafer.

The last total eclipse in Hawai'i had been in 1850, and at the time the Hawaiians had felt that their chiefs had abandoned them, that the gods were angry, and that the sun—the great *Lā*, which they worshipped—had lost its *mana*. The stars appeared in daytime, the temperature dropped, flower blossoms closed, birds stopped singing.

People flocked to Hawai'i to experience this total eclipse of 1991. There would not be another one like this for 142 years. Fifteen hundred Japanese crouched on the first fairway of the Hyatt Waikoloa, clutching "sunpeeps" which would prevent them from being blinded.

The astronomer Edward Krupp said, "Eclipses are the most awesome inspiring events on earth. No one should go through life without witnessing one."

It was also a marketing opportunity. The hotels were serving a special omelette called an "egg-clipse." There were eclipse towels, eclipse mugs and jewelry, t-shirts saying *Eclipsomania*! and *Totally Umbra!* and *I was there*! A young man named Miles Okimura of Honolulu sold specially sealed commemorative cans of tinned darkness. The *Honolulu Advertiser* pointed out that "the darkness had been canned before the eclipse."

Walking groggily to the roof of my hotel in the early morning darkness I bumped into a man with a flashlight, who was unmistakably Portuguese.

"It's cloudy," he said, sounding vindictive.

Louis Schwartzberg, time-lapse photographer, had been on the roof since four, assembling two 35 mm cameras. He had brought fourteen large crates of equipment.

"I usually bring 30," he said. "But I'm alone."

We ate grapes. Louis looked anxiously at the cloudy skies over Mauna Kea.

"You're not going to need that," he said, indicating my welder's mask.

"What time will sunrise be?"

"It happened twenty minutes ago," he said.

A cloudless day had been forecast. Most days were cloudless here. This freaky haze was connected with the volcanic ash from the eruption of Mount Pinatubo in the Philippines. Louis fell silent. I walked to the edge of the roof and saw people assembling on the driving range half a mile away.

"What can we do?"

Louis said, "Pray." I thought he was going to scream: his jaw tensed. Screaming is uncool. Louis (from Los Angeles) said, "I accept the clouds. I won't get a good shot. I accept that. At least the eclipse brought all these nice people together."

I hurried to the driving range where little family groups squatted on the grass, peering at the bright clouds, aiming cameras. Bryan Brewer, a tall, pale man from Seattle wearing an *Eclipsomania* t-shirt, paced the grass. He was the author of a book about eclipses called *Totality*. He had seen his first eclipse in 1979 and was hooked. He traveled the world, observing eclipses. This, he had predicted, would be one of the greatest. I greeted him, I asked him how he was.

"Nervous," he said.

It was as though he was personally taking the blame for this Act of God.

"We won't see this cloud cover for another 142 years," a photographer said.

No one laughed, though I found this very funny.

A woman named Charlene had come to Hawaii to give lectures on cosmic consciousness and solar vibrations linked to the eclipse—*mana* in fact, emanating from the shadow of the sun. Charlene had long hair and a gownlike dress, and she had attached herself to a group of chatty photographers. She had a sense of urgency, and she walked among the group of men and women saying, "Listen, guys" or "I've got an idea, guys."

The sky was filled with pearly gray clouds and on the ground the gloom was palpable.

"Guys, there's an answer," Charlene said. "When the Dalai Lama escaped from Tibet he needed cloud cover. He and his followers linked their arms together and chanted '*Om*' over and over."

Having nothing to lose we tried this, and the clouds seemed to thicken. Wasn't that what had happened in Tibet? No one said so, but nearly everyone had spent thousands of dollars to come here. Besides the Japanese, there were French and Germans, there were people from Brazil, from California, from Canada.

A photographer said, "We should go back to the hotel and watch this on CNN."

On the roof, Louis Schwartzberg was saying, "I accept this."

"So what happened to the eclipse?" a man asked Bryan Brewer.

"I don't know," Mr. Brewer said, guiltily. "I'm still hoping."

"Did you see the sign in Kona?" a woman asked. "'The eclipse has been cancelled due to unforeseen difficulties.'"

"The eclipse has been eclipsed."

Tedious early morning jollity had begun.

Someone said breathlessly, "The cloud's moving."

People were willing the clouds to shift. And some of the clouds were shifting—sludgy layers of them jostled, allowing sunlight to burst from their seams. It was ten minutes to seven.

Hopefully, I put on my welder's mask and was in total darkness. I took it off and saw that clouds were passing across the sun, ravelling like great hanks and skeins of wool.

No one spoke, there was scattered applause and intense concentration, as the sun burned through the fragmenting cloud, illuminating the woolly shreds. And when it emerged, still in haze but visible, it was not a perfect disc. There was a smooth measured bite out of the top of the sun. And while we watched, the bite grew, until the sun looked like a moon crescent, a fat one, glimmering in daylight.

"What's your setting?"

"One-twenty-fifth at F-eight, 100 ASA."

It was like a command to fire, for as soon as the words were spoken there was a sucking sound of shutters and winders, a shooting that was like bolts being shot from crossbows in furious gulps.

"Check for focus."

"Look at that shadow."

"Anybody got an exposure?"

I was putting on and taking off my welder's mask. With it, I saw a dim crescent. Without it, the glare dazzled and almost blinded me. I scrunched my eyes and glanced and then looked away, as though peering at a forbidden thing. The time was 7:24 and the sun was a golden banana, and two minutes later, the air had already begun to grow cool, and the banana had narrowed to a bright horn that kept thinning and was soon a brilliant splinter, and finally a sliver of intense whiteness. The rest was a dark disc, with specks of light glimmering at its edges, a phenomenon known as Bailey's Beads.

At last the sun was in total darkness, as though a dinner plate had been slid across it—the hand of God, someone had predicted, and that was how it seemed, supernatural. There was brief, hesitant applause, some worried whooping, and then silence, as a chilly shadow settled over us. In Hawaiian Pidgin, the expression for goose pimples is "chicken skin," and I could hear this word being muttered: cheecken skeen.

By 7:29 the world had been turned upside down. Again the stars appeared in daytime, the temperature dropped, flower blossoms closed, birds stopped singing, and we sat transfixed on our cooling planet, watching light drain from the world.

We stared blindly at the black sun until there was a sudden explosion at its top edge that showed a flare of red light.

Our amazement was not pleasurable—not fascination: it was compounded of fear and uncertainty, a feeling of utter strangeness. It was like the onset of blindness. I looked around. There was just enough light to scribble by if I held my little notebook near my face. It was not pitch darkness, but the eeriest glow around the entire horizon, a 360-degree twilight. The silence continued, and in the large crowd, all looking upward, the mood was somber, though the morning air was unexpectedly perfumed by night-blooming jasmine.

It was a world of intimidating magic in which anything could happen.

Before the sun emerged again from its shadow, making the earth seem unmeasurably grander than it ever had before. I kissed the woman next to me, glad to be with her. Being happy was like being home.

Paul Theroux is the author of many works, among them travel books such as The Great Railway Bazaar, The Old Patagonian Express, Riding the Iron Rooster, *and* The Happy Isles of Oceania, *from which this story was excerpted.*

*

The menacing shadow approached us across the water at breakneck speed, then we were suddenly surrounded in a sort of deep twilight...as all on deck gasped or shouted. I was so taken by the enormity of the experience that in three minutes I only managed to take one decipherable photograph. It showed another ship, its lights suddenly visible while our own ship's passengers on two decks were silhouetted against a gray sky with the mysterious black but shining orb above. No photograph, perhaps no verbal depiction of the event could do justice to the experience itself. Later many of us spoke to those positioned at various points on land. They had found it "interesting." But none reported the same heart-stopping, almost religious experience of those of us who had a clear, unobstructed view in the path of totality.

—Robert W. Bone, "A Sight to See"

PART FOUR

In the Shadows

STEVE WILSON

Down and Out in Honolulu

Low life or high life, it's all life in the Islands.

WHEN I ARRIVED IN HAWAI'I I WAS BROKE. THE LAST OF MY money had been spent on the Australian "Departure Tax," and when I walked off the plane in Honululu I had ten cents, and two weeks in which to spend it. After a three-hour walk from the airport—a trek in which I threw up twice—I reached the Ala Wai Boat Harbor, near the hotel strip, where I planned to bang on back doors until I found a job washing dishes. Or was given a meal. Or anything.

I was resting in the shade of a nightclub that had a huge mural of a blue whale painted on one wall when somebody hissed at me. I turned to see an old wooden sailboat, layered with rags and used sandpaper. A man was pacing the deck smoking a cigarette.

"How's it going, man?" he asked.

"It's been better," I said.

"Yeah, want to buy some speed? Crystal?"

I told him that drugs were not on my list of priorities at that moment.

"Do you know if anybody is looking for someone to work on their boat?" I asked.

"Sure—right here, man," he said.

"Can I sleep on the boat too?"

"Sure."

The man's name was something that sounded like Char, at least that's what I called him. He was in his mid-30s, short and wiry like a flyweight boxer. A thick black mustache curved over the edges of his mouth, into which he popped little white pills several times a day. He talked, gestured, ate, worked, and probably shaved and shat, at top speed. We agreed on the ridiculous wage of $20 a day.

The boat, he told me while making lunch, was owned by a bigshot lawyer named Bruce, who had a large estate in the hills behind the city. Char was his gardener. "But I do whatever needs to be done, you know, man?"

He gave me a sandwich made of substances I had forgotten people actually ate: white bread, sandwich spread, sliced bologna and individually wrapped pieces of processed American cheese.

This was not what I expected. I had imagined scores of pineapples awaiting me in Honolulu. Nice, sweet, ripe, juicy pineapples. I knew that pineapples grew in Hawai'i, and I was sure that everybody ate them, cooked with them, drank their juice, and kept dozens of emergency back-up pineapples in their pantries. The thought of eating a fresh pineapple was driving me insane.

"Pineapples? Man, that shit's for the tourists."

"But I am a tourist!"

"You're not a tourist," he scoffed. "Tourists have money. You're practically homeless, man!"

"I'm sure homeless people eat pineapples," I murmured.

Instead of a pineapple I was given a jar of paint remover and sent below. The project Char was involved in was the complete removal of old white paint from the interior of the boat, to be replaced with new white paint. My job was to sand, scrape, grind, chafe, and apply noxious chemicals to the old white paint to encourage its departure. I worked in the only clothes I owned—threadbare white cotton pants and t-shirt—breathing in fumes from paint and paint remover through a thin cotton bandanna tied over my face. The sun and humidity made it fiercely hot inside the cabin. Just breathing was a risk sport. My height of six feet, taller than the cabin, forced me to work for hours with my head bent to one side.

Still, I felt pretty pleased with myself. I was intrepid, a real traveler. I had come into town with no money, found work and a place to sleep, all in one morning. I was surviving on my wits.

That night Char explained the sleeping arrangements to me.

"Hey, man, you can sleep on the front bunk, right, but like, you've got to stay away from the boat until ten tonight."

"Why?"

"My girlfriend is coming over, dude, you know? And she's loud."

He gave me a lewd smile.

I asked him for some money for the day's work. He shook his head, saying, "Hey man, I'm really sorry, but I can't do that. I haven't got any. But, you know, I'm going to see Bruce tomorrow, and he'll give me some cash."

I protested, but he shook his head.

"Tomorrow," he said, "you'll get it all tomorrow."

Char's girlfriend was a thin brunette, maybe eighteen years old, who greeted me with the words, "Let's party!"

That night I walked the streets of Honolulu thinking, this is what it's like to be homeless. You eat lousy food, you don't get much sleep, and complete strangers tell you what to do. As I wandered along, in and out of hotel lobbies, I realized that people were giving me that sidelong glance reserved for the potentially dangerous and unpredictable.

I wanted sleep more than I had ever wanted anything. Walking into one of the big, busy hotel lobbies, sat down on a very soft couch in the lobby, and passed out. I was awakened by two Honolulu policemen, who politely escorted me outside. I blinked at them stupidly: it was a fight to wake up. They helped me to the sidewalk and set me free after warning me about the consequences of a repeated meeting.

When I got back to the harbor, I saw a black Corvette parked in the slot nearest to the boat's slip. I had been warned about this eventuality. The black Corvette belonged to Char's dealer. Char's dealer did not like strangers. If I ever saw the black Corvette, Char said, I was forbidden to be onboard.

Wearily I turned around and walked back to the nightclub by the harbor parking lot. A row of bushes hid the rear wall, and I pushed through them, lay down in the dirt, and fell asleep to the sound of music, laughter, and flushing toilets. I woke up several times to peer out, but the black Corvette was still there. Finally, after the club went quiet, the Corvette was gone. I climbed aboard and collapsed into my bunk. It was 3 a.m.

Char woke me at dawn, gave me some coffee, and set me back to work. Before lunch he vanished, admonishing me to work while he was gone.

"I don't pay you to take breaks, dude."

Indeed, he didn't, for during the two days I worked there we didn't take any breaks. Lunch was a ten-minute interruption, then it was back to scraping, sanding, and painting. The moment he drove off I stopped, ate all the food I could find, stared out the portholes, and didn't start again until Char shook me awake.

"Oh, man, you haven't done shit. This is bullshit, man. How do you expect to keep a job when you don't work?"

"Did you go visit Bruce?" I asked.

"Yeah, man."

"I want my pay. For yesterday and today." I held out a hand.

"Oh, yeah, sure." He gave me ten dollars.

"What's this?"

"Well, dude, you know, Bruce was kind of short on cash. He only had $40 to give me, so I'm giving you half. That's pretty generous, because it means I've only got twenty, too."

Something was wrong with Char's math.

"Well, I took out money for all the food you ate, man. You don't think I'm paying for your meals, do you?"

I put the ten in my pocket, furious. For the rest of the day I sulked and sanded the same one-foot stretch, mostly when Char was yelling at me. He popped pills and jumped in and out of the cabin, complaining about my lack of work ethic.

There were two reasons I didn't leave right then. One was that I didn't know where else to go. The second was that Char had told me he would see Bruce again later that day, and I hoped to get at least another ten dollars out of him. When we finally quit for the day, after working almost fourteen hours, I fell asleep and Char left. He greeted me the next morning in his usual way, shaking me awake with the gray light of dawn behind his head.

"Wake up man. You are fucking lazy, you know that? All you do is sleep. Guess you were plenty tired, eh? Hey, I hope you got enough sleep, because my girlfriend's coming over again tonight. You gotta be gone."

"As long as she's gone by ten or eleven."

"Oh, no, dude, my dealer's coming over too."

"So, tell him to leave. Tell him you've got a tenant."

"No, I can't do that man. Besides, he and my girlfriend, they got a thing going. She gives him some and he gives her a little free, you know?" His feet were walking back and forth while the rest of his body stayed in place.

"What?"

"Yeah, right there where you're sleeping."

"In my bunk?"

He laughed. "Yeah, dude."

"Did you see Bruce?" I asked as I crawled out of my sleeping bag.

"Oh, no, man, he wasn't home. I'll see him today. C'mon."

"I'm not working until I get paid."

"What? Man, you're lucky I give you a place to stay, and you can't work for shit. You're lucky I give you anything."

"I want my pay."

Cursing my ineptitude, my laziness, my lack of respect, he gave me another ten dollars and showed me his empty wallet.

"You see, man, I'm giving you all my money. You think I'm trying to con you, I'm not."

"Good," I said, "because I'm leaving."

Char spent a fruitless ten minutes trying to convince me not to go. He insulted me, praised me, offered me drugs, his girlfriend, and the afternoon off. I put my few belongings in my pack and left. I was surprised he wanted my services so much, but I guess ten dollars for a day's labor is enough to get most businessmen excited.

We left on good terms, Char promising to hire me if I came back and me offering not to contact his boss, the police, and the harbor master. Before the boat was out of view I looked back, and saw his dark shape frenetically careening around the deck.

I felt pretty good as I walked away from the boat. I had money in my pocket, I had eaten, showered, and had a night's rest. A speed freak had not beaten me. I strolled around town, bought supplies (bread, cheese, pineapple) and sat on the beach to eat.

That afternoon I took a bus ride, circling the Island. I saw pineapples growing, for the first time. They looked like artichokes, low to the ground and circled by spines, which surprised me. I had always thought pineapples grew on trees.

About halfway around the Island we passed a resort, the name of which triggered a chain of memories that culminated with the realization that I knew somebody who lived on O'ahu, a man named Shaun whom I had last seen in high school.

After a lot of phone calls, I reached him at work. He sounded very harried.

"Hey, I'd like to help you, you know, but I'm working every day here for the next three weeks. I'm training for this new job, you know, and I've got no free time."

Something, pride or politeness, deterred me from asking to sleep on his floor. I had already decided I could sleep at the airport, or on the beach.

"But, hey," Shaun continued. "Maybe I can help you out. My grandmother, she lives here too, and she's a real sweet old lady. I'll call her and have her meet you somewhere, give you a feed. She's a great cook."

This was welcome news. I spent the next few hours in the library, hiding from the rain, and when I called Shaun that night he told me he'd set a time for noon the next day.

"You go to Macy's, in the mall, you can get there by bus. She'll be waiting for you outside the front entrance."

"How will I know it's her?" I asked.

"She's a little Filipina woman, about as big as a peanut. She'll be standing outside the main entrance."

What Shaun didn't tell me was that Honolulu is home to thousands of legume-sized Filipina women, and that shopping at Macy's is one of their favorite activities. When I arrived there the next day I saw an amazing sight: 50 women fitting Peanut's description were loitering around the front entrance to Macy's. Some were standing, some were sitting around the planter boxes, eating lunch and talking, and some were showing off their purchases to friends. They were all small and brown and had black hair and carried Yves St. Laurent handbags. I stood there before the group wondering how I would ever find Peanut.

Then one of the women approached me, gradually taking on a look of calm concern.

"Are you Steve?" she asked.

I admitted to this and shook her hand. Peanut was in her early 60s, spoke with slightly accented English, and was around four and a half feet tall. She was absolutely unflappable. When I told her that I had been sleeping in the homes of drug dealers, she said it was important to have friends in times of need. She spoke in short, commanding sentences.

"Okay," she said, "now we take the bus." I followed her, feeling tall and gangly. "Shaun said to feed you, so I have lots of food at home. You will have lunch and tell me why you're here."

I have the fondest memories of Peanut. She took me in, treated me like a member of her family, fed me huge amounts of delicious food and would accept nothing in return. I was able to do some minor repairs around her apartment, about which she was overly enthusiastic. She even offered to wash my clothes, which I had to reluctantly decline, since I had nothing else to wear.

"Eat some more," she said when I finished the first plate.

"Oh, no, really, thank you," I said.

Peanut scowled at me. She ordered me out of the chair and over to the stove. There were four pots on it, each of them half full. Then she commanded me to open the fridge. Inside were several bowls of cold salad and noodles.

"Listen," she said, "I grew up in a large family. I have sons and grandsons and I know how much they eat. Look how tall you are. Look how small I am. You think I'm going to eat all this food?"

Feeling gluttonous, I ate two more platefuls. She was an excellent cook.

When I left there I was carrying two plastic bags, each containing three aluminum pie tins filled with teriyaki chicken, sweet and sour pork, salad, fried rice, potstickers, noodles, things made with coconut milk, things made with ginger. I lived off Peanut's food for four days, carefully supplementing it with food bought with my tiny savings.

Peanut had commanded me to return five days later, and when I did, she piled even more food into my stomach and into plastic bags. When I protested she told me to stop being silly.

"You just return the favor to somebody else," she said.

By the time I finished eating her food, I had four more days left in Hawai'i. I had spent a week relaxing on the beach when it was sunny, taking the bus or sitting in the library when it was raining, and sleeping either in the airport or in one of the free state parks. I found a movie theater that played films nonstop, all day, and spent two days in there, with all the other poor. I saw *Platoon* twelve times. (Even today, I can't hear the song "Tracks of My Tears," without remembering waking up in a dark room to the smell of popcorn and body odor.)

The day before I left, with my pack stored safely in an airport locker, I was walking past a big pink hotel when a tour bus pulled up. Twenty-two identical old women with blue hair and bulging handbags piled into it.

"Would you like to join our tour of the Hawaiian macadamia nut factory?" a man asked me, as I watched them board.

"Yes, I would," I said quickly.

We drove for about fifteen minutes, then the bus stopped and the 22 identical old women with blue hair, and myself, got out of the bus and were herded into the macadamia nut factory, where we saw macadamia nuts shelled, sorted, cut, cooked, salted, chopped, diced, dipped in chocolate, mixed with other nuts, covered in honey, fitted into candy bars, poured into plastic, glass, and tin containers, and finally, sold for outrageous prices. The macadamia nut, they told us, is a very versatile food.

At the end we got to the free samples. I ate as much of everything as I could, and when the tour guides looked the other way, I filled up my pockets.

When we got back to the hotel the bus driver switched on the P.A. system and thanked us, then spent several minutes going into the details of his low income and twelve children, and all the purses opened and each of the 22 little old ladies with blue hair gave him a dollar or two when they disembarked. When I left the bus, pockets bulging with macadamia nuts, I smiled, and offered him one.

Steve Wilson has written for Sunset, Blue, Big World, *and* Transitions Abroad, *and at last sighting was getting on his bicycle to finish a trans-Asia ride that he and his girlfriend started in Singapore. They hope to reach their ultimate destination, the coast of Portugal, at which point he will, again, be broke.*

*

It was not long after we moved to Hawai'i, that we learned the true meaning of the aloha spirit.

We were at the airport, waiting to welcome some friends, a couple who was coming to visit us from the Mainland. In our arms, we held two flower *lei*, the traditional welcoming gifts of the Islands.

Nearby was a young, dark-skinned maiden dressed in hula costume—short, ti-leaf skirt, coconut bra. In her arms she held a half-dozen plumeria *lei*.

The plane was running late, and we struck up a conversation with an older Oriental woman. She also held a *lei*, an especially lovely one, composed of some unusual and beautiful flowers. She explained that she was there to welcome her cousin, who was visiting from California.

Then the doors opened and passengers began to pour into the terminal. Someone began singing and playing a *'ukulele*. The costumed young woman sprang into action, placing a yellow plumeria *lei* over the heads of all the *malihini* (newcomers) who were wearing a button of a certain color and design signifying their (paid) membership in a particular tour group.

When her job was finished, she left and the crowd began to move on to collect their suitcases. At that moment one more passenger, a tall man, emerged into the terminal. Although not connected with a group, he was apparently unaware of any difference between himself and those who had immediately preceded him.

"Hey!" he said, looking around but speaking to no one in particular. "What about me? Don't I get some flowers, too?"

The woman at our side hesitated for just a second. Then she stepped forward with the *lei*—the one she had brought for her cousin. The tall passenger stooped low so she could place the flowers over his head.

Then he smiled, thanked her, and strode off toward baggage claim, unaware that anything special had happened to him. The woman then turned, glanced at us, and then shrugged her shoulders.

"What else could I do?" she asked. "He just looked so unhappy!"

It was right there that we learned the meaning of the Aloha Spirit.

—Robert W. Bone, "The Aloha Spirit"

MADELYN HORNER FERN

Moonless Night in Kona

Anything can happen out there on the lava of the Big Island, especially if you're Hawaiian.

IT HAPPENED DURING ONE THANKSGIVING WEEKEND IN KONA. I was working for a travel organization in Waikīkī. My job entailed offering recommendations on places to see, things to do, hotels to stay in, for visitors.

About three times a year, my two coworkers, Juanita and Aulani, and I would plan a trip to one of the Neighbor Islands for a long weekend to keep abreast of new hotels and tours.

We had spent about two weeks planning our upcoming trip to the Big Island. Because of its size, we drew a map and marked off all the places where we would be stopping around the Island, figuring this would make finding them much easier once we were on the road.

I kept the map in a safe place. Aulani and Juanita asked their husbands to join us. Airline reservations were tight: Juanita and I were able to get on a 5 p.m. flight to Kona, but we had to wait until 9 p.m. for Aulani and the two husbands, who were arriving on a private plane.

Juanita and I sat in the old Kona airport talking and passing the time watching people come and go. I pulled our map out of my bag a couple of times to review some of the stops we'd be making.

As darkness fell the crowds thinned out. By 8 p.m. the final commercial flight had come and gone, and workers were locking up for the night. An Aloha Airlines employee came up to see if we needed assistance; when we told him we were waiting for a private plane, he smiled and told us we were in the perfect spot as the private planes landed right outside.

After he left, we felt spooked. No one else was in the terminal. I decided to sit across from Juanita so she could watch my back and vice versa. It was eerie, pitch black in the parking lot and the lights on the runway were dull and looked like they were dancing. And the quiet—it was oh, so quiet. I kept looking at Juanita and she kept looking at me, both of us trying to put up a brave front.

I turned to the right and looked out on the runway. It was a moonless night, the ocean was calm, and I could see the silhouette of a *kiawe* tree against the dark sky. I was mesmerized by this scene. Lo and behold, there was a movement down by the *kiawe* tree. I blinked my eyes to make sure I wasn't seeing things. Yup, there was movement down there. I could see figures walking along the shoreline at the edge of the runway.

I could see men wearing *mahiole* and feather capes. They looked like warriors. There was no sound. It hit me like a lightning bolt. These were night marchers, a long procession of them. The hair on the back of my neck stood up, and I was as white as a sheet. Juanita was trying to talk to me, I kept telling her to be quiet, not to make a sound.

All the stories I had heard from my *tūtū* and my dad came to mind. I kept pointing to the procession and telling Juanita about the movement, but she kept telling me there was nothing there. I don't know how she could have missed them.

I was quite shaken after this experience. I sat completely still in my chair and would not look out at the runway. Juanita and I were both scared. I was looking straight ahead and could see someone approaching. He was walking toward me. It was an older Hawaiian gentleman, slim, with white hair and dark skin, with a white long-sleeved shirt, a *lauhala* hat, and long pants. He was walking but he wasn't making a sound.

I was trying to tell Juanita that he was coming from behind her, but no sound would come out of my mouth. This gentleman walked right up and said, "Aloha." He had a dazzling smile. I answered by saying, "Aloha, how are you?" He came right up to me and said, "I came to get the map that you have in your purse." I was dumbfounded.

Juanita, in the meantime, asked him where he came from. He replied, "I come from Hilo and I have to get the map." With that, I got the map out of my purse and handed it to him. He took it and thanked me. Juanita asked him where he was going and he said, "I'm going back to Hilo." Then, he turned and began to walk away from me. He walked about ten feet and then disappeared into thin air

This completely unraveled us. We didn't know where to turn or what to do because we were the only people at the airport. Soon thereafter we heard a plane approaching. The plane landed and we ran to greet our friends.

Upon overhearing our story, an elderly Hawaiian woman walked up and told me not to fret.

"Those night marchers were your *'ohana*, welcoming you to the place of your family's beginnings. Don't fear them, embrace them, for they will watch over you during your stay here.

"As for the gentleman who took your map, he was your *'aumakua* who took the form of a human. There was danger awaiting you at one of the sites marked on your map and he was protecting you."

Having said that, she got into a car and drove off.

Madelyn "Maddie" Horner Fern, a native of Waimānalo on O'ahu, is Human Resources Manager at the Sheraton Maui Hotel.

*

We were at camp deep in South Kona one night. Our fronts were warm from the fire. Around us it was cold and black. It was a night for stories and this is one Wayne Collins told:

"I was hiking, high up in the ranch country. It was a cold and I was working along through a depression in the pasture, taking it easy, certainly thinking I was very much alone, then suddenly I heard a noise and looked up.

"There was this Hawaiian, on a horse, and he held a rifle on me. It was a Winchester '94, of all things, and the man was glowering. I stopped, there were more hoof scrapings, and soon there were about eight of them on horseback, all Hawaiian or part-Hawaiian cowboys. And they looked upset and serious.

"I just stood there, wondering what the hell was going to happen. One of the last to arrive was an older man who I knew slightly. He said something in Hawaiian to the others, and they rode off, waiting at some distance. He got off his horse and walked down to me. In effect, he told me I was a good guy and he was a good guy and he didn't want to see me get hurt. He said all this in a roundabout Hawaiian style, but there was no mistaking the message: I was going where the Hawaiians didn't want me to go and I was to leave, right then, and stay away. There was no explanation. That was it, and they watched for a long time as I went back down the slopes.

"I have no idea what they were guarding. It might have been an old burial place of the chiefs, or a temple site or religious shrine of some sort. I don't know.

"The curious thing is that I'm not sure they knew. I've often wondered about this. In the ancient system, the *kahu*, the guardian, had a sacred charge. And it was passed on from generation to generation. But over the centuries it seems almost certain that the sites themselves would be lost or buried—by earthquakes, flash floods, lava flows. A grove of trees that held great significance in long ago days is now dust. Nothing remains. These men may be simply guarding memories of vague places. But it doesn't matter. It is a great privilege that they are the Selected. and they will pass the commission on to their children and children's children and the youngsters will know even less...."

—Ed Sheehan and Gavan Daws, "Encountering the Selected," *The Hawaiians*

DANIEL DAVID MOSES

Rain in Hawai'i

A red man discovers a blue Hawai'i.

THE GRADUATE STUDENT GREETS ME AT THE AIRPORT WITH apologies for the rain.

We haven't seen blue sky for six weeks, sighs his girlfriend.

But I can't complain. I'm just in from Canada, where we talk, mocking our situation, even in the temperate south, about six months of winter. It's March, the first week of spring, and though the snow's gone and frost is coming out at last in Toronto, colour has yet to come back.

The Island of O'ahu under rain was a warm body, green and flowered, even through clouds from the plane. And now the city of Honolulu, drizzled on in the distance, seems organic, rocks in a tropical garden.

And I'm the guest here, the exotic one, a red Indian.

On the short walk to the lot and the graduate student's sturdy little car, for the first time in seasons, my skin feels damp, my forehead drips, and suddenly I'm sure I'm shining with sweat.

The car swings onto the expressway, and overhead through the see-through, snapped-down sunroof, the clouds part and show just for a moment the blue of the sky.

What a tease, the girlfriend mutters from her front seat.

✶

But later it's begun again, the downpour a rushing noise on the roof of the restaurant where my new friends and I are eating Japanese.

We're talking about my work and theirs, about the reading I'm here to do tomorrow night at the University, about what I should see of Hawai'i in my bit of time here. We're talking about the life in my home city, and New York, and how isolated they feel here.

It really is the frontier, she says.

All I need to do at this end of the long day, after the hours of flight and the hours added by time zones, and in this twilight of paper lanterns, is close my eyes—I'm that ready to dream. But the sake clarifies my hunger, and the flesh colours of sushi bloom on my plate, my palate.

So the Japanese are the cowboys? The student grins.

And the rain plays the car for a drum when we drive, seeing the sights of the night city. It also beats against the ocean face and the leaves, against the flat and the mountainsides, against houses and their eaves.

So how is it that, in the dark off Diamond Head, lights glow in the rain? Is it phosphorescence?

No, the girlfriend tells me. The true surfer goes out boarding the waves at every opportunity.

So why are so few tourists here, a mere scattering dodging drops on the slick streets along the strip? Isn't there usually more spending of the green stuff at the feet of the famed tall hotels of Waikīkī? The lights here are lit but so few of the crowd are.

The fear of war in the Gulf, the girlfriend tells me, keeps the people away.

But that war's on the other side of the world—I begin.

We're Americans, the grad student sighs, as if explaining everything.

We swerve away from the strip and up a street to the heights as the rain comes down, the center line reflectors like electric fish under the rushing water.

And up there we shelter beneath the gutters of the girlfriend's house, and watch a blackness, a cloud of whispers and winds, moving in from the night and the ocean. It blows between the mountains and covers up first a hill of stars—a suburb where smaller streets and houses are. Then it's closing in on the bright towers downtown, putting their stories of light out too.

The clouds finally part for me four days later on Hawai'i, the Big Island.

My guide to the Kīlauea Crater welcomes me like a brother, says one of his foremothers was Algonquin, from Canada too.

In the orientation center, a display pictures the volcano as a goddess, Pele, and as a tornado of heat rising through the earth's crust, a storm of magma.

Prayer sticks have been placed at the edge of the crater, just beyond the wooden barriers. Under my fingers the grain of that wood is risen, weathered by acid air, by a frost of sulfur.

So somehow both of us do end up red-faced, burned, from the sun glaring there off the bare fields of lava or from the vog, the volcanic fog, or maybe from both.

On my last afternoon on the Island, I seek shelter from that high sun under palms.

I'm at a beach on the south coast, hoping with my hosts for the success of the handsome young man I met and ate dinner with the evening before, a Native Hawaiian who had tried, he said, to be an American. He did school and business like he was supposed to, but ended up in his twenties divorced, a recovering alcoholic. Now he was trying just to be Native again.

I scramble from rock to rock a short way out into the bay, and look back and up at the green fields and mountain. How hard it must be to learn now how to carve, how to drum and sing, to remember a way of life, with all this land overturned into plantations.

Down on the beach, my hosts are easy to spot, two light faces among all the dark ones, all crowded along that narrow strip of lava-black sand by No Trespassing signs.

And here in the loud, bright surf at my feet, great sea turtles are riding in on the tide, eyes wide and steady as many grandfathers'.

Much later, my wonder is how we manage to keep on living so absorbed in ourselves, with the storms of creation right under our feet.

Daniel David Moses is a Toronto poet, a playwright, and coeditor of An Anthology of Canadian Native Literature in English. *His works include poetry* (Delicate Bodies, Nightwood Editions) *and plays (*Coyote City, Almighty Voice and His Wife *and* The Indian Medicine Shows, Exile Editions, *winner of the 1996 James Buller Memorial Award for Excellence in Aboriginal Theater). "I'm the homebody who prefers to stay in his own territory." When he visited Hawai'i and wrote this story, however, he says, "I'd already been in Rotterdam for a storytelling festival...and then I was so suddenly on the other side of the planet that it seemed I was awake in my own dream time. Gradually glimmers of the politics of the place and a bit of rest assured me I was in the same old new world."*

⋆

I was one of those rare Californians who had never been to Hawai'i. The Islands hold a special allure for Californians—who are not a particularly loyal breed. We have mostly come from someplace worse, and we are always looking for someplace better. For easterners, moving west represents a chance to start again, free of the social pressures, the long winters, the crowds. But where do you run to when you're already in California? The choices are few: either into therapy or to Hawai'i.

Every Californian to whom I mentioned my first trip to the Islands wanted to give me the lowdown on Hawai'i—which invariably meant telling me about their favorite beach. Now, I've got nothing against beaches—I was hoping to visit as many as I could. But my real purpose was not just to immerse myself in Hawai'i's warm waters but also to learn something about the local island traditions, about the grass roots sovereignty movement and the renaissance of native culture.

Californians reacted to this as if I'd said I was going to the Sahara to learn how to ski. "Culture?" one Hawai'i buff said. "There isn't any culture in Hawai'i."

—Joel Simon, "The New Paradise: Turning The Tides,"
Condé Nast Traveler

JOANA VARAWA

Lāna'i's Last Cowboy

A plantation community overwhelmed by modern change grieves for a man and the way of life that died with him.

AFTER HE DIED, PEOPLE GATHERED UP AT THE "RANCH." FAMILY, friends, people who had known one another for 30, 40, 50 years, gathered to remember and cry and laugh and tell stories about the man. Everyone had a story to remember him by. The kids played around under the trees and swung from the fences and were warned away from the horses by the old folks. The horses, patient as they had been all their lives, stood and stamped and tossed bridles and reins in the empty air.

"You can't write about him for there is nothing to write. The writing would never end, the stories would just go on and on, and as soon as you told one, there would be another to tell."

"He and Mama took care of all those kids, they just scooped them up, all those kids, the ones the parents didn't have time for, or had to work—took them when they were babies, and raised them and taught them to listen, to ride horse, to be respectful and learn."

"Mama nursed two babies at once, her own and a neighbor's. She held them both in her arms at the same time."

After so many years, the life of a man and wife cannot be separated, the life becomes one life and in the telling of the man or the woman, one tells the story of both.

So it is with Ernest and Rebecca Richardson. While he reigned as the last cowboy on Lāna'i, she made the world clear and orderly for everyone who came around. And come around they did, for there was something compelling and wondrous about "Uncle" Ernest and the "Ranch." It was his sureness, his solid conviction born of his own experience, his specific and focused abilities. He made tack and carved saddles. He braided reins and stretched hides. He planted vegetables and flowers, tended to his horses, and trained everyone else's horse. He was available at all hours if something was needed.

"We walked Colin's horse around all night, eight or ten of us, trying to hold him up, for if he ever went down, he would never get up again. Uncle rigged a sling under the tree to hold up the horse. We walked all night holding up the horse. In the morning it died and Colin cried."

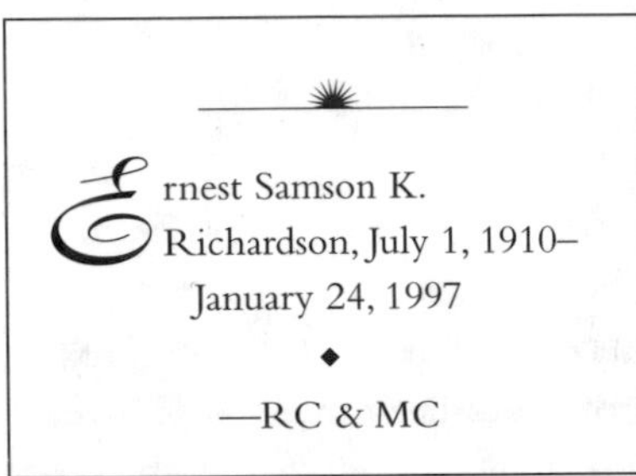

"We rode in the plowed field on the young horses; it was hot and muddy, the sky all smoky and strange looking. Uncle took them to the plowed field so they would get tired and couldn't get out of hand, and he looked at the sky and said, 'Pele's smoke'—the first and last time I ever heard anyone say anything like that."

"He didn't talk that much. If you wanted to learn something from him you just had to watch and be quiet. It was no sense in asking questions; you just stayed quiet and watched."

"He talked this wonderful Pidgin; it was his own. Nobody else talked like Uncle did."

"I used to go with my father when I small-boy time...My mother used to scold me every time I follow him. But him, every time like take me go. He like make me one cowboy. I never think about school. I like only ride horse. When my father leave me home, I cry. And I know where they go. I like go follow them. I no go school. I walk, walk, go find. My father, he only tell me, 'You gotta go school tomorrow.' That's only what they tell me, but that time, I never like go school. I like ride horse. Every time I like follow. I come over here. I learn cowboy. I work with the cowboys. The cowboys, they talk Hawaiian. Then I learn from them. I learn from the way I work. I look, I make, I look, I make, I watch and then *bumbai,* I make and come out."

Their house was right behind the big banyan that is now behind The Lodge at Kō'ele. There was a rope hanging from the banyan and a ring on the end of the rope and that's where Uncle would tie the horse to cool down, there in the enveloping shade of the tree.

The garage was just behind the tree, a long iron-roofed shed with two old military jeeps, saddles, stacked cardboard boxes, tools, cupboards, benches. Uncle would sit on a wood bench in front of the garage and work at something. He was always working at something, making, planting, digging, watering, tending horses. There were horses staked out around the house in the tall grass, a goat pen in back and in front of the house, a sandbox with a tin roof for shade. There was an atmosphere of peace and dignity about the place. Even if you were a stranger, you sensed the order that prevailed there.

Old photos of Kō'ele show a line of trees along the back, parallel with the ridge line, the reflection of the reservoir that is now the reflecting pond behind The Lodge, and some small houses clustered under the trees. The big circular drive in front of The Lodge was a circular drive then, and just there, where the great old Cook Pine tree still stands, was the ranch manager's house.

For a long time there was a proper arena and corral, with rodeo events. One year Uncle Ernest won the "dollar" competition. You had to put a dollar bill under your butt and then ride bareback in a number of events until every man except one had lost his dollar. Uncle was the one who still had the dollar under him at the end. There is a photograph of him sitting on a slim young Hawaiian horse, wearing a cowboy hat trimmed with braided rope and a braided rope *lei* around the neck of the horse. He is holding the dollar.

There is another, even older photo of a very young man, almost a boy, slight and smooth of skin. He is wearing full wide leather chaps, a bandolier across his chest with bullets slotted neatly in it and a bandanna. The chaps were necessary to ride through the Pālāwai (Basin) when it was full of *pānini* cactus; the bandanna became a part of him. A photo taken 50 some years later shows a man with a strong, calm face and a long white beard, wearing a white t-shirt and a bandanna.

Rebecca Kaopuiki Richardson and her family came up from Keōmuku when the ranch moved its headquarters to Kō'ele. Ernest and Rebecca's kids were born in the house at Kō'ele, brought into the world by Rebecca's aunty, a Hawaiian midwife, or by her father, Daniel Kaopuiki Sr.

Of their seven children, three survived. Two died in childbirth, the rest died young. There were no doctors and very little medicine. Rebecca and Ernest took on other children; Rebecca's younger brothers and sisters, eight Morita kids who were neighbors, others. All in all, they raised twenty children as their *'ohana.*

Ernest always was a cowboy. When the Lāna'i Ranch at Kō'ele closed in 1950, they sold the remaining horses to the former cowboys. Uncle Ernest went to work driving a truck, carrying pineapples down to Kaumalapau. But he stayed a cowboy, stayed up at the Ranch and continued the life he knew. He kept his horses, kept going. When he celebrated his 76th birthday, the family sat around outside the house and talked and ate, sang songs and joked. In front of the house, the bulldozers were clearing away the tall grass and the wild bushes, the ferns and flowers, in order to build The Lodge at Kō'ele. Not long after, the Richardsons were moved over toward the graveyard road into an old ranch house that also came from The Lodge site, and they started a new garden, put in banana and ti plants, planted flowers, kept going, kept to the way they knew. The morning they left, the old house was torn down.

When Ernest Richardson died, his physical body was cremated and his ashes carried in a memorial procession on Lāna'i by his riderless horse. Thirty-two horses were gathered up at the house early Saturday morning. Thirty-two family and friends rode down the road, past The Lodge, between the Norfolk Pines, down Lāna'i Avenue, past the post office and the old Dole labor yard, and turned in, where the seasonal workers used to live, to the Cafeteria. There a service was held and some of the stories were told. There were photos of his life and his family and marvelous *lei* of ti-leaf roses. Uncle's saddle was exquisitely decorated with flowers and looped rope. There was a small polished wood box with a small brass plaque.

What is left of his body is in that box. What is left of his spirit is alive in the hearts of the hundreds of people who knew and loved him.

Joana McIntyre Varawa was educated at UCLA and Berkeley. She has written three books and has contributed to Travelers' Tales: Love and Romance. *She lives with her husband Malé in Hawai'i.*

*

We all experienced a sense of loss when the plantation was shut down. Pineapple is gone. Pineapple as we knew it is *pau*. The things we knew which symbolized plantation days are nothing more than a memory now. No more labor trucks rolling out of the labor yard at 6 a.m., and no more picking machines set to harvest what we believed to be the best-tasting pineapple in the world.

You don't see people walking home from the labor yard with their big bags and large hats any more. No need for cover pants and arm guards for work any more and no more *kaukau* tins. The lunch table used to be old newspapers in the middle of the dirt road, and the bathrooms were wherever you felt comfortable going.

Everybody used to start work at the same time and *pau hana* at the same time. Most everyone had Saturday and Sunday off so we had plenty of time to get together, talk story, and have the occasional wedding or baby *lū'au*. We had *luna*, field bosses, and a plantation manager. We were the largest pineapple plant in the world.

Today, we have The Lodge at Kō'ele and the Mānele Bay Hotel as our major employers. We work in housekeeping, transportation, laundry, pastry shop, private dining service, Hulopo'e Court, the Pool Grill, front desk, and concierge. We have movie stars and sports personalities visiting on a regular basis, private jets, helicopters, even butlers.

The town square still looks the same, but we have new names and different uses for the shops. The banana patch at the end of Fraser Avenue is gone due to the development of Iwiole Hale apartments. But no worry, still get chicken fights every weekend, and it is still in one banana patch...."

—Kurt Matsumoto, general manager of The Lodge at Kō'ele,
from his "Reunion Speech" at Lāna'i High School's
55th anniversary, March 1993

RICK CARROLL

Last Dance at the Palace

In changing times, taxi-dancing is gone from Chinatown.

THE SLIM CHINESE GIRL IN THE CLINGY WHITE GOWN WANTED ONE dollar to dance on the last night at the Palace Ballroom. I had a dollar, so we danced. She was light as a feather but she never smiled, just gazed out the dusty windows on Chinatown.

The regulars, Jesus, Boy, and "Crazy" Charley, were there. So were the girls who danced for 50 cents a dance. The band played as if the night would never end.

Imae Kobayashi collected the money; there were no free dances. Someone brought chicken *adobo*, and the regulars tried to put on a happy face like people do at wakes. Then as the four-piece band swung into a hot Latin medley, everyone danced until the music stopped.

The lights came up at 2 a.m., and the old men and the young girls stood there, blinking. They knew it was all over. The slim Chinese girl in the clingy white gown vanished with a bouquet of red roses. The musicians put away their instruments. The old men filed down the steps into Chinatown early on a Sunday morning. After 27 years of countless waltzes and real short romances, the Palace Ballroom was finally closed. They knew it couldn't go on forever.

The taxi-dance ballrooms of Honolulu, for 60 years the pay-day night spots of plantation workers, are all gone now. In their heyday, after World War II, eight dance halls with 70 girls each attracted thousands of lonely men. The Casino, Crystal, The King, The Royal, and The Liberty packed them in every night of the week except Mondays. So did The Sampuagita and The Orchid. Only The Palace Ballroom on Maunakea Street, up above Tin Tin Chop Suey, survived, and then only until 1984.

I learned all this from Warlind Kealoha Jr., the man who closed the last taxi-dance ballroom in Honolulu.

"It was big business after the war," Kealoha told me. "Everybody came, sailors and soldiers."

We met the day of the last dance. He was putting up a hand-lettered sign: "Last Night For Palace Ballroom" on the front door.

Inside, up a narrow staircase, the ballroom looked out of focus in the afternoon glare, an illusion caused by thick dust that blurred the edges of reality. A strand of red, orange, and yellow Christmas lights dropped from the ceiling over an ancient black piano that entertained termites. The dance floor, ringed by 42 faded red theater chairs and two wooden church pews, looked like a gray dishrag.

"It looked better at night," Kealoha said.

At 23 and a business major at UCLA, it fell to him to close the ballroom, which his father had run for 27 years until his death.

"We had no choice—someone had to run it," his widow, Beatrice Kealoha said. She wanted no part of it. "A bundle of nerves. Too many painful memories."

Instead of inheriting a thriving business, young Warlind found himself the caretaker of old men and a dying diversion. "It wasn't making a big profit," he said. "Hardly any at all; soft drinks and coffee. It was a break-even situation." He kept it open anyway.

"It's nice to do things for people," he said.

Taxi-dance ballrooms opened in the 1920s after thousands of young Filipino contract laborers came to Hawai'i to work in the sugarcane fields. The girls, young and pretty, Filipino, Chinese, and local, soon followed. They were skilled ballroom dancers, not prostitutes—although arrangements, Kealoha said, could be made. A fast-stepping taxi-dancer could earn $50 a night and more. The taxi-dance hall was just about the only place a single man could enjoy social contact with women. The music never stopped and the girls never said no, so long as a fellow had cash.

It started out a dime a dance but inflation took care of that. Dances soon cost 50 cents each (the girls got half) and lasted a full minute. A woman with a stopwatch kept tab. The bands played old standards, lots of cha-chas and tangos and cheek-to-cheek ballads.

In the 1930s, two University of Hawai'i sociology students observed the scene and wrote a thesis entitled, "The Taxi-Dance Hall In Honolulu." The scholars, two women, found that the average age of a dancer was 22, although most girls were 18 and a few were 38.

"Out of about 300 girls, 40 are Portuguese, 31 are Filipino, 28 are pure Hawaiian, 27 are Hawaiian-Chinese, 24 are Japanese, 15 are Korean, and 12 are pure Chinese. The older dancers are of the Caucasian races, and they are old hands at the game.

"One distinguishing characteristic of the taxi-dancer is the inevitable permanent wave. This, added to plenty of mascara and eye shadow, rouge, and lipstick, is supposed to render her sexually attractive.

"She usually chooses a dinner or cocktail dress of clinging form, revealing lines, and of medium length, worn with sandals for comfort and durability."

Nearly 50 years later, the last taxi-dancers at the Palace were mirror images of their sisters of the '30s, minus the permanent wave.

In all those nights of a thousand tangos nobody ever took a picture inside the Palace of the old men and young girls dancing. "I never saw such a picture," Kealoha said.

Years ago, he said, Honolulu Police took mug shots of the girls. "The girls had to have their picture taken. All the girls were registered. Most dancers had day jobs in banks or stores. They came and they went," he said. He said he never knew their last names.

The slim Chinese girl in the clingy white gown said her name was Mei. It took two dollars to get that far with her on the last night at the Palace as we danced. She didn't want to talk, only dance.

After our third dance, she excused herself and dashed off to the powder room. I went in search of a soft drink and stood on the sidelines watching old men and young girls dancing. The next time I saw the slim Chinese girl in the clingy white gown, she was in the arms of an old Filipino man. He arrived just before the last dance with a bouquet of red roses. He was smiling through tears as they danced.

Rick Carroll also contributed "At the Bishop" in Part Two.

⋆

Mary Lou wanted red, roasted, hung-out-to-dry Chinatown ducks, five in all, for her open house the day after Christmas, so Michael and I rose before dawn the day of the party to hunt duck.

First, we bought four dozen fresh *bao* (buns) at a hole-in-the-wall bakery next to the Zamboanga Theater, then arrived at O'ahu Market, seventeen stalls under one tin roof, minutes after it opened. We were the only *haole* shoppers amid old Chinese ladies with fast-filling market baskets.

Michael and I surveyed the aquariumlike displays of fresh yellow and blue and gold fish, some still shimmering on ice, grimaced at the sight of a freshly decapitated hog's head, paused before overflowing bins of shrimp of every size.

We laughed at odd, erotic-looking Asian vegetables, bought two fresh young coconuts and a bag of almond cookies.

Vendors began displaying Hong Kong-style noodles, steamed *manapua* (Chinese pastry filled with sweetened pork), Korean ribs, Thai ginger fish, flaky Vietnamese croissants, Filipino chicken *adobo,* and Hakka-style Chinese seafood.

Finally, we found Chinatown ducks, hanging by their necks in a glass case on King Street.

"You want duck?" asked the young Chinese girl with cleaver in hand.

"Five ducks, please," I told her.

She held up five fingers of her free left hand.

I nodded and she began hacking the first duck into precise bite-sized pieces—hack, hack, hack—without looking.

She saw that I was watching her hack.
"Peking duck," she said. Hack, hack, hack.
"Beijing duck, now," I said, being politically correct.
"Peking duck," she replied, "always."

—RC

RON YOUNGBLOOD

Not on an Island

Noise, and how you deal with it, is a peril of local life on Maui.

IT WAS A SCENE THAT IS REPEATED ALL OVER THE ISLANDS. A GROUP of motorheads standing around in a garage, working on machines, talking story. Except this scene included a nasty element.

D. D. is a longtime wrench. He'll work on anything that has wheels, from riding lawn mowers to Harleys to big diesel rigs. He has a place near the end of a narrow residential street.

It's an old neighborhood. The houses sit cheek by jowl. The street is barely wide enough to allow two compact sedans to pass each other.

At the entrance end of the street, the houses are mostly occupied by retirees, folks who spent years laboring for one of the plantations or the county or the state.

The houses are old and small but they glisten in the sunlight. The yards are as neat as a front-room carpet. The vehicles parked in the garages are older but in mint condition, showing the effects of short trips and frequent washings and waxings.

Here and there are households with families and small kids who, naturally, think of the narrow street as an asphalt adjunct to their yards. Then, there are the cats and dogs who live in the neighborhood.

It's a pleasant place. But it takes accommodations.

Veterans of the plantations' old housing camps know what is involved. So do folks with experience in non-air-conditioned apartment houses. Noise and traffic can be problems in the confines of such a neighborhood. There is a level of noise that is acceptable. A level of traffic that is tolerable. Everyone has to be considerate of everyone else. Real noisy activities such as running big compressor rigs or banging on metal gets done during the day and as quickly as possible.

Behind D. D.'s place is a little cul de sac. Down there, another group of motorheads often gather to talk about and work on an eclectic collection of muscle cars, trucks, and jeeps.

Lots of vehicles coming and going.

D. D. had just finished welding up an exhaust pipe on his truck. A couple of friends were hanging around. The atmosphere was as light as the day was clear. Wisecracks and banter flew back and forth. Laughter competed with a neighbor's radio. Then the rumble of an unmuffled Harley drowned out both.

D. D. looked up as the rider pulled up at the end of the driveway and parked his scooter. He left it idling and walked away from the 800 rpm thudding.

The rider—a slight acquaintance who had once gotten some help for his ride from D. D.—was about ten yards away.

"Goin' kinda fast, yeah, bro," D. D. said as amiably as he says anything.

"Not that fast," the rider said with a hint of bristle.

"Gotta lot of retired folks living up that way," D. D. said. The two friends just stood and watched. It was D. D.'s place and his play.

"It's the loud pipes," the rider said, coming to a stop still some yards away.

"Yeah, well.... Gotta keep it down. Just ride real easy. Let it...."

The rider spoke with surprising heat as he spun on his heel.

"Expletive you. No one is going to tell me how to ride my bike."

"Yeah, I will. On my street," D. D. shot back.

The rider straddled his bike. D. D. glared at the man's back. The rider revved the engine and went screaming down the street. The bike could be heard moving out on the main street several blocks away. The sound continued for several minutes as the angry rider blasted down the main road.

D. D. sighed then he talked about doing violent things to "that expletive expletive." But his heart wasn't in it. The friends understood. Old-time motorheads on Maui are well aware of the trouble loud engines can cause in neighborhoods. You do what you can to keep the noise and the heat down.

The sky was clear but a cloud floated by, dousing the dazzle of the day.

D. D. went back to doing what he was doing before the rider showed up.

"I've talked to the brothers about that guy. They all say he's a jerk."

The damage had been done.

D. D. would have to live with the repercussions.

The two friends talked about the flash response from the rider.

"Ahh, that bike is probably the only neat thing in his life," said one.

"You'd think he'd have enough sense to walk easy until he knew what was happening. That's the way to handle that kind of situation,"said the other.

"Or just climb on your scoot and blast off," said the first. "That's the other way to deal with it."

"Not for long, though," said the other. "Not on an island."

Born on the plains of northern Illinois, Ron Youngblood was raised in Indiana and educated by United Press International in Indianapolis and Chicago. Cold winters drove him to Hawai'i, in 1968 where he worked for the Honolulu Advertiser *before moving to Maui. He worked as a freelancer, county information officer, editor of a weekly newspaper, broadcaster, and, columnist, and theater reviewer for* The Maui News, *was principal writer for* On the Hana Coast, *and has had two plays produced on Maui. He lives in Haiku with two cats (the steers stay outside), enjoys scuba diving, motorcycles, music, and "the glories of the best people in the best places in the world."*

✶

On every Island, I suppose, there's got to be a practical place where you can commit retail—you know, get gas, find film, eat pizza by the slice, sip a latte, shop for Nikes, get fast cash at the ATM, and otherwise hang out at the mall. There never used to be all this Mainland stuff on Maui until recently.

While everybody was snorkeling, I guess, it all seemed to surface overnight in Kahului; the failed sugar mill town was a pushover for developers.

Now, Kahului looks like the place you went to Maui to get away from. It's got a big new mall, streets lined with used car lots, fast-food joints, pizza parlors, and blocks of schlock with traffic lights and traffic jams. What used to be a wide spot in the road is now an excellent example of bad urban planning—there's a Costco next to a wildlife preserve, with Maui's three main roads ending in a killer intersection that puts deplaning tourists at direct odds with home-bound locals. Now, they're talking about extending the runway and adding direct flights from Tokyo and Los Angeles.

Unless you're a serious mall rat on holiday, or need to fill up your rental car on the way out of town, I can think of no reason to visit Kahului, the least Hawaiian place.

—Rick Carroll, *Frommer's Hawai'i*

LEE QUARNSTROM

One Way to Get Laid in Honolulu

Sticking your nose into someone else's business.

UNTIL AMERICAN MISSIONARIES BROUGHT WESTERN CULTURE, which mainly consisted of prohibitions against almost everything Hawaiians did and believed, to the Islands in the 1820s, sex was apparently as popular as dancing the hula. In fact, to the horror of the New England Puritans who brought the word of Jesus to the archipelago, much of the hula was *about* sex—and consequently had to be banned post haste.

Zealous in their efforts to cover bare breasts and genitals of what they believed to be demonically sex-crazed natives, the prim Congregationalists quickly invented that godly piece of haberdashery, the *mu'umu'u*.

Today, not quite two centuries after contact with the censorious *haole* fashion mavens, many Hawaiians are, indeed, quite proper in the expected manner of repressed converts whose souls have been properly saved. Yet, one need not be a detective nor even a keen observer to discover that it's pretty easy, in Honolulu, to whoop it up!

My pal C., a local boy, tells me I'm not gonna believe the scene at the Rock-Za. And in truth, the half dozen stages spread throughout the smoky room, each with several nude women "dancing" with their nether regions not only exposed but in fact presented for inspection millimeters away from the gynecologically astute male customers' faces, is a bit overwhelming at first.

We order a drink from the *mama-san* who runs the bar while keeping a sharp eye on each dancer and each engrossed man at the same time. Then we try, and fail miserably, to look cool, disinterested, even above it all as we sit on stools at the edge of one of the little stages. But damn, this sloe-eyed brunette with the gigantic breasts and the pubis shaved but for a tiny vertical strip of hair sort of like Hitler's mustache turned on edge, is standing right above me with her...well, her labia pulled open with fingers that sort of ask me to stick my nose into somebody else's business.

I give C. a "side-eye," as he calls the method used by prowling Japanese businessmen to observe the Waikīkī streetwalkers without showing immediate interest on Kalākaua Avenue just a few blocks away. But C. is watching a reedy blonde with breasts that could not possibly have any true genetic legacy grinding out a slow hootchie-kootchie unrelated to the loud, jazzy rock music blaring through this remarkable Honolulu cultural center.

Later, outside, sated with the show but certainly not sated in the more traditional manner, we split, he to drive home to the missus, me to decide the rest of my evening's itinerary. I could head over to the "body shampoo" parlors a few blocks away for a Japanese-style rubdown to relieve *all* the stress in this body. I know that a few blocks up the way there's a peep-show arcade where two bucks worth of quarters and a fiver slipped through a slot will inspire a model who'll assume just about any pose for anyone wanting to relieve his own stress. I understand that at several clubs between the Rock-Za and downtown there are so-called Korean bars where practitioners of the old expensive-drink B-girl schemes promise but rarely deliver quality time in one of the dark booths at the back of the club.

And, of course, there's the Club Hubba Hubba, a World War II–era joint on notorious Hotel Street in Chinatown, a place where slatternly strippers will sit with horny males and, if one is lucky, do the same thing prostitutes did on Hotel Street during the days when Navy swabbies and Army guys on R&R stood in long lines outside cribs occupied by overworked girls.

But I decide to get to Waikīkī on the double.

It's not far away, a ten-minute walk across the Ala Wai Canal (and it's going to move closer once the new Hawai'i Convention Center draws thousands of men away from home with money to burn right across the street from the Rock-Za).

Night after night during my two dozen-plus trips to Honolulu, I've observed the nubile honeys who make their Kalākaua Avenue appearances after 8:30 p.m. Most are *haole*, although there's a smattering of Asian and "chop-suey" or "all mix-up" ethnic Hawaiian blends among the streetwalkers who stroll singly or in pairs along this famous tropical boulevard.

All of these pretty young women, it seems, are fluent in Japanese. At least, they speak enough to engage the omnipresent Japanese men out on the town in preliminary discussions about what they might do to make the evening more pleasant.

Some of the young women dress demurely. Most, however, affect the hooker look that not only makes the statement, "I gotta be me," but offends the rubes from mid-America who often stop and gape at these little angels of the night.

How many times I have heard hefty middle-aged women snarkily say to bowling-pin-shaped hubbies, "Well, will you look at that!" What a stupid thing for wives to say to husbands who are already half-blind from side-eye inspections.

Now don't get me wrong: I knew from numerous evening walks along the promenade that the young ladies don't just date men from the western edge of the Pacific Rim. Although some ignore their fellow Americans, others are likely to ask a lonely guy, "Wanna date?" "Maybe later," has been my usual response.

This time, though, it was quite late, and the pool of potential bed mates had thinned out for the night, when a lovely young lady of some exotic ethnic heritage wondered whether I was booked for the next half hour. I listened, visions of Rock-Za *artistes* quickly being replaced by anticipation.

"My girlfriend and I," and here she pointed to a pal who turned out to be Chinese and Filipina, "will do you for 200 dollars."

Jesus, 200 bucks, I thought to my cheapskate self.

But I responded, of course, "Sure, that sounds good."

So we walked, my new friends and I, a couple of blocks inland to a quieter street where one of them hailed a taxi. We drove five dollars' worth of time, my five bucks, to a small hotel on an obscure corner not too far from the Ala Moana shopping mall. I paid the driver, tipped him a buck, and followed the gals inside. Despite the sign outside advertising this place as a hotel, there was no front desk, just an elevator that took us to our third-floor love nest.

I can make this long story shorter by reporting this: It was the best $200 I ever spent. Call me sometime and maybe I'll give you some details.

As former executive editor of Larry Flynt's notorious Hustler Magazine, *Lee Quarnstrom was the perfect professional to write this piece. Now a staff writer and columnist with the* San Jose Mercury News, *Quarnstrom has visited Hawai'i more than two dozen times. Prior to taking trips to the Islands, he took trips in the 1960s as one of author Ken Kesey's Merry Band of Pranksters, whose trips in those days were mostly into Inner Space.*

*

From the moment I stepped off the plane, I knew that Maui was a lovers' paradise. The second thing that came to mind was that I was without a lover.

I was traveling with a family as their nanny. My reality shifted from the seductive smell of plumeria *leis,* mind-altering trade winds, and soul-capturing tropical waters to swimming-pool toys, bedtime gecko hunts, and Cheeseburgers in Paradise. Both irresistible, but worlds apart.

On my night off, the need for amour returned. I hit the streets of Lahaina in search of a fulfillment I didn't know I didn't need. I had heard great things about a certain restaurant. Its dining room and bar were set on an open-air wooden deck right over the water.

One of the two bartenders there looked like the ever-so-handsome Aidan Quinn. Without hesitation I chose to sit on his side of the bar. It didn't take long before we were charming each other. With some effort,

I managed to make my dinner and drinks last till the end of his shift. That night we had a drink together, and we made a date for my last night in town.

I bounced around for two days, then paced and fiddled with my hair the last hour before he picked me up. We went for drinks, and I found out he'd left the Mainland ten years ago and had no intention of going back. I wondered if I could move to an island for the love of a man—this particular man before me.

"I want to show you something," he said, distracting me from my fantasy.

He drove me through hidden farm roads walled by sugarcane. Up the side of the mountain, we climbed toward the big "L." An owl flew across our path and he told me its Hawaiian name, *pueo.* What a rare occurrence this was, he said; good luck was on its way.

The road ended at an old hunting lodge. We sat on the porch steps and gazed at the moon. I pretended to be cold in hopes that he would put his arm around me. No such luck. Where was that owl anyway? This was a perfect romantic setting in my mind. Why wasn't he kissing me? Instead, we talked and talked.

It was past midnight when he suggested we move down to the beach. I eagerly agreed.

Kapalua Beach was an even better place for love to light a fire. He'll surely kiss me now, I thought, sitting next to him in the sand, moving closer. Finally, he made the motion. He gave me a sweet short kiss. Then another. And another.

"Want to go to my place?" he blurted out. We hadn't kissed more than six times—believe me I was counting—and he wanted to take me to bed? That's not romantic. I wasn't even warmed up! No rolling around in the sand first? What about second and third base? There are rules of progression to this business. Well, at least on the Mainland.

Seeing the look on my face, he said it was best to take me home. My quintessential island romance cooled as quickly as the night breeze.

Jennifer Leo, "Island Romance"

PART FIVE

The Last Word

MARCIE CARROLL

Beauty and the Beach

A secret shared by the faithful.

I HAVE BECOME ADDICTED TO NATURAL BEAUTY AND PARTICULARLY, to the beautiful beach where I live. I came to Hawai'i yearning to live as close to the warm, clear sea as I could get, close enough to see it, smell it, and jump in, anytime, any day. I moved here, a mountain away from the city, because I wanted to walk to the beach and drive anywhere else. O'ahu is ringed with spectacular beaches, but none is more enticing than Lanikai Beach, on the morning side of the Ko'olau mountains, as lovely a spot as the planet has to offer and my home for the past fifteen years.

For better or worse, Lanikai was memorialized by a Maryland marine researcher as America's Best Beach of 1996. Dr. Stephen Leatherman liked the silky coral sands and awesome scenic views, and he wanted to highlight the problems of seawall-prompted beach erosion shared by Lanikai and many other shores.

Fortunately, he did not include a map (and neither will I), so this notoriety has not changed my out-of-the-way beach too much.

My beach defines the odd little Windward neighborhood of Lanikai, misnamed by a 1920s-era developer who wanted to call his creation "heavenly sea" (that would have been "Kailani"). Lanikai is a few hundred homesites squeezed between the sea and rocky Ka'Iwa ridge, formed like the wing of the mighty *'iwa* (frigate bird). The ridge hides my neighborhood from view.

Yet people inevitably find it. Even people who can take or leave beaches seek out Lanikai; often, however, they go away unfulfilled. Others like me fall in love with the place and brave the winding drive over green peaks day and night in order to live here, while city friends visit every chance they get to escape the hot pavement. Travelers from afar who missed the turn for Kailua Beach Park and stumbled onto Lanikai, or who were led to Buzz's Steak House and the beach beyond by local friends, know the way now, and they return year after year. All these are beach people, and Lanikai is that kind of beach. A secret shared by the faithful.

There are broader strands, with better access and more onshore amenities, but perhaps they make Lanikai even more special. Its fine golden sands are ephemeral, shifting always with the tides and storms and seasons, settling offshore to give Lanikai's share of the Pacific distinctive, brilliant aquamarine hues. Sometimes the beach vanishes under high tides, while low tides leave it bare and defenseless.

Nearly a mile offshore, a fringe of reef breaks the force of the waves and pokes above the horizon in the form of two little islands called the Mokulua ("two islands"), part of a great sunken crater whose edges include other neighboring islets and land ridges in the area. So picturesque are the Mokulua against the azure waters, so typical of the tropical dream that photos of the scene show up in the oddest places: masquerading as Australia in Down Under tourism ads, for instance, or featured as the view to expect from your room in ads for a chain whose Waikīkī hotels are miles away.

The Mokulua, locally known as The Mokes, are inhabited by wedge-tailed shearwaters, seabirds that moan in the night like fretful babies. They dig burrows and raise families. I can see them with a telescope that reveals a Moke hillside pocked with fluffy white chicks and roosting birds above a sandy beach jammed on sunny weekends with Hobie cats, windsurfers, and kayakers.

Lanikai Beach borders a large lagoonlike channel formed by the reef. Sheltered waters, twenty feet at the deepest, flow over a drowned beach dotted with chunks of coral-crusted reef rock left behind by old tidal waves. Turtles and eels and colorful reef fish cruise among the rocks at will, while schools of silvery *'oama* and darting *papio* are born and caught along the shallows. Wavy red Spanish dancers—nudibranchs—wash up periodically and on soft summer nights, the stars above are echoed by tiny phosphorescent creatures in the sand below.

The beach is the core of our neighborhood, the place where strangers meet and children grow up. We proudly claim a famous *hula hālau* and a champion outrigger canoe team, but the beach is what cements Lanikai. People get married, baptized, and eulogized on the beach. Toddlers learn to swim here without fear of the waves that pound nearby beaches. Bodies in scanty attire, ranging from young and perfect to old and lumpy, supine to sauntering, are regularly displayed on the warm sands.

The beach has been my joy, inspiration, and solace, a place to turn cartwheels, learn tai chi, plot novels, comfort friends, and mourn my dead mother.

While the beach and the sea offshore are only crowded on Sundays and holidays, they are almost always in use, good weather or bad. Winter storms are most impressive when I venture out on the beach to look for glass fishing floats from Japan and see the placid pool whipped to froth, tearing viciously at the land. When the white noise roar of offshore surf wakes me in the middle of the night, I know the devout will be up before the sun to paddle out to Lefts, Rights, or No Can Tells for the ritual of dawn patrol.

This is where the day is born. Dawn comes with a symphony of bird song: dainty chattering from red bills, noisy mynah conversations, shrill wake-up calls from the cardinals, clumsy bulbul whistles, and above it all, the heartstopping melodic contralto of the shama. The skies are streaked with reds and golds before the sun blasts out of the sea. On the beach, early swimmers, walkers, and runners glory in the sunrise and watch for the green flash. Nothing is so bad that a Lanikai dawn can't make it better.

All through the day, mothers and children, vacationers and others bring towels and chairs to the sand and bake, basting themselves periodically in the warm green sea. Mothers bring newborns here for a first touch of lapping seawater and swimming lessons. Snorkelers regularly inspect the deeper coral heads. Film crews bring their models and actors to pose before the natural Technicolor of Lanikai. Winter days bring passing humpback whales, which spout and cavort outside the reef and seem to hang out around the Mokulua.

Now and then, howling trade winds blow up a cloud of pastel, plastic butterflies, and my windsurfer neighbors streak back and forth until they collapse on shore to rest before they carry home their rigs on their heads. Shoreline fishermen bring their families, poles and bait, and sometimes sizzling woks to the beach early in the day or after the sunbathers retire to their showers. Night divers go out in search of fish and lobster, their underwater lights creating strange blue-green blooms in the dark sea.

The moon rises here, drawing nocturnal beach strollers. I have walked the strand in moonlight when ghostly boys whooshed by on skateboards with sails. Moonlight silvers the waters and silhouettes the Mokulua and coco palms. In the bright, mercurial waters, you can see colors, at least echoes of blue—perhaps the inspiration of the song "Blue Hawaiian Moonlight." We can't bear to shut out this scene with shades. Once I awoke and saw a moonlit rainbow over the Mokulua, an unforgettable pearly rendition of the daytime classic. Sights like this elude film; they can only be absorbed through the eyes and stored in the heart.

Someday, inevitably, I will have to leave Lanikai, packing my tattered pareu and albums of sunrise pictures and relinquishing my place on the beach to another aficionado. I'm not sure I really can live without it. But every day is richer for having had the beauty of the beach and the ebb and flow of the sea to comfort my spirit.

Marcie Carroll also contributed "Birdland: Lullaby of Midway" in Part Two.

Other islands may call you to their shores, but in the Pacific, only Hawai'i has all the elements of an earthly paradise. The old, the new, and the fantastic all may be found in all the Hawaiian islands from Kaua'i's velvet Nā Pali cliffs in the north to the black lava coast of the Big Island's South Point. Even in Honolulu, travelers experience a sense of well-being derived from the Polynesian concept of wealth—you are what you feel, not what you have—and they return time and again for reality checks, as if Hawai'i were a dream. In a way, it is—one that almost always comes true.

What You Need to Know

If you're a *malahini* (newcomer) you need to know some basic information on Hawai'i. Like where it is, how far it is, what time it is there, what the weather's like, when's the best time to go, and important stuff like if it's okay to drink the water.

The Basics

- The water's fine (it's filtered for centuries through volcanic rock), you don't need a passport, or a visa or shots like in a Third World country. American greenbacks are the currency, but Hawai'i does accept Japanese yen.
- Natives are friendly—if you can find one. Everyone speaks English here. No topless maidens will meet you in canoes with flower *lei*. Nobody thinks you look funny wearing a *lei*. There are no diamonds on Diamond Head.
- The volcano goes off whenever it feels like it. Rainbows appear whenever you are between the sun and a rain cloud.
- Waikīkī is $15 by taxi from the airport. Folks tip here. People don't live in grass shacks anymore. The pink hotel is the Royal; the white one is the Moana.
- Nobody lives in the Royal Palace. The last king died in 1891, and the last queen died in 1917. The average wait to see Pearl Harbor by boat

is 90 minutes. Yes, Japanese tourists go there, but most are too young to remember the day of infamy, December 7, 1941.

- Moloka'i is an island, not something to eat; that's a *loco moco*, not to be confused with a local *moke*. Tongans are the big guys in skirts, so no make fun. That's pidgin for don't poke fun. Pidgin is that funny language everyone speaks that you don't understand at first. Byumby, you talk li'dat.
- Interisland planes (Aloha and Hawaiian) leave about every 20 minutes. Often, they arrive on time. Everything costs more because Hawai'i is in the middle of the Pacific. Sharks are friendly, some are people's relatives. James Michener wrote *Hawai'i* (Hawai'i's all-time best-selling book), but he lived in Florida and died in Austin, Texas. Nobody thinks "I Got *Lei*-d In Hawai'i" t-shirts are funny anymore.

Where Is Hawai'i?

Hawai'i is near the center of the Pacific Ocean about 2,390 miles southwest of California, or five hours by jet from the West Coast. The seven inhabited islands—Hawai'i, Maui, O'ahu, Kaua'i, Moloka'i, Lāna'i, and Ni'ihau—lie southeast to northwest across the Tropic of Cancer between 154°40' and 178°25' west longitude and 18°54' to 28°15' north latitude. That puts it in the North Pacific not, as most people believe, in the South Seas. The error persists; I just saw Hawai'i misplaced in the South Pacific in *The New York Times* travel section.

Hawai'i is just inside the tropical zone and shares the same latitude with Mexico City, Havana, Hong Kong, Calcutta, Mecca, and the Sahara Desert; it's full of sunshine, balmy trade winds, and temperatures in the low 80s.

...In Relation to Botswana?
Honolulu is 2,498 miles from Denver, 3,850 miles from Japan, 4,829 miles from Washington, D.C., 4,900 miles from China, and 5,280 miles from the Philippines. It is 1,700 miles north of the equator. Its antipodes—places on the other side of the globe—are Botswana and southwest Africa.

Quick Geography Lesson
In the vast reaches of the North Pacific a great range of volcanic mountains

rises from the sea floor. The mountain range is nearly 2,000 miles long, and one of its peaks is the highest on earth. The peaks of those mountains comprise the Hawaiian archipelago, the world's longest island chain. It stretches 1,305 miles from the barren, windswept cliffs of South Point on the Big Island of Hawai'i to the pale green lagoon of Kure Atoll, the last peak in the Hawaiian chain. The chain includes Midway, and it points like a bent finger toward Japan where it's moving about as fast as fingernails grow on the shifty Pacific plate.

Some day, in 70 million years or so, the Hawaiian Islands may end up next to Japan. At present, the geographic center of the island chain is the island of Lāna'i, about 2,400 miles from Japan, California, and Alaska.

An infinity of deep, open ocean stretches in every direction from the Hawaiian Islands, the most remote inhabited island group on the planet. It sits at the head of Polynesia, a vast triangle defined by Hawai'i in the north, New Zealand in the southwest corner, and Easter Island (or Rapa Nui) in the southeast corner. (Easter Island, incidentally, is the *single* most isolated island of Polynesia; it is 1,400 miles east of Pitcairn, its nearest inhabited neighbor island and 2,400 miles off the west coast of Chile.)

How to Tell *Mauka* from *Makai*

There is no north and south on an island, it's leeward or windward, like on a ship. In Hawai'i, it's also *mauka* and *makai*. It means to the mountain or to the sea. On O'ahu, directions are: Diamond Head and 'Ewa, *mauka* and *makai*. Diamond Head is the volcano and 'Ewa is the once great plain of sugarcane, now sprouting three-bedroom, two-bath tract houses.

Ask a Honolulu police officer for directions and he may say: "It's on the Diamond Head *mauka* corner"—which would be southeast to you. Officers also carry compasses, so they can show you, in case you still don't get it.

Get a map. The best maps of Hawai'i, bar none, are published by University of Hawai'i Press. Full-color topos, they are a bargain at $2.95. Each map includes a detailed network of island roads, large-scale inset maps of towns, points of interest and historical importance, both natural

THE NEXT STEP

and cultural; hiking trails, parks and beaches, waterfalls, peaks and ridges (with altitudes); and many other amazing details.

What Flag Is Hawai'i Under?

Even though you've flown five hours across the Pacific, you are still in the good old USA. Check out the flag. Stars and stripes. The other one is the Hawai'i state flag. It looks like Great Britain's Union Jack because the islands were first claimed by the British. Hawai'i is the last and 50th state, admitted to the union on August 21, 1959, as The Aloha State.

WHEN TO GO/WEATHER

Go anytime you can. There are so-called high and low seasons, but Hawai'i is a popular world destination year-round. Peak tourist traffic from the U.S. Mainland occurs between Christmas and April and July and August, so plan your visit before or after those months and you'll enjoy Hawai'i more.

The temperature for all islands is seldom below 72°F or over 90°F. The normal daily mean temperature is 77°F—best in the United States.

Hawai'i doesn't have the traditional four seasons. Since it's just inside the tropical zone, Hawai'i technically has only two seasons—wet and dry. The dry season corresponds to summer, and the rainy season is like winter.

Many believe the weather never changes in Hawai'i, but the Islands, isolated as they are in the middle of the Pacific, are subject to an incredible range of weather conditions from tropical to alpine, often dramatic, sometimes disastrous, like Hurricane 'Iniki, the most powerful in Pacific history, which crushed Kaua'i in 1992 with 225-mph winds.

Tsunamis, huge tidal waves generated by distant earthquakes in Alaska and Chile, have swept Hilo and the south shore of O'ahu. Such occurrences are rare. Mostly, days pass in glorious sunny procession, one quite like the other, and you have only to decide where and how to spend the day.

What Should I Wear?

Just wear a smile and a swimsuit. You'll fit in everywhere at the beach. A block or two *mauka*, you may want to dress up: shorts, a t-shirt, flip-flops. Summer dresses, short-sleeve blouses, shorts, and sandals. A *mu'umu'u*, if you mu'ust. Blue jeans, polo shirts, and tennis shoes are usually too hot.

Most of the time in the Islands, it's BB (basic beach)—swim trunks, shorts, t-shirts and "aloha attire"—bright-tropical-print shirts worn untucked over white or khaki pants, and sandals.

Pack light, one carry-on, skip Baggage Claim, be the first one on your plane at the beach. Most people bring too much or clothing that's too warm or inappropriate. Like neckties. Or those rectangular rock-hard cosmetic cases some men schlep around for their wives. Leave it behind.

VISAS/PERMITS

Citizens of most European countries, Australia, and New Zealand require only a valid passport to enter the USA for 90 days. They must also have enough money to support themselves during their stay.

Citizens of other nations must check with their local American embassy or consulate about obtaining a visa. Besides a valid passport, minimum requirements often are a round-trip air ticket, enough money to make the visit possible, or a letter and various official documents (e.g. a bank statement) if the visit is being funded by a friend or a relative in the U.S.

CUSTOMS AND ARRIVAL

If you are not a U.S. citizen or legal resident and are over 21, you are allowed to bring a one-liter bottle of alcohol; if you are over 17, you can bring 200 cigarettes and 100 cigars (but not Cuban), and $400 worth of gifts. Declare at Customs if you plan to bring in or take out more than $10,000.

The customs officers will also want to know if you are bringing in any fruits, vegetables, seeds, cooked meat, or exotic plants and animals. All these are forbidden and you must notify the Customs people. If you try to smuggle any of these items (as a special surprise gift to your American friend or cousin), you will be fined and perhaps even jailed. So get rid of that smelly durian, the moldy cheese, baby python, or special herb before the full weight of the United States Department of Justice bears down upon you.

Getting Around Hawai'i

Taxis, rental cars, and inter-island airlines, are available on O'ahu and the outer islands.

Honolulu is served by TheBus seven days a week with most routes beginning and ending at Ala Moana Center, a short walk from Waikīkī. Kaua'i and the Big Island of Hawai'i offer public bus service. Maui and Moloka'i have no public transportation. The Island of Lāna'i offers guests a shuttle van from the airport to the two resort hotels.

Taxi service is available 24 hours a day, seven days a week at Honolulu International Airport. Just step outside Baggage Claim and look for a person wearing a TAXI shirt and holding a cell phone who most likely will find you first and ask if you want a taxi. Fares are based on mileage, about $15 from the airport to Waikīkī hotels.

Taxis also may be found at airports on outer islands but service may be random, sketchy and possibly adventurous.

All major rental car agencies are represented at Honolulu International Airport as well as airports on outer islands, although you may encounter a lack of available cars on Kaua'i, Moloka'i and Lāna'i, especially on holiday weekends when locals are traveling interisland.

To rent a car you must be 25 years old, have a valid driver's license in your home state, and a credit card.

Unless you rent a Ferrari (available for hire in Waikīkī and Lahaina) all rental cars look alike. When you park next to other rental cars, leave some

personal item—a sea shell, a flower *lei,* or even this book—on the dashboard or front seat and you can easily find your car wherever you park.

If you lock your camera or other valuables in the trunk, it probably will get stolen at the beach. Wiser to take it with you and leave the car unlocked—a clear sign to local *mokes* that nothing of value is on board.

Interisland jet and prop service is available daily on Hawaiian Airlines and Aloha Airlines from Honolulu to Maui, Kaua'i, Moloka'i, Lāna'i and the Big Island of Hawai'i. Each airline offers about 200 flights daily to five major Island airports. The planes depart from Honolulu almost every 20 minutes. If you miss one don't worry, another will be along shortly. Service begins at 6 a.m. and ends about 9 p.m. There are no late night flights between Islands.

If you plan to take a small plane or helicopter in Hawai'i always catch the first flight of the day. The tropic air is still and the sky is usually cloud-free. You'll see more and enjoy the flight.

Health

You can BYOW (bring your own water) to Hawai'i but it's redundant. Some of the world's finest, purest, cleanest water is readily available in Honolulu and Waikīkī. Just turn on the tap. The water's been trickling for years through volcanic rock and it tastes so good it should be bottled.

All prescription drugs are available in Hawai'i drug stores, usually a ubiquitous Long's Drugs, where pharmacists stand ready seven days a week, year-round to fill prescriptions. Although you will need a note from your doctor back home.

Hawai'i has some of the healthiest, longest-lived people in the United States. Excellent health care is available on O'ahu, but falls off on outer islands.

If you take ill or are seriously injured on an outer island, you may be evacuated by helicopter to Queen's Medical Center in Honolulu, the central receiving hospital in the Islands.

THE NEXT STEP

Travel Insurance and Assistance

Unlike Britain, Canada, and some European nations, there is no national health service in America. Consequently, health care is very expensive. We recommend that you buy an insurance policy to cover any health problems that might occur during your trip. Several companies in the U.S. and Europe provide emergency medical assistance for travelers worldwide, including 24-hour help lines. Travel agents and tour companies can recommend policies that can work for you.

TIME

Hawai'i is in its own time zone. It's called Hawai'i Standard Time or (HST). Hawai'i does *not* observe daylight saving time like the U.S. Mainland does between April and October. With nearly 12 hours of sunshine daily almost year-round, there's no need. Hawai'i's longest and shortest days—in June and December—are 13 hours and 26 minutes and 10 hours and 50 minutes, respectively. (During daylight saving time on the Mainland, there is a three-hour difference to the West Coast and six to the East Coast.)

Greenwich Mean Time (GMT) is 10 hours ahead of Hawai'i Standard Time. Thus, when it is noon in Hawai'i, it is:

2 p.m. in San Francisco
5 p.m. in New York
10 p.m. in London
11 p.m. in Paris
6 a.m. the following day in Hong Kong
7 a.m. the following day in Tokyo
8 a.m. the following day in Sydney

Business Hours

The workday starts before sunrise in Hawai'i, a vestige of plantation days, and ends in the early afternoon. Many people work two jobs and some ferry their little darlings to (and from) school, so there's a treble-commute, and traffic is busy day-long in Honolulu, often, more recently in Līhu'e,

Kaua'i, and Kahului, Maui. Honolulu television news readers report the traffic with glee, since they arrive hours ahead of crunch-time.

MONEY

The Yankee dollar and Japanese yen are accepted in Hawai'i along with traveler's checks, sometimes even personal checks from the West Coast, and all major credit cards. Since automated teller machines were first tested in Honolulu's multiethnic mélange in the 1970s, every inhabited island, except Ni'ihau, has an ATM now.

ELECTRICITY

Power runs on 110–120 volts AC, 60 cycles. If you come from a country that uses 220-250 volts AC, 50 cycles, bring your own adapter with two flat vertical plugs because converters that change from 220 to 110 are difficult to find here.

The Big Island of Hawai'i suffers rolling brownouts, and outages are frequent when there's a hard wind, but power and lights remain in play despite arcane utility systems on all islands. Be prepared. Pack a small pocket flashlight, candles, and matches to light mosquito coils.

MEDIA: LOCAL NEWSPAPERS AND RADIO

If you think the IQ of a place is in direct proportion to its distance from *The New York Times,* you'll be disappointed in Honolulu. It's not a great newspaper town, although two dailies, the morning *Advertiser* and evening *Star Bulletin*, offer brief national reviews but seem to focus on two car crashes, hotel mattress fires, and the latest scandal involving Bishop Estate trustees.

Some hotels, like the Four Seasons, Halekulani, and Ritz-Carlton, offer a fax copy of *The New York Times* or provide day-old copies of the *San Francisco Chronicle, San Francisco Examiner,* and *Los Angeles Times*—when you need a hometown fix. The *Wall Street Journal* and *USA Today* can be found in supermarkets.

THE NEXT STEP

Hawai'i magazine is the only national magazine to focus on the Hawaiian Islands. The California-based magazine provides readers with illustrated articles by Hawai'i's writers on beaches, resorts, restaurants, nightlife, and the great outdoors. With the demise of *Aloha: The Magazine of Hawai'i & The Pacific*, this journal now best captures the joy of Islands life. *Honolulu Magazine* is a slim, old-fashioned "city" magazine that's almost lost its audience; occasionally it has a story of interest beyond the reef, but its otherwise narrow take on Hawai'i lacks journalistic vision. Amusing restaurant reviews, annual "Sour Poi Awards," and profiles of local heroes are featured. *Maui* is a slick, growing magazine dedicated to promoting the rural island as the "sophisticated" alternative to cosmopolitan Honolulu, but it's a little too stuck on itself (and Maui); full of pretty pictures, glossy ads, scant content.

On O'ahu, two local radio stations are worth lending an ear: KHPR, the public radio station; and KINE which plays Hawaiian music 24 hours a day. The rest, alas, are pre-formatted stations owned by mainland conglomerates.

TOUCHING BASE: PHONE, FAX, POSTAGE, E-MAIL

Communication is simple, easy, very reliable, and not very expensive. You can use the U.S. Post Office to mail letters or parcels to anywhere in the world. Nearly every town in Hawai'i has a post office. Most efficient, according to a local poll, is Ala Moana Post Office at the mall, but Kailua Post Office is very friendly, and Waimanalo Post Office is a breeze. My favorite is the one-man office in Ka'a'awa, on O'ahu's windward side. If you want your package or letter to arrive faster, you can contact private companies such as Federal Express, UPS, or DHL that promise delivery within the USA in 24–48 hours. Worldwide delivery takes a little longer.

The local area code is 808. Local telephone calls made from a public phone booth cost a minimum of 25 cents. If you are calling beyond your immediate area, you dial "1," the three-digit area code, and then seven digit numbers. Dial 0 or 411 for the local operator.

Many businesses such as hotels, car rentals, airline offices, government

departments, travel agencies, etc., have toll-free numbers, so you can call them for free. These numbers usually begin with 800 or 888. Call 1-800-555-1212 to get the toll-free number of the company you want to contact.

If your credit card cannot be used to make phone calls, buy a phone card. These can be purchased at airports, post offices, many supermarkets, and other convenience outlets. To make international calls, dial 011 first, followed by your country and city codes, and then the local number. To contact the international operator, dial 00. You can make international calls from most public phones.

And don't forget fax and E-mail. Many hotels and photocopying stores have fax and E-mail facilities.

Cultural Considerations

Local customs

- When you're in Hawai'i, don't say "back in the States" because you are in a state, the 50th. Everyone here calls the continental U.S., "the Mainland."
- Don't honk your horn, it's considered rude.
- Rubbing your chopsticks together is bad manners.
- Make sure you wear a flower behind the correct ear. If you're available, it goes behind the right ear, if you're not, it's the left.
- Never go topless on Waikīkī beach; it's against the law for women to go topless anywhere on beaches in Hawai'i although by some quirk it's perfectly acceptable for adult performers to dance totally naked indoors in Honolulu nightclubs.
- Try to distinguish Japanese from Chinese, never say they all look alike.
- Never laugh and point at Samoan or Tongan men wearing *lava lavas*.
- Try to say Hawaiian words correctly; it's easy—just pronounce every vowel.

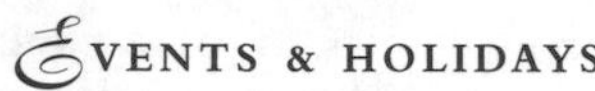

EVENTS & HOLIDAYS

If you arrive in Hawai'i and everything is shut down and the surf's not up, it's not a tsunami alert, it's just a local holiday. Hawai'i celebrates holidays the rest of the world has never heard of such as Prince Kūhiō Day and Buddha's Birthday as well as observing, of course, America's traditional holidays such as New Year's Day, Memorial Day, and Labor Day.

January or **February** brings **Chinese New Year.** The actual day of Chinese New Year changes each year, according to the Chinese Calendar. Call the *Honolulu Advertiser* or *Star-Bulletin*, or Chinese Chamber of Commerce (808 533-3181) to find date and time of public events, lion dances, fireworks, food booths, and ceremonies held each year in Honolulu's Chinatown.

March 26th is **Prince Kūhiō Day**, honoring Hawai'i's first delegate to the U.S. Congress. (State and county offices are closed.)

April 8th is **Buddha's Birthday**.

April 15th is **Father Damien's Day.** Joseph Damien de Veuster, a Belgian priest arrived on Moloka'i in 1873, and spent the next 16 years caring for the lepers of Kalaupapa until he died of the disease in 1989. He was 49 years old. He was buried in the settlement. In 1937, his remains were exhumed and reinterred at Louvain, Belgium where he trained for the Catholic priesthood. Nominated for sainthood, he awaits canonization, pending a miracle. A statue of Father Damien stands on the *mauka* side of the Hawai'i State Capitol where remembrance events are held each year on his day.

May 1st is **May Day** is ***Lei* Day** in Hawai'i, a celebration of the flower garland inspired by poet Don Blanding.

June 11th is the birthday of **King Kamehameha the Great** who united the Islands and ruled from 1795 to 1819. (State and county offices closed.)

July 4th is **Independence Day**—Fireworks on all islands but especially on windward O'ahu at Kailua Beach Park, also Waikīkī.

August brings **Admission Day** on the third Friday in August. This celebrates Hawai'i's admission as the 50th state of the United States on August 21, 1959. (State and county offices closed.)

September celebrates **Aloha Week** during the third week of the month. The statewide celebration of Hawaiiana involves floral parades, crowning of the king and queen and their court, royal balls, banquets, hula festivals.

October 12th may be Columbus Day elsewhere but the man who is believed to have discovered America never came to Hawai'i, so here October 12th is called **Discoverer's Day** and has no local meaning whatsoever. No holiday has ever been declared in honor of Capt. James Cook, the Briton who "discovered" Hawai'i and on a return voyage was killed by Hawaiians at Kealakekua Bay, Big Island of Hawai'i, on February 14, 1779.

October 31st is **Halloween** and it is celebrated on all islands, but especially in Lahaina, Maui.

November celebrates **Thanksgiving**, which falls on the fourth Thursday of the month.

December 7th is **Pearl Harbor Day** commemorating the Japanese surprise attack that caused America to enter World War II.

IMPORTANT CONTACTS

Besides the state tourism office, most cities and towns have an official visitor center that will hand out free information and maps and brochures. The Chamber of Commerce often offers free information to visitors.

Hawai'i Visitors & Convention Bureau
808-923-1811
www.gohawaii.com

THE NEXT STEP

Big Island Visitors Bureau
808-961-5797
www.gohawaii.com

Maui Visitors Bureau
808-244-3530
www.gohawaii.com

Moloka'i Visitors Association
808-553-3876
www.Moloka'i-hawaii.com

Kaua'i Visitors Bureau
808-245-3971
www.gohawaii.com

O'ahu Visitors Bureau
808-524 0722
www.visit-oahu.com

IMPORTANT TELEPHONE NUMBERS

(area code is 808 for all)

Coast Guard Rescue
  O'ahu 536-4336
  Maui 244-5246
  Kaua'i 245-4521
  Hawai'i 935-6370
Directory Assistance 1+411
Emergency (police, fire, ambulance) 911
Hyparbaric Center (bends treatment) O'ahu 523-9155
Interisland Directory Assistance 1-808-555-1212
Lifeguard Service 922-3888
National Weather Service (recorded messages)
  Marine 836-0121
  Surf 836-3921

Pacific Tsunami Warning Center 689-8207
Pilot Weather-FAA 734-6677
Plant Protection & Quarantine 541-2951
TheBus (it's spelled "likethat") 531-1611
Time of Day 983-3211
Volcano Hotline 967-7977 (24-hour recorded updates)
Weather Forecasts
  Honolulu 833-2849
  O'ahu 836-0121
  Hawaiian Waters 836-3921
  Haleakalā Crater (808) 572-7749
Whale Hotline (808) 879-4253

ACTIVITIES

REAL HAWAI'I

At a time when Hawaiians are trying to revive their own ghost culture, the Islands are being smeared under a new veneer of chain restaurants, tacky outlet stores, and upscale Euro boutiques that only cater to Japanese visitors and otherwise have nothing to do with Hawai'i's culture. There's even a new Neiman-Marcus and such misfits as Nike Town, Starbucks, and something called the Texas Rock 'n' Roll Sushi Bar which serves raw fish in a country-and-western karaoke bar with an Elvis-clone deejay.

Now, this rash of retail is spreading to the outer islands where a naked, life-size, Fiberglas statue of Sylvester Stallone soars above the bar at Planet Hollywood in Lahaina, Maui.

What happened to the real Hawai'i? Where did it go?
To obtain the best possible experience in Hawai'i, the intelligent traveler will avoid the obvious, the familiar, and the crass, seek out differences instead of similarities, discover the unusual in arts, crafts, cuisine, and culture; look for the essence of each Island; and savor the authentic experience.

THE NEXT STEP

Otherwise, why go to Hawai'i?

Everyone who arrives in Hawai'i should be required to spend at least three days in quarantine in Waikīkī while overcoming jet lag so when they find their bearings, shed Mainland ways, and get in sync with Hawai'i, they can then press on and discover the real reason they came to the Islands.

It's easy if you:

- Avoid Waikīkī
- Live on Hawaiian time, or, rise with the sun, like most Islanders do
- Have a cooler full of cold drinks
- Always go windward
- Stay in old hotels and B&Bs
  Luxury resorts are spectacular but the real Hawai'i lies beyond their gates. Seek out old hotels, historic places like Waikīkī's Moana, Lahaina's Pioneer Inn, the Big Island's Manago Hotel and Volcano House on the rim of Halema'uma'u crater, or Waimea Plantation Villages on Kaua'i. Or stay in bed and breakfasts that have popped up on all Islands. Go, explore.
- Visit National Parks & Historic Sites
  Hawai'i has the most unusual national parks. One floats over a sunken battleship. Another surrounds an erupting volcano. Yet another features one of the biggest craters on earth. Three are uniquely Hawaiian—a free zone for royal offenders, an exile for lepers, and one of the largest temples of worship in Polynesia. Each national park protects invaluable resources to present important chapters in Hawai'i's history. Seek out parks.
  National Park Service facilities in Hawai'i are:
  - *Arizona* Memorial at Pearl Harbor, O'ahu
  - Haleakalā National Park, Maui
  - Kalaupapa National Historical Park, Moloka'i
  - Hawai'i Volcanoes National Park, Big Island of Hawai'i
  - Pu'u honua O Hōnaunau National Historic Park, Big Island of Hawai'i

- Kaloko-Honokōhau National Historic Park, Big Island of Hawai'i
- Pu'u Koholā *Heiau* National Historic Site, Big Island of Hawai'i

- Get Wet

If you go to Hawai'i and don't go in the water, you've missed two-thirds of the experience. It's the water that makes any island great, especially the Hawaiian Islands where the water temperature is in the 70s almost year-round. Take a dip at dawn, learn to windsurf, go snorkeling, catch a wave on a Waikīkī outrigger canoe, kayak up the Hulēia river, plunge in a waterfall pool, or take a shower under a waterfall. Get wet.

- Look at Hawai'i's Night Sky

If you wake up jet lagged in the middle of the night, go outside and look up. Hawai'i's night sky is like no other—pollution free and clear. You'll never see the Milky Way so big and bright. Look for shooting stars, and planets, night rainbows. Watch the full moon rise over off-shore islets. Look for the endangered Hawaiian *pueo* (owl) as it stalks its prey. Beware night marchers, Hawaiian spirits who wander after dark.

- Meet Local People

If you go to Hawai'i and only see people you see back home, you might as well stay home. Extend yourself, leave the resorts and tourist quarters, go out and make a new friend, learn about Hawai'i and her people. Smile and say aloha.

- Go to the Beach

Hawai'i's beaches are America's best—but who can name 10 or more? Everybody knows Waikīkī and Sunset and, maybe even Makaha because of *Endless Summer* surf flicks and old Beach Boy songs. Maui lovers claim Kā'anapali and Kapalua, and Kaua'i fans will add Hanalei and Poipū (San Francisco's favorite), but that's just about as far most people go with beach identification unless they live in the Islands. The littoral extant of Hawai'i is literally unknown to most. With 132 islands, shoals, and reefs in the tropical Pacific and a general coastline of 750 miles, Hawai'i has beaches in all different sizes, shapes, and colors. The variety on the seven inhabited islands is astonishing. You can go to a different beach every day for a decade (there's no two alike) and still not see them all.

THE NEXT STEP

ODD & UNUSUAL HAWAI'I

The days of kings and queens are gone but Hawai'i still has a real-life princess. Princess Kinoiki Kekaulike Kawananakoa, who lives in Honolulu, is a direct descendant of King David Kalākaua and may have ascended to become Queen Kawananakoa if the Hawaiian monarchy hadn't been overthrown by the U.S. in 1893.

Hawai'i is the endangered species capital of the world but Honolulu's the nation's healthiest city. Average life span for men and women at birth in Hawai'i is 77.98 years; on the U.S. Mainland, it is 74.7 years. Honolulu is second only to San Francisco in restaurant spending yet it's favorite meat is Spam.

Hawai'i doesn't have billboards; outlawed since 1926, billboards are absent from Hawai'i's landscape, so you can see Hawai'i.

The humpback whale is the official state marine mammal. The yellow hibiscus is the official state flower. The *nēnē* goose is the state bird. The *humuhumunukunukuāpua'a* is the state fish. You will see them all, if you're lucky.

Snakes are *kapu* in Hawai'i, they only appear in the Honolulu Zoo. Efforts to keep out the snake begin at Honolulu Airport where detectives, man and dog, have so far prevented the dread Guam brown tree snake from invading the Islands. It hitchhikes on landing gear of jets and in cargo on trans-Pacific ships.

No poison ivy, poison oak, poison sumac. Lowland and even rain forests of Hawai'i are free of poisonous plants, but carnivorous plants eat insects, and mango and Christmas berry cause an itchy rash to the hypoallergenic.

Biggest threat at the beach is sunburn although big waves often litter the sand with "blue bottles"—the nickname of stinging jellyfish known as the Portuguese man-of-war. It stings like a bee; rub on papaya to rid the pain.

Chances of a meteorite striking an island as small as O'ahu in the middle of the Pacific about 10 million to one. Yet, a 30-pound meteorite struck

September 27, 1825, near Punchbowl Crater, alarming the citizens who thought a Russian sea captain had attacked Honolulu. The meteorite broke into pieces and rusted. The largest piece, about 1 1/4 pounds, is at Yale University.

Hawai'i's ski season may be brief, but it occurs whenever it snows, usually in February and March on 13,796-foot Mauna Kea. Hawai'i is the only place in the world where you can snow ski and snorkel a tropical lagoon on the same day.

Hawai'i, believe it or not, has a glacial lake; Lake Waiau, only 10 feet deep and two acres wide, is on the Big Island of Hawai'i at the 13,020 elevation mark of Mauna Kea; it's the highest lake in Hawai'i, third highest in the U.S., and it's considered glacial because it never thaws.

Hawai'i is America's rainbow capital. They arc across the sky with alacrity on all islands day or night. Yes, there are night rainbows. It happens when the moon is full. There are many different types of rainbows—singles, doubles, circles, and stripes. It's all because of sun- (or moon-) light and moisture. The skies of Hawai'i have plenty of each.

Rainbows appear in Hawai'i's brightly lighted, moisture-laden sky whenever the sun is directly opposite a collection of raindrops. Suddenly, you see a graceful arch with seven colors—red, orange, yellow, green, blue, indigo, and violet. A traditional rainbow is sunlight spread out into its spectrum of colors and diverted to the eye of the observer by water droplets.

Sir Isaac Newton figured that out in the 17th century when he noted that when white light enters and leaves a raindrop, it breaks out into the primary colors and is reflected back from the rear of the raindrop at its own optimal angle of refraction. The bigger the raindrops, the more brilliant the rainbow. The "bow" is an optical illusion, first clearly discussed by René Descartes in 1637, and far too complicated to explain here, but it has to do with spheres, radii, and the antisolar axis all of which create a circle of color which we can't see because the earth gets in the way. Trust me.

THE NEXT STEP

Too bad Newton and Descartes never came to Hawai'i, where rainbows appear with such dramatic frequency the Hawaiians came up with dozens of different names to describe nature's own spectacular light show.

Here are 10 names for Hawaiian rainbows:

anuenue	rainbow
anuenue kau po	lunar rainbow
po makole	night of a lunar rainbow
leiokamahina	rainbow ring around the moon
pio ke anuenue	rainbow's arc
ua alaea	reddish rainbow
hakahakaea	greenish rainbow
lehopulu	low-lying, earth-clinging rainbow
kahili	standing, rainbow shaft
ala muku	rainbow fragment
luahona	rainbow around the sun or moon

Green Flash (Explained) & How to See It

Everybody talks about the "green flash," but few have actually seen it. I am not among the privileged, so what follows is not an eyewitness account but a report based upon the expert advice of others, notably astronomers.

For more than a dozen years now, I have been looking for the green flash in Hawai'i. Others standing right next to me claim they have seen it. All I ever see is another gorgeous Hawaiian sunset. So I asked several experts exactly what to look for and how to see the elusive green flash, and this is what they said:

- Hawai'i is supposed to be the best place to observe the green flash.
- Scientifically speaking, the green flash is an atmospheric refractive phenomenon where the light of the sun bends and momentarily turns green. It happens at sunrise or sunset and usually can be seen from ships at sea, especially in the Pacific.
- To see the green flash, you need a clear, pollution-free view of the horizon. It must be uncluttered by objects like palm trees in the foreground and clouds on the distant horizon.

- You need to see a distance of several miles "out," almost to the point where the curvature of the Earth begins—somewhere between 15 and 20 miles.
- The green flash, reportedly, is best seen when the sun sets or rises over the ocean and only when it is absolutely clear all the way to the horizon.
- There is no "flash," although it lasts a fraction of a second, sometimes longer. It's supposed to show as a fleeting spot of intense green light on the horizon just after sunset.
- Look for a west-facing shore with an unobstructed sunset view. The best time to look is from September to early March

Don't think for a moment that you can just step out on your *lāna'i* at sunset, look off toward sun sinking on the ocean's horizon and see it. Even if you know where and when to look, you may not see the green flash. Or you may blink and miss it. This has happened to me. If you're watching another Hawaiian sunset, and everyone near you suddenly starts jumping up and down, screaming or yelling, do not be alarmed. They probably have just seen the elusive green flash. Da buggahs.

Where to Find the Perfect Mai Tai

Bright as a tropical moon, smooth as summer surf, rich as old *Lurline* passengers, cool and fresh as green limes, the mai tai is Hawai'i's favorite drink. One sip and it's paradise. Or, should be. Most mai tais served in Hawai'i today are too strong, too sweet, and, at $7 and up, too expensive. They are pale imitations of the original, created by Trader Vic Bergeron in Emeryville, California, in 1944 and exported to Hawai'i. Some taste like gasoline, others like cough syrup. They burn the throat, produce terrible headaches, and generally give Hawai'i a bad name. They should be served with a Surgeon General's warning. The worst mai tais are served in Waikīkī. They contain cheap rum, bottled pre-mixes, canned pineapple juice, and orange juice concentrate. Weak and syrupy, they look murky in a plastic glass brightened only by a red maraschino cherry and pineapple wedge skewered on a plastic sword. These tacky concoctions have little in common with a real mai tai and should be avoided at all costs. Some variations on the original theme are excellent because they don't alter the basic ingredients.

THE NEXT STEP

The classic mai tai is an unforgettable cocktail, an icy Jamaican rum and fresh lime juice drink with a subtle hint of orange and almond and a sprig of fresh mint for garnish. Now that's a mai tai.

Where you sip a mai tai is almost as important as the ingredients. This tropical drink always tastes better in a thatch hut on a lagoon with coco palms lining the shore. A great mai tai in the Tonga Room of San Francisco's Fairmont Hotel is not the same as a great mai tai on Waikīkī Beach. The search for the perfect mai tai ends at the House without a Key (mentioned below in Fun Things to Do). It's as close to the original as you will find in Waikīkī. This sophisticated version is comprised of a fine blend of two rums, lemon and lime juice, and sweet orange curaçao. A purple vanda orchid adds a splash of color. Other noteworthy concoctions can be found at:

- Jameson's by the Sea, Hale'iwa
  Up on O'ahu's North Shore, big waves draw surfers from around the world but mai tai connoisseurs pack the *lāna'i* at Jameson's at sundown to catch the wave of mai tais prepared by head barman Jim Bragaw; the best in Surf City.
- New Otani Kaimana Beach Hotel
  Go on Aloha Friday when the exotic sounds of Arthur Lyman waft across the golden sand. Ask veteran bartender Clara Nakachi for a classic mai tai. Sit under the tree where Robert Louis Stevenson wrote poems to Princess Kaiulani. Take a sip, stare out to sea, and wonder, is this not paradise?
- The Bay Club, Kapalua Bay Hotel & Villas, Maui
  Maui may be the Chardonnay capital of Hawai'i (all those ex-pat California wine-bibbers), but you can find a great mai tai at the newly renovated Bay Club overlooking Kapalua Bay where head barman James "Kimo" Tagupa knows how to make a good one.
- *'Ōhi'a* Lounge, Kulakoi Hotel & Golf Club, Moloka'i
  At the end of a hot, dusty trail ride on the Moloka'i Ranch, nothing tastes finer than a mai tai in the *'Ōhi'a* Lounge, an airy seaside bar on Moloka'i's biggest gold-sand beach. Mai tais taste original here because hardly anything ever changes on Moloka'i, thank goodness.

- Tahiti Nui, Hanalei, Kaua'i
  Tahiti Nui got smashed by Hurricane 'Iniki but its world-famous mai tai lives on. It's Auntie Louise Marston's secret 30-year-old family recipe imported from Tahiti. Only change over the years—no vanilla beans. The new Nui has now reopened—same place, same mai tais, the best on Kaua'i.
- Shipwreck Bar, Kona Village, Big Island of Hawai'i
  Johnno Jacko wrecked his 42-foot schooner on the reef at Ka'upūlehu in 1959 and stayed on in the Islands to build Kona Village. The hull today serves as the Shipwreck Bar where host Fred Duerr still serves the traditional mai tai, according to Trader Vic's original recipe.

FUN THINGS TO DO

- Tropical Cocktails at Sunset, Waikīkī
  Sip a classic Mai Tai at sunset at the Halekūlani's famed House without a Key on the beach at Waikīkī; listen to the old-time Hawaiian music and enjoy the hula dancers, then adjourn to a private booth at La Mer (ask for table 25), the finest restaurant in Waikīkī's only five-diamond hotel. The romantic, teak-paneled, open-air, seaside dining room features a Provence-style menu of Hawai'i's freshest seafood, fruits, herbs, and vegetables to create masterpieces for the table. Savor each bite, sip fine French wine, stare into each other's eyes as moonbeams dance on the waves. Halekūlani, La Mer, 800-367 2343, 808 923-2311, www.halekulani.com
- Catch a Wave, Waikīkī, O'ahu
  I am flying across O'ahu's Māmala Bay like an ancient Polynesian mariner in an outrigger canoe. The 30-foot canoe surfs down the face of a big Pacific wave. We are one with the wave, paddles digging on the ancient sea route called "Canoes." From offshore, Waikīkī is all skyline, palm trees, and thousands of prone people roasting in coconut oil. On the beach stands the statue of Duke Kahanamoku, Hawai'i's 1912 Stockholm Olympic gold medalist, and most famous beachboy. We surge past Queen's Beach surfers, then head back out to sea to do it again. Waikīkī is the only place in the world you can catch a wave on an

outrigger canoe. Three waves for $5. It's the best deal on the beach. Aloha Beach Services, 808-922-3111, ext. 2341

- Recall the Monarchy, Honolulu, O'ahu
Visit I'olani Palace, the 1882 Italian Renaissance jewel box that's a museum full of "national treasures of the sovereign kingdom of Hawai'i." Inside are found relics of the last days of the Polynesian kingdom, including *koa* thrones and gold crowns in the red- and gold-draped Throne Room. Built by King David Kalākaua (1836-1891) in 1882 for $360,000, the four-story, 10-room palace had electricity four years before the U.S. White House. Restored at a cost of $7 million, America's only royal palace stands in the historic heart of Honolulu as an ornate symbol of Hawai'i's Monarchy Period. In 1893, Queen Lili'uokalani, Hawai'i's last monarch (1838-1917), was deposed and held prisoner in the palace where she wrote *"Aloha 'Oe,"* the lament for a lost kingdom that is the state anthem today. I'olani Palace 808-522-0832
- Gain a Sense of the Whole, Honolulu, O'ahu
Go to the Bishop Museum to gain a sense of the whole. See how a hot spot on the earth's submarine crust pumps these islands out like fresh biscuits on tectonic plates that keep slip-sliding to Japan. Gaze upon a bas-relief map of the Hawaiian archipelago, and realize you are standing on the most remote inhabited chain of islands in the world that stretches 1,900 miles across the Pacific, roughly the same distance as from Atlanta, Georgia, to Salt Lake City, Utah. For 2,400 miles around you in every direction, north to Alaska, west to Japan, and east to California, there is only open ocean. Bernice Pauahi Bishop Museum 808-847-3511, www.bishop.hawaii.org
- Enter the House of the Sun, Maui
Tiptoe into Maui's sleeping volcano and hear your sneakers grind against clinkers, *crunch crunch*, as Sliding Sands Trail betrays your presence. Shhh, don't wake this old volcano. Haleakalā, officially called dormant, last erupted in 1790, a blink of the eye in geologic time. Some drive up the mountain, others coast down on a bike. To really experience its grandeur you have to go to the summit of 10,023-foot high mountain then enter the 3,023-foot-deep, 33-square-mile crater.

Once inside Haleakalā, you feel like the last person on earth. Haleakalā National Park 808-572-4400, www.nps.gov/hale

- Hike Pu'u Kukui, Maui

One of the biologically richest areas in Hawai'i, Pu'u Kukui's 5,871-foot summit in the West Maui Mountains, is a pinnacle wreathed in clouds that's been *kapu* for a century. People of old believed the mountain, one of the last cloud forests in Hawai'i, was the intersection between Heaven and Earth.

Up here, a dozen lucky hikers each year discover a native forest full of silverswords and sedges, little daisies, and scores of ferns that flourish in an 8,661 acre arboreal sanctuary untouched by humans. In hanging valleys at the edge of bogs, a dozen different species of ferns and shade plants found nowhere else flourish along with rare Hawaiian daisies, wild orchids, greenswords and silverswords, and who knows what remains undiscovered? Kapalua Nature Society 808-669-8088, www.kapaluamaui.com

- La Pérouse Pinnacle, Maui

In 1786, French explorer Jean-François de Galoup de La Pérouse set foot near Makena Beach, but the first European to visit Maui sailed on never to be seen again. His stopover is memorialized by a three-foot stone cairn with a brass plaque on La Pérouse Bay, just south of Makena, but another, natural monument lies hidden underwater, unseen by all except snorkelers and divers. La Pérouse Pinnacle rises 60 feet above the sea floor to about 10 feet below the surface of the azure water. It's just off the south coast of Maui in the middle of La Pérouse Bay, a scenically-endowed place where black fingers of lava run to turquoise tide pools. The submarine landmark attracts schools of damselfish, triggerfish, and even the timid bird wrasse. Here, amid coral forests, the deadly fugu puffs up its porcupine quills while goatfish graze day-long in this real fantasy land. Ed Robinson's Diving Adventures 800-635-1273, 808-879 3584, www.mauiscuba.com

- Above Wai'ale'ale/Kaua'i

It's not easy to see "the wettest place on earth"—the 5,148-foot summit of Mt. Wai'ale'ale—on the island of Kaua'i. A collapsed caldera, this multipronged, cloud catcher wrings record torrents down to keep the

THE NEXT STEP

Garden Island green. Up there, it rains daily, year-round. Since 1910, the U.S. Geological Survey has measured the rainfall. Records show it rains 435 inches (or 37 feet) a year. One year it rained 950 inches, or almost 80 feet! Ancient Hawaiians built a *heiau* on Wai'ale'ale, which means "rippling or overflowing water"—and probably prayed to stop the rain. Early geologists rode mules to the summit to check the rain gauge, a 55-gallon drum.

Often as I can, I go into the clouds on a bumpy helicopter ride to see the Earth's wettest spot, not always with great success. Once, all I saw was the inside of a storm cloud. On another, rare, sunny day, the waterfalls showed as bone-dry grooves. But one rainy day, the clouds parted only for a moment to reveal the full spectacle of Wai'ale'ale—countless waterfalls lacing the spiky, cathedral-like peaks of the old volcano. Ohana Helicopter Tours 800-222-6989, 808-245-3996

- Hike Kalalau Trail, Kaua'i

Ten inches wide in places with sheer, 1,000-foot drops to the sea. One misstep and it's *limu* time—that's seaweed, in Hawaiian. Only fear keeps you on the Kalalau Trail, an 11-mile footpath down Kaua'i's Nā Pali coast, the fastest eroding real estate on Earth. A true wilderness, the 6,500-acre Nā Pali Coast State Park is irresistible with hanging valleys, steepled cliffs, splashy waterfalls, and dense jungle topped by 5,148-foot Mt. Wai'ale'ale, the world's wettest spot. The trail starts where the road ends just past Ha'ena's Ke'e Beach. Ascend the rocky trail to the Bali Hai cliffs to enter a place of extreme beauty. Self-guided

- Seeing the Red/Big Island of Hawai'i

My boots give off the telltale scent of burnt rubber. I am trekking across the Earth's newest land. The eerie night is punctuated by bobbing flashlights wielded by others hot-footing it across rumpled rivulets of newly cooled lava. Everyone is going to the edge of the burning island to see the red-hot molten lava run into the sea. It's the main attraction after dark in Hawai'i Volcanoes National Park. Silhouettes against fire, we stand like primal souls witnessing the schist act of creation and destruction. Lava hisses, spits, and crackles as it enters the Pacific Ocean, advancing in black and red fingers big as logs

into blue waves. The 2,500°F lava burns underwater until the cooler sea puts out the fire and in a cloud of white smoke—presto!—transforms it into a new black-sand beach. Is anything more awesome? Hawai'i Volcanoes National Park 808-985-6000, www.nps.gov/havo

- Hunt for Granders, Big Island of Hawai'i
The fish exploded out of the sea like a rocket. It flashed and thrashed and fought the line. An *ono*, also known as wahoo, is one of Hawai'i's great sport fishes to catch—and eat. We had just wet a line outside Honokohau Harbor where the big Pacific blue marlin roam in deep, cold water off the Big Island's Kona Coast. No marlin today, just a quick catch of-the-day dinner entrée for a fisherman on his first sea hunt. If you want to catch fish, it doesn't get any better than Kona. They hook 1,000-pound fish called "granders" here. That night back at the Shipwreck Bar at Kona Village, an architecturally keen collection of thatched-roof South Seas *hales* under coco palms, the sports started swapping fish tales. I stopped them cold when I told them about the guy I know who caught a trophy marlin with a brass doorknob. Kona Charter Skippers Association 808-329-3600
- Summer to Winter in 90 minutes, Big Island of Hawai'i
Hawai'i is the only place you can snorkel in a tropical lagoon and ski down a mountain all on the same day. Summer and winter here are only 90 minutes apart on the Big Island. All four seasons can occur in one day on top of Mauna Kea, at 33,476 feet from sea floor to summit, "the tallest mountain on Earth," according to the *Guinness Book of World Records*. Avalanches, blizzards, and whiteouts are common in this tropical conundrum. No wonder ancient Hawaiians named it "white mountain."
- Visit to "Forbidden" Island
I am sitting on the beach on the "forbidden" island of Ni'ihau, plucking tiny white shells out of the sand with Momi, a young island girl who has keen eyes and quickly finds the pearly shells. Never before possible, this encounter on the last, true Hawaiian island 17 miles off the coast of Kaua'i is of my favorite adventures in paradise. You cannot go easily to Ni'ihau like Lāna'i, Hawai'i's other privately owned island, because Ni'ihau is the last Hawaiian enclave where people still speak the native tongue and pay little heed to the great world beyond. The

THE NEXT STEP

20-minute flight on Ni'ihau Helicopters takes you back a century or more to a museum-piece island right out of the pages of Captain Cook's journal. It's eerie and wonderful all at once. Ni'ihau Helicopters 808-335-3500

- Five Islands in a Single Glance, Lāna'i
On a clear day up on Lanai'hale, you can see all the main islands in the Hawaiian chain, except Kaua'i and Ni'ihau. Take a jeep to the peak or take a hike. No sign marks the spot. Nothing says "Summit 3,379 feet," so you have to keep an eye out yourself. Look for a wide spot in the road and a clearing that falls sharply to the sea. I remember some wind-bent *'ōhi'a* trees, a lot of ferns, and some little red flowers that looked like begonias, but I can't give you a better clue. The view's the reason. Once you see it, everything else fades in memory. Out there on the flat, blue sea stood the islands like a real-life topographic map: Kaho'olawe. Maui. Molokini's tiny crescent. The Big Island of Hawai'i. The faint outline of O'ahu more than 30 miles across the sea. Lāna'i City Service 808-565-7227, www.golanai.com
- Spotting Native Birds, Big Island of Hawai'i
Until I ventured into the Pu'u O'o forest on Mauna Kea's southern slope with Big Island naturalist Rob Pacheco I thought Hawai'i's native birds could only be seen, stuffed under glass, at the Bishop Museum. Now, even rank amateurs can see Hawai'i's rara avis in the wild.

We set off down lava rocks to a Saddle Road *kīpuka*, the Hawaiian word for a green island in a sea of black lava. In the forest we trade bright hot sun for the cool half light under tree ferns, and almost immediately see native birds.

We spy several *'elepaio* (*Chamsiempis sandwichensis*), a chubby brown-and-white striped flycatcher whose voice seems tied to its flirty tail. And the *'i'iwi* (*Vestiaria coccinea*), a scarlet flash with a curvy pink bill. We also hear the haunting warble of the solitary *'ōma'o* (*Phaeornis obscurus*), found only here.

Binoculars ready, Rob spots a squadron of *'apapane* (*Himatione sanguinea*), little red birds that rocket overhead. He counts—"five, six, seven, eight"—before I see one. "There they go," Rob says. Finally, I see where the whir/blur stops—in an *'ōhi'a* tree full of showy red blossoms. I watch the *'apapane* dip its curved beak deep into an *'ōhi'a* blossom. Never again will the red bird elude me. Hawai'i Forest & Trail 800-464-1993, www.hawaii-forest.com

AVORITE BEACHES

- Lanikai Beach, O'ahu

  If there's a finer sunrise beach anywhere in Hawai'i I have yet to see it. Golden sand fine as talcum powder, framed by swaying palms on a turquoise lagoon with two signature islands offshore, Lanikai is *"hapa-haole"* for heavenly sea (it should be: Kailani, but the *haole* developer transposed the words heavenly sea to make it sea heaven). Either way, this windward O'ahu beach lives up to its name.
- Kapalua Beach, Maui

  A gold-sand crescent on a wave-swept bay full of yellow butterfly fish, Kapalua Beach is a postcard, a marine preserve, and the home of the Kapalua Wine Symposium, the most sophisticated beach party on Maui.
- Hulopo'e Beach, Lāna'i

  It's not just the spinner dolphins that crease the azure bay or the rolling swells that tumble you ashore, or even the black-lava tide pools that make this Lāna'i's premiere beach. It's the location: on the island's sunset side.
- Kauna'oa Beach, Big Island of Hawai'i

  Oh, the good times here: sunrise walks, early morning plunges, long hot summer days laced with frozen margaritas, beach parties under the volcanoes, après-dinner visits to see Mauna Kea's manta rays, the roar of the surf in your room at night. Some beaches are more than sand; they're memories of a life well spent.
- Hāmoa Beach, Maui

  Half-moon-shaped Hāmoa stunned James Michener ("the only beach I have ever seen that looks like the South Pacific was in the North Pacific—Hāmoa Beach, on Maui"), and it will dazzle you. The beach is nestled at the foot of lush-green, 30-foot sea cliffs on Hāna's awesome coast.

THE NEXT STEP

- Māhā'ulepū Beach, Kaua'i
  Sometimes I close my eyes and hear again the wind in the ironwood trees, feel the reddish-gold, grainy sand between my toes, smell the salty tang of the far Pacific, and realize I'm dreaming of Māhā'ulepū Beach on Kaua'i's western shore.
- Waikīkī Beach, Oahu
  A great urban beach, this too-thin sliver of sand imported from Moloka'i is a year-round beach party that's been going on for centuries. There's far too many people and too little sand for me, but Waikīkī is one of those places to see and be seen. Surf's not bad, either.
- Āhihi-Kina'u Marine Preserve, Maui
  Not exactly a beach, more like little patches of sand between chunky fingers of black *a'ā* (lava) that spilled into the sea in 1790, Āhihi-Kina'u Marine Preserve is one of Hawai'i's natural wonders. Green tide pools in black lava. Nothing like it anywhere.
- Hāpuna Beach, Big Island of Hawai'i
  Big enough to have its own beach, Hāpuna is the Big Island's most popular beach, a wide, half-mile-long idyllic strand full of fun on weekends. Those who seek privacy head for the north end of the beach to a pocket cove and tiny bay full of tropical fish. I never want to leave.
- Wailea Beach, Maui
  Big, wide, and sheltered on two sides by black-lava points, this exceptional gold-sand beach in the front yard of the Four Seasons offers five-star views of Kaho'olawe and Lāna'i, unreal ocean sunsets, and splashy whales in season (December to April).
- Polihale Beach, Kaua'i
  For its size, 12 miles long, end-of-the-world isolation and Sahara-like dunes, Polihale is a grand spatial experience. Hawai'i's biggest beach wraps around Kaua'i's northwestern shore and includes a channel view of the "forbidden" island of Ni'ihau.
- Kama'ole Beach Park III, Maui
  If every small town in America had a beach this good, nobody would ever come to Hawai'i. Kama'ole Beach Park III is a long, wide, golden-sand beach in the heart of Kihei with a tree-shaded grass park, views

of the West Maui Mountains, the islands of Lāna'i and Kaho'olawe, and affordable beach condos.

- Kalalau Beach, Kaua'i
  I once spent several glorious days without a dull care on Kalalau Beach, sleeping in sea caves, showering under the waterfall, hiking *mauka* to bouldered streams, picking wild fruit, cooking on campfires, living the life. I thought of staying forever, but my prior life called and I left with great reluctance.
- Kailua Beach, O'ahu
  Two miles long with golden sand under coco palms and casuarina at a 35-acre beach park, busy Kailua Beach is home to windsurfers, kayakers, sunbathers, the annual sand castle contest, Buzz's Original Steak House, the legendary Kalapawai Market, and a "wish you were here" view of O'ahu's windward side.
- Sandy Beach, O'ahu
  On the H-1, past Hawai'i Kai's suburban cul-de-sacs and around the bend from Hanauma Bay, the empty, raw natural beauty of O'ahu's south coast begins to show. There you find Sandy Beach. Its shore break is dangerous, offshore currents stiff, but I love this beach because it always reminds me how good an island looks when its saved from the greedy clutch of developers.

OTHER SITES OF NATURAL AND HISTORIC INTEREST

- Puako Petroglyph Park, Kohala Coast, Big Island of Hawai'i
  See the Big Island petroglyphs of Puako on the Kona Coast where a cast of 3,000 characters carved in stone appears in the smooth black slate of *pāhoehoe* lava at your feet. Come see dancers and paddlers, a fisherman with pole and fish, a chief and 209 marchers all in a row. Self-guided.
- Mo'omomi Dunes, Moloka'i
  Mo'omomi Dunes, a two-mile stretch of always shifting sand dunes on Moloka'i's north shore, is said to be "the place of the dead." The dunes, among the biggest in Hawai'i, hold a treasure trove of clues to evolution. Here, Smithsonian Institute ornithologists have found bones of prehistoric birds, some of them flightless, which exist nowhere else

THE NEXT STEP

on earth. Archaeologists discovered rock enclosures where it was planted, caves that held *lauhala* baskets full of salt and other amazing relics of life in old Hawai'i—adze quarries, burial sites, and shelter caves. Botanists have identified five endangered plant species. The secrets of the dunes are revealed on a free guided nature tour to the 920-acre preserve. The Nature Conservancy of Hawai'i 808-553-5236, 808-524-0779

- 'Iao Valley State Park, Maui

Ancient Hawaiians named the valley 'Iao (literally Supreme Light) in honor of the creator. In 1790, King Kamehameha and his men engaged in the bloody battle of 'Iao Valley to gain control of Maui. When the battle ended, so many bodies blocked 'Iao stream the battle site was named Kepaniwai—"Damning of the Waters." Today, this peaceful valley, the eroded volcanic caldera of the West Maui Mountains, is a state park full of tropical plants, rainbows, waterfalls, swimming holes, and hiking trails. 'Iao Needle, a stone basaltic finger which juts 2,250 feet above sea level is often lost in misty clouds or backlighted by gold rays in the afternoon. Self-guided.

- Captain Cook's Monument. Kealakekua Bay, Big Island of Hawai'i

Exact spot of "the fatal encounter," as the Brits say, is now underwater on Kealakekua Bay's north shore. Onshore, on a plot of land deeded to England by Princess Miriam Likelike, stands a white obelisk ringed by cannons.

A brass plaque reads: "In memory of the great circumnavigator Captain James Cook. R.N. who discovered these islands on the 18th day of January AD 1778 and fell near this spot on the 14th day of February 1779. This monument was erected in November AD 1874 by some of his fellow countrymen." Self-guided.

- Pu'u honua O Honaunau National Historic Park, Big Island of Hawai'i

With its fierce, haunting idols, this sacred site on the black lava Kona coast looks forbidding. To ancient Hawaiians, however, it must have been a welcome sight, for Pu'u Honua O Honaunau served as a 16th-century place of refuge, providing sanctuary for defeated warriors and

kapu violators. A great rock wall—1,000 feet long, 10 feet high, and 17 feet thick—defines the refuge where Hawaiians found safety. Hale O Keawe Heiau holds bones of 23 Hawaiian chiefs. Other archaeological finds include burial sites, old trails, an ancient village. You can see reconstructed thatched huts, canoes, and idols, and feel the *mana* (power) of old Hawai'i. Self-guided.

SEVEN NATURAL WONDERS OF HAWAI'I

- Haleakalā Crater, Maui (Biggest Dormant Volcano)
  Once inside Haleakalā (Hawaiian for "house of the sun"), you feel like the last person on Earth. Some call it the eighth wonder of the world. Unreconstructed hippies call it a "power center." It is all that and more. NASA used the seven-mile-long, two-mile-wide, 30,230-foot-deep crater as a training ground for Apollo moon men. The U.S. Air Force today uses a 3.7-meter telescope on Haleakalā's summit to keep an eye on spacecraft, domestic, foreign, and otherwise. Just going up the mountain is quite an experience. Nowhere else can you climb from sea level to 10,023 feet in 45 minutes and never leave the ground. Officially considered dormant, Haleakalā last spewed lava about 1790, and could go off again, any day.
- North Shore Waves, O'ahu (World's Best Surfing Waves)
  The big waves snarl out of the Pacific on O'ahu's North Shore like a tsunami and they roar like a freight train to form a perfect barrel-shaped wave before smashing almost at your feet in foam. You may have seen the Banzai Pipeline, the world's most famous surfing wave, on television reruns of *Hawai'i Five-O* but it's not the same as seeing a 20-foot wave in person. Bring binoculars or your surfboard, if you dare.
- Mauna Loa, Big Island of Hawai'i (Biggest Sea Mountain on Earth)
  Fifty miles long, as high as the Alps, Mauna Loa is a multi-layered, monster volcano that appears less than it is. It's so big you almost don't notice its looming presence. The biggest sea mountain on Earth, Mauna Loa created one-sixth of the Big Island of Hawai'i which is big as Connecticut and growing daily. Mauna Loa, or "long mountain," as Hawaiians call it, is reputed to be the largest single mountain mass on

THE NEXT STEP

Earth, rising 30,000 feet above its base on the ocean floor. Of course, you can only see the 13,679 feet that are above sea level.

- Mauna Kea, Big Island of Hawai'i (Highest Peak in the Pacific)
I am standing on top of Mauna Kea, the tallest peak in the tropical Pacific, achieving an only-in-Hawai'i fantasy. Two hours ago I was snorkeling a tropical lagoon, now I'm making snowballs on Mauna Kea, "the tallest mountain on Earth," according to *The Guinness Book of World Records*. It's 33,476 feet from sea floor to summit. In this tropical conundrum, summer and winter are 90 minutes apart.

    Take a 4x4 to the top, and take your time—altitude sickness can strike the elderly or faint of heart. Pregnant women, small children, the obese or unfit should stay below at the 9,000-foot Onizuka Visitor Center (808 961-2180) named for Hawaii's first astronaut. You can peer at the night sky through a nine-inch telescope at 7 p.m. every Friday and Saturday at the center.

    Early Hawaiians who named it white mountain hit the slopes on sleds they called *holua*. Dick Tillson, a Honolulu engineer who surveyed Mauna Kea on skis in 1965 and named the popular and easily accessible Poi Bowl (it's a three-quarters of a mile run with 500 feet of vertical drop), discovered that old Hawaiian trails converge at the ski bowls.
- Kīlauea Volcano (Most Active Volcano on Earth)
Down on the lava coast of the Big Island of Hawai'i the lava from Kīlauea Volcano runs like strawberry jam into the cobalt sea. It hisses and spits and crackles as it moves like a black snake to the sea. It burns under water, unfolding from the inside out until the ocean finally douses its fire and turns the lava into coarse black sand, fine as gravel, smooth as glass—the stuff of Hawai'i's famous black sand beaches.

    On its seven-mile flow from the summit caldera to the sea, the lava has crossed Chain of Craters Road several times, smothered the National Park Visitors Center, destroyed the famous black sand beach at Kalapana in 1989, and the Waha'ula heiau, built in 1275 A.D. by the Polynesian navigator Pa'ao, who introduced human sacrifice. More than 100 homes have gone up in smoke, causing more than $20 million damage.

THE NEXT STEP

This has been going on almost around the clock since 12:31 a.m., January 3, 1983, when Kīlauea Volcano began its current, continuous eruptive phase at Pu'u O'o vent on the southeast rift zone.

In the longest eruption in recorded Hawaiian history, Kīlauea Volcano has been pumping out 650,000 cubic yards of lava every day—enough to build a four-foot-wide, four-inch-deep sidewalk from Honolulu to New York in two days. No one knows when it will stop.

- Wai'ale'ale Summit, Kaua'i (Wettest Spot in World)

Moisture-laden clouds from every point of the compass collide with Mt. Wai'ale'ale and drop the rain in this crown-like caldera that sends torrents coursing down Kaua'i's seven river valleys. It's not the highest peak on Kaua'i. That honor belongs to its neighbor, Kawaikini, which is "90 feet higher, three-fifths of a mile south (and) too small and slippery to stand on," according to nature photographer Robert Wenkam, who knows. Kawaikini, by the way, means "the multitudinous water."

A collapsed caldera, this multi-pronged, cloud catcher acts as a cloud snare to wring record torrents of rain down on Kaua'i. The 5,148-foot summit of Mt. Wai'ale'ale, is supposed to be "the wettest place on earth" although I have heard some place in India also claims it is during the monsoon season. Here, it rains every day, year-round, and the U.S. Geological Survey has measured the rainfall since 1910. Records show it rains at least 435 inches (or 37 feet) a year on Wai'ale'ale. One year it rained 950 inches, or 79.16 feet!

Wai'ale'ale, according to the Hawaiian dictionary, means "rippling or overflowing water." The mountain was sacred to Hawaiians who scaled its slippery summit and built terraces, house platforms, and temples, or *heiau*.

You cannot go easily to Wai'ale'ale's summit and unless you have a local guide you should not try. On a rare, clear day, take a helicopter to see the wettest place on earth or all you will see is the inside of a rain cloud.

- Moloka'i Sea Cliffs, Moloka'i (Highest Sea Cliffs in World)

The breathtaking sea cliffs tilt 3,500 feet almost perpendicular out of the Pacific and they stretch 14 majestic miles along Moloka'i's forbidding north shore. Laced by waterfalls, creased by five Eden-like valleys—Hālawa, Pāpalaua, Wailua, Pelekunu, and Waikolu—the cliffs are listed in *The Guinness Book of Records* as the highest in the world. You can see them from a small plane like I did the first time, or kayak down the coast in summer when seas are calm. You can ride a mule 1,600 feet down a trail with 26 switchbacks to Kalaupapa National Historic Park or simply stand in awe at the edge of Moloka'i's grand precipice and take in the awesome vista from Pālāau State Park. It's the best free show on Moloka'i.

SEVEN MAN-MADE WONDERS OF HAWAI'I

- Grande Wailea, Wailea, Maui
  The biggest, most expensive resort in the world, it cost $600 million to build in the 1980s. The Grande Wailea includes waterfalls, lagoons, swinging rope bridges, wild animals and exotic birds, dolphin encounters, an Asian art collection, a Japanese "bullet" train in the lobby, and motorboats to take you shopping at French boutiques.
- The W. M. Keck Telescope, Mauna Kea, Big Island of Hawai'i
  World's biggest telescope, this eight-story, 150-ton, $94 million Keck telescope is a mosaic of 36 hexagonal mirrors that peers into deep space at 13,796-feet above sea level on top of Mauna Kea, the highest point in the Pacific. A second scope, Keck II, is now being built next to it.
- The Reef Runway, Honolulu, O'ahu
  Two miles long, built on landfill in a lagoon, the reef runway was designed as an emergency landing strip for the space shuttle but has never been used for that purpose. It serves only as Honolulu International's biggest, longest, and most expensive runway.
- The Hilton Dome, Waikīkī, O'ahu
  Buckminster Fuller's first public geodesic dome, erected in 1959, has survived hurricanes, screaming blue-haired ladies attending the Don Ho Show, and now serves as a showcase for a local magic act although it's slated to disappear soon in favor of, yes, another Hilton hotel tower.
- Hāna Highway, Maui
  Switchbacks, bridges, waterfalls, rainbows, sudden showers, incredible

vistas, 56-mile Hāna Highway is like no other road, a journey not a destination. Built in 1926, it's an unforgettable two-lane road celebrated in song and hula that, like the road, goes "up and down the hills and around the bend."

- Pearl Harbor, Honolulu, O'ahu
  Where pearl oysters once thrived, nuclear subs now stand ready. Pearl Harbor, the biggest, deepest, most strategic harbor in the Pacific, was a prime target of Japanese air raiders in 1941, now a graveyard of 1,100 sailors who perished aboard the battleship USS *Arizona*, and one of Hawai'i's most visited sites. The USS *Missouri*, known as Mighty Mo, is now anchored in Pearl Harbor 1,000 yards from the *Arizona* and, together, the relic vessels form an iconic bookmark to World War II. The Japanese sank the *Arizona* but surrendered three years, eight months, and 25 days later in Tokyo Bay on the teak decks of the battleship *Missouri*. USS *Arizona* Memorial (808-422-2771)
- The H-3 Highway, Kāne'ohe Marine Corps Base–Pearl Harbor, O'ahu
  More than three decades in construction, the $1.2 billion, 16.1-mile freeway is a pork barrel project spearheaded by U.S. Sen. Daniel Inouye (Democrat-Hawai'i) that links Pearl Harbor and Kāne'ohe Marine Corps Base. The highway pokes through the Ko'olau mountains, trespasses a once *kapu* Hawaiian *heiau* (which resulted in a *kapuna* imposing a curse), and is considered an eyesore by many. The freeway does little to alleviate Honolulu's traffic congestion which flows mostly from Diamond Head to 'Ewa instead of to and from the windward side of the Island.

ADDITIONAL RESOURCES

VIRTUAL HAWAI'I

If you search for Hawai'i on the net—just type in "Hawai'i"—you get, at last count, 210,206 matches. That's surely a record for seven small, inhabited islands in the middle of the Pacific. And more Hawai'i websites appear every day.

THE NEXT STEP

Nothing comes close to actually being in Hawai'i (even Apple's sexy new iMac can't emit the sweet fragrance of a night-blooming cereus), but the net does offer a virtual facsimile at your fingertips.

You can visit the Bernice Pauahi Bishop Museum (www.bishop.Hawai'i.org/), watch Lōihi, the undersea volcano, bubble up off the Big Island's south coast (www.soest.Hawai'i.edu), check out a live shot of the Pipeline (www.surfline.com), preview your next Lanikai Beach retreat (www.flyhi.com), search for native birds with Rob Pacheco on the Big Island (www.Hawai'i-forest.com), or download Chef Allen Tsuchiyama's recipe for sweet potato crab bisque with pernod cream and macadamia nuts.

The net now delivers Hawai'i faster and better than any guidebook with up-to-the-minute info, high-res color, live cams, and full-on stereo. However, the path to paradise is indirect, full of technological obstacles and bad information. In the free-fall rush to cyberspace, Hawai'i home page creators have developed a tsunami of information too big to surf in a single lifetime. Hawai'i is one of America's most wired states. It has home pages for everything from Aloha shirts and Kona coffee to Waikīkī condos.

When I need to check news, weather, and sports, I always browse the *Honolulu Star Bulletin*, the locally owned daily fishwrap (www.starbulletin.com) or, in the alternative, *Honolulu Weekly* (www.honoluluweekly.com) which rakes muck, honestly reviews city restaurants, and keeps a cool calendar of events. I also read *Pacific Business News* (www.amcity.com/ pacific/), but wish they'd post John McDermott's wry travel column.

When I really want to know what's happening in the Islands, I catch the H4, (www.hotspots.Hawai'i.com), a pioneering web site by Rabbit Abbott, a veteran Honolulu disc jockey, who's created a net version of Arthur Godfrey's old-fashioned radio talk show.

The H4, connects the world's displaced Hawaiians via the Internet. The name's an ironic play on the "interstate" freeways that don't connect Hawai'i to the other 49 states.

Always evolving, H4 is Rabbit's "expression of a personal love affair with this very special place," an eclectic, interactive pastiche of Hawai'i featuring beaches, bikinis, sunsets, backyard lūa'u, recipes, and important info like surf reports, current temperatures, and volcanic eruptions.

Here are a few of the best:

- Virtual Hawaii

  You can visit Kaho'olawe, the least-visited and most Hawaiian Island, at http://db1.bishop.hawaii.org/KAHO/index.htm and discover a Hawai'i most people have never seen. Photographer Rowland Reeve captures ancient house sites, ceremonial structures, fishhook and goat petroglyphs (the goat was introduced by Captain George Vancouver), and sorry evidence of bomb damage. In 1975, the Navy simulated a nuclear explosion and blasted a crater that spoiled the Island's fresh water supply. Originally a Bishop Museum exhibit seen only in Hawai'i, this web site enables everyone to glimpse an Island lost in time.
- Chinatown, my Chinatown.com

  It's easy to solve the mysteries of Chinatown by visiting its home page (www.chinatownhi.com/). Tour the historic 17-block district, visit open markets, drop in on Havana Cubana, pick up Alan Lau's herbal remedy for the common cold at Tak Wah Tong in the Chinese Cultural Center, even read about the adventures of Charlie Chan. Don't forget to click on your fortune cookie.
- Visit Virtual Maui

  Maui Visitors Bureau's home page (www.vistmaui.com/index.html) is so cool, it makes you want to go there, right now. No heavy graphics, just lots of solid info and cool links, including views from seven remote cameras. My favorite focuses on Ho'okipa's windsurfers. Check out surf and daily temperatures, order a free Maui Vacation Planner and create a vacation. Click on the Pacific humpback whale and hear what it thinks about Maui.
- Thy Kingdom.com

  Need proof America claimed Hawai'i in a colonial expansionist bid to take the Philippines? Check out hawaiiankingdom.org. This new home page won't win any prizes for graphics but the content is of

THE NEXT STEP

great historical importance, especially as Hawaiians today strive to regain a remnant of their lost kingdom. The best sovereignty home page, however, is Hawaiian Nation (info@hawaii-nation.org) which is virtual headquarters for the movement. I get almost daily E-mail reports from Hawaiian Nation to stay informed on what's really going on in the once and former kingdom.

- Mighty Mo in Cyberspace

  Easy to navigate, this official, by-the-book site of the historic battleship USS *Missouri* (www.ussmissouri.com/) is full of nostalgic details about the dreadnought's role in World War II. Click on Mighty Mo's wheel to take a tour, visit the Surrender Deck, see combat photos, (the ship saw action in WWII, Korea, and the Persian Gulf during its 50-year life), and even a video of Mighty Mo's nine, 16-inch guns roaring. Or, take a 20 question quiz, order the ship's blueprints, join a chat room, and sign the ship's log. The Ship's Store wasn't open when I stopped by but look for Mighty Mo souvenirs there.

Related Reading

Ambrose, Greg. *Surfers Guide to Hawai'i: Hawai'i Gets All the Breaks*. Honolulu: Bess Press, Inc. 1991.

Barnard, Walther M., ed. *Mauna Loa—A Source Book Historical Eruptions and Exploration Vol 3: The Post-Jagger Years (1940-1991)*. Fredonia: State University of New York College at Fredonia, 1992.

Beaglehole, J. C., ed. *The Journals of Captain Cook on His Voyages of Discovery*. New York: The Syndics of the Cambridge University Press, 1967.

Bird, Isabella L. *Six Months in the Sandwich Islands*. Rutland, Vt.; Tokyo: Japan, Charles E. Tuttle Co., 1974.

Brennan, Joseph. *The Parker Ranch of Hawai'i: The Saga of a Ranch and Dynasty.* New York: HarperCollins, 1974.

Brown, Desoto. *Hawai'i Recalls: Selling Romance to America*. Honolulu: Editions Limited, 1982.

THE NEXT STEP

Bushnell, O. A., Gavan Daws, and Andrew Berger. *Atlas of Hawai'i.* Honolulu: Island Heritage, 1983.

Carroll, Rick. *Chicken Skin: True Spooky Stories of Hawai'i.* Honolulu: Bess Press, Inc., 1996.

Carroll, Rick, and Joceyln Fujii, eds. *Frommer's Hawai'i* (lst Edition). New York: Simon & Shuster/Macmillan Press, 1997.

Carroll, Rick. *Great Outdoor Adventures of Hawai'i.* San Francisco: Foghorn Press, 1991.

Carroll, Rick. *Hawai'i Best Beach Vacations.* New York: MacMillan.

Carroll, Rick., ed. *Hawai'i's Best Spooky Tales: True Local Spine Tinglers.* Honolulu: Bess Press, 1997.

Carroll, Rick., ed. *Hawai'i's Best Spooky Tales 1, 2, 3.* Honolulu: Bess Press.

Cho, John Nagamichi. *Spam-Ku: Tranquil Reflections on Luncheon Loaf.* New York: HarperPerennial, 1998.

Clarke, Thurston. *Pearl Harbor Ghosts: A Journey to Hawai'i Then and Now.* New York: William Morrow & Company, 1991.

Davis, Lynn Ann, with Nelson Foster. *A Photographer in the Kingdom: Christian J. Hedemann's Early Images of Hawai'i.* Honolulu: Bishop Museum Press, 1988.

Daws, Gavan. *Shoal of Time.* Honolulu: University of Hawai'i Press, 1974.

Day, A. Grove, ed. *Stories of Hawai'i by Jack London.* New York: Appleton-Century, 1965.

Emory, Kenneth P. *The Island of Lāna'i: A Survey of Native Culture.* Honolulu: Bishop Museum Press, 1969.

Farber, Thomas. *On Water.* Hopewell: The Ecco Press, 1994.

Forbes, David W. *Encounters with Paradise.* Honolulu: Honolulu Academy of Arts, 1992.

Hemmings, Fred. *The Soul of Surfing is Hawai'i.* Burlingame, Calif.: Round Mountain Media, 1997.

Hiroa, Te Rani. *Arts and Crafts of Hawai'i.* Honolulu: Bishop Museum Press, 1957.

Hongo, Garrett. *Volcano: A Memoir of Hawai'i.* New York: Borzoi Books, 1995.

THE NEXT STEP

Houston, James D. *In the Ring of Fire: A Pacific Basin Journey*. San Francisco: Mercury House, 1997.

Jenkins, Bruce. *North Shore Chronicles*. Berkeley: North Atlantic Books, 1990.

Jones, James. *From Here to Eternity.* New York: Avon Books, 1951.

Kaeppler, Adrienne L., ed. *Directions in Pacific Traditional Literature: Essays in Honor of Katherine Luomala.* Honolulu: Bishop Museum Press, 1972.

Kalakaua, David. *Legends and Myths of Hawai'i*. Honolulu: Mutual Publishing, 1990.

Kamaka'eha, Lydia Lili'uokalani. *Hawai'i's Story*. Rutland, Vt.: Charles E. Tuttle Co., 1990.

Kamakau, Samuel Manaiakalani. *Ruling Chiefs of Hawai'i*. Honolulu: Kamehameha Schools Press, 1961.

Kamakau, Samuel Manaiakalani. *The Works of the People of Old.* Honolulu: Bishop Museum Press, 1976.

Kingsolver, Barbara. *High Tide in Tucson: Essays From Now or Never.* New York: HarperCollins, 1995.

Kirch, Patrick Vinton. *Feathered Gods and Fishhooks: An Introduction to Hawaiian Archaeology and Prehistory.* Honolulu: University of Hawai'i Press, 1985.

Law, Anwei Skinsnes. *Kalaupapa: A Portrait*. Honolulu: USS *Arizona* Memorial Museum Association, 1989.

Lodge, David. *Paradise News*. New York: Viking, 1991.

London, Charmian K. *Our Hawai'i: Islands and Islanders*. New York: Macmillan Publishing Company, 1922.

London, Jack. *Tales of Hawai'i,* Seattle: Press Pacifica, 1984.

McPhee, John. *The Control of Nature.* New York: Farrar, Straus and Giroux, 1989.

Michener, James. *Hawai'i.* New York: Random House, 1959.

Nelson, Victoria. *My Time in Hawai'i: A Polynesian Memoir.* New York: St. Martin's Press, 1989.

Nollman, Jim. *The Charged Border: Where Whales and Humans Meet*. New York: Henry Holt and Company, 1987.

THE NEXT STEP

Pukui, Mary Kawena. *'Olelo No'eau: Hawaiian Proverbs and Poetical Sayings.* Honolulu: Bishop Museum Press, 1983.

Pukui, Mary Kawena, and Samuel H. Elbert. *Hawaiian Dictionary.* Honolulu: University of Hawai'i Press,1986.

Ronck, Ronn. *Ronck's Hawai'i Almanac.* Honolulu: University of Hawai'i Press, 1984.

Rooke, Constance, ed. *Writing Away: The PEN Canada Travel Anthology.* Toronto, Ontario: McClelland & Stewart Inc., 1994.

Sheehan, Ed. *The Hawaiians.* Norfolk Island: Island Heritage Limited, 1970.

Sutherland, Audrey. *Paddling Hawai'i.* Seattle: The Mountaineers, 1988.

Stewart, Frank. *A World Between Waves.* Washington D.C.: Island Press, 1978.

Takaki, Ronald. *Pau Hana: Plantation Life and Labor in Hawai'i, 1835-1920.* Honolulu: University of Hawai'i Press, 1983.

Theroux, Paul. *The Happy Isles of Oceania: Paddling the Pacific.* New York: G. P. Putnam's Sons, 1992.

Tregaskis, Moana. *Hawai'i.* New York: Compass American Guides, 1993.

Twain, Mark. *Letters From Hawai'i.* Honolulu: University of Hawai'i Press, 1975.

Twain, Mark. *Roughing It.* New York: The Lakeside Press, 1911.

Wesselman, Hank. *Spiritwalker: Messages from the Future.* New York: Bantam Books, 1995.

Winchester, Simon. *Pacific Rising: The Emergence of a New World Culture.* New York: Prentice Hall Press, 1991.

THE NEXT STEP WAS COMPILED BY RICK AND MARCIE CARROLL.

Glossary

'a'ā	rough lava
'ahi	tuna fish
ali'i	nobility
Aloha 'Oe	song written by Queen Lili'uokalani, literal meaning: May you be loved
ama	outrigger float
'amakihi	native Hawaiian honey creeper
'apapane	native Hawaiian honey creeper
'au'au	to bathe
'aumakua	family or personal god
haku	to braid, as in a type of *lei*
hālau	long house for hula instruction, new hula school
hānai	foster child, adopted child
haole	Caucasian person
hapa haole (hula)	hula danced to song with both English and Hawaiian words
heiau	Pre-Christian place of worship, shrine
ho'omana	place in authority
ho'oponopono	to resolve
holokū	Victorian-style long dress with a yoke and usually a train
hula	Hawaiian dance
hula 'auana	modern hula

hula kahiko	ancient or traditional hula
humuhumunukunukuāpua'a	Hawaiian state fish (type of trigger fish)
'iiwi	scarlet Hawaiian honey creeper
'ilima	native shrubs with yellow, orange flowers
'iwa	frigate bird
ka'ai	sennit casket
kahakō	macron
kahu	guardian
kahuna lapa'au	healer, medical practitioner
kai	sea, sea water, area near the sea
kapū	taboo
kaukau	food
kīpuka	oasis within a lava bed where there may be vegetation
kiawe	algaroba tree
koa	largest of native forest trees
kukui	native candlenut tree
kūlolo	pudding made of baked grated taro and coconut cream
kumu hula	hula instructor
kūpaianaha	surprising, strange
lānai	veranda
lau hala	pandanus leaf
laulau	steamed packet of taro leaves with beef (or pork) and salted fish
lei	necklace of flowers, leaves, shells, feathers given as symbol of affection
le'ie	a tree
lo'i	irrigated terrace, especially for taro

lomilomi	referring to Hawaiian dish of tomatoes, salt salmon and onion rubbed together (literal meaning: to massage)
lū'au	Hawaiian feast
luna	boss
mahimahi	dolphin fish
mahiole	feather helmet, helmet
māhū	homosexual of either sex
maka'āinana	commoner
malihini	newcomer
malo	loincloth
mālolo	Hawaiian flying fish
mana	supernatural or divine power
mauka	toward the mountain, or inland
moi	threadfish
mu'umu'u	a loose, long "Mother Hubbard" style dress
nēnē	Hawai'i state bird (goose)
'ō'ō	black honey eater with yellow feathers under each wing
'oama	young goatfish
'ohana	family
'ōhelo	small native shrub in the cranberry family
'ōhi'a	native tree
'okina	glottal stop
ono	large mackeral
'opihi	limpet
pāhoehoe	smooth, unbroken lava
pakalolo	marijuana
pali	cliff
pānini	the prickly pear
paniolo	cowboy

pāpio	type of fish
pau hana	to finish work
pīkake	jasmine
pōhaku	rock, stone
pōpolo	black
pueo	Hawaiian native owl
pūkiawe	plant known for its small round red and black seeds
pūpū	appetizer
pūpū kani oe	a land snail
ti	a long-leaf plant in the lily family, native to tropical Asia and Australia
tūtū	Grandma, or Auntie
'uhane	soul, spirit
wahine	woman, lady
wai	fresh water

Index

Index of Contributors

Acknowledgements

One day four years ago James O'Reilly traveled to Lana'i, where he met Gigi Valley, who lives on the island and knows many things; it was a very lucky encounter for me and you.

Lana'i is a very small island in the middle of the Pacific and Gigi is not very big, and James could have been looking at petroglyphs, and she might have gone to Honolulu that day. They might never have met at all but they did, and James talked of many things but she recalled he mentioned something about his search for the right editor of an anthology of Hawai'i stories to be called *Travelers' Tales Hawai'i.*

Without hesitation Gigi nominated me, then called to see if I possibly might be interested. She had no idea I'd been collecting stories about Hawai'i for years, and even then was looking for the right publisher for just such a book. It turned out well as you shall see. For her ability to make the most of a random encounter, I thank Gigi Valley, one of the nicest, smartest, most thoughtful people I know in Hawai'i. *Mahalo nui loa*, Gigi, Aloha.

And I am full of thanks for:

James O'Reilly, who at Stanford over espresso and bagels one June morning somehow managed to convince my reluctant wife, Marcie, into being co-editor of the book, which brought a total of 30 years of Hawai'i insight from two quite different points of view into the collecting and editing process and prompted many heated discussions which we appear, so far, to have survived.

Larry Habegger, who seconded the motion in San Francisco that summer, after we met at Perry's, that great watering hole on Union Street, where many outstanding goals are conceived and sometimes actually achieved. For their talent in turning this vision into reality, James and Larry deserve a thank you not only from me but from all whose work appears in this unique collection of Hawaiiana.

Susan Brady, a juggler on a tightrope over a bonfire, whose grace under pressure in the production department is unequaled, and Jennifer Leo and Deborah Greco in the San Francisco office of Travelers' Tales whose good humor over long-distance and time kept the journey with a million possible little detours smooth to the end.

Mary Lou Foley and Michael Dalke of Ka'a'awa, Benjamin Bess, Cheryl Chee Tsutsumi, Sheila Donnelly Theroux, Ruth Ann Becker, Nancy Daniels, Candy Bahouth, Ruth Limtiaco, Donna Jung, Joyce Matsumoto of Honolulu; Brooke Dunbar of Lahaina, Maui; Judy Sawyer in New York City, Yvonne Landavazzo of Wailea; Linn Nishikawa of Kapalua, Maui; John Flinn, George Fuller, Michelle Corbin, and Molly Cahill in San Francisco; John Hollon in Los Angeles, Eddie Sherman, Dave Donnelly and Don Chapman for their generous and enthusiastic support of my work in Hawai'i.

The contributing authors whose stories reveal a Hawai'i seldom experienced by even those who live in the Islands.

Joyce Miyamoto of the Hawai'i State Library who found old books, rare first editions and made my research a cool breeze.

Darralene Carroll, my mother, who gave me my first Aloha shirt in the 1950s (a red-and-white silkie with parasols that's probably worth a fortune now) and took me to Honolulu on the way home from Japan in 1961; and encouraged me to write, write, write; my sister, Conni, who married a Hawai'i boy from Kula in the '70s, and inspired me to see Maui through Hawaiian eyes which influenced me try always to write from that perspective; and my co-editor/wife, Marcie, who caused me to take early retirement from the *San Francisco Chronicle* in the 1980s, buy a one-way ticket to Hawai'i and take up the writer's life with a laptop under the coco-palms.

Without each and every one of you, I am only sitting on the beach, staring out to sea, dreaming of a book like this.

Aloha.

"Fire in the Night" by James D. Houston excerpted from *In the Ring of Fire: A Pacific Basin Journey* by James D. Houston, published by Mercury House. Copyright © 1997 by James D. Houston. Reprinted by permission of the author.

"Coming Home" by Thomas Farber excerpted from *On Water* by Thomas Farber. Reprinted by permission of the Ellen Levine Literary Agency. Copyright © 1994 by Thomas Farber.

"Paradox in the Sun" by Jan Morris reprinted from the October 1990 issue of *Travel Holiday.* Copyright © 1990 by Jan Morris. Reprinted by permission of the author.

"A Sea Worry" by Maxine Hong Kingston excerpted from *A World Between Waves* edited by Frank Stewart. Copyright © 1978 by Maxine Hong Kingston. Reprinted by permission of the author.

"Infernal Paradise" by Barbara Kingsolver excerpted from *High Tide in Tucson* by Barbara Kingsolver. Copyright © 1995 by Barbara Kingsolver. Reprinted by permission of HarperCollins Publishers, Inc. and Frances Goldin Agency.

"The Last Wave" by Walt Novak reprinted from the December 1995 issue of *Honolulu Magazine.* Copyright © 1995 by Walt Novak. Reprinted by permission of the author.

"*Kapu* Tube" by Garrett Hongo excerpted from *Volcano: A Memoir of Hawai'i* by Garrett Hongo. Copyright © 1995 by Garrett Hongo. Reprinted by permission of Alfred A. Knopf, Inc. and Darhansoff & Verrill Literary Agency.

"For the Love of Hula" by Lei-Ann Stender Durant published with permission from the author. Copyright © 1999 by Lei-Ann Stender Durant.

"David and the Mango Tree" by Niles B. Szwed published with permission from the author. Copyright © 1999 by Niles. B. Szwed.

"Travels with Bird" by Sally-Jo Keala-o-Ānuenue Bowman originally appeared as "Bird in Hand" in the September 1996 issue of *Aloha* magazine. Copyright © 1996 by Sally-Jo Keala-o-Ānuenue Bowman. Reprinted by permission of the author.

"Cliffhanger in Kaua'i" by Tony Perrottet reprinted from the July 1996 issue of *Escape.* Copyright © 1996 by Tony Perrottet. Reprinted by permission of the author.

"The Tropic of Spam" by Robb Walsh reprinted from the March 15, 1998 issue of *American Way* magazine. Copyright © 1998 by Robb Walsh. Reprinted by permission of the author.

"Kalaupapa, an Inspirational Outpost" by Betty Fullard-Leo published with permission from the author. Copyright © 1999 by Betty Fullard-Leo.

"Swimming with Dolphins" by Jim Nollman excerpted from *The Charged Border: Where Whales and Humans Meet* by Jim Nollman. Copyright © 1999 by Jim Nollman. Reprinted by permission of Henry Holt and Company, LLC and Literary Agency.

"Birdland: Lullaby of Midway" by Marcie Carroll published with permission from the author. Copyright © 1999 by Marcie Carroll.

"Doing Battle with One Tough Plant" by Jo Broyles Yohay reprinted from the June 15, 1997 issue of *The New York Times*. Copyright © 1997 by Jo Broyles Yohay. Reprinted by permission of the author.

"At the Bishop" by Rick Carroll excerpted from *Chicken Skin: True Spooky Stories of Hawai'i* by Rick Carroll. Copyright © 1996 by Bess Press, Inc. Reprinted by permission Bess Press, Inc.

"Going to Hāna" by Larry Habeggar published with permission from the author. Copyright © 1999 by Larry Habeggar.

"Where the Whales Play" by Elgy Gillespie originally appeared as "Where the Humpbacks Learn to Make Whoopee" reprinted from *Worldview's Travelocity*. Copyright © 1997 by Elgy Gillespie. Reprinted by permission of the author.

"Searching for *'O'ō*" by Simon Winchester originally appeared as "Kaua'i" excepted from *Pacific Rising: The Emergence of a New World Culture* by Simon Winchester. Copyright © 1991 Simon Winchester. Reprinted with the permission of Simon & Schuster and A M Heath & Co. Ltd.

"Valley of Ghosts" by Steve Heller excerpted from *Chicken Skin: True Spooky Stories of Hawai'i* edited by Rick Carroll. Copyright © 1996 by Steve Heller. Reprinted by permission of the author.

"Pretending to be Rich" by John Flinn originally appeard as "The Butler Did It" in the March 15, 1998 issue *San Francisco Examiner*. Copyright © 1998 by *San Francisco Examiner*. Reprinted by permission of *San Francisco Examiner*.

"Tropic Bird" by Dustin W. Leavitt published with permission from the author. Copyright © 1999 by Dustin W. Leavitt.

"Honolulu Mamas" by Robert Strauss published with permission from the author. Copyright © 1999 by Robert Strauss.

"Spiritwalker" by Hank Wesselman excerpted from *Spiritwalker: Messages from the Future* by Hank Wesselman. Copyright © 1995 by Hank Wesselman. Used by permission of Bantam Books, a division of Random House, Inc., and the author.

"In Praise of Lipstick Red Convertibles" by Shirley Streshinsky. This article first appeared in *SALON.com, at http://www.salon.com*. Reprinted by permission of the author.

"Afternoon at Lake Waiau" by Nyla Fujii-Babb published with permission from the author. Copyright © 1999 by Nyla Fujii-Babb.

"Spirit of the Lodge" by Babs Harrison published with permission from the author. Copyright © 1999 by Babs Harrison.

"Chinaman's Hat" by Maxine Hong Kingston reprinted from the *East West Magazine*. Copyright © 1977 by Maxine Hong Kingston. Reprinted by permission of the author.

"Sail of a Lifetime" by Linda Kephart Flynn published with permission from the author. Copyright © 1999 by Linda Kephart Flynn.

"Learning Curve" by Emily Ackles reprinted from the November/December 1996 issue of *Islands Magazine.* Copyright © 1996 by Islands Publishing Company. Reprinted by permission of Islands Publishing Company .

"Phallic Rock" by Anna Johnson reprinted from the July, 1995 issue of *Condé Nast Traveler*. Copyright © 1995 by Anna Johnson.

"In My Father's Footsteps" by Carole Terwilliger Meyers published with permission from the author. Copyright © 1999 by Carole Terwilliger Meyers.

"Pizza Night at the Pau Hana Inn" by Jane Albritton published with permission from the author. Copyright © 1999 by Jane Albritton.

"Hawai'i with Julia" by Jonathan Raban reprinted from the September 14, 1997 issue of *The New York Times Magazine*. Copyright © 1997 by *The New York Times Magazine*. Reprinted by permission of *The New York Times Magazine*.

"Eclipse" by Paul Theroux excerpted from *The Happy Isles of Oceania: Paddling the Pacific* by Paul Theroux. Copyright © 1992 by Paul Theroux. No changes shall be made to the above work without the written consent of the The Wylie Agency, Inc.

"Down and Out in Honolulu" by Steve Wilson reprinted from *Big World Magazine*. Copyright © 1997 by Steve Wilson. Published by permission of the author.

"Moonless Night in Kona" by Madelyn Horner Fern published with permission of the author. Copyright © 1999 by Madelyn Horner Fern.

"Rain in Hawai'i" by Daniel David Moses excerpted from *Writing Away: The PEN Canada Travel Anthology* edited by Constance Rooke. Copyright © 1994 by Daniel David Moses. Reprinted by permission of the author.

"Lana'i's Last Cowboy" by Joana Varawa originally appeared as "The Last Cowboy" in the March 15, 1997 issue of *Lana'i Times*. Copyright © 1997 by Joana Varawa. Reprinted by permission of the author.

"Last Dance at the Palace" by Rick Carroll originally appeared as "Taxi Dancing" in the February 18, 1985 issue of *The Honolulu Advertiser*. Copyright © 1985 by Rick Carroll. Reprinted by permission of the author.

"Not on an Island" by Ron Youngblood reprinted from the January 9, 1997 issue of the *Maui News*. Copyright © 1997 by the Ron Youngblood. Reprinted by permission of the author.

"One Way to Get Laid in Honolulu" by Lee Quarnstrom published with permission from the author. Copyright © 1999 by Lee Quarnstrom.

"Beauty and the Beach" by Marcie Carroll reprinted from the Winter 1997 issue of *Aloha* magazine copyright © 1997 by Marcie Carroll. Reprinted by permission of the author.

Additional Credits (arranged alphabetically by title)

Selection from "The Aloha Spirit" by Robert W. Bone published with permission from the author. Copyright © 1999 by Robert W. Bone.

Selection from "Bobby and Lou! Bobby and Lou! Go Over by the Plant. OK, Now, Smile!" by George Fuller reprinted from *Honolulu Magazine*. Copyright © 1989 by George Fuller. Reprinted with permission of the author.

Selection from *Burning Island: A Journey Through Myth & History in Volcano Country, Hawai'i* by Pamela Frierson copyright © 1991 by Pamela Frierson. Reprinted with permission of Sierra Club Books.

Selection from "Cooling the Lava" by John McPhee excerpted from *The Control of Nature* by John McPhee. Copyright © 1989 by John McPhee. Reprinted by permission of Farrar, Straus and Giroux, Inc. Published in Canada by MacFarlane Walter & Ross.

Selection by Jerry Camarillo Dunn Jr. reprinted from the November/December 1990 issue of *National Geographic Traveler*. Copyright © 1990 by Jerry Camarillo Dunn Jr. Reprinted by permission of National Geographic Society.

Selection from "The Far Side of Paradise: Hawaii's Big Island" by K. M. Kostyal reprinted from the January/February 1991 issue of *Islands* magazine. Copyright © 1991 by Islands Publishing Company. Reprinted by permission of Islands Publishing Company.

Selection from *Feathered Gods and Fishhooks: An Introduction to Hawaiian Archaeology and Prehistory* by Patrick Vinton Kirch copyright © 1985 by University of Hawai'i Press. Reprinted by permission of University of Hawai'i Press.

Selection from "The Fireball in Hawaiian Folklore" by William K. Kikuchi excerpted from *Directions in Pacific Traditional Literature: Essays in Honor of Katharine Luomala* edited by Adrienne L. Kaeppler. Copyright © 1972 by Bishop Museum Press. Reprinted by permission of Bishop Museum Press.

Selection from "Going 'Ewa" by Joan Didion reprinted from the issue of New West magazine. Copyright © by Joan Didion.

Selection from *Great Outdoor Adventures of Hawai'i* by Rick Carroll copyright © 1991 by Rick Carroll. Reprinted by permission of the author.

Selection from *"Haku Mele"* by James O'Reilly published with permission from the author. Copyright © 1999 by James O'Reilly.

Selection by Ron Hall reprinted from the July 1996 issue of *Condé Nast Traveler*. Courtesy *Condé Nast Traveler*. Copyright © 1996 by Condé Nast Publications, Inc.

Selection from *The Happy Isles of Oceania: Paddling the Pacific* by Paul Theroux copyright © 1992 by Paul Theroux. No changes shall be made to the above work without the express written consent of the Wylie Agency, Inc.

Selection from "Hawai'i Calls" by Carol Baker published with permission from the author. Copyright © 1999 by Carol Baker.

Selection from "Hawai'i on Foot" by Dewey Schurman reprinted from the January/February 1996 issue of *Islands* magazine. Copyright © 1996 by Islands Publishing Company. Reprinted by permission Islands Publishing Company.

Selection from "Hawaiian Highball" by Robert Sullivan reprinted from the September 1995 issue of *Condé Nast Traveler*. Copyright © 1995 Robert E. Sullivan Jr. Reprinted by permission of the author.

Selections from *The Hawaiians* by Ed Sheehan and Gavan Daws copyright © 1970 by Island Heritage Limited. Reprinted by permission of Robert B. Goodman.

Selection from *The Soul of Surfing* by Fred Hemmings. Copyright © 1999 by Fred Hemmings. Reprinted by permission of Thunder's Mouth Press and the author.

Selection from "Honolulu Days" by Joan Didion reprinted from the July 14, 1980 issue of *New West* magazine. Copyright © 1980 by Joan Didion.

Selection from *The Island of Lana'i: A Survey of Native Culture* by Kenneth P. Emory copyright © 1969 by Bishop Museum Press. Reprinted by permission of Periodical Service Company.

Selection from "Island Romance" by Jennifer L. Leo published with permission from the author. Copyright © 1999 by Jennifer L. Leo.

Selection from *The Journals of Captain James Cook on His Voyages of Discovery* edited from the Original Manuscripts by J. C. Beaglehole copyright © 1967 by The Syndics of the Cambridge University Press. Reprinted by permission of The Syndics of the Cambridge University Press.

Selection by Helen Keao excerpted from *Kalaupapa: A Portrait,* text by Anwei Skinsnes Law. Copyright © 1989 by Arizona Memorial Museum Association.

Selection from "Kona Dreamtime" by James O'Reilly published with permission from the author. Copyright © 1999 by James O'Reilly.

Selection from *Mauna Loa—A Source Book Historical Eruptions and Exploration Volume Three: The Post-Jagger Years (1940–1991)* edited by Walther M. Barnard copyright © 1992 by Denby Fawcett. Reprinted by permission of Denby Fawcett.

Selection from "Midway" by Kenneth Brower reprinted from the May/June 1997 issue of *Islands* magazine. Copyright © 1997 by Islands Publishing Company. Reprinted by permission of Islands Publishing Company.

Selection from "The Mindless Vacation" by Art Hoppe reprinted from the December 7, 1994 issue of *The San Francisco Chronicle.* Copyright © 1994 the *San Francisco Chronicle.* Reprinted with permission.

Selection from *My Time in Hawai'i: A Polynesian Memoir* by Victoria Nelson copyright © 1989 by Victoria Nelson. Reprinted by permission of the author.

Selection from "The New Paradise: Turning the Tides" by Joel Simon reprinted from the September 1994 issue of *Condé Nast Traveler.* Copyright © 1994 by Joel Simon. Reprinted by permission of the Richard Parks Agency.

Selection from "O'ahu" by Emily Ackles reprinted from the March 1993 issue of *Islands* magazine. Copyright © 1996 by Islands Publishing Company. Reprinted by permission Islands Publishing Company.

Selections from *'Olelo No'eau: Hawaiian Proverbs and Poetical Sayings* by Mary Kawena Pukui copyright © 1983 by Bishop Museum Press. Reprinted by permission of Bishop Museum Press.

Selections from *On Water* by Thomas Farber. Reprinted by permission of the Ellen Levine Literary Agency. Copyright © 1994 by Thomas Farber.

Selection from *Our Hawai'i: Islands and Islanders* by Charmian K. London copyright © 1922.

Selection from *Paradise News* by David Lodge copyright © 1992 by David Lodge. Used by permission of Viking Penguin, a division of Penguin Putnam Inc. and Curtis Brown London.

Selection from "Paradise Rising" by Rick Bass reprinted from the June 1993 issue of *Condé Nast Traveler.* Copyright © 1993 by Rick Bass. Reprinted by permission of the author.

Selection from "Pearl Harbor: From Here to Eternity" by John McDonough published in the November 1991 issue of *Travel & Leisure.* Copyright © 1991 by John McDonough.

Selection from *Pearl Harbor Ghosts: A Journey to Hawai'i Then and Now* by Thurston Clarke copyright © 1991 by Thurston Clarke.

Selection from *A Photographer in the Kingdom: Christian J. Hedemann's Early Images of Hawai'i* edited by Lynn Ann Davis with Nelson Foster copyright © 1988 by Bishop Museum Press. Reprinted by permission of Bishop Museum Press.

Selection from "Reunion Speech" by Kurt Matsumoto published with permission from the author. Copyright © 1993 by Kurt Matsumoto.

Selection from *Roughing It* by Mark Twain copyright © 1911 by Mark Twain.

Selection from "Roy and Pele" by Helen Fujie excerpted *from Hawai'i's Best Spooky Tales: True Local Spine Tinglers* edited by Rick Carroll. Copyright © 1997 by Helen Fujie. Reprinted by permission of the author.

Selection from "Shangri-La for Tourists" by Steve Rubenstein published with permission from the author. Copyright © 1999 by Steve Rubenstein.

Selection from "A Sight to See" by Robert W. Bone copyright © 1999 by Robert W. Bone. Published with permission from the author.

Selection from *Stories of Hawai'i* by Jack London edited by A. Grove Day copyright © 1965.

Selection from *Surfers Guide to Hawai'i* by Greg Ambrose copyright © 1991 by Greg Ambrose. Reprinted by permission of Bess Press, Inc.

Selection from "Swimming with Turtles" by Art Hoppe reprinted from the September 28, 1998 issue of the *San Francisco Chronicle*. Copyright © 1998 the *San Francisco Chronicle*. Reprinted by permission.

Selection by Jan TenBruggencate reprinted from the October 7, 1992 issue of *Honolulu Advertiser.* Copyright © 1992 by *Honolulu Advertiser*. Reprinted by permission of *Honolulu Advertiser*.

Selection from *The Works of the People of Old* by Samuel Manaiakalani Kamakau copyright © 1976 by Bishop Museum Press. Reprinted by permission of Bishop Museum Press.

Selection from "Unifinished Hawai'i" by James O'Reilly published with permission of the author. Copyright © 1999 by James O'Reilly.

Selection by Nathaniel Emerson excerpted from *Unwritten Literature of Hawai'i: The Sacred Songs of the Hula* published by Smithsonian Institute Bureau of American Ethnology. Copyright © 1909.

Selection from "What do Tom Selleck, Patrick Swayze and Elvis Have in Common?" by Richard J. Pietschmann originally published in *Travel & Leisure* September 1991. Copyright © 1991 by American Express Publishing Corporation. All rights reserved.

Selection from "Where Hawai'i Began—and Ends" by Rick Carroll excerpted from *Frommer's Hawai'i* edited by Jocolyn Fuji and Rick Carroll. Reprinted by permission of Macmillan General Reference USA. Copyright © 1997 by Simon & Schuster, Inc.

Selection from *The Works of the People of Old* by Samuel Manaiakalani Kamakau copyright © 1976 by Bishop Museum Press. Reprinted by permission of Bishop Museum Press.

About the Editors

Rick and Marcie Carroll were both working for the *San Francisco Chronicle* in 1983, when she spotted a bulletin board notice announcing Asian Studies journalism fellowships at University of Hawai'i and applied. Fortune smiled, and they bought one-way tickets to Honolulu. She went to class and stumbled through beginning Japanese. He sailed and windsurfed until the money ran out, then joined the daily morning newspaper. When the school year ended, after a month-long study trip to Japan, it was too late to go home to San Francisco; they were already hopelessly in love with Hawai'i and the Pacific.

They shared a flair for great assignments and knew a good story when they saw one. *Honolulu Advertiser* editors sent him to Manila and the pirate-infested Southern Philippines with volunteer surgeons on a risky medical mission. His illustrated series, "Surgeons of the Sulu Sea," won a National Headliner's Award. His prize-winning reports from such exotic datelines as Nuku'Alofa, Huahine, Tawi Tawi and Rapa Nui have appeared in newspapers around the world. He has interviewed the Sultan of Sulu, the King of Tonga, the former Premier of China, three governors of Hawai'i, and Imelda Marcos.

She went to work for a local magazine, *Discover Hawai'i*, and traveled extensively throughout the Islands to write about people, destinations, and the travel industry, the engine that runs Hawai'i's economy. She joined the Hawai'i Visitors Bureau as director of communications and created prize-winning publications. She worked with writers and broadcasters from around the world in pursuit of Hawai'i stories. Her duties took her to Japan, Singapore, and Australia on marketing missions.

In the late 1980s and early 1990s, they both became freelance travel writers, working from their Windward O'ahu home, reporting on Hawai'i and the Pacific for United Press International and a variety of publications. Author of six Hawai'i guidebooks, his *Great Outdoor Adventures of Hawai'i*, (Foghorn Press, San Francisco) was the first eco-adventure guide to the Islands and inspired an award-winning column that ran five years in *Aloha: The Magazine of Hawaii & The Pacific*. His Hawaii adventure stories have appeared in many newspapers and magazines, including the *Los Angeles Times*, *San Francisco Examiner*, *Outside,* and *Forbes FYI*.

His anthology, *Chicken Skin True Spooky Stories of Hawai'i* (The Bess Press, Honolulu), became one of Hawai'i's best sellers along with sequels, *Hawai'i's Best Spooky Tales* and *Hawai'i's Best Spooky Tales 2*. The trilogy brought nearly 100 new authors to print.

Marcie Rasmussen Carroll was born in New Orleans and grew up in the South and the Midwest before her family moved to Maryland. She graduated from Bucknell University and earned a master's in journalism from Stanford University, where she won a reporting fellowship some years later. She started reportage on the women's pages of the *San Jose Mercury*, moved to Atlanta to work for United Press International covering primarily politics, moved back to the Bay Area and the *Mercury News* to cover city hall, wandered south to the *Monterey Herald* to cover environmental and energy news, joined the *Chronicle* and wrote about energy, science, suburbs, and politics before becoming the "plague editor" (assistant city editor in charge of politics, law, and government coverage).

Born in Fort Dodge, Iowa, Rick Carroll, son of a World War II pilot, grew up in Massachusetts, Florida, Washington, Texas, California and Japan. He first sailed across the Pacific when he was fourteen (and survived a typhoon at sea), His first newspaper job was at the *Okinawa Morning Star.* He returned to California in time for the '60s, studied journalism at San Jose State University, and wrote for the *San Jose Mercury News* before joining the *San Francisco Chronicle.*

The Carrolls, married in 1980, live at Lanikai Beach on O'ahu and in Friday Harbor on San Juan Island in Washington's Puget Sound.

BODY & SOUL

THE ROAD WITHIN:
True Stories of Transformation and the Soul

Edited by Sean O'Reilly, James O'Reilly & Tim O'Reilly

ISBN 1-885211-19-8, 459 pages, $17.95

Small Press Book Award Winner and Benjamin Franklin Award Finalist

LOVE & ROMANCE:
True Stories of Passion on the Road

Edited by Judith Babcock Wylie

ISBN 1-885211-18-X, 319 pages, $17.95

FOOD:
A Taste of the Road

Edited by Richard Sterling

Introduction by Margo True

ISBN 1-885211-09-0

467 pages, $17.95

Silver Medal Winner of the Lowell Thomas Award for Best Travel Book – Society of American Travel Writers

THE FEARLESS DINER:
Travel Tips and Wisdom for Eating around the World

By Richard Sterling

ISBN 1-885211-22-8, 139 pages, $7.95

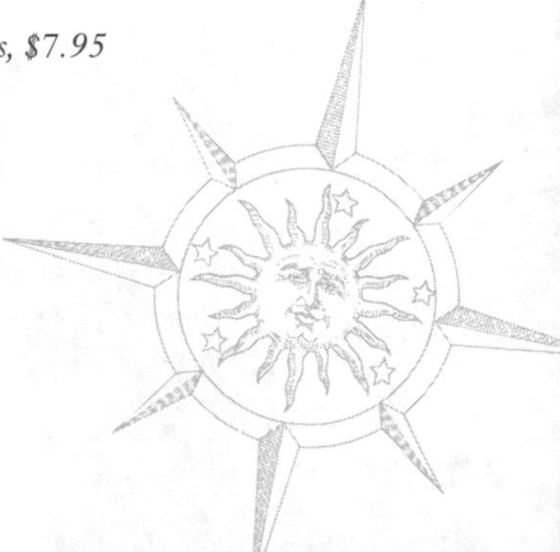

COUNTRY GUIDES

AMERICA
Edited by Fred Setterberg
ISBN 1-885211-28-7, 550 pages, $19.95

JAPAN
Edited by Donald W. George
& Amy Greimann Carlson
ISBN 1-885211-04-X, 437 pages, $17.95

ITALY
Edited by Anne Calcagno
Introduction by Jan Morris
ISBN 1-885211-16-3, 463 pages, $17.95

INDIA
Edited by James O'Reilly & Larry Habegger
ISBN 1-885211-01-5, 538 pages, $17.95

FRANCE
Edited by James O'Reilly, Larry Habegger
& Sean O'Reilly
ISBN 1-885211-02-3, 517 pages, $17.95

COUNTRY GUIDES

MEXICO
Edited by James O'Reilly & Larry Habegger
ISBN 1-885211-00-7, 463 pages, $17.95

THAILAND
Edited by James O'Reilly
& Larry Habegger
ISBN 1-885211-05-8
483 pages, $17.95

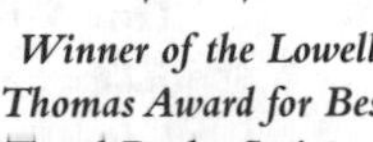

Winner of the Lowell Thomas Award for Best Travel Book–Society of American Travel Writers

SPAIN
Edited by Lucy McCauley
ISBN 1-885211-07-4, 495 pages, $17.95

NEPAL
Edited by Rajendra S. Khadka
ISBN 1-885211-14-7, 423 pages, $17.95

BRAZIL
Edited by Annette Haddad & Scott Doggett
Introduction by Alex Shoumatoff
ISBN 1-885211-11-2
452 pages, $17.95

Benjamin Franklin Award Winner

REGIONAL GUIDES

HAWAII
True Stories of the Island Spirit
Edited by Rick & Marcie Carroll
ISBN 1-885211-35-X, 375 pages, $17.95

GRAND CANYON
True Stories of Life Below the Rim
Edited by Sean O'Reilly & James O'Reilly
ISBN 1-885211-34-1, 375 pages, $17.95

CITY GUIDES

HONG KONG
Edited by James O'Reilly, Larry Habegger & Sean O'Reilly
ISBN 1-885211-03-1, 439 pages, $17.95

PARIS
Edited by James O'Reilly, Larry Habegger & Sean O'Reilly
ISBN 1-885211-10-4, 417 pages, $17.95

SAN FRANCISCO
Edited by James O'Reilly, Larry Habegger & Sean O'Reilly
ISBN 1-885211-08-2, 491 pages, $17.95

TRAVELERS' TALES GUIDES

LOOK FOR THESE TITLES IN THE SERIES

FOOTSTEPS: THE SOUL OF TRAVEL

A NEW IMPRINT FROM TRAVELERS' TALES GUIDES

An imprint of Travelers' Tales Guides, the Footsteps series unveils new works by first-time authors, established writers, and reprints of works whose time has come... again. Each book will fire your imagination, disturb your sleep, and feed your soul.

KITE STRINGS OF THE SOUTHERN CROSS

A Woman's Travel Odyssey

By Laurie Gough

ISBN 1-885211-30-9, 400 pages, $24.00, hardcover

A TRAVELERS' TALES FOOTSTEPS BOOK

THE PENNY PINCHER'S PASSPORT TO LUXURY TRAVEL

The Art of Cultivating Preferred Customer Status

By Joel L. Widzer

ISBN 1-885211-31-7, 253 pages, $12.95

DANGER!

True Stories of Trouble and Survival

Edited by James O'Reilly, Larry Habegger, & Sean O'Reilly

ISBN 1-885211-32-5, 336 pages, $17.95

Check with your local bookstore for these titles
or visit our Web site at www.travelerstales.com

SPECIAL INTEREST

FAMILY TRAVEL:
The Farther You Go, the Closer You Get

Edited by Laura Manske

ISBN 1-885211-33-3, 375 pages, $17.95

THE GIFT OF TRAVEL:
The Best of Travelers' Tales

Edited by Larry Habegger, James O'Reilly & Sean O'Reilly

ISBN 1-885211-25-2, 240 pages, $14.95

THERE'S NO TOILET PAPER ON THE ROAD LESS TRAVELED:
The Best of Travel Humor and Misadventure

Edited by Doug Lansky

ISBN 1-885211-27-9, 207 pages, $12.95

A DOG'S WORLD:
True Stories of Man's Best Friend on the Road

Edited by Christine Hunsicker

ISBN 1-885211-23-6, 257 pages, $12.95

WOMEN'S TRAVEL

SAFETY AND SECURITY FOR WOMEN WHO TRAVEL

By Sheila Swan & Peter Laufer

ISBN 1-885211-29-5, 159 pages, $12.95

WOMEN'S TRAVEL

WOMEN IN THE WILD:
True Stories of Adventure and Connection
Edited by Lucy McCauley
ISBN 1-885211-21-X, 307 pages, $17.95

A MOTHER'S WORLD:
Journeys of the Heart
Edited by Marybeth Bond & Pamela Michael
ISBN 1-885211-26-0, 233 pages, $14.95

A WOMAN'S WORLD:
True Stories of Life on the Road
Edited by Marybeth Bond
Introduction by Dervla Murphy
ISBN 1-885211-06-6
475 pages, $17.95

***

Winner of the Lowell Thomas Award for Best Travel Book–Society of American Travel Writers

GUTSY WOMEN:
Travel Tips and Wisdom for the Road
By Marybeth Bond
ISBN 1-885211-15-5,123 pages, $7.95

GUTSY MAMAS:
Travel Tips and Wisdom for Mothers on the Road
By Marybeth Bond
ISBN 1-885211-20-1, 139 pages, $7.95

Submit Your Own Travel Tale

Do you have a tale of your own that you would like to submit to Travelers' Tales? We highly recommend that you first read one or more of our books to get a feel for the kind of story we're looking for. For submission guidelines and a list of titles in the works, send a SASE to:

Travelers' Tales Submission Guidelines
330 Townsend Street, Suite 208, San Francisco, CA 94107

or send email to ***guidelines@travelerstales.com***
or visit our Web site at **www.travelerstales.com**

You can send your story to the address above or via email to ***submit@travelerstales.com***. On the outside of the envelope, ***please indicate what country/topic your story is about***. If your story is selected for one of our titles, we will contact you about rights and payment.

We hope to hear from you. In the meantime, enjoy the stories!